ABKHAZIA 1992-2022

REFLECTIONS ON ABKHAZIA SERIES

Metin Sönmez
(*Comp. & Ed.*)

George Hewitt
(*Ed.*)

AUTHORS

Aivar Jürgenson, Alexander Iskandaryan, Aslanbek Mirzoev, Beslan Kobakhia, Cem Kumuk, Charlotte Hille, Christopher Langton, Clayton Payne, Dieter Boden, Dodge Billingsley, Donnacha Ó Beacháin, Edward Mihalkanin, Elçin Başol, Fehim Taştekin, Giulia Prelz Oltramonti, Inal Khashig, Jade Cemre Erciyes, Karlos Zurutuza, Ketevan Murusidze, Kieran Pender, Marina Elbakidze, Maxim Gvindzhia, Natella Akaba, Paata Zakareishvili, Patrick Armstrong, Paula Garb, Ramesh Ganohariti, Rick Fawn, Stanislav Lakoba, Stephen Shenfield, Thomas de Waal, Timothy K. Blauvelt, Ucha Nanuashvili, Uwe Klussmann, Ümit Dinçer & Yasemin Oral, Vadim Mukhanov, Vitaly Sharia, Vladislav Bugera, Zaira Khiba

Project website: https://www.abkhazia.co.uk

Cover design

Lorenzo Mariotto

Page layout

Koyusiyah Publishing, Turkey
www.koyusiyahkitap.com

Cover photo

Abkhazian fighters sit in a hallway. September, 1993.
Photo by Malcolm Linton.

First Printing, 2022

Printed in the United Kingdom

Available from Amazon.com and other retail outlets.

ISBN: 9798353949220

Audi alteram partem

Editors

Metin Sönmez, Independent Researcher. Founder of www.circassian-world.com, founder and administrator of www.abkhazworld.com & www.reflectionsonabkhazia.net.

George B. Hewitt, Emeritus Professor of Caucasian languages at the School of Oriental and African Studies (SOAS) and a fellow of the British Academy.

Authors

Aivar Jürgenson, Senior Research Fellow in School of Humanities, Tallinn University. Senior Research Fellow in Literature Museum. Estonia.

Alexander Iskandaryan, Political scientist, the Director of the Yerevan-based Caucasus Institute. Armenia.

Aslanbek Mirzoev, Historian. Institute for Humanitarian Studies - branch of the Kabardino-Balkarian Scientific Center of the Russian Academy of Sciences, Nalchik. He was a former Circassian volunteer from Kabarda. Kabardino-Balkaria, Russia.

Beslan Kobakhia, The public and political figure of Abkhazia. During the 1992-93 Georgian - Abkhazian War, he was head of the government commission for the exchange of prisoners of war and the protection of the civilian population. Abkhazia.

Cem Kumuk, Independent researcher and writer on the history of the Caucasus for about 40 years. Turkey.

Charlotte Hille, Assistant professor at the Department of Political Science, University of Amsterdam. Dr Hille is specialised in State building, conflict resolution and international mediation. Netherlands.

Christopher Langton, Director of The Independent Conflict Research & Analysis (ICRA). He spent thirty-two years in the British Army. In that time he served as the Deputy Commander of the UN Observer Mission in Georgia (UNOMIG) as well as holding various attaché posts in Russia, the South Caucasus, and Central Asia. United Kingdom.

Clayton Payne, Researcher on environmental governance in Abkhazia and South Ossetia. SOAS, University of London. United Kingdom.

Dieter Boden, Ambassador (ret) Former Special Representative of the UNSG in Georgia (1999 - 2002). Germany.

Dodge Billingsley, Director, Combat Films & Research and Global QRF. Editor and Contributor: OE Watch (FMSO), Author: Fangs of the Lone Wolf: Chechen Tactics in the Russian Chechen Wars 1994-2009. United Kingdom.

Donnacha Ó Beacháin, Professor of Politics at the School of Law and Government, Dublin City University (DCU) where he lectures on post-Soviet politics, unrecognised states, Irish studies, and foreign policy. Ireland.

Edward Mihalkanin, Associate Professor in the Department of Political Science at Texas State University. U.S.A.

Elçin Başol, Lecturer at Aydin Adnan Mendered University, PhD Candidate at Kadir Has University, International Relations Department. Turkey.

Fehim Taştekin, Turkish journalist and a columnist for Turkey Pulse who previously wrote for Radikal and Hurriyet. Tastekin specializes in Turkish foreign policy and Caucasus, the Middle East, and EU affairs. France.

Giulia Prelz Oltramonti, Assistant Professor in International Relations at ESPOL, Université Catholique de Lille, France. She has written on the political economies of conflict in the Caucasus and on informality in eastern Europe and the former Soviet Union. France.

Inal Khashig, Journalist. Founder and editor of Chegemskaya Pravda, an independent newspaper in Sukhum, Abkhazia. Earlier he worked at the State Information Agency "Apsny Press." Abkhazia.

Jade Cemre Erciyes, Editor of the Journal of Caucasian Studies (JOCAS). Turkey.

Karlos Zurutuza, Freelance correspondent specializing in the Caucasus and the Middle East regions. He has reported for numerous publications including Al Jazeera, IPS, Vice, Deutsche Welle, and The Diplomat. Basque Country.

Ketevan Murusidze, Peace Researcher and Practitioner. Georgia.

Kieran Pender, Writer for the Guardian. Australia.

Marina Elbakidze, Project Coordinator at the Caucasus Institute for Peace, Democracy and Development and coordinator of the 'Memory Project' in Tbilisi. She is a lecturer in psychology at the Department of Organisational Psychology, Tbilisi State University. Since 1997 she has participated in a range of peacebuilding activities and has played a key role in Georgian-Abkhaz dialogue processes. Georgia.

Maxim Gvindzhia, Former Minister of Foreign Affairs of Abkhazia. Abkhazia.

Natella Akaba, Historian, Chairperson of the board of the Association of Women of Abkhazia. Abkhazia.

Paata Zakareishvili, Georgia's former Minister of Reconciliation. Georgia.

Patrick Armstrong, Political analyst. He was an analyst in the Canadian Department of National Defence specialising in the USSR/Russia from 1984 and a Counsellor in the Canadian Embassy in Moscow in 1993-1996. Canada.

Paula Garb, Senior Fellow at the Center for Peacemaking Practice, George Mason University. For twenty years she co-directed the Center for Citizen Peacebuilding which she co-founded at the University of California, Irvine (UCI). USA.

Ramesh Ganohariti, Ph.D. Researcher, Dublin City University, Ireland.

Rick Fawn, Professor of International Relations. University of St Andrews. Scotland.

Stanislav Lakoba, Professor in Archeology, Ethnology and History at the Abkhazian State University. Former Secretary of the Security Council of Abkhazia. Abkhazia.

Stephen Shenfield, Specialist on politics and society in Russia and the post-Soviet region. For several years he produced the Research and Analytical Supplement to Johnson's Russia List. USA.

Thomas de Waal, Senior fellow with Carnegie Europe, specializing in Eastern Europe and the Caucasus region. United Kingdom.

Timothy K. Blauvelt, Professor of Soviet and Post-Soviet Studies at Ilia State University in Tbilisi. Georgia.

Ucha Nanuashvili, Founder at Democracy Research Institute DRI; Project Director at Human Rights Center; Former Public Defender of Georgia. Georgia.

Uwe Klussmann, Freelance Journalist. He was a correspondent for the magazine "Der Spiegel" in Moscow from 1999 until 2009. Germany.

Ümit Dinçer, President, **Yasemin Oral**, Vice President of the Federation of the Caucasian Associations (KAFFED). Turkey.

Vadim Mukhanov, Head of Caucasus Department of The Institute of World Economy and International Relations of the Russian Academy of Sciences (IMEMO). Russia.

Vitaly Sharia, Honoured Journalist of Abkhazia. Editor-in-chief of the independent newspaper Echo of Abkhazia and author of the Ekho Kavkaza. Abkhazia.

Vladislav Bugera, Philosopher, political publicist, and independent left-wing activist. Russia.

Zaira Khiba, Linguist & Translator. United Kingdom.

Table of Contents

ix

Preface

Metin Sönmez

Independent Researcher. Founder of www.circassianworld.com, founder and administrator of www.abkhazworld.com - www. reflectionsonabkhazia.net

The 14th August 2022 is the 30th anniversary of the beginning of the war between the Georgians and the Abkhazians in the decades-long dispute over ownership of the small territory known to the autochthonous Abkhazians as *Apsny*, to the Georgians as *apxazeti*, and to most of the world as *Abkhazia*. A place remains for much of the world either a thoroughly unknown or, at best, poorly known country, or for many, a disputed region...

First of all, I would like to point out some basic facts about Abkhazia and the Abkhazians, which will help to understand the origin of the Georgian-Abkhazian Conflict.

- Abkhazians are one of the autochthonous peoples of the Western Caucasus. Abkhazia is their unique homeland.
- They have a language, distinct from that of the Georgians, which belongs to the North-West Caucasian language-family group, and they are ethnically related to Circassians.

- Between 780 and 978: The Kingdom of Abkhazia flourished and the Abkhazian Dynasty extended its sway over much of what is now Western Georgia.
- After the Russian-Caucasus wars, Abkhazia was the last Caucasian principality to be forcibly annexed to the Russian Empire. Russian oppression was so severe that over the next few decades more than half of the Abkhazian population fled to Turkey and the Middle East.
- After 1864 (when the Russian-Caucasus wars ended) and the Russo-Ottoman War of 1877/78, the question arose as to who would make the most appropriate substitute-population. One of the leading Georgian intellectuals of the time, the educationalist Iakob Gogebashvili, wrote an interesting article in *Tiflisskij Vestnik* in 1877 entitled (in Georgian) *vin unda iknes dasaxlebuli apxazetshi?* (Who should be settled in Abkhazia?). In this article he argued that the neighbouring Mingrelians would make the best *k'olonizatorebi* (colonisers)... And this is precisely what they subsequently became.
- In 1917 Abkhazia joined The Mountainous Republic of the Northern Caucasus. In 1918 the Mensheviks came to power in Georgia and succeeded in annexing Abkhazia.
- In 1921 the Bolsheviks overthrew the Mensheviks in Georgia. The Abkhazian Soviet Socialist Republic was established, separate from Georgia, and headed by Nestor Lakoba.
- In 1931 Stalin (Georgian) and Beria (Mingrelian) reduced Abkhazia to the status of an autonomous Republic within Georgia.
- Between 1937 - 1953 mass-immigration of Kartvelians (mostly Mingrelians) into Abkhazia was carried out from Western Georgia (Mingrelia) by Stalin and Beria. This period is called the 'Stalin-Beria Terror in Abkhazia'. During this period Abkhaz's script was then altered from a roman to a Georgian base. Abkhazian intellectuals were killed. The Abkhaz alphabet was changed to a Georgian base. Abkhaz place-names changed to Georgian ones. Abkhaz-language schools

were summarily closed in 1945-6, followed by a ban on broadcasting and publications.

These are some of the important points that we should know in order to understand the origin of the conflict.

14 August 1992

On 14 August 1992, Georgian troops entered Abkhazia with tanks and combat helicopters. Thus began the Georgian-Abkhazian war, which would last 13 months. Today Abkhazians are deeply grateful to the inhabitants of the North Caucasus, who arrived in Abkhazia in the first days of the war and fought on the Abkhazian side. Many Armenians, Russians and other nationalities who lived in Abkhazia also took part in the war on the Abkhazian side. Of course we should not forget the Confederation of the Peoples of the North Caucasus, members of the Abkhaz-Adyghe diaspora who came to fight (principally from Turkey) to defend their ancestral lands.

The war ended on 30 September 1993 with victory for the Abkhazians. As with all wars, tragedy was experienced by thousands of people on both sides. Thousands died on both sides. Abkhazians lost 4% of their population; each Abkhazian family lost at least one member during the conflagration. About 200,000 Georgians became refugees by fleeing to Georgia. Also many volunteers from the North Caucasus and diaspora died in the fighting.

Immediately after the war, Abkhazia was subject to a CIS embargo led by Georgia and, be it noted, Russia. In the following years, Georgia tried several times to reconquer Abkhazia by force, but without success. At the same time, direct talks with Abkhazia continued. That is until 2008.

On the night of 7/8 August 2008, when President Mikheil Saakashvili issued the order for Georgian troops to attack South Ossetia. This was Georgia's "final" mistake. After Georgia's defeat and the recognition (on 26 August) of the independence of South Ossetia and Abkhazia by the Russian Federation, the Georgian-Abkhazian conflict entered a new phase. Direct talks between Georgia and Abkhazia ended, and, following the recognition by Russia, the Georgian Parliament adopted a law on Abkhazia as a territory occupied by Russia.

Since 2008, both in Georgia and the international arena, attempts have been made to resolve the Georgian-Abkhazian conflict without the Abkhazians, thereby ignoring one of the two parties to the conflict. The West, in particular, has chosen to be a party instead of a mediator. This naturally results in no progress being made in the resolution of the conflict.

In recent years, we see that many experts and journalists have written articles as if everything started in 2008. So, one might imagine from what they wrote that Abkhazia was a part of Georgia before 2008. While I hope this is due to a lack of information, it can surely be interpreted as part of some black propaganda.

Georgia completely lost its control over Abkhazia after the 1992-93 war. By the way, it should be noted that even in the period of 1931 to 1991, when Abkhazia was (a notionally autonomous) part of the Georgian SSR, they both together were parts of the administrative structure of the USSR. Abkhazia was, thus, not at this time part of an independent Georgian polity.

Another misconception is that Abkhazia declared independence before the war. In fact, just before the Georgian invasion, the Abkhazian side proposed a confederate state-structure to Georgia. Even after the war, the Abkhazian side still discussed this proposal, but the Georgian side ignored this; finally, Abkhazia officially declared its independence in 1999.

Abkhazia and Georgia in the Battle of International Powers

It is very clear that, after all their many experiences over long years, Abkhazians do not trust the Georgians, who have only themselves to blame for their woes in the disputed regions of both Abkhazia and South Ossetia. But the Mingrelians, who (following Georgian practice) are widely viewed as a 'sub-ethnic' Georgian group, still live in the border Gal District of Abkhazia.

Abkhazians are also suspicious of the West, which has tended from the very start to ignore them completely and to offer blind support to the Georgian side.

Currently, Georgia is a country used by the West against Russia. Likewise, Abkhazia is a country used by Russia against the West, and at the same time Russia uses both contested territories as pressure on Tbilisi. It is clear that both the West and Russia are acting only in their own interests, and both Abkhazia and Georgia use these powers in their own interests too.

As Sergey Shamba, one-time Foreign Minister of Abkhazia, has said to *Der Spiegel*: *"The true battle is between the large international powers. On the one hand, Abkhazia and Georgia are levers in this fight, and on the other, Abkhazia and Georgia also use these powers for their own gain. The exploitation is mutual."* [1]

When the late Andrei Sakharov described the relationship between Abkhazia and Georgia, he wrote: "I tend to justify the Abkhazian position. I think we should regard with special attention the problems of small peoples: freedom and rights of big nations should not be exercised at the expense of small ones" (*Znamya*, 1991, No.10, p.69). Unfortunately, both Sakharov's own country and the western / EU states that created the Sakharov Prize for Freedom of Thought in his memory ignore the problems of small peoples and prefer to use them for their own ends.

Indeed, Abkhazia is certainly a fine piece of territory, not least because it is especially important strategically. Russia always wanted to be in the Caucasus, in the Black Sea. Russia will not happily relinquish its influence in the Caucasus and Black Sea, whilst the West would prefer to see that influence lost at the expense of the small nations.

So, how will the Georgian-Abkhazian conflict, in which the interests of the great powers seem to come first, be resolved? No progress has been made by the methods that have been tried for the past 30 years. Attempting to solve a problem by essaying the same means while waiting for a different result is (as has been often observed) the mark of insanity.

First of all, it should be understood that under no circumstances will either Abkhazia or South Ossetia agree to be placed once again within the former Soviet borders of Georgia, which were after all created by the Georgian Stalin (Dzhughashvili). Difficult and painful as it must be for some to accept this simple fact, such is the REALITY.

Despite what we have heard recently from Georgia's President Salome Zurabishvili, what the vast majority of Georgians, whether among the political and intellectual élite or in wider social circles, seek is not to repair relations with the Ossetians and Abkhazians but (and this is their exclusive concern) the restoration of their lost "territorial integrity" (as understood in Soviet terms).

What do Georgia and its supporters demand of Abkhazia?

1. Give up independence and become again part of Georgia.

There is not a single example in history where a people after being invaded, losing 4% of their population, and yet finally winning the war have meekly resigned themselves to returning to the *status quo ante*. Abkhazia will not be the country to set this precedent.

Also, the question of territorial integrity is actually associated not with Georgia proper but with the former minor Soviet Empire, i.e. with the Georgian Soviet Socialist Republic, into which on 19 February 1931 the former Soviet Socialist Republic of Abkhazia (1921-1931) was included as an autonomy by Stalin's dictat[2]. So, regrettably, we have to say that the UN and certain circles in the West are actually attempting to preserve the Stalinist pattern[3] of dividing peoples into ranks. Otherwise, it is difficult to understand why the former union-republics are recognised while the autonomous ones are not. Is this not a clear manifestation of double standards?

2. Allow all Georgians (including the ones who fought against Abkhazia) who fled to Georgia after the war to return to Abkhazia, which in 1999 did actually accept more than 40,000 largely Mingrelian refugees.

Those refugees are not living in a third country but in their own country. Let's assume the entire former 'Georgian' population are allowed to return. Who will guarantee that this mass-return will not cause severe consequences and a new war? Do we need another experiment? Because the whole non-Georgian population perfectly remembers from past history how Abkhazia was when part of Soviet Georgia.

For Georgians there is a country called Georgia, their motherland, where they may live freely, but the Abkhazians have no other home.

Before the 1992-93 war, despite everything that had happened in the past, there was still a chance to live together, but right now we cannot talk about this option any longer, after the war, after both sides lost their loved ones and after the hatred instilled toward each other. As a war-veteran **Esmeralda Arshba said** in the Finnish documentary film "Ei-toivottu valtio": "How could a woman who has lost four children tolerate it, if the killers of her children would move to become her neighbours? How could one understand that!"[4]

Another example is Nagorno-Karabakh. Let's remember what the Azerbaijani government and their Western friends were saying before and during the 2020 war.

> Both Armenians and Azerbaijanis can live in peace and harmony.[5]
>
> Armenians can live in Azerbaijan as citizens of our country, just as they did before the conflict. They can live in our country just as they live in all other countries of the world — in Russia, France, America

— *Rovshan Rzaev, Chairman of the State Committee for Refugees and Internally Displaced Persons.[6]*

We all have to be realistic. This will not be possible either in Karabakh, or in South Ossetia, or in Abkhazia. Even in Chechnya... Soon or later we shall see it. As long as we insist on the so-called 'resolutions' while ignoring the people who suffered from the conflict, from the war, there will be no peace. I know this is hard to accept for some people, but this is the reality.

What does the West want? A solution or to please Georgia?

When I listen to the EU and US officials, once again some questions arise in my mind: Why do all the solutions offered by Western powers focus on, and respect, only Georgia's interests?

How many western ambassadors have visited Abkhazia to listen, to learn what the Abkhazian side is saying? Perhaps we should ask another question before that: are they really brave enough to pay such a visit, despite Georgian objections?

Why are no Abkhazian officials ever invited to present their views at international *fora*, at the United Nations, at the EU Parliament? Aren't these people part of the conflict? How will one solve this problem by ignoring them and not listening to them?

We always hear about Georgia's losses, sufferings and solutions to please only one side of the conflict. Why does no-one talk about compensation to Abkhazia(ns) for the losses they suffered in the war that Georgia imposed upon them? In 2010, Vice-President Aleksandr Ankvab estimated the damage done to Abkhazia's agriculture, industrial base and resorts in the 1992–93 war to be no less than US $13–14 billion. And, of course, this does not take into account the human losses, which must not be forgotten. As mentioned above, every Abkhazian family lost at least one member. If justice is what is being sought, how can there be talk of justice when one side in the conflict is totally sidelined?

Russia: Abkhazia's Only Gate to the World

Many commentators, while accusing Abkhazia of being more and more dependent on Russia, for some reason, do not talk about the circumstances that led to this.

In 2008, Sergey Shamba, Abkhazia's one-time Foreign Minister, asked about Russia›s influence over Abkhazia and whether he is concerned about this or not.

Shamba was said:

> It is difficult for us, but the European states don't provide us with any alternative. They have closed all the doors to us. What should we do? Our ties with Russia solve practically all of our problems. For small Abkhazia, the large Russian market, Russian tourists or the security guarantee is enough. We have the right to dual citizenship. In order to travel to different countries outside of Russia, our citizens also have Russian passports. [7]

Indeed, Russia is happy with this situation. For instance, I do not think that Moscow would be happy to see Abkhazia recognised by the international community, since that would negatively affect its influence not only in Abkhazia but the North Caucasus too. Imagine that the USA recognises Abkhazia. I am sure that Russia would indirectly resist this recognition, simple because this does not suit the national interests of Russia...

If one wants to go on complaining about Russian influence in Abkhazia, they had better engage with Abkhazia to open another door to integrate it with the rest of the world. This does not necessarily entail recognition of their independence but a policy of 'engagement without recognition'.

Otherwise, the Abkhazians and Ossetians will continue having to rely mainly on Russia and its military strength as the main factor in their stability and security.

Seeking a new war: The Second Front

Since Russia launched its invasion of Ukraine, there have been repeated appeals to Georgia to open a "second front" against "Russia" by launching a war against Abkhazia and South Ossetia. Such advocates are manifestly so devoid of conscience that they are ready to sacrifice these two small nations for their own gain.

After 30 years this is where we are: freedom and independence for their own people and oppression and injustice towards others. Can this be called modern democracy?

As Liz Fuller said:

> *The international community may have forgotten (or chosen to overlook) Georgia's earlier attempts to reconquer Abkhazia by force in May 1998 and September-October 2001, and South Ossetia in the summer of 2004, and the Georgian incursion into the upper reaches of the Kodor Gorge in the summer of 2006. The Abkhazians and South Ossetians have not forgotten.[9]*

The concern of these people is neither to solve the problems of Georgia with Abkhazia and South Ossetia, nor to provide peace to the Caucasus. Their sole purpose is to weaken their great enemy to their own benefit. All else can easily be sacrificed for this goal.

A new war will not only affect South Ossetia and Abkhazia but will involve the entire North Caucasus and all the countries where the North Caucasus diaspora lives. This new front, which some seem to view as desirable, may also bring the end of Georgia, contrary to expectations. These are realities that need to be understood.

Abkhazia: 1992-2022

This project is the continuation of the earlier 'Reflections on Abkhazia: [14 August] 1992-2012', which I completed 10 years ago[10]. It aims to bring together different points of view on Abkhazia and the Georgian - Abkhazian Conflict.

The authors were given complete freedom regarding the content of their texts. The views they express in their contributions for this project do not necessarily reflect the views of the AbkhazWorld.com website. The texts have been listed alphabetically according to the names of the authors.

In fact, this project, which was supposed to have 50 authors, did not manage to reach this number due to the fact that some of the authors could not complete their writings As a result (in same cases) of their busy schedule.

I hope that the published material will help to bring a new perspective on the Georgian-Abkhazian conflict, which has not been resolved for 30 years.

I would like wholeheartedly to thank all of the following who have contributed to this project by allowing their valuable thoughts to be included on this site.

Also, for his endless help in editing all the texts and making any necessary translations many thanks to Prof. Emeritus George Hewitt. This project could not have been completed without his help.

Finally, I would like to thank Mr. Beslan Agrba, head of the Moscow Abkhazian Diaspora and trustee of the Amshra Charitable Foundation, who sponsored the publication of this project both online and as a book.

Let us hope there will never be another war between the peoples discussed in what follows.

Note on editorial practice

George B. Hewitt

Emeritus Professor of Caucasian languages at the School of Oriental and African Studies (SOAS) and a fellow of the British Academy. www. georgehewitt.net

Whilst AbkhazWorld normally uses the forms of toponyms approved in Abkhazia, whatever forms were used by contributing authors have been left as written in their submitted texts. So, whereas AbkhazWorld would typically write: Sukhum, Ochamchira, Gal, Kodor, readers will here see such versions as: Sukhum/i, Sukhum(i), Sokhumi, Ochamchire, Gal/i, Gal(i), Kodor/i, Kodor(i), etc... However, if an article was submitted in Russian, toponyms appear in the translations that are standard on AbkhazWorld.

As an Englishman, I have used UK (and not US) spellings and dates (e.g. 14 August 1992, and NOT August 14, 1992) in translated articles. Also, my preference is for 's' over 'z' in such words as: organise, organisation. I also have a strong liking for the hyphen, and readers might notice that it appears far more frequently in my edits than they will have encountered (or willl encounter) elsewhere. If any of these (what some might see as) idiosyncracies have made their appearance in non-translated articles, I apologise to relevant authors and hope they will happily accept my occasional tinkering with their submissions.

Endnotes

[1] https://www.spiegel.de/international/world/tbilisi-aggravating-the-situation-abkhazia-threatens-georgia-with-second-front-a-570829-amp.html (accessed 17 July 2022)

[2] https://abkhazworld.com/aw/history/1869-how-the-s-s-r-abkhazia-became-an-autonomy-within-georgia (accessed 17 July 2022)

[3] https://abkhazworld.com/aw/history/499-stalin-beria-terror-in-abkhazia-1936-53-by-stephen-shenfield (accessed 17 July 2022)

[4] https://www.youtube.com/watch?v=Mls-aHCKBko (accessed 17 July 2022)

[5] https://www.dailysabah.com/opinion/op-ed/long-term-peace-in-karabakh-is-possible (accessed 19 July 2022)

[6] https://haqqin.az/news/211413 (accessed 19 July 2022)

[7] https://www.spiegel.de/international/world/tbilisi-aggravating-the-situation-abkhazia-threatens-georgia-with-second-front-a-570829.html (accessed 19 July 2022)

[8] https://abkhazworld.com/aw/analysis/842-engagement-without-recognition-by-a-cooley-l-mitchel (accessed 19 July 2022)

[9] https://abkhazworld.com/aw/analysis/536-why-can-georgian-president-mikheil-saakashvili-not-emulate-willi-brandt-by-liz-fuller (accessed 19 July 2022)

[10] https://www.reflectionsonabkhazia.net (accessed 19 July 2022)

Estonian Orientalist Linnart Mäll and His Role in Activities of the UNPO During the Georgian-Abkhazian Conflict

Aivar Jürgenson

Senior Research Fellow in School of Humanities, Tallinn University. Estonia; Senior Research Fellow in Literature Museum, Estonia.

On September 8, 1992, Linnart Mäll (1938-2010), an orientalist and head of the Laboratory of Oriental Studies of the University of Tartu, started his course "History of Indian Religions". I was a history student at the University of Tartu and took notes during the lecture. In the first lecture, Mäll described India's cultural and ethnic diversity and predicted the imminent political collapse of the Indian state, because there are nations who would rather be separate. However, it was typical of Mäll's lectures that he loved to expand the topics and to compare different phenomena and regions. In this lecture, Mäll also looked comparatively at US regions and predicted the imminent secession of California and, in the long run, the emergence of independent Native American states. As we can see, quite utopian thoughts but as we know, the Soviet Union had just collapsed and many of its successors became independent, which may have inspired Mäll's bold predictions. Such themes and visions reflected well Linnart Mäll's sympathy and strong support for oppressed and deprived nations.

As a leading figure in the Unrepresented Nations and Peoples Organization (UNPO), he visited the fact finding missions in crisis areas and participated in international conferences dedicated to conflict resolution. When the Georgian-Abkhaz war broke out, he told in an interview to the Estonian newspaper "Postimees": "I have no doubt that the fight will result in the fall of Shevardnadze and the liberation of the entire Caucasus."

The UN, the CSCE, later the OSCE, and many other organizations were involved in the fact finding and peace mediation missions in the Georgian-Abkhazian war (1992-1993), among them UNPO, one of the leaders and founders of which was Linnart Mäll. As we know, the UNPO unites indigenous nations whose right to self-determination is more or less restricted and are therefore unable to be members of the UN or to participate in the discussions concerning them in the international arena. Since its inception, the organization has sought to provide the oppressed or silenced nations of the world the opportunity to address the international community.

Linnart Mäll and the Estonian city of Tartu played an important role at the inception of the UNPO. The UNPO Preparatory Committee was established at a meeting held in Tartu on 5-6 September 1990. At this meeting, Linnart Mäll became the chairman of the UNPO Preparatory Committee. At the UNPO Founding Assembly in The Hague on 11 February 1991, the representatives of 15 nations signed a treaty establishing the organisation. Linnart Mäll was elected as the Chairman of UNPO and Michael C. van Walt van Praag, a Dutch lawyer and Adviser to the Tibetan Government-in-Exile, as Secretary General. Separate regional coordination centres were set up as UNPO institutions in the early 1990s. One of these was the Tartu Coordination Office, which coordinated UNPO´s activities in the Eastern European and North Asian regions, including the former Soviet Union.

When on August 14 1992 Georgian troops entered the territory of the Republic of Abkhazia and the Georgian-Abkhazian war broke up, UNPO began actively gathering and disseminating information about the conflict. It is worth emphasizing that Georgia and Abkhazia were both members of UNPO. While Georgia was a founding member of the UNPO, Abkhazia officially became a member in August 1991 at the II General Assembly of the UNPO (as did Kosovo, for example).

After the Georgian forces had occupied much of Abkhazia, Vladislav Ardzinba, the Chairman of the Abkhaz Supreme Soviet, invited Linnart Mäll, the UNPO Chairman, to come to the crisis area on a peace mission. One of the initiators of the visit was Dzhokhar Dudayev, the President of the Chechen Republic. It is also worth mentioning the interpersonal relations that existed at the time, i.e. Mäll knew Ardzinba from the 1970s, when both had studied at the Moscow Institute of Oriental Studies and Dudayev was a familiar person for Mäll from the time when Dudayev was the commander of the heavy bomber division in Tartu (1987-1990). Dudayev also tried to mediate a meeting between Mäll and Georgian leader Eduard Shevardnadze. However, Shevardnadze ignored Dudayev's attempts at mediation and refused to meet with Mäll, or to guarantee his security if he flew by helicopter over the territory of Georgia. In the end, Mäll did not go to Abkhazia for security reasons. Thus, in essence, the peace mediation mission failed, but Mäll received important information about the background of the conflict.

This information he needed in the next trip to the conflict area which took place from 31 October to 8 November 1992, when Mäll was a member of an official UNPO mission. The other members of the mission were Michael van Walt van Praag from UNPO, as well as Lord David Ennals, a member of the House of Lords and former British Foreign Secretary, Margery Farrar, a member of the US Congress, and Alvaro Pinto Scholtbach, a member of the Dutch Parliament. This mission was also helped by Chechen President Dzhokhar Dudayev, who invited the members of the mission to Chechnya, where they met with Dudayev and other leading politicians in the Chechen Republic, as well as with Zviad Gamsakhurdia, the legitimate President of Georgia, who had sought refuge in Chechnya at the time. In Abkhazia, great emphasis was placed on meetings with both Abkhazian and Georgian refugees, prisoners of war and the residents of various settlements. The UNPO mission highlighted the serious incidents of violence perpetrated by Georgian forces in Abkhazia, in particular against the Abkhazians.

In further UNPO activities related to the Georgian-Abkhaz conflict the UNPO Tartu Coordination Office began to play an increasing role. When a UNPO regional meeting was held in Pärnu, Estonia from 1-3 June 1993, with the participation of sixteen delegations, Georgia's aggression against Abkhazia was condemned and the rights of Abkhazians clearly supported. It is also worth noting that, at the same meeting, the leadership of the Russian Federation was called upon to recognise the right of the Chechen people for self-determination. In the eyes of UNPO, both the Chechens and the Abkhazians fought fairly for their independence, and the hegemony demands of the larger neighbours of both nations, i.e. Georgia and Russia, equally deserved condemnation.

The UNPO continued to support Abkhazia after the Georgian-Abkhaz war. The next UNPO regional meeting was held on 26-29 November 1993 in Estonian town of Pühajärve. An appeal to the Russian president Boris Yeltsin was composed, which called on him to end the economic blockade on Abkhazia, which Russia had begun in support of Georgia. And because Abkhazia had a well-founded fear that a war might break out again, the UNPO called on Yeltsin to stop providing military equipment to Georgia and not to use its army to fight Abkhazia. Taras Shamba, who represented Abkhazia at the meeting at Pühajärve, gave an overview of the recently ended Georgian-Abkhazian war in an interview to the Estonian newspaper *Eesti Aeg*, emphasizing Russia's support for Georgians, but also highlighting the role of North Caucasus volunteers as allies of Abkhazia. In the interview, Shamba also pointed out that many international peace mediators represent Georgia's interests and wish to impose on Abkhazia autonomy as part of Georgia.

Shamba later published an article in the Estonian newspaper *Postimees*, in which he invited Estonians who had left Abkhazia during the war to return to their homes. By that time, Abkhazia had appealed to the Greek, Israeli and Estonian governments to help the Greeks, Jews and Estonians who had evacuated to return to Abkhazia. Shamba also expressed hope, which has not been fulfilled to date: "We take into account that Estonia will soon recognise the Republic of Abkhazia diplomatically as well."

Shamba's statement may seem provocative today, but in the early 1990s, the principles of recognition of states had not been clearly fixed in Estonian political discourse. Although the international community had generally agreed that political entities attempting to leave the former Soviet republics would not be recognised, this was not clearly stated. In any case, a year earlier, on October 11, 1992, the UNPO Tartu Coordination Office had turned to the Estonian Parliament with an appeal, the third paragraph of which proposed to recognise as a subject of international law countries that had declared their national independence and to support nations that strive for self-determination and independence. As a representative of the Estonians, the appeal was signed by Linnart Mäll. Later a member of Estonian Parliament Jaanus Raidal, a person closely related to Mäll, presented a draft declaration "Support for the self-determination aspirations of the peoples of the former Soviet Union" with 26 signatures. According to the project, the Parliament of Estonia should have express support for the aspiration of all peoples of that region to realise their inalienable right for self-determination. On the proposal of the Speaker of the Estonian Parliament Ülo Nugis, the draft was voted out of the agenda. Linnart Mäll reacted painfully to the vote, saying it was a blow to many discriminated nations. Outraged, he promised to do everything possible to ensure that the decision of the Parliament was not announced outside Estonia. He later reiterated this idea in an article, stating that during his visit to Chechnya he did not talk about the decision of the Parliament, because as an Estonian he was ashamed.

On 19 May 1993, on the initiative of the UNPO, a softer draft petition "For the Protection of Indigenous Peoples' Rights in the Territory of the Former USSR" was submitted to the Estonian Parliament. It stated: "The Parliament supports the protection of human rights and self-determination efforts of the Yoked Peoples in the Territory of the Former Soviet Union." However, on 25 November 1993, a day before the start of the UNPO Pühajärve meeting, the draft was excluded from the agenda of the Parliament.

It is possible that the information about the vote was not quickly reached by the participants of the UNPO meeting, which would explain the aforementioned statement of Taras Shamba. However, there is no reason to consider the statement of Shamba itself too curious, considering Linnart Mäll's lobbying in UNPO. Encouraging Estonian state officials to recognise the peoples of Russia was undeniably one of his goals at the time. Later, when it was clear that his efforts would not succeed, he stated with regret: "Estonia was the biggest loser in terms of the policy of non-recognition of small peoples. In the early 1990s, he played down the chance to become the leader of small nations."

At the UNPO General Assembly from 20 to 26 January 1995 it was emphasised that UNPO missions to the region in 1992 and 1993 proved Georgia's abuses against the UNPO's core principles, incl. against the Abkhazia's right for self-determination and the fundamental rights of Abkhazians. In this context, the General Assembly adopted a resolution to suspend Georgia's supporting member status in the UNPO.

A great deal of UNPO's relations with Abkhazia focused on providing the young country with legal advice on drafting their legislation. In 1995 and 1996, the UNPO Tartu Coordination Office led by Linnart Mäll advised Abkhazian representatives on legislative issues and Russian translations of the legal acts of the Republic of Estonia were sent to the mission of the Republic of Abkhazia in Moscow as examples for the Abkhazian laws that were being drafted.

Linnart Mäll and his personal contacts

UNPO's support for Abkhazia in the 1990s was based on the UNPO's statutory positions. The organisation of specific events, mediation of contacts and formulation of appeals was mainly organised by the UNPO Tartu Coordination Office and its director Linnart Mäll. In this regard, Mäll's previous contacts played a significant role. Linnart Mäll became acquainted with Vladislav Ardzinba, the leader of the Abkhaz resistance, and later, the head of the Abkhaz state, during Mäll's time at the Institute of Oriental Studies of the USSR Academy of Sciences in Moscow, and later, when he defended his dissertation. While Mäll was a well-known Buddhologist, Ardzinba's field of research was the ancient Hatti culture in Asia Minor. He was a postgraduate student at the same institution and also worked there for many years after graduation. Since the Hatti language is considered to be related to the Abkhazian-Adyghe languages, i.e. he sought explanations for the origins of the Abkhazians in the ancient cultures of Asia Minor.

Also important were Linnart Mäll's good relations with Chechen leader Dzhokhar Dudayev, who had previously served in the Soviet military in Tartu, which was also the home city of Mäll. The Mäll and Dudayev families were also friends. At the same time, friendly relations existed between Dudayev and Ardzinba, who were allied in the Confederation of Mountain Peoples of the Caucasus. The Chechens played a significant role in the UNPO's activities during the Abkhaz–Georgian conflict. Dudayev helped organise Linnart Mäll's visit to the crisis area in August 1992 and the UNPO mission to Abkhazia in the autumn of the same year. In addition to Dudayev, a UNPO visit to Georgia was also organised by Dudayev's Special Representative Zelimhan Jandarbiyev. He was the same man, who had visited Dudayev in Tartu in the spring of 1991 and invited him to lead the national movement in Chechnya. Dudayev supported the Abkhazian struggle against the Georgians, but when Russia launched hostilities in Chechnya in December 1994, this was fiercly criticised by V. Ardzinba, the Abkhazian leader, and he offered to mediate peace with the Kremlin. Needless to say, Dudayev's success in the First Chechen War was based on a professional army, one of the most important parts of which was the so-called "Abkhaz" battalion, i.e. Chechen fighters hardened in the war against the Georgian aggressor in Abkhazia. In the Chechen War, Abkhazians also fought against the Russians on the Chechen side.

While Linnart Mäll had excellent relations with the leaders of Abkhazia and Chechnya, Mäll treated the Georgian leader Shevardnadze with undisguised contempt, which probably did not help the UNPO conduct impartial mediation. In one interview, Mäll describes Shevardnadze as a "cunning, cold and cruel fox." It is difficult to say whether this assessment may have been due to Georgia's aggression in Abkhazia or something else. Linnart Mäll had a negative attitude towards the communist partocracy, which Shevardnadze had represented during the Soviet era. Mäll was caught in the gears of the Communist machinery during the Soviet era, when, in 1973, he lost his job as a senior lecturer in the Department of General History of Tartu State University for political reasons. Mäll's connections with Moscow dissidents dated back to his early years in Moscow, his contempt for those who toadied to the Soviet authorities. In the early 1990s, in addition to UNPO, Mäll was also a leading figure in many Estonian social and political organisations. The Estonian writer Arvo Valton calls Mäll "a great scientist and truth-seeker, an uncompromising Estonian patriot and someone who showed compassion to all the world's distressed nations". Ivar Tröner, publisher of Mäll's writings, calls him a "humanist-visionary" and patriot.

As an Estonian patriot, Mäll was very knowledgeable about the struggle of other small indigenous peoples for survival and political self-determination. He has stated the following: "Nationality is of great value. I

34

would say that the longer the human history lasts, the more nationalism will become a universal value." Or also, "If the nineteenth century was the age of great powers, if the twentieth century is the age of states, then the next century will be the age of peoples. A time will come when every nation can develop its own culture and cultivate its own language." The following excerpt from one of Mäll's interviews conveys the same spirit: "If, in the last century, there was a widespread belief that national cultures must disappear in order for a unified human civilisation to develop, and both the United States and later the Soviet Union strove so hard to achieve this, then it has now become clear throughout the world that it is only through national identity that universal values can be expressed. A totally homogeneous culture is impossible if only because this would become very boring."

It is not only a patriot who is speaking these lines, but also an empathetic person who perceives the common ground with the patriots of other countries, further, we meet here an optimistic visionary, in whose eyes ethnic cohesion is the optimal form of human organisation. Against this background, he predicted the disintegration of political colossuses, such as the United States and India, and the emergence of smaller national entities based thereupon. He called Russia, as one of the largest colonial empires of the modern age, an unnatural formation, and predicted that the entire Caucasus would become free. He supported the Chechens in their fight against the Russian imperialism and the Tibetans against the Chinese imperialism. In 1991, Mäll invited Dalai Lama to visit Estonia. China's anger was ignored although there was a danger that it could harm Estonia's foreign policy and economic interests. Linnart Mäll's international activities were largely focused on supporting the right of peoples for self-determination. For Linnart Mäll, it made no difference whether the empire was big or small – he was criticised those who stood in the way of peoples' rights to self-determination. As I have experienced many times in Abkhazia, Linnart Mäll is still warmly remembered there.

Geopoliticisation of the Unrecognised: Change of Paradigms in the Developmental Trajectories of Post-Soviet de facto States

Alexander Iskandaryan

Political scientist, the Director of the Yerevan-based Caucasus Institute. Armenia.

E thnopolitical conflicts in the post-Soviet space arose almost immediately, as soon as the central government began to weaken in the late 1980s. The first in time was the Karabakh or Armenian-Azerbaijani conflict, then the South Ossetian, Abkhazian, Transnistrian, Chechen. There were conflicts that managed, albeit after bloody clashes, to be stopped, for example, the conflict in Tuva, the Prigorodnyj district of North Ossetia and in the Kadar zone of Daghestan. There were conflicts that did not progress into a hot phase, for example, in the western part of the North Caucasus. But there was something in common between all these conflicts. All of them were territorial, that is, their essence was that representatives of ethnic groups came forward with demands to change the status of certain territories. These demands led to the politicisation of ethnicity and the ethnicisation of politics, which in the conditions of a weakening Centre often led to bloody dénouement.

It is logical to look for the reasons behind similar processes in different parts of the decaying empire in the structure of this empire. The boundaries of Soviet administrative units were drawn and changed voluntaristically, without regard for the desires and moods of the population. The purely formal nature of borders and repeated changes in the status of administrative units – all this could be levelled out within the framework of a single, yes, even a totalitarian state. However, at the time of its collapse in each of the republics into which the USSR fragmented, the problems of nation-building became actual, and besides, it became necessary to draw between these republics no longer formal, but real borders. A role here was played by the fact that the administrative division of the USSR, firstly, was a nesting doll, that is, it consisted of units of different levels included in each other in different, often bizarre configurations, and secondly, it was ethnicised, that is, these units in were mainly created along ethnic lines and had the so-called "titular nations". As a result, even in the USSR itself, these administrative units were perceived as ethnic domains, and even under Soviet rule, the concept of "hosts and guests" arose there, viz. representatives of the titular ethnic group of the administrative unit as against all the other ethnic groups living there.

Thus, the bloody conflicts of the late 20th century, which in some places escalated into wars, can be perceived not as random events divorced from the general logic, but as part of a global process of creating political identities and ethnic demarcation at the time of the collapse of the *Imperium*.

Path to secessions

The formation of the first generation of *de facto* states took place in the conditions of the collapse of the USSR against the background of the weak legitimacy of the newly formed post-Soviet republics and the incompletely formed rules of the post-*Białowieski* space.[1] The collapse of a multinational country took place along institutionalised ethnic boundaries. It is characteristic that almost all conflicts took place not just in places of the compact settlement of certain ethnic groups, but in formally autonomous Soviet administrative formations. For example, in Georgia there are the regions of Dzhavakheti Javakheti and Kvemo Kartli, densely populated, respectively, by Armenians and Azerbaijanis, who are more numerous there both in relative and absolute terms than Abkhazians in Abkhazia or Ossetians in South Ossetia. However, ethno-political conflicts did not arise in Javakheti and Kvemo Kartli. There are many such examples. It can be assumed that the existence of ethnicised autonomies back in Soviet times contributed to the consolidation of ethnic groups that received the status of "titular nations", the formation of ethnic élites and corresponding mental maps in them. We can say that the ground for self-determination was being prepared back in the days of the USSR.

The only exception in this respect in the former Soviet Union is the Transnistrian conflict. In Soviet times, there was no autonomy in Transnistria, it was an ordinary part of Moldova, just lying on the left bank of the River Dniester, while the rest of the territory of Moldova, the former Bessarabia, lies on the right bank. In addition, the Transnistrian conflict was distinguished by a lesser degree of ethnicisation: both Moldovans and Russians lived and live on both sides of the Dniester. Presumably due to the lower level of ethnicisation, the Transnistrian conflict is also characterised by less isolation of the two communities from each other (it is still possible to travel from Chisinau to Tiraspol without hindrance), and a lower level of fierce hostilities during the period of aggravation of the conflict in the nineties. In fact, the Transnistrian conflict was originally socio-cultural, not ethnic, and these socio-cultural differences have historical reasons: Transnistria was in the USSR since its creation in 1921 and was then an autonomy within the Ukrainian SSR. The rest of the territory of Moldova, which was part of Romania, ended up in the USSR only in 1940 after the Molotov-Ribbentrop Pact. Accordingly, having been in the USSR for twenty years longer, Transnistria was not only more Sovietised, but, unlike the rest of Moldova, was largely Russified. In addition, many enterprises of the Soviet economic complex operated on its territory. It can be assumed that it was sociocultural differences that played the role of a simulacrum of ethnic autonomy in Transnistria.

The conflicts in the Caucasus also differed from one another. In South Ossetia, from the very beginning, there was a strong irredentist component in the form of the desire of the Ossetians of the south to unite with the Ossetians of the north and become part of Russia. This was originally due to the existence of two Ossetians bordering each other, inhabited by the same ethnic group – one as part of Russia, the other, much smaller, as part of Georgia. Accordingly, the South Ossetian project began in the Soviet paradigm, so that even South Ossetia's statement of self-determination, which occurred on 20 September 1990, took the form of a declaration of "sovereignty within the USSR". South Ossetia's movement towards independence began already after the collapse of the USSR and the war of the early 1990s in the light of the obvious impossibility of joining Russia. Such tendencies persist in South Ossetia to this day. From time to time, desires to join the Russian Federation are voiced there at various levels, albeit still without finding any response in Russia.

The situation in Karabakh was similar. The movement of the Karabakh Armenians from the very beginning was also irredentist and for the same reason: the Armenian SSR was nearby, which was also an order of magnitude larger than Karabakh both in terms of territory and population. As in South Ossetia, the movement that began in Karabakh under the slogan of reunification (in Armenian *miatsum*) was only relevant before the dissolution of the USSR, since it was an attempt to annex Karabakh to Armenia within the framework of the USSR. When it became clear that this attempt had failed and the USSR was doomed, a referendum was held in Karabakh a few weeks before the formal collapse of the USSR and independence was proclaimed, rather than reunification with Armenia.

Along with *de facto* independence, Nagorno-Karabakh gained a war with Azerbaijan, which ended by 1994, and eventually became a classic unrecognised state. Reunification with Armenia was no longer seen as a relevant political prospect. There was a negotiation-process within the framework of the OSCE Minsk Group – the immediate joining of Karabakh to Armenia in the eyes of the international community would look like an annexation, and so even Armenia has not yet officially recognised the Nagorno-Karabakh Republic.

But in Abkhazia, a fully-fledged secession took place, since from the very beginning it fought precisely for secession from Georgia. When this struggle took the form of a war, representatives of the ethnic groups of the North Caucasus who are kindred to the Abkhazians also fought alongside the Abkhazians, but there was no question of union with the republics inhabited by these ethnic groups. The problem of the Abkhazians was that, unlike South Ossetia or Karabakh, they did not make up the majority of the population in the republic of which they were the titular nation. There were almost three times more Georgians in Soviet Abkhazia than Abkhazians. However, most of these Georgians had to leave Abkhazia as a result of war, as was the case in other conflict zones in the Caucasus.

Thus, by the beginning of the 21st century, four *de facto* states in the post-Soviet space created an inertia of existence, built political systems of varying degrees of internal legitimacy and found ways of economic survival, usually with the support of third states (Russia in the case of Transnistria, South Ossetia and Abkhazia, Armenia in the case of Nagorno-Karabakh). A reality has emerged that is fairly typical of the collapse of large multinational empires, with numerous border problems from Silesia and Alsace to East Timor and Eritrea. In none of the agreements on peaceful settlements of the conflicts of the early nineties (Dagomys Agreement on South Ossetia, Moscow Agreement on Transnistria and Abkhazia, as well as the Bishkek Protocol on an indefinite ceasefire in Karabakh) are these entities mentioned as separate states.

Geopolitically, the existence of these states did not play a special role, although it created problems for major actors, but still not on such a scale as to require serious intervention. These states remained unrecognised, and it was customary to treat the borders formed after the collapse of the USSR as sacrosanct, at least in legal terms. This also applied to Russia itself, in which there were periods of political sponsorship of some unrecognised states, which did not, however, affect their status. "I think it is immoral to encourage separatist tendencies," Russian Foreign Minister Sergej Lavrov said in a March 2008 interview with *Rossijskaja Gazeta*, specifying that the "Kosovo precedent" had already encouraged separatists in other regions of the world, and that "we see only the beginning of an extremely explosive process". Literally five days after the declaration of Kosovo's independence, President Putin called this act a "terrible precedent" that "essentially ruins the entire system of international relations that has evolved not even over decades, but over centuries. And without any doubt, it can lead to a whole chain of unpredictable consequences".[2]

Revisionism and geopoliticisation

Problems started a few months later and had nothing to do with Kosovo. The reason was the crisis in relations between Russia and Georgia, which had been deteriorating since President Saakashvili came to power. Georgia's unambiguously pro-Western stance had long irritated Moscow, and its emerging orientation towards NATO and EU membership was perceived by Russia as a threat. Relations were on the verge of breaking down several times. The result was the Russo-Georgian War of 2008, also known as the *Five Day War*. There is no need to analyse in detail the causes and course of this war, as there is already a lot of literature on this topic (the Tagliavini report, for example) – in this context it is not the war itself that is important, but Russia's subsequent legal recognition of the independence of South Ossetia and Abkhazia. This act actually changed the paradigm of Russia's behaviour in the post-Soviet space from traditionalist to revisionist. Russia considered it possible, based on political considerations, to encroach on the inviolability of post-Soviet borders.

It is extremely important here that, in an effort to punish Georgia, Russia, following the outcome of the *Five-Day War*, recognised not only South Ossetia, where this war began, but also Abkhazia. Thus, the recognition of the independence of the two unrecognised republics stemmed from Russia's attitude towards Georgia (and not towards these republics themselves), and Russian-Georgian contradictions turned out to be more important than the principle of the inviolability of the borders of the states of the former USSR. An indirect confirmation of just such a motivation was the fact that Russia did not recognise Nagorno-Karabakh and Transnistria, thereby differentiating entities that are completely identical from a legal point of view.

As a result of Russian recognition and its consequences (viz. the opening of Russian military bases on the territory of South Ossetia and Abkhazia; the complete and final closure of their borders with Georgia; as well as Georgia's deprivation of any tools to influence this situation), Abkhazia and especially South Ossetia are actually migrating from the South Caucasus to the North, not, of course, in a geographical but in a political sense. Their complete unilateral dependence on Russia in terms of finance, investment, security and other respects leads both to internal political changes and to the absence of even a theoretical option to establish relations with third countries, as well as to a deterioration in the conditions for the activity of civil society, etc.

The next step towards revision of post-Soviet borders was the Russian annexation of Crimea in 2014. As a result of the sharp confrontation after the Euromaidan, Russia's relations with Ukraine deteriorated to such an extent that Russia decided, and was able, to carry out an operation to annex Crimea. A referendum was held ignoring the Ukrainian constitution, and the union was thus legitimised (from Russia's point of view) .

In this collision, we are again interested in the change in Russia's position from traditionalist to revisionist, which again occurred for political reasons that have nothing to do with Crimea itself and the aspirations of its population. Before the conflict with Ukraine, Russia had no territorial claims against it. In an interview in 2008, Putin said bluntly that even the question of Russia's possible claims to Crimea is provocative: "Crimea is not a disputed territory... Russia has long recognised the borders of today's Ukraine.... I believe the question about Russia having such goals implies a provocative meaning".[3]

At the same time, a conflict began in eastern Ukraine, mainly in the Donbass, which resulted in the creation of two new unrecognised entities – the Donetsk and Luhansk People's Republics. Of course, the conflict also had its own internal causes, but from the very beginning the Russian state provided the new entities with substantial material and military assistance, at the very least condoning the recruitment and sending of groups of mercenaries and volunteers from its territory to the conflict zone. It is unlikely that the self-proclaimed republics would have been able to hold out for any length of time in opposition to a country of the size of the Ukraine.

The DPR and LPR are already unrecognised states of the second generation, radically different from those formed in the early nineties. There is less ethnicisation here than in the Caucasus or even than in Transnistria: the population on the two sides of the newly formed borders does not differ at all in an ethno-cultural sense. The desire to create independent states in the Donetsk and Luhansk regions has never existed even at the level of ideas and discourses. In a new twist, the logic has become reversed. This is not secession and attempts to build viable states which then become a problem for the surrounding recognised states, but on the contrary, the creation of unrecognised entities as one of the forms of confrontation between major regional, or even global, players.

The latest event in this series was the Second Karabakh War of 2020, in which, for the first time in the history of post-Soviet conflicts, a non-post-Soviet player directly supported one of the parties to a post-Soviet conflict, thus entering the territory that was previously considered purely the territory of the national interests of the Russian Federation. Nothing like this had ever happened before in the former Soviet Union: there was no direct intervention of an external force in any of the conflicts. The extent and even type and manner of Turkish assistance to Azerbaijan during the Second Karabakh War are still the subject of controversy and research, but it is certain that without Turkey's participation, the outcome of the war might have been different.

Thus, we can conclude that conflicts in the post-Soviet space are being geopoliticised, while turning into their opposite: from a problem for external actors, these conflicts have been transformed into an instrument of influence and rivalry between major players.

Endnotes

[1] https://www.imemo.ru/index.php?page_id=1248&file=https://www.im-emo.ru/files/File/magazines/meimo/12_2021/10-MARKEDONOV.pdf (Accessed 5 August 2022)

[2] https://www.bbc.com/russian/features-43061604 (Accessed 5 August 2022)

[3] https://ria.ru/20080830/150807671.html (Accessed 5 August 2022)

Volunteer-Movement and the Circassian Factor During the Patriotic War of The People of Abkhazia in 1992-1993: Historical and Political Significance

Aslanbek Mirzoev

Candidate of Historical Sciences, Senior Researcher in the Department of Mediaeval and Modern History of the Department of History of the Institute for Humanitarian Research of the Kabardino-Balkarian Scientific Centre of the Russian Academy of Sciences. He was a former Circassian volunteer from Kabarda. Kabardino-Balkaria, Russia.

The mass volunteer-movement in support of the Abkhazian people has no analogues in the post-Soviet space in the recent history of the 20th century.

The Georgian-Abkhazian military conflict (14 August 1992 – 30 September 1993), officially called in Abkhazia "The Patriotic War of the People of Abkhazia", and "The Georgian-Abkhazian War" among the public of the republics of the North Caucasus, was one of the largest in the post-Soviet space [Kushkhabiev, p. 3].

The cause of the war was an attempt by the leadership of Georgia to create a national-unitary state by abolishing two of the autonomous entities that were part of it, namely the Autonomous Republic of Abkhazia and the Autonomous Region of South Ossetia. The policy of Georgia received support from the United States and a number of Western European states, in which the actions of the State Council of Georgia in relation to the Republic of Abkhazia were considered as an internal affair of Georgia [Kushkhabiev, p. 3].

Before the start of the Georgian army's incursion into Abkhazia, Russian-Georgian negotiations took place on 24 June 1992 in Dagomys, where Boris Yeltsin and Eduard Shevardnadze signed an agreement on the creation of peace-keeping forces in South Ossetia and the freezing of the conflict. There were other tacit agreements behind Abkhazia's back. According to this agreement:

a) Georgia agreed to join the CIS, but in return Russia had to turn a blind eye to the invasion of the Georgian armed forces into Abkhazia;

b) Georgia received a large amount of military equipment from the Transcaucasian Military District [Khalidov, p. 28].

On 14 August 1992, the Abkhazian people found themselves facing a national catastrophe that threatened not only the loss of national statehood but also their very physical existence. This was the fate that was predicted for them in many political and intellectual circles around the world, who were aware of the correlation of the capabilities of the warring parties, but at the same time underestimated the strength of the spirit of the small Abkhazian people and did not expect strong support from the peoples of the Caucasus [Khagba, p. 3].

The Georgian-Abkhazian conflict went far beyond the borders of Transcaucasia. Citizens and organisations were drawn into it from the Russian Federation, the CIS states, the USA, the countries of Europe, the Middle East, all countries in which the large Abkhaz-Adyghean diaspora is accommodated.

The aggression of the troops of the State Council of Georgia against Abkhazia provoked protests in many regions of Russia. In defence of the people of Abkhazia, the peoples of the North Caucasus spoke out, and above all, representatives of the ethnic group closely related to the Abkhazians, namely the Circassians [aka Adygheans, though in the North Caucasus West Circassians are rather known as 'Adyghes', whilst the East Circassians, such as Kabardians and Besleneys, are generally termed Cherkess(ians), though the self-designation of ALL Circassians is A:dygha – Trans.], both those living in the Russian Federation as well as representatives of the large Circassian foreign diaspora [Kushkhabiev, p. 3].

On the first day of the war, 14 August 1992, the President of the International Circassian Association (ICA), Yuri Khamzatovich Kalmykov, made an appeal with "a petition to the Adyghe and Abaza peoples, to all the peoples of the North Caucasus, the Cossacks of the South of Russia to announce a call for volunteers to protect the fraternal Abkhazian people" [Keshtov, p. 16–17]. Immediately in the city of Nalchik, where at that time the headquarters of the International Circassian Association was located, there was convened the Council of the Adyghe Khase and the Congress of the Kabardian People (KKN), at which decisions were made to assist the leadership of Abkhazia. On the same day, representatives of the KKN and Adyghe Khase met with the President of the KBR V.M. Kokov, where he was presented with demands: to give the opportunity to read the appeal of the President of the ICA Yuri Kalmykov on republican television, to make a statement on behalf of the republican authorities to the President of the Russian Federation B.N. Yeltsin, to provide a helicopter for the first group of volunteers to fly to Abkhazia, headed by the chairman of the Defence Committee of the Confederation of the Mountain Peoples of the Caucasus (KGNK), Colonel of the Reserve of the USSR Air Force Sultan A. Sosnaliev. Valery M. Kokov agreed to all these measures and on the same day, 14 August 1992, the announcer of the Kabardino-Balkarian radio, a member of the KKN, Ali Pshigotyzhev, read out the address of the President of the ICA Yuri Kalmykov to the Circassian and Abaza people, to all the peoples of the North Caucasus, the Cossacks of the South of Russia [informant Khatazhukov Valerij

Nazirovich, born in 1956, in the village of Shordakovo, Zolskij district, KBR]. The registration of volunteers for the helicopter-flight was begun. While the issue with the helicopter was being resolved, night fell, and the flight was rescheduled. In order not to waste time, it was decided to leave by bus. On 14 August at 23.00, the first group of volunteers, representatives of the KKN and Adyghe Khase, headed by S.A. Sosnaliev, left the building of the Congress of the Kabardian People on a tourist-bus. Having passed the territory controlled by the Georgian troops, on 15 August at 17:15 the group arrived in the city of Gudauta, where S.A. Sosnaliev took control of the Headquarters of Defence of the People's Militia [informant Kushkhov Mukhamed Ismailovich, born in 1938, in the village of Zalukokuazhe, Zolskij district of the KBR].

It should be noted that the statement of the President of the International Circassian Association Yuri Kalmykov was made even before the official appeal of the leadership of the Republic of Abkhazia to the leaders and peoples of the North Caucasus with a request for immediate assistance.

Chairman of the Supreme Council of the Republic of Abkhazia Vladislav Ardzinba issued a statement on 16 August 1992, addressed to "Parliaments, presidents, peoples of the world", which contained a request "to urgently put pressure on the State Council of Georgia and its head, Shevardnadze, to force him to withdraw troops and equipment from the territory of sovereign Abkhazia, to stop the bloodshed and robberies, and to send humanitarian aid to Abkhazia" [Kushkhabiev, p. 12]. The leadership of Abkhazia also turned to the leaders and peoples of the North Caucasus with a request for immediate assistance [Kushkhabiev, p. 12]. In an appeal to the leadership and peoples of Kabardino-Balkaria 15 dated August 1992, the following was noted: "In the hour of mortal danger, the Presidium of the Supreme Council of the Republic of Abkhazia asks the President of the Kabardino-Balkarian Republic and the fraternal peoples of Kabardino-Balkaria for help by all available means" [Kushkhabiev, p. 12].

On 18 August 1992, in the Chechen Republic, in the city of Grozny (where the Central Headquarters of the KGNK was located), the 10th extraordinary expanded session of the KGNK parliament was held. The resolution adopted by the 10th session strongly protests against the policy of the State Council of Georgia and the Russian leadership in Abkhazia. The resolution also contains fundamental points: "In the event of the continuation of the occupation of Abkhazia, to declare the start of military operations by the KGNK against Georgia, with all the ensuing consequences. To support the initiatives of the International Circassian Association and other national movements and parties in the region to start the formation of volunteer-units to protect the just cause of the Abkhazian people and send armed units of the KGNK to Abkhazia" [Kushkhabiev, p. 13].

From the very beginning of the war, Nalchik and Grozny were the collection-points for volunteers. Armed detachments of volunteers were already leaving from Grozny.

The contradictions in the Russian political élite and the confrontation that began between the Supreme Council of the Russian Federation and President Boris Yeltsin allowed in the first days of the war armed detachments of volunteers from the Kabardino-Balkarian Republic, the Chechen Republic - Ichkeria, the Republic of Adyghea, and the Karachay-Cherkess republics to arrive in Abkhazia literally a few days after the aggression of the Georgian State Council.

It was then, in the most difficult period, from the 15th to the end of August 1992, that several international detachments of North Caucasian volunteers came to Abkhazia – on 15 August: Kabardian group under the command of Sultan Sosnaliev; on 15 August: the second group of Kabardian volunteers, who flew by helicopter to Adler and managed to pass through the cordons of Georgian troops in the villages of Leselidze and Gantiadi; on 22 August: two Chechen detachments under the command of Shamil Basaev and Khamzat Khankarov, one Kabardian de-

51

tachment under the command of Ibragim Yaganov, one detachment of Circassians from Adyghea under the command of Adam Huade, 1 detachment of Circassians and Abazins from Karachay-Cherkessia under the command of Mukhamed Kilba (all armed groups); on 22 August: an armed group of Kabardian volunteers (30 people under the command of Aslan Iritov), who took off by helicopter from the Kanzhal mountain-plateau in the KBR to the Damkhurts Pass; on 27 August: an armed detachment under the command of Ruslan Gelaev from Chechens, Kabardians, Adyghes and Circassians.

It was important that they were armed volunteers, since the Abkhazian militias had few weapons. On the first day of the war, Georgian troops had captured in the barracks, along with weapons, a significant part of the so-called "Abkhazian Guard" (Separate Regiment of the Internal Troops of the Republic of Abkhazia). It was also important that it was timely assistance – if the Georgian army, which entered the city of Sukhum and became consumed with sacking the city, had not lose a few days but had immediately developed an offensive against Gudauta, the situation could have been different. With the help of the armed detachments of the North Caucasian volunteers who arrived in the first days of the war, the Abkhazian militia reliably secured defences immediately behind the city of Sukhum on the River Gumista. When already on 31 August/1 September the Georgians came to their senses and attempted a tank-breakthrough in the direction of Eshera, the Abkhazian militia, together with the North Caucasian volunteers, successfully repulsed it, and from then until the end of the war, the Georgians did not attempt any breakthrough in this direction. It was important that the North Caucasian volunteers were armed with anti-tank weapons – grenade-launchers; they also carried across the passes with them air-defence systems (MANPADS), anti-tank mines, and ammunition left in warehouses by the Russian army during the withdrawal from the Chechen Republic. Abkhazian militias in the first days of the war were mainly armed with small arms.

In order to imagine the role of volunteers in the Patriotic War in Abkhazia, one must have a clear idea of the situation that had developed in the republic by the beginning of the aggression of the Georgian State Council on 14 August 1992.

On 14 August 1992, the troops of the State Council of Georgia invaded the territory of the Republic of Abkhazia and launched Operation Sword, which envisaged the conquest of the territory of Abkhazia within a few days. The number of the invading group of Georgia was 2,000, with 60 tanks, infantry fighting vehicles, armoured personnel carriers, as well as artillery installations and air-cover. Georgian troops crossed the border at the River Ingur, capturing the towns of Gal and Ochamchira, and entered the capital of Abkhazia, the city of Sukhum. On 15 August, Georgian troops landed in the village of Gantiadi (in Abkhaz, Tsandripsh) and captured the north-western regions adjacent to the border with Russia. As a result of the hostilities, the Georgian troops, having broken the resistance of the few detachments of the Abkhazian militia and home-guard, captured the city of Sukhum on 18 August, and the city of Gagra on 19 August [Kushkhabiev, p. 11].

The Abkhazians and other nationalities of the republic found themselves surrounded in a small area from the River Gumista (in the South) to the village of Colchida (in the west). The leadership of the republic, headed by V.G. Ardzinba, left the city of Sukhum after its occupation and moved to the town of Gudauta, which became the centre of the national liberation war of the Abkhazian people. The problem was that Abkhazia was not ready for such an unfolding of events. What could the Abkhazians put up in opposition to the well-armed Georgian military which consisted of several thousands. It took time to form combat-ready units, but there simply was no time [Khalidov, p. 58].

Among some officials and former party-workers could be observed a mood of capitulation, whilst some were on the verge of poorly concealed panic. Some deputies of the Supreme Council of the Republic of

Abkhazia considered resistance to be inexpedient and called for capitulation [Kushkhabiev, p. 49]. Nevertheless, the leadership of the Republic of Abkhazia took urgent measures to repel the aggression. On 14 August, the Presidium of the Supreme Council of the Republic of Abkhazia adopted a resolution on the mobilisation of the Republic's population aged 18 to 40 inclusive and sending them for regimental deployment as internal troops. The leader of the nation Vladislav Ardzinba and his associates, like the main part of the Abkhazian people, were firm in their intention to defend the independence of the country. When, literally on the second day of the Georgian aggression, the Chairman of the Defence Committee of the KGNK, Colonel Sultan Sosnaliev with his small group, and after him several armed detachments of North Caucasian volunteers miraculously broke through into Abkhazia, this was of great moral and political importance, for the morale of the Abkhazian nation thereby received powerful reinforcement [Khalidov, p. 53].

S.A. Sosnaliev launched activities for the immediate formation of the people's militia and actually took command. The People's Militia Defence Headquarters (SHONO) was created.

Particularly strong moral and psychological shock was experienced by Georgian soldiers against the backdrop of their euphoria after the capture and several days of looting of the Abkhazian capital as victors, after the counter-attack of detachments of North Caucasian volunteers on the night of 25-25 August both in the village of Achadara (by a combined group of Chechens under Shamil Basaev and Circassians under Adam Khuade) and in the area of the city of Gagra on Mount Mamzyshkha (by two Kabardian groups under the command of Ibragim Yaganov and Aslan Iritov) [Kushkhabiev, p. 52–53].

In the most difficult and decisive minutes and days of the war, the Abkhazian people received the necessary military support from the peoples of the North Caucasus. The plans of the Georgian command for an easy victory in a short-term war were frustrated [Kushkhabiev, p. four].

In the first stage of the war, the role played by several hundred North Caucasian volunteers was significant. It was they who ensured a change in the public mood of a part of society, and shifting the initial feelings of panic among certain bureaucratic circles in the direction of confidence in final victory [Khalidov, p. ten].

The most massive volunteer-movement took place in the Chechen and Kabardino-Balkarian Republics. More than 1,000 volunteers from Chechenia and about 700-800 from Kabardino-Balkaria went through the war in Abkhazia. These are the data of V. Pachulia, colonel of the Ministry of Defence of the Republic of Abkhazia, Candidate of Historical Sciences, former employee of the General Staff of the Armed Forces of the Republic of Abkhazia [Khalidov, p. 54]. True, volunteers relieved one another and, at any one time, there were no more than 600–800 of them in Abkhazia. The exact number, for example, of Kabardian volunteers who took part in the Georgian-Abkhazian war has not been established. According to the Union of Abkhazian Volunteers of the KBR, over 1,500 Circassian volunteers from the KBR passed through Abkhazia. In addition to the Kabardians, among the volunteers from the KBR there were nine Russians and three Balkars [Kushkhabiev, p. 80].

The North Caucasian volunteers arrived in Abkhazia on subsequent days as well. Some groups made their way through the passes, others on boats. Volunteers also arrived in Abkhazia from the Abkhazian and Circassian diasporas of Turkey, Syria, and Jordan.

It is rather difficult to establish the exact number of North Caucasian volunteers in those days. It was constantly changing. They would leave Abkhazia injured and and having carried out various assignments. New groups of volunteers would arrive regularly. By the end of August, the total number of North Caucasian volunteers was approximately 800. Of these, over 200 were Kabardians, over 200 were Chechens, over 200 were Adyghes, about 50 were South Ossetians, about 50 were Abazins, Karachays and Cherkess(ians), about 50 were foreign Abkhazians and

Circassians. There were also Ingush, representatives of the peoples of Daghestan, and others [Kushkhabiev, p. 51]. Volunteers from the Don, Terek and Kuban Cossacks, from different regions of Russia also arrived in Abkhazia.

Speaking about the motivation of volunteers, it should be noted that the vast majority of them went to Abkhazia not for the purpose of material enrichment, but out of a sense of justice – "at the call of the heart", as they say. Kabardians, Adyghes, Circassians and Abazins arrived to help the ethnically related Abkhazian people. Chechens, South Ossetians and representatives of other peoples of the North Caucasus – out of solidarity with a small neighbouring people, an ally in the KGNK [Confederation of the Mountain Peoples of the Caucasus]. During the period under review, among the peoples of the North Caucasus, the ideas of Caucasian solidarity and the organisation reflecting these ideas, represented by the Confederation of the Mountain Peoples of the Caucasus, were quite popular. Supporters of the KGNK viewed the attack on Abkhazia by Georgian State Council troops as an attack on the Confederation itself. Don, Kuban and Terek Cossacks, as well as Russian volunteers, arrived to help the Russian population of Abkhazia [Kushkhabiev, p. 52].

In the first three weeks from the beginning of the war, with the help of North Caucasian volunteers, the Abkhazian militia managed seriously to cool the ardour and excitement of the Georgian units. The command of the troops of the State Council of Georgia at first did not perceive the North Caucasian volunteers to be any serious force [Kushkhabiev, p. 54]. The head of the State Council of Georgia, E. Shevardnadze, called the KGNK a "paper tiger", and the commander of the Georgian troops, G. Karkarashvili, in his infamous television address (25 August 1992) stated: "I can immediately assure especially the supporters of Mr. Ardzinba, those separatists who, under the name of some "Highlander Union" want to harass civilians ... they will find a mass-grave here" [Kushkhabiev, p. 55]. However, after the very first battles, the Georgian command came to appreciate the North Caucasian volunteers and began to seek their withdrawal from the territory of Abkhazia.

Volunteers took part in virtually all the military operations of the Armed Forces of the Republic of Abkhazia from the beginning to the end of the war, but they played a particularly important role in the initial stage, when the Abkhazian army was just being formed. The contribution of volunteer formations in major offensive operations of the Abkhazian army until January 1992 was at least 50 percent.

North Caucasian volunteers took an active part in the battles on the Gumista front in August 1992, and, in October 1992, in the liberation of the city of Gagra and the western regions of Abkhazia.

With the onset of cold weather, the season of storms, the blockade of the territory controlled by the leadership of Abkhazia could lead to catastrophic consequences. Maritime communication with Russian ports became more difficult, and communication with the North Caucasus through mountain-passes became impossible. There was a threat of economic "strangulation" of Abkhazia's blockaded territory [Kushkhabiev, p. 55]. In this situation, the leadership of the Republic of Abkhazia made a decision – to proceed with the liberation of the city of Gagra and the regions adjacent to the Russian border (the north-western regions of the Republic of Abkhazia).

By 17:30 on 3 October, Gagra was liberated. The losses on the Georgian side amounted to: several hundred soldiers and officers killed, whilst over 100 soldiers were taken prisoner. On the Abkhazian side, 24 fighters were killed. Abkhazian militia units seized a significant quantity of weapons, ammunition and 20 armoured vehicles [Kushkhabiev, p. 58]. The tens of armoured vehicles and the hundreds of small-arms weapons obtained during this operation as trophies made it possible to equip the emerging units of the Abkhazian army.

On 4 October, the Abkhazian international militia continued its offensive in the direction of the Russian border. On 6 October, at 6:40 am, the state-flag of the Republic of Abkhazia and the flag of the KGNK were raised on the border with Russia. The north-western part of Abkhazia had been liberated from the occupying troops [Kushkhabiev, p. 58].

The liberation of the north-western regions of Abkhazia was of great strategic and political importance. This was the first large-scale victory of the Abkhaz-North Caucasian militia over the regular Georgian army, which destroyed the plans and forecasts of the State Council of Georgia for an easy and rapid victory [Kushkhabiev, p. 59–60]. The unblocking of the territory and the access to the Russian border made it possible to transport humanitarian cargo freely from the republics of the North Caucasus to Abkhazia, which had previously been delivered by boat from Sochi. Now automobile-convoys could deliver food to Abkhazia in large quantities across the Russian-Abkhazian border. The food-problem was by that time very serious. V. Ardzinba had to think about how to feed not only the Abkhazian army, but also the large number of refugees from the regions occupied by the Georgian army. In the eastern regions of Abkhazia, by the winter of 1992-1993, there was already famine and an acute shortage of food. If not for the successful July and September operations of the Abkhazian army, which ended in victory, there was even the question of evacuating the civilian population from Eastern Abkhazia.

North Caucasian volunteers dominated in the divisions of the Armed Forces of the Republic of Abkhazia which carried out the Shroma operation on 3-4 November 1992 [Kushkhabiev, p. 61].

Although this operation was not successful for the Abkhaz-North Caucasian militia, the losses sustained in it by the Georgian army, despite the fact that they were the defenders, were twice the losses of the attackers (56 against 26).

Such was the result of the first stage of the war, in which the formations of the North Caucasian volunteers played a huge role [Khalidov, p. 61].

The second stage of the war was fundamentally different from the first both in terms of the role and the number of Abkhazian combat-units in the liberation of their homeland. At that time (from the autumn of 1992), the formation of the RA Armed Forces was completed on the basis of the people's volunteer-corps. They were created according to the system of the Armed Forces of the Soviet Union [Khalidov, p. 61–62]. On 11 October 1992, the Ministry of Defence and the General Staff of the Republic of Abkhazia were established by a Decree of the Presidium of the Supreme Council of the Republic of Abkhazia. The ministry was headed by Colonel Vladimir Arshba. Colonel Sultan Sosnaliev was appointed First Deputy Minister of Defence and Chief of the General Staff of the RA Armed Forces.

It was in the first stage that volunteers from the North Caucasus, primarily from Chechenia and the KBR, played an important role. In the second stage, the factors of the North Caucasian volunteer-movement and its political "core" in the person of the Confederation of the Peoples of the Caucasus receded into secondary roles, although they were still of considerable importance [Khalidov, p. 65].

The policy of the Federal Centre and the republican authorities in the North Caucasus in relation to the activities of the Congress of the Kabardian people, the International Circassian Association, the Adyghe Khase of the KBR, the Confederation of the Mountain Peoples of the Caucasus - public organisations that acted as organisers of the volunteer-movement can be divided into two stages. If the leadership of the Chechen Republic, in the person of Dzhokhar Dudaev, like the Chechen people, unambiguously supported the liberation-movement of the Abkhazian people, then the policy of other leaders of the republics of the North Caucasus from the very beginning was ambivalent. Some of them (in particular, Aslan Dzharimov, the leader of the Republic of Adyghea) warned Boris Yeltsin against unilateral support for Tbilisi. In general, they were facing difficult circumstances: on the one hand, the position and demand of the Kremlin, which were distinguished by their pro-Geor-

gian orientation; and on the other hand, a sufficiently powerful movement "from below" in support of the Abkhazians in their republics. On
the one hand, they had to manoeuvre between public expectations and
demands to provide real assistance to Abkhazia, and on the other hand,
to pursue a policy that would not greatly irritate Moscow. In such a situation, the only thing they could do without prejudice to their political
careers was the provision of humanitarian aid to Abkhazia, which in fact
was done throughout the war [Khalidov, p. 50].

Georgia demanded the withdrawal of volunteers. The Russian leadership also demanded from V.G. Ardzinba the withdrawal of volunteers
from the territory of Abkhazia in exchange for the promise of a political
settlement of the conflict.

By the beginning of September 1992, a rather acute situation had
developed in the KBR. Kabardian public organisations and state-au-
thorities characterised the events in Abkhazia as an aggression of the
State Council of Georgia against the Republic of Abkhazia. In this their
positions coincided. The position of the authorities of the KBR was to
make efforts to resolve the situation in Abkhazia by peaceful means, to
provide its people with all kinds of political and moral support, as well
as humanitarian assistance. The positions of the Kabardian public organisations and the leadership of the KBR diverged on one of the main
issues – and that was the formation of volunteer-detachments to be sent
to Abkhazia to the places of hostilities. The position of the Kabardian
public organisations was that the Abkhazian people were on the verge of
physical annihilation and sending volunteers to Abkhazia was the most
effective help to be given to the people of Abkhazia. The leadership of
the KBR in this matter took a negative position, agreeing with the leadership of the Russian Federation [Kushkhabiev, p. 23].

On 27 August 1992, an emergency-session of the Supreme Council
of the Kabardino-Balkarian Republic was held, dedicated to the situation in the Republic of Abkhazia. Among the proposed measures for the

peaceful settlement of the conflict and the provision of humanitarian assistance to the Abkhazian people, the resolution of the Supreme Council of the KBR contained a requirement for socio-political organisations and national movements to "stop illegal actions in acquiring weapons, campaigning and forming volunteer-detachments" [Kushkhabiev, p. 20].

At the emergency-session of the Supreme Council of the KBR, a deputy-group was formed consisting of deputies of the Supreme Court of the Russian Federation M.Sh. Mamkhegova, F.A. Kharaev and deputy of the Supreme Council of the KBR K.A. Murzakanov to be sent to the area of the Georgian-Abkhazian conflict on a peacekeeping mission. In Georgia, the deputies were received by E.A. Shevardnadze, who demanded putting a stop to the sending of volunteers to Abkhazia. The representatives of the Supreme Council of the KBR replied that they had nothing to do with the volunteer-movement [Kushkhabiev, p. 21].

The press-service of the President of the KBR issued a statement noting that the President of the KBR and the Presidium of the Supreme Council of the KBR condemned the solution of problems by force of arms and adhered to the principle of non-interference in the affairs of a sovereign state by armed means [Kushkhabiev, p. 21]. The statement also says that the position of the Government of the KBR was to provide the people of Abkhazia with political and moral support as well as humanitarian assistance. The following statement by the press-service of the President of the KBR (dated 4 September 1992) noted: "... the government, the authorities in the KBR firmly adhere to the position of a peaceful settlement of the Georgian-Abkhazian conflict and oppose the sending of volunteers to Abkhazia ... The Government of the KBR ... will carry out the decision of the Supreme Council of the Kabardino-Balkarian Republic and will continue to provide political, moral and humanitarian support to Abkhazia" [Kushkhabiev, p. 22].

The prosecutor's office of the KBR issued a sharp statement against Kabardian public organisations, accusing the leadership of the KKN of violating a number of laws and destabilising the situation in the republic [Kushkhabiev, p. 22].

Prosecutor of the KBR E.G. Denisov turned to the Chairman of the KKN Yuri Kalmykov with a presentation in which he qualified as illegal actions conducted in support of the people of Abkhazia (viz. blocking the Rostov-Baku highway, rallies, etc.). The prosecutor suggested to the chairman of the KKN, Yuri Kalmykov "to take measures to stop the illegal actions of the KKN executive committee when organising actions in support of the Abkhazian people in the Georgian-Abkhazian conflict, to carry out this work within the framework established by the current legislation" [Kushkhabiev, p. 22]. The prosecutor also said that the prosecutor's office instructed the Ministry of Internal Affairs of the KBR to conduct a thorough investigation to identify specific perpetrators and bring them to justice [Kushkhabiev, p. 22].

The Ministry of Justice of the KBR also stated that "the activity of public associations aimed at creating formations with the aim of providing military assistance to Abkhazia is illegal. They will be held fully responsible for the dangerous consequences of such actions" [Kushkhabiev, p. 22].

On 3 September 1992, a meeting was held between the President of the Russian Federation B.N. Yeltsin and the leaders of the republics, territories and regions of the North Caucasus. At this meeting, a decision was taken on the need to introduce a state of emergency in the North Caucasus region and to transfer internal troops from other regions of the Russian Federation in connection with the explosive situation. With regard to the Georgian-Abkhazian military conflict, the participants in the meeting proposed a plan, the essence of which was that Russia should take on a mission of mediation. The first step was to ensure the cessation of hostilities and to introduce peacekeeping forces into Abkhazia. The second stage was the organisation of negotiations between the parties in order to develop conditions for peace and an acceptable status for Abkhazia within Georgia [Kushkhabiev, p. 25].

On the same day, a meeting was held between the President of the Russian Federation Boris Yeltsin, Chairman of the State Council of the Republic of Georgia Eduard Shevardnadze, Chairman of the Supreme Council of the Republic of Abkhazia Vladislav Ardzinba and leaders of the republics, territories and regions of the North Caucasus. Its final document called for cessation of fire on both sides and of any use of force, starting from 12:00 on 1 September 1992, as well as the creation of a commission for control and inspection from representatives appointed by the authorities of Georgia, Abkhazia and Russia. The following tasks were entrusted to the commission: disarmament, disbandment and removal from Abkhazia of illegal armed formations and groups, as well as the prevention of their entering Abkhazia. The document enshrined the provision of the territorial integrity of Georgia [Kushkhabiev, p. 26].

The leadership of the Russian Federation took a number of measures to resolve the situation in the North Caucasus, connected with the events in Abkhazia. Under the Security Council of the Russian Federation, a special Commission was formed to resolve the situation in the North Caucasus, and especially on the border with Abkhazia. Already by 19 August the border-guards of the Novorossijsk border-detachment began to serve on the Russian side of the Psou River, blocking the border between Russia and Abkhazia. Additional contingents of troops were transferred to the North Caucasus. The border with Abkhazia was strengthened by units of the internal troops (VV), whose tasks included preventing groups of North Caucasian volunteers from crossing into Abkhazia.

The transfer of additional contingents of troops to the North Caucasus and the strengthening of the border with Abkhazia, which complicated the ties of the North Caucasian public organisations with this republic, caused a sharp reaction from the KGNK. The leaders of the

KGNK stated that, if the authorities tried to resist the formation of volunteer-detachments by military force, "then military operations will be deployed here ..." [Kushkhabiev, p. 26].

The situation in Kabardino-Balkaria acquired an "explosive" character. The entry of a significant contingent of internal troops and special police units (OMON) was perceived by a part of the population as a measure of the federal authorities to counter the movement in support of the people of Abkhazia.

On 12 September 1992, at a meeting of the KKN, a resolution "On the Socio-political Aituation in the KBR" was adopted. The resolution says that the KKN considered the introduction of special-forces' battalions into the territory of the republic unreasonable and qualified their actions as "insulting the dignity of citizens". It is noted that the KKN demanded the withdrawal of all special-purpose battalions of internal troops from the territory of the republic.

On 24 September 1992 in Nalchik near Government House there began an indefinite rally organised by Kabardian public organisations. The rally was attended by thousands of residents of the KBR (mainly Kabardian settlements) and representatives of neighbouring republics. The protesters demanded of the leadership of the republic the release of the arrested President of KGNK Musa (Yuri) Shanibov and appearances on air of the KKN and Adyghe Khase. Attempts by law-enforcement agencies to disperse the protesters were unsuccessful. On 26 and 27 September, in a number of districts of the city of Nalchik, protesters clashed with units of the internal troops (VV) and special police units (OMON), who used tear-gas and then firearms. There were wounded on both sides. The transfer of army-units to the KBR continued. In Nalchik, in Government House, the special "Alpha" forces of the Federal Security Service of the Russian Federation were located. Supporters of the Kabardian national movement blocked roads and the airport in Nalchik. As the situation worsened, the number of protesters increased [Kushkhabiev, p. 28]. They put forward demands: to withdraw units of the VV riot-police and OMON special forces from the territory of the KBR; to remove the president of the KBR V.M. Kokov; to dissolve the Supreme Council of the KBR; to re-elect the Central Election Commission of the KBR; to launch a campaign to collect signatures to terminate the Federative Treaty of the KBR with the Russian Federation, etc. The rally in Nalchik was supported in neighbouring republics. Rallies demanding the release of the president of the KGNK began in Cherkessk and Maykop [Kushkhabiev, p. 29].

The situation was becoming critical. Only as a result of long and extremely difficult negotiations between the leadership of the KBR and Kabardian public organisations on 1 October 1992 was an agreement was reached providing for the termination of the open-ended rally, the dissolution of the Supreme Council of the KBR before 1 December 1992, and the withdrawal of units of the Ministry of Internal Affairs and special forces from the territory of the republic. In those days, the KBR was on the verge of civil war. The situation was saved by Yuri Kalmykov, authoritative public figure, scholar and later appointed Minister of Justice of Russia. He played the role of mediator and a kind of "lightning rod", thereby saving the face of both the authorities and the leaders of the opposition. The inevitable managed to be avoided [Khalidov, p. 51]. The rally did not disperse until Yu.M. Shanibov was released on 27 September and arrived in Nalchik, where he addressed the protesters.

The agreement between the authorities of the KBR and the opposition was that the authorities should provide humanitarian and political support to Abkhazia and turn a blind eye to the activities of the opposition in terms of organising a volunteer-movement. President of the KGNK Confederation and leader of the KKN Musa Shanibov himself left the republic in the autumn of 1992 and went to Abkhazia, where he continued his political activities, leading the KGNK. On 4 October, the open-ended rally in Nalchik dispersed.

The rallies and demonstrations consisting of many thousands that took place in August-September 1992 in the republics of the North Caucasus, especially the protests in Nalchik, which were accompanied by clashes with internal troops and which exacerbated the situation to the limit, demonstrated to the leadership of Georgia and the world-community the determination of the North Caucasian peoples to provide real assistance to the victims of aggression, namely the people of Abkhazia [Kushkhabiev, p. 29]. In general, the KBR, along with the Chechen Republic, remained throughout the war one of the main rear bases, serving a humanitarian role and as a centre for organising the volunteer-movement.

From that time, the authorities no longer tried to impede the volunteer-movement or to aggravate relations with national public organisations. Every time when there was an aggravation of the military-political situation through the fault of Georgia, the ICA [International Circassian Association] reserved the right to appeal to the Circassian people with a request to mobilise volunteers. Thus, in response to the mobilisation of the population announced in Georgia, the ICA Executive Committee at its meeting on 10 November 1992 in Maykop issued a declaration: "The International Circassian Association considers it necessary to warn that, in the event of a repeated escalation of military operations by Georgia in Abkhazia, it will be forced to re-announce the formation of volunteer-detachments and provide the fraternal Abkhazian people with all the assistance they need" [ICA, p. 32].

A barbaric action in Abkhazia produced a wide public outcry in the KBR: on 14 December 1992, Georgian units shot down a Russian helicopter with a surface-to-air missile – it was carrying out a humanitarian mission to evacuate refugees, sick, wounded, women and children from the besieged city of Tkvarchal. As a result, 58 people died, including 13 women and 20 children. Among the dead were three Kabardian volunteers who were taking part in the evacuation of the refugees. A funeral-meeting was held in Nalchik [Kushkhabiev, p. 31].

At a meeting of the Supreme Council of the Russian Federation on 24 December 1992 V.Zh. Mastafov, a deputy from the KBR, made a speech on behalf of a group of deputies of the North Caucasian republics as well as of the leaders of the Republic of Abkhazia. Addressing the President of the Russian Federation B.N. Yeltsin, he noted that the foreign Circassian (Adyghe) and Abkhazian diasporas were providing assistance to the people of Abkhazia, including sending volunteers to participate in hostilities as part of the Armed Forces of Abkhazia. He also stated: "And it is quite natural that inaction on the part of the Russian Ministry of Foreign Affairs, the Ministry of Defence and the Supreme Council of the Russian Federation has provoked a new wave of mobilisation of compatriot-volunteers not only from Turkey but also from the republics of the North Caucasus, ready to fight for the just cause of the Abkhazians. Literally the other day, after the tragedy with the Russian helicopter, I received information from the leadership of Kabardino-Balkaria, Adyghea and Karachay-Cherkessia that mobilisation of volunteers has begun again in these republics" [Kushkhabiev, p. 31].

On 27 February 1993, a meeting of representatives of the national-democratic movements, public and socio-political organisations of the republics, territories and regions of the North Caucasus was held in Nalchik, dedicated to the situation in Abkhazia. The meeting was attended by 66 organisations of the North Caucasus region. Documents were adopted at the meeting – a resolution, a statement, an appeal to the President of the Russian Federation Boris Yeltsin and Chairman of the RF Armed Forces Ruslan Khasbulatov, UN Secretary General Boutros Ghali. They contained a call to stop the war in Abkhazia, cut off economic ties with Georgia, recognise the independence of Abkhazia, etc. The resolution of the meeting contained the following fundamental points:

1. "Recognise the entry of the Armed Forces of Georgia into the territory of Abkhazia as an act of military aggression on the part of the Republic of Georgia against Abkhazia, and the actions

carried out by them in the occupied territory as genocide of the Abkhazian people."

2. "Two. Demand the immediate withdrawal of Georgian troops, without any conditions, from the territory of Abkhazia. Otherwise, the peoples of the North Caucasus will consider themselves obliged to expand their assistance, including military assistance, to the fraternal Abkhazian people" [Kushkhabiev, p. 32].

In connection with the aggravation of the situation in Abkhazia and the special measures taken by the leadership of Georgia in March 1993, ICA President Yuri Kalmykov sent a telegram to Eduard Shevardnadze, to whom it was stated in particular: "It has become known from the mass-media that in connection with the aggravation of the situation in Abkhazia, a general mobilisation of reservists in Georgia is expected. The ICA Executive Committee considers this measure to be an error and extremely dangerous. If it is implemented, the ICA will be forced to appeal to the entire Circassian (Adyghe) people, including the five millionth Circassian diaspora, to stand up for the fraternal Abkhazian people in order to save them from genocide" [Kushkhabiev, p. 33].

On 27 July 1993, a ceasefire-agreement in Abkhazia was signed in Sochi. The document, signed by representatives of the leadership of Georgia, Abkhazia and Russia, provided for the withdrawal from the territory of Abkhazia of Georgian troops and armed formations, groups and individuals located in the conflict-zone within 10-15 days from the date of the ceasefire.

It was also planned to use international observers and peacekeeping forces in the conflict-zone [Kushkhabiev, p. 35].

However, the truce did not last long. Fulfilling the Sochi Agreement, on 17 August 1993, the leadership of the Republic of Abkhazia sent groups of North Caucasian volunteers to their homeland. At the same time, according to the RA Ministry of Defence, the Georgian leadership left more than 80% of its military equipment in the occupied territory of Abkhazia and continued to import ammunition. Officers and soldiers of the Georgian Armed Forces were re-registered as police- and commandant-officers. During August, the Georgian side repeatedly violated the terms of the truce and opened fire on Abkhazian positions. These actions were regarded by the Abkhazian side as a demonstration of the unwillingness of the Georgian leadership to implement the Sochi agreement [Kushkhabiev, p. 35].

On 14 September 1993, on the initiative of the KKN and *Adyghe Khase*, a press-conference was held in Nalchik with the participation of representatives of the Supreme Council of the Republic of Abkhazia and representatives of the leadership of the Kabardino-Balkarian Republic. A joint-statement of the Executive Committee of the KKN and *Adyghe Khase* was announced, which contained an appeal to the President of the Russian Federation B.N. Yeltsin - «to take all necessary measures to ensure that Georgia fulfils its obligations» [Kushkhabiev, p. 36–37].

The statement notes: "The Kabardian people and their valiant sons will never leave our Abkhazian brothers in trouble. If hostilities resume due to the fault of the Georgian side, then the volunteer-movement in Kabardino-Balkaria will take on an even wider scope. The KKN and *Adyghe Khase* will appeal to all socio-political and national-patriotic movements of the North Caucasus with an appeal to resume the volunteer-movement and the provision of humanitarian assistance in Abkhazia" [Kushkhabiev, p. 37].

In the then-current impasse, the leadership of the Republic of Abkhazia was forced to resume the fight against the occupying forces. At dawn on 16 September 1993, units of the armed forces of the Republic of Abkhazia went on the offensive [Kushkhabiev, p. 37].

On the initiative of the KKN and *Adyghe Khase*, on 20 September an open-ended rally began in Nalchik in support of the people of Abkhazia fighting aggression. [Kushkhabiev, p. 38]. Volunteers went to Abkhazia after taking part in the rally. During the week, about 150 volunteers went to the places of hostilities.

The participants of the open-ended rally also adopted a resolution (21 September 1993). The resolution contained calls: to the peoples of the KBR, to the heads of regional and city-organisations and enterprises, calling on them to strengthen the provision of humanitarian assistance to the people of Abkhazia; and to all volunteers "regarding an immediate return to Abkhazia and continuation of the armed struggle against the Georgian fascists to the bitter end" [Kushkhabiev, p. 38].

The open-ended rally in Nalchik and other actions in support of the people of Abkhazia, which took place in the KBR and other republics of the North Caucasus, ended after 27 September 1993, when a message was received about the victory of the armed forces of the Republic of Abkhazia over the troops of the aggressor [Kushkhabiev, p. 39].

The mass volunteer movement in support of the Abkhazian people has no analogues across the post-Soviet space in the recent history of the 20th century.

Among the factors that determined the mass-character and strength of the volunteer-movement are:

1. The volunteer-movement did not emerge out of nothing; its appearance was facilitated by the huge preparatory work of public organisations (*Ajdgylara* of the Republic of Abkhazia, *Adyghe Khase* of the Kabardino-Balkarian Republic, the Republic of Adyghea, the Karachay-Cherkess Republic, the Congress of the Kabardian People, the International Circassian Association, the Confederation of the Mountain Peoples of the Caucasus) and specific individuals (Musa Shanibov, Yusup Soslanbekov, Issa Arsamikov, Gennadi Alamia, Guram Gumba, Khamzat Khankarov, Denga Khalidov, Ruslan Gvashev, Amin Zekhov, Ibragim Naurzhanov, etc.) in the pre-war period (from 1989 to 1992).

2. The justice of the struggle of the Abkhazian people against aggression and the imperial, unitary policy of the Georgian state
became the moral and psychological basis for the participation
of volunteers in the war. The concepts of truth and justice in-
herent in the mentality of the North Caucasian peoples became
one of the motives for participation in the war. The youth of the
Caucasus, and the volunteers, according to statistical data, were
mainly young people, marked by a keenly felt sense of justice.
At the same time, they did not feel hatred or enmity towards
Georgia and Georgians. The ancient history of the Caucasus, its
customs and traditions created a certain archetype and specific
phenomena within social life – the functions of protecting national honour and dignity, speaking out against the arbitrariness
of the strong over the weak.

3. The desire of the North Caucasian peoples for national independence, the spirit of freedom they have preserved, is also a
factor in the mass-participation in these events. The freedom
and independence of the Abkhazian people was considered by
the leaders and active participants in the national movements
of the North Caucasus to be an important precedent that could
later become a model and example of the independent existence
and state-building of the small peoples of the North Caucasus.

4. The phenomenon of the role of the individual in history played
an important role. The personalities of Vladislav Ardzinba and
Yuri Kalmykov were accepted and recognised as national leaders
of the Abkhazian and Circassian peoples. No less important was
the role of the personal qualities of Sultan Sosnaliev and Yuri
(Musa) Shanibov, the former as a military leader, the latter as a
politician and ideologist.

5. The absence of a confessional orientation in this war ensured
the support and participation in it of volunteers not only of
the North Caucasian peoples, but also representatives of the

Cossacks, Russian and other peoples from different regions of the Soviet Union and the Russian Federation.

The massive nature of the volunteer-movement in the North Caucasian republics of the Russian Federation forced both the leadership of these republics and the political leadership of the Russian Federation to change their attitude towards the conflict.

The prolongation of the war in the conditions of limited human, military-technical, material-, and food-resources of Abkhazia, coupled with a significant superiority of Georgia according to these indicess, and also coupled with a complete blockade of Abkhazia by Russia, could have rendered the outcome of this conflict different. The broad and powerful (political, material, military) support of the peoples of the North Caucasus, primarily the Circassian and Chechen ethnic groups in the Caucasus, as well as the Abkhaz-Adyghe diaspora, in the form of organising the volunteer-movement did not allow the then-Russian leadership to blockade Abkhazia, leaving the Abkhazian people face to face with the aggressor. There was a real threat, if not of the defeat of Abkhazia in the war then of the freezing of this conflict for many years, with the occupation of the eastern regions of the republic, in line with the Cypriot scenario.

A frozen, unresolved conflict would have allowed the Russian Federation to keep Georgia in its sphere of influence and prevent its withdrawal from the CIS. In this regard, military victory by either side did not seem expedient.

Volunteer-detachments played an important role in the first period of the war. This made it possible during that time (from August to November 1992) to create a fully-fledged Abkhazian army. In the offensive operations carried out during that period, the proportion of volunteer-detachments was at least half.

Right up to the present time, there is no consensus among scholars and the public of the republics of the North Caucasus regarding the significance of the assistance provided by the peoples of the North Caucasus to the people of Abkhazia in the fight against aggression. Supporters of the sceptical approach argue that this assistance was not significant and could not influence the course of events in Abkhazia. Supporters of the opposite point of view believe that the fate of Abkhazia was largely decided in the North Caucasus [Kushkhabiev, p. 90].

In this matter, one should take into account the opinions of both the participants in the events – the volunteers and representatives of the leadership of Abkhazia. According to the results of a 2008 survey conducted in the KBR, the question: "How significant was the political, moral and humanitarian support for Abkhazia from the KBR and other North Caucasian republics?", 96% of the combatants answered that without this support Abkhazia would not have been able to repel the aggression, whilst 4% found it difficult to answer. Regarding the significance of the participation of North Caucasian volunteers in hostilities, 95% of respondents noted that without the participation of North Caucasian volunteers, the people of Abkhazia would have been defeated, and 5% indicated that the participation of North Caucasian volunteers in military operations hastened the victory of the people of Abkhazia [Kushkhabiev, p. 91].

At the same time, all the interviewed volunteers noted that the victory in the war was undoubtedly won by the people of Abkhazia. The political and moral support provided to Abkhazia by the peoples of the North Caucasus, as well as the participation of North Caucasian volunteers in hostilities, hastened the victory of the people of Abkhazia [Kushkhabiev, p. 91].

Lieutenant General S.A. Sosnaliev believed: "The role of the North Caucasian volunteers in the victory of the people of Abkhazia was significant, and especially in moral and psychological terms. Their very appearance in Abkhazia helped raise the spirit of the Abkhazian militia. No less important was the political and humanitarian aid to the people of Abkhazia, which came from the republics of the North Caucasus" [Kushkhabiev, p. 91].

The position of the Abkhazian leadership on this issue was expressed by the President of the Republic of Abkhazia Vladislav Ardzinba in his report at the II World Congress of the Abkhaz-Abazinian (Abaza) people on 24–27 July 1994: "The reaction to the events in Abkhazia in the North Caucasus broke through the information-blockade and contributed to a change in official Russia's attitude towards us. But this help was not only moral, although the thousands-strong rallies in Nalchik, the broadcasting of the meetings of the parliament of the Confederation of Mountain Peoples of the Caucasus, the speeches of its leaders ..., the leaders of other social movements of the Caucasus and the South of Russia instilled courage and faith in the defenders of Abkhazia; but it was also direct – in the form of the participation of volunteers, representatives of the peoples of the North Caucasus, the South of Russia – Cossacks, Russians ... We are rightfully proud of the heroism and courage of the entire multinational people of Abkhazia, but the dedication and feat of our volunteer-brethren should be doubly and triply appreciated. Many of them entered the land of Abkhazia for the first time but fought for it as well as they would have done for their homeland" [Kushkhabiev, p. 91–92].

In summation, it should be noted that there can be no doubt that the victory in the Georgian-Abkhazian war of 1992-1993 was won by the people of Abkhazia. Without exaggerating or underestimating the importance of the participation of the North Caucasian volunteers in the hostilities as part of the Armed Forces of the Republic of Abkhazia, one can agree with the above point of view that it was really timely and effective and that it contributed to the victory of the people of Abkhazia. The very fact of the North Caucasian volunteers' non-compulsory and disinterested participation in the hostilities in order to assist the numerically small people of Abkhazia who were being subjected to aggression, coupled with the nobility and heroism they displayed, is a striking phenomenon in the recent history of the Caucasus [Kushkhabiev, p. 92].

Literature

Kushkhabiev, A.V.: *Kabardian volunteers in the Georgian-Abkhazian war 1992–1993*. Nalchik. Publishing-house of M. and V. Kotljarov. 2008.

Khalidov, D.Sh.: *The North Caucasus in the Patriotic War of Abkhazia (1992–1993)*. Sukhum. 2014.

Khagba, L.R.: *Their Souls are Melting over the Mountains... An Essay on the Volunteers of the North Caucasus, Participants in the Georgian-Abkhazian War of 1992-1993*. Sukhum, 2013.

Keshtov, T.M., & Tsulaja, G.V. (Compilers): *Volunteers in the Patriotic War of Abkhazia (1992–1993). Documents and Materials*. Sukhum. 2014.

I[nternational] C[ircassian] A[ssociation] 1991–2011. Collection of Documents. Nalchik. Tetragraf. 2011.

We Abkhazians Have Failed to Spread an Understanding of Our Aspirations Internationally

Beslan Kobakhia

The public and political figure of Abkhazia. During the 1992-93 Georgian-Abkhazian War, he was head of the government commission for the exchange of prisoners of war and the protection of the civilian population. Abkhazia.

Despite the abundance of material about what happened 30 years ago, we, the Abkhazians, have failed, in my opinion, to convey to the whole world around us what happened to our people 30 years ago and what grave consequences this had and continues to have for them today.

According to the results of the last war, the Abkhazian people lost about six percent of their population killed. These were mainly losses among young men, whose average age was 23. Approximately three times as many people were severely injured and permanently disabled. A large gap formed in the ratio between women and men, as a result of which many girls of post-war Abkhazia did not have suitors left inside the country whom they could marry.

The hardest blow was dealt to the economy of Abkhazia, which was completely destroyed. Huge damage has been done to the scientific and educational system of the country. As is well-known, most schools, place of higher learning, and scientific institutions were simply wrecked and destroyed. In addition, most of the archives of our country in which many unique historical documents of the centuries-old history of Abkhazia were concentrated were put to the torch. Museums, theatres, cultural monuments were looted. In the city of Sukhum, not a single monument to the figures of the Abkhazian state, representatives of its culture and art, many of which cannot be restored, has remained undamaged.

The whole of Abkhazia was turned into a cemetery 30 years ago. Our whole country is littered with the graves of innocent people. In every district and town of Abkhazia today there are monuments to the fallen defenders of the motherland, which are sacred to all the people of our small country.

Everything that I list has been known for a long time and has been published many times in the free press. And yet, this does not impress the outside world, which cannot fully appreciate what happened in Abkhazia 30 years ago.

Therefore, I will try to compare the numbers of our losses with other countries, if such a large-scale tragedy were to happen to them.

If this happened in the United States, then the figures for loss in that country might be about 18 million individuals, i.e. about 45 thousand people would die every day of the war. For the European Union, the figures would be roughly comparable to those for the United States.

For China, if such a situation arose, the death toll might be approximately 90 million individuals, i.e. approximately 230 thousand people on each day of the war.

For Georgia, if this country suffered the same losses as Abkhazia, the death toll could be estimated at about 300,000, which would equate to about one thousand individuals per day of the war.

At the same time, it should be understood, as I said above, that among the dead were mostly men aged 23, most of whom were not married.

I apologise for playing with numbers, but it is precisely such an analysis that can help one fully to understand the tragedy of the situation in which the small Abkhazian people found themselves.

The history of mankind knows many examples of such tragedies. The most striking example is World War II, which is comparable in scale and consequences to what happened in Abkhazia at the end of the 20th century. We all remember from history how difficult it was for mankind to recover from the consequences of that terrible war, how many years it took to overcome the legacy of the horrors of the mid-20th century, how much effort was needed to restore the economy, culture, and educational system. But the most important thing is that humanity of that period was able both to condemn everything negative that gave rise to the Second World War, and to create an uncompromising attitude towards all types of manifestations of fascism. As a result, today's world and its human values are based on that very basis. That is to say, our fathers and grandfathers found the strength not only to end the catastrophic war but also to overcome the legacy of the past, creating and passing on the modern world to us.

What helped Abkhazia survive in such a difficult situation 30 years ago? There are many components of this phenomenon, but there is one simple explanation of the reasons for the victory of Abkhazia in the war against an unequal enemy. That is the unconditional awareness of the rightness of their cause, unconditional faith in the justice of that war on the part of Abkhazia, and unshakable confidence on this basis in their subsequent victory. It was this attitude that helped our people survive 30 years ago. It was this attitude that helped our society avoid turning into a criminal enclave, in which we could well have found ourselves after such a monstrous war and its dire consequences. It is this attitude that helps us build our state today. And we see this state as open to all our friends in this world. The very model of the state under construction is based on democratic values, as indicated by all our fundamental documents adopted at different times, including the Referendum, and confirmed by subsequent decisions of the Parliament of the Country. Suffice it to say that all elections at all levels of power in our country take place at the appointed time and, without fail, on the basis of choice.

What do we expect from the world around us?

From Europe as a whole and from the entire Western World, we expect an understanding of what has happened to us over the course of the last 20-30 years. We do not ask for anything for ourselves that could exceed the usual actions of all the countries of the European Union. Abkhazia has never found itself outside world-processes throughout its centuries-old history. Suffice it to say that Abkhazia has in practice been part of all the universal integration-formations created in the world over the entire history of mankind. Abkhazia was part of the Roman Empire, the Byzantine Empire, the Ottoman Empire, the Russian Empire, and was part of the Soviet Union. An Abkhazian delegation took part in the first Christian Nicaean Council in 325 A.D... Based on the results of the work of that First Council, a decision was taken to open an Orthodox Seat in Abkhazia, in the city of Pitsunda.

We expect Europe to recognize the current realities. In the last 30 years, the map of Europe has undergone significant changes, resulting in the emergence in the world of many new independent states. And Abkhazia too is amongst them. But towards Abkhazia, on the part of Europe, some kind of selective policy is being pursued which ignores reality. I believe that such an approach is not correct and does not meet the humanistic ideals of today's world. Suffice it to say that citizens of Abkhazia are often denied visas to EU countries, as a result of which many of our students are deprived of the opportunity to receive education in the best European universities, and sick people who need urgent treatment cannot get to the corresponding European clinics. Therefore, I would like to take this opportunity to appeal to the deputies of the European Parliament and ask them not to ignore Abkhazia, and give it the opportunity to be integrated into the world-community.

Unfortunately, we have more than enough problems. According to the most conservative estimates, the damage caused by the war and the post-war blockade of our country is at least 120 billion US dollars. It is clear that Abkhazia cannot cope with such problems and costs on its own. We need real economic and financial assistance to our country. We need a Grand Plan for the restoration of everything destroyed, which can only be possible with the consolidated assistance of the countries of the world. Today, only the Russian Federation is providing such assistance in relation to Abkhazia, for which we are extremely grateful. But the funds coming to Abkhazia are way insufficient to solve our problems. At the same time, looking back at world-history, one can recall how post-war Europe was restored, how post-war Japan was restored, developments which were made possible only with the consolidation of the leading world-powers.

Abkhazia, as a state, does not pose a threat to the outside-world. The very name of our country contains its essence, for one of the interpretations of it is "Country of the Soul". And the soul of our country is open to all people of the surrounding world who come to visit us with pure thoughts. Perhaps it is this name of our country that most fully reveals its mentality, which allows our people to survive in any situation, retaining their own sense of being and not losing the most important thing that is in the soul of every Abkhazian – Love of Humanity.

Abkhazia and Georgia on the Verge of Independence (1917 - 1921)

Cem Kumuk

Independent Researcher and Author on the history of the Caucasus. Turkey.

Abstract

Abkhazia and Georgia have confronted each other in every period when the cards were shuffled in the history of the Caucasus. One of these challenges came at a time when the Romanov dynasty in Russia was ending and the independence-hopes of the peoples of imperial Russia were blooming. Including many Georgian intellectuals and politicians, large Caucasian masses idealised a Great Caucasian Confederation as the only solution to save the Caucasus from Russian imperialism. However, the chauvinistic Georgians, who could not understand that they could not be free until the whole Caucasus was liberated, again played a facilitating role in Russia's domination of the Caucasus. We witnessed a similar scene when the Union of Soviet Socialist Republics was disintegrating in 1991. The events that this article reveals and which took place between the years 1918-1921 will sound extremely familiar to those who have witnessed what has happened since 1991 in Abkhazia, because the path followed by the chauvinist Georgian policies in the period after 1991 was not very different from the path followed in the period of 1918-1921. The article aims to draw the attention of the reader to the exemplary resemblance between what happened during the period of the existence of an opportunity for independence when the Russian monarchy collapsed and the experiences of the recent past and the present.

Those who have witnessed the last thirty years will understand the striking similarity between the period on which the article focuses and what is happening today, and how historical scholarship sheds light on our future.

Keywords: *Abkhazia, the Abaza, the Republic of the North Caucasian Mountaineers Union, the Caucasian Confederation, Georgia, Menshevik Georgians, Bolshevism, the Russian Revolution*

While the Romanov dynasty had fallen into the course of collapse in the early 1900s, Abkhazia, living a completely rural life, remained alien to most of the events taking place in Russia. The revolutionary ideologies that Alexander Herzen had spread found supporters in Georgian society through liberal nationalists such as Niko Nikoladze. A few intellectuals among the Caucasian Mountaineers who were educated in the well-known ideological centres of the Russian empire and who had the opportunity to be more integrated into the events in Russia were also struggling to ensure that the Caucasian Mountaineers would not be left out of this process. Wassan Girey Jabagiev in his article published in the St. Petersburg *Vedomosti* newspaper stated that the arrogant Russification policies of the tsarist regime, with its lawlessness, and bureaucracy that denied individuals and even entire nations, had aroused national consciousness and nationalist sentiments in the border-regions of the empire. Jabagiev also emphasised that, if the revolutionaries succeeded in capturing Daghestan and Chechnya, the once majestic strongholds of Imam Shamil, they would not be obliged to re-conquer the Caucasus. In another article published in the same newspaper two weeks later, as if to denounce Jabagiev, Georgian Menshevik Mikhail Mirianishvili was claiming that the turmoil in the Caucasus was caused by so-called Muslim separatists who acted entirely under the influence of the Young Turks. Mirianishvili's approach alone was a striking example of the effort of Georgian chauvinism to dominate all independence-attempts when Russia's immune system was weak and the opportunity for independence for the Caucasian peoples had been aroused.

Contrary to the chauvinistic Georgian approaches, the Caucasian Mountaineers in this period not only unified against Russian imperialism but also established strategic partnerships with other Caucasian peoples to save the entire Caucasus from the Russian yoke.

When the initiative called the Caucasus Committee was established in Istanbul by the leading figures of the North Caucasian immigration during the First World War, Georgian figures such as Kamil Tavdgiridze and Prince Giorgi Machabelli were also included in that committee. A delegation of the Committee, that included Aziz Meker, an Abaza intellectual, and also the Georgian figures together went to European capitals such as Vienna and Berlin to hold talks and requested support from the representatives of the Central Powers for the independence of the Caucasus.[3] The initiative was also supported by the Ottoman intelligence service, where the North Caucasians immigrants were very influential and the delegation was furnished with broad diplomatic powers. [4] These efforts were rewarded with the following statement of the German Foreign Minister Gottlieb von Jagow;

> *"As a proof of its sincere interest in the cause of independence of the Caucasus, the Imperial Government from the very beginning of the war was in contact with organizations aiming to establish a confederation of independent states to liberate the Caucasus from the Russian yoke, and is ready to support the peoples of the Caucasus for the realization of their national ideals and the establishment of an independent Caucasian state."[5]*

As the outcome of these contacts, the Caucasian Committee was given the right to select personnel to form the core army of the future Caucasian state among the prisoners-of-war of Caucasian origin in the hands of the German and Austro-Hungarian Empires. The prisoner-of-war status of the chosen ones would end and they would be released.[6] After the Committee representatives returned to Istanbul, severe disagreements arose between the North Caucasian and Georgian members. The Georgians, thinking that the Germans, rather than the

Ottomans, were a more suitable partner for their independence, undermined the cooperation. Despite such a Georgian manoeuvre, the North Caucasus immigrants voluntarily teamed up with the Ottoman forces to contribute to the liberation of Georgia.[7] The leading figures of the North Caucasus immigration in Istanbul conveyed a similar offer to the Germans, but the Germans, who were making insidious plans against their Ottoman Empire ally by using the Georgians, rejected such an offer. [8] The 3rd Conference of Nationalities, which was held in Lausanne in 1916, was another important opportunity to start a common struggle for the liberation of the Caucasus from Russian imperialism.[9] The North Caucasus delegation was presided over by Prof. Aziz Meker at this conference. There, the Georgians again pursued their priorities instead of joining in a block with other Caucasian nations, and the opportunity to form a single front against Russian imperialism was missed once again due to their attitudes.[10]

With the February Revolution, the monarchical system collapsed. Meetings and conferences were held, and enslaved nations started to discuss the options for future road-maps. Naturally, North Caucasian Mountaineers, with similar concerns, were holding congresses one after the other to seek ways to overcome the chaotic days most safely, in close contact with each other and with neighbouring peoples. They formed an overarching structure called the Provisional Central Committee of the Union of the Mountaineers and decided to hold a congress in Vladikavkaz on 1 May 1917 (O[ld] S[tyle]), with the participation of authorised representatives of all Mountain elements.[11] The National Democrat fraction of the Georgians, unlike their Menshevik compatriots, followed a more friendly policy with other Caucasian nations and tried to find ways to establish a common future with them. They organised a conference in Vladikavkaz on 9 May 1917, with the participation of representatives of Mountaineers and Azerbaijan, to prepare the ground for the formation of a possible Caucasian Confederation.[12] Although we have not yet been able to obtain any concrete evidence regarding the outcomes of this conference, it is understood through the German archival documents that projects of the Georgian National Democrats for initiating anti-Russian rebellions in the Caucasus were not considered reliable enough by the Germans. Hence, it may be presumed that the conference did not have any practical results.[13]

After the first congress held in Vladikavkaz in May, the Mountaineers decided to hold the second congress in Andi on 20 August 1917 (OS) to make more tangible decisions and invited their Georgian neighbours to this congress. While no response was received from the Menshevik Georgians, Shalva Amiredzhibi, one of the prominent figures of the National Democrats, attended the event in Andi. One of the items on the agenda at the congress in Andi was rapprochement with the Georgian people and eliminating the misunderstandings between the Mountain people living in the region and the Georgians.[14] Shalva Amiredzhibi, who was deeply impressed by the determination of the Mountaineers to free themselves from the yoke of Russian imperialism, talked about the majestical atmosphere in Andi in an article he wrote during his years in Paris immigration.[15] The well-known political figure and cleric of the North Caucasus, Najmudin Gotsinski, who was elected as the Mufti of all Mountaineers at the Andi Congress, in an interview, instructed the public to be careful not to harm any Georgians in such a chaotic and anarchic environment.[16] Since the Andi Congress ended without the desired outcomes, a second congress was held soon after in Vladikavkaz, on 21 September 1917 (OS). The Abkhazian representatives who attended the Second Congress of the Caucasian Mountaineers in Vladikavkaz applied to join the Union of Mountaineers, and their accession was confirmed unanimously by the participants of the congress.[17]

Meanwhile, on 25 October 1917 (OS), the Bolsheviks seized power in Petrograd, which went down in history as the "Great Russian Revolution". Without wasting time, just the day after the revolution, Lenin declared Russia's withdrawal from the First World War and started negotiations with the Central Powers in Brest-Litovsk, where the

German headquarters was located, on 22 December 1917. The Brest-Litovsk treaty did not please the Transcaucasian nations, and neither did the Georgians. During the negotiations started on 14 March 1918, in Trebizond, the Transcaucasian Sejm was presided over by the Georgian leader Akaki Chkhenkeli, while the Ottoman delegation was headed by Rauf Bey (Orbay), an Ottoman statesman of Abaza origin. Chkhenkeli had claims on the Ottoman-Georgian border to be drawn as per the treaty of 1914 according to the pre-war Ottoman-Russian frontier and insisted that they would not resile from their demands on Batumi. Rauf Bey, on the other hand, insisted that since the Transcaucasian Sejm had not declared independence, they were subject to the articles of the Brest-Litovsk Treaty.[18] The parties did not in any way step back from their demands, and the Trebizond talk ended without any specific results. The representatives of the Sejm-delegation returned to Tbilisi to evaluate the situation and to find a way out from such a vicious circle.

The Transcaucasian Sejm declared independence and announced the newborn Federal Transcaucasian Republic on 22 April 1918. The Government, headed by Akaki Chkhenkeli, decided to carry on the talks with the Ottoman side in Batumi on 26 April 1918. The negotiations that started in Batumi on 11 May 1918 had reached a dead-end from the very first day due to the disagreements between the parties. Pleasing the Menshevik Georgians, the German Ambassador to Moscow, Count von Mirbach, manipulated the Soviet Foreign Commissar Chicherin and requested him to send a representative to Batumi to participate in the talks.[19] The Menshevik Georgian administration was relying on the Bolsheviks to implement their plans in the region. Due to the uncertainty between the Central Powers and the Transcaucasian Government and the growing Bolshevik danger, the North Caucasian delegation declared the independence of the Republic of the Union of the Mountaineers of the North Caucasus on the same day. On the map presented with the declaration of independence, Abkhazia, which at the 2nd Congress of Mountain Peoples linked its fate with the Union of North Caucasian

Mountaineers, was also included within the borders of the young repub-lic.[20] The declaration of independence of the Republic of the Union of the North Caucasian Mountaineers was followed by successive agree-ments with the representatives of the Ottoman and German empires. The clauses of the agreement were as follows:[21]

> "The Imperial German government on the one hand and the government of the Republic of Mountaineers of the Caucasus on the other, deciding to establish friendly relations between their countries on legal, economic and political grounds, have concluded among themselves the following:
>
> Contract:
>
> 1. A permanent peace and indestructible friendship are established be-tween the Imperial German government and the government of the Republic of the Mountaineers of the Caucasus.
>
> 2. The Imperial German Government undertakes to come to the aid of the government of the Republic of the Mountaineers of the Caucasus by armed force if the latter will ask to ensure peace and tranquillity in his country.
>
> Note: Representation of the specified armed force up to two battalions should follow if the circumstances so require and before the ratification of this treaty.
>
> 3. Given the conclusion of this treatise, in the absence of any agree-ments, conditions, acts, and other legal relations of international na-ture between the Imperial German government and the Government of the Republic of the Mountaineers of the Caucasus, both contracting parties contracted to conclude a consular convention, a commercial treaty and other acts that are not finding it necessary for the estab-lishment of legal and economic relations. The Consular Convention will be concluded two years from the date of the exchange of ratifi-cations. During this transitional period, the Consul General, Consul, and the vice-consuls of the said states shall enjoy, in respect of their

privileges and duties, favoured nation position based on international law.

4. *Until the Republic of the Mountaineers of the Caucasus enters the international postal telegraph union, postal and telegraphic relations between the German Empire and the Republic of the Mountaineers of the Caucasus will be established immediately after the exchange of ratifications of these contracts, according to the terms of the contracts, orders, and rules of the international postal telegraph union.*

5. *The Imperial German Government itself recognises the independence of the Republic of the Mountaineers of the Caucasus and provides diplomatic assistance to the recognition of this independence by other states.*

6. *The Imperial German Government likewise undertakes to render to the Government of the Mountaineers of the Caucasus support through diplomatic means to establish the borders of the republic based on the national principle, and in particular to the establishment in the north of the border, passing through Gelendzhik - Kubanskoje (20 versts north of Armavir), Stavropol, Svjatoi Krest (Karabalyk) the course and mouth of the Kuma River, and in the south of the border, passing along the Ingur River, along the main ridge of the Caucasus Mountains (along the watershed) and with the inclusion of the Zakatalskyj district and the Dagestan areas.*

7. *The number of German troops within the Republic cannot be increased without the consent of the government of this republic.*

8. *The Government of the Republic of the Mountaineers of the Caucasus undertakes to take effective measures to remove from the borders of the Republic of missions and agents of countries at war with the Central Powers.*

9. *The contracting parties mutually undertake to establish economic re-lations and organise the exchange of goods based on provisions to be established, possibly soon by additional agreements.*

10. *This treaty will be approved and the exchange of ratifications will take place in Berlin not later than one month, or, if possible, earlier."[22]*

The sixth article of the agreement was unmistakably explicit enough to expose the liabilities of the Imperial German Government. However, the Germans did not provide any opportunity for the ratification of this agreement. While they were negotiating such a treaty with the North Caucasian Mountaineers, at the same time they were making secret plans with the Georgians and Cossacks in order not to lose control in the Caucasus to her ally, the Ottoman Empire. The diplomatic talks between General von Lossow, Head of the Delegation of the State of Emergency of the Imperial German Government, and Haydar Bammat, the Minister of Foreign Affairs of the Republic of North Caucasus, result-ed in Germany's *de facto* recognition of the independence of the North Caucasus; von Lossow asked Bammat about the status of the relations between the Republic of the North Caucasus and Moscow, and added;

> *"The situation regarding the Terek and Daghestan regions is clear. Nobody has any doubts about the belonging of these lands to the Republic of North Caucasus. But the Cossacks of the Kuban region are ethnographically close to Ukraine. The German Government does not want a new source of conflict to emerge in this region and cannot allow such a thing. In addition, the recognition of Kuban as the territory of the Republic of the North Caucasus would mean breaking the Brest-Litovsk Peace Treaty. Therefore, this issue should be left open for now. If you agree to this, I am ready to invite the representatives of the Ottoman Empire and the Transcaucasian Republic to establish the parts of the peace-treaty related to the North Caucasus."[23]*

So, neither in the context of the agreement nor in von Lossow's words was there a single mention of Germany's territorial objection to Abkhazia. Moreover, Georgian and Abkhazian representatives, who met in Tbilisi on 9 February 1918, shortly before the start of the Trebizond and Batumi talks, stated that the future political structure of Abkhazia will be determined in the Abkhazian Constituent Assembly under the principle of self-determination. Besides, Georgian and Abkhazian representatives had signed a treaty about the territorial integrity of Abkhazia, confirming the recognition of the Georgian National Council that the area between the Mzymta and Ingur rivers was Abkhazians' historical boundaries. As an indicator of the ideal of uniting all Caucasian peoples under a confederative roof in the future, and to prevent any problem at that stage, the parties also promised that they would not engage in commitments with third parties without informing each other.[24] The ink was not dry on the signed agreement when the Georgian troops of the Federal Transcaucasian Republic under the command of Valiko Dzhugheli, who used the Bolshevik structures in Abkhazia as an excuse, occupied Sukhum on 17 May 1918. After the occupation, they began to manipulate the structure of the Abkhazian People's Council through some traitors whom they suborned for various personal gains.[25]

Georgia left the Federal Transcaucasian Republic on 26 May 1918, because they were under the threat of the Ottoman Empire, and declared independence. The fact that Georgia's declaration of independence was made by the Marxist Mensheviks, who aimed to remain a federal part of Russia during the days of the February Revolution, revealed an interesting contradiction. After the declaration of independence of Georgia was echoed in Sukhum, the Abkhazian People's Council convened on 2 June 1918, and issued a statement:

1. *With the declaration of Georgia's independence, all legal ties between Abkhazia and Georgia became null.*

2. *The power of the Abkhazian People's Assembly in Abkhazia declares that the conditions of the agreement dated 9 February 1918, must be improved.*

3. *Solidarity is an essential element to establish a strong state-structure in both countries. If the Georgian Government misses this historical opportunity, Turkey will certainly invade Abkhazia soon.*

In addition, it was emphasised that the Abkhazian side must participate on equal terms with the other elements in the process of the disintegration of the Transcaucasian Government.[26] On the other hand, the Tbilisi administration made individual agreements with some members of the Abkhazian People's Council on 8 and 11 June 1918, in return for personal benefits, and began to drag things into a dead-end by claiming that these individual agreements bound the Abkhazian People's Council. While preparing to invade Abkhazia, the Menshevik Georgian Government signed a friendship-treaty with the Government of the Republic of the Union of the Mountaineers of North Caucasus. Despite repeated proposals of the representatives of the Government of the Republic of North Caucasus for the establishment of a Caucasian Confederation, the members of the dispersed Federal Transcaucasian Republic left the issue tabled due to their hidden agendas with the British, German, and the Ottomans.[27] The Menshevik Georgian Government occupied Sukhum on 13 June 1918, with the support of the German army. Haydar Bammat's ultimatum to the Head of the Diplomatic Mission of the German Empire, F.W. Schulenburg, which strongly condemned the invasion, did not change the attitudes of the Germans and the Georgians, who were determined to stand by their own guns.[28]

The Georgian armed forces, led by General Mazniashvili and supported by the Germans, seized full control of the territory of Abkhazia between 17 and 19 June. Mazniashvili declared martial law on 23 June and declared himself the governor-general of Abkhazia, asking the people to obey Georgian laws unconditionally.[29] Menshevik Georgians tried to legitimise the occupation by distorting the treaty of 9 February 1918. They claimed that the agreement in question consisted of autonomy granted by the Georgians to the Abkhazian side. However, this was not a convention between two sovereign powers. Neither the Georgian side nor the Abkhazian had the status of a sovereign state yet. Therefore, the Georgians did not have the status required to offer autonomy to the Abkhazian side. Neither the Georgian National Council nor the Abkhazian People's Council was a governmental body.

Against the growing Bolshevik threat in Abkhazia and the invasion of Menshevik Georgians, an armed group called the Sukhum Detachment, consisting of about 800 individuals from the Abaza and Circassian elements among Ottoman subjects, prepared a landing in Ochamchira. However, a part of the detachment, which failed to reach the Ochamchiran shores in stormy weather, had to disperse and landed at different points, while a part of it had to return to Ottoman lands. 120 people who were able to get ashore engaged in fierce battles against the disproportionate German-backed Georgian forces, but they were defeated.[30] Due to Mazniashvili's threats of collective punishment, the civilian population was hesitant to help the members of the platoon. [31] The operation had also caused a diplomatic crisis. Georgian leader Akaki Chkhenkeli sent a protest-note to Hakkı Pasha at the Berlin embassy of the Ottoman Empire at the beginning of July 1918. Ignoring the ethnic identities of the platoon personnel, Chkhenkeli described them as "Turks". Chkhenkeli also played the German card and threatened the Ottoman state not to interfere in the Abkhazian issue.[32]

While some of the surviving personnel of the detachment were captured by the Menshevik Georgians, some of them were able to return to Batumi by their own means. Some of the survivors in the mountains were rescued by the Abaza Bolsheviks, while some succeeded in crossing to the North Caucasus and joined the forces of the North Caucasus Mountaineers' Union.[33]

The invading Georgian forces began to engage in serious plundering. They loaded all the cattle and horses on vessels and shipped them out of Abkhazian territory. The civilian population, who could not get help from anywhere, was in a desperate situation.[34] The Mensheviks, proponents of Marxist socialism, fuelled the class-conflict, but the Abaza were generally not swayed by such provocations. However, Megrels [aka Mingrelians] and Gurians joined the Mensheviks in hopes of taking possession of the lands of others. When disagreements started between the Abaza, the Megrels, and others, the Mensheviks launched a boycott, repression, and terror. The Russians took advantage of the situation in the first place and deepened ethnic distinctions. They humiliated non-Menshevik Georgians and manipulated their influence and reputation with provocations. The Abaza distanced themselves from the other groups a little more each day. Despite all the negativities caused by the Menshevik Georgians, there were also Abazas, such as Tatash Marshania, who insisted on keeping themselves distant from the Russians. He, as a well-known Russophobe, wanted the freedom of Georgia and Abkhazia. The Russians knew this very well and were very much afraid of him. However, the Georgians, who did not learn from their mistakes and eventually lost his sympathy too. Due to the terror of Georgian Mensheviks on civilians, Tatash Marshania did not oppose the Bolsheviks during their first temporary reign in Abkhazia despite his great influence on the people. Marshania always looked for a way out of the Russian traps, but the attitude of the Georgian Mensheviks always discouraged his efforts.[35] Simon Basaria, representative of Abkhazia in the Union of North Caucasian Mountaineers, in his message to Haydar Bammat on 5 September, with the code "top priority", stated that the Abkhazians were in danger of being completely annihilated if they did not deliver help immediately and that he, like other Abkhazian patriots, would be arrested by the Georgian Mensheviks.[36]

Today, many historians claim that the Abaza were always on the side of the Bolsheviks during the years of the Russian civil war, and the detachment known as the "Sukhum Platoon" was called to help the Bolsheviks against the Georgians. Therefore, based on this allegation, they defend the idea that Abkhazia's initiative to take part in the Union of North Caucasian Mountaineers had no practical value. However, the

Abkhazians would declare at the Vladikavkaz Congress on 21 September 1917 that it was not just something that remained on paper. When the Menshevik Georgian forces invaded Abkhazia, the Abkhazians did not appeal to the Bolsheviks but to the Mountaineers' Government, which was fighting both the Bolsheviks, on the one hand, and the White Volunteer Army, on the other. Menshevik Georgian leader Noë Zhordania portrayed this situation in the memoirs as follows;

> *"Prince Shervashidze, dissatisfied with us, fled to the North Caucasus and at one rally presented them with all of Abkhazia. Instead of asking him by what right or by whose authority he speaks, they immediately accepted this gift and made a complaint to us: "Abkhazia is ours, get out of there!" These are the kind of neighbours we had."[37]*

The Germans appointed General Kress as the representative to Tbilisi in June 1918.

In the name of serving the interests of the Georgian Government, Kress left the North Caucasian Mountaineers alone in the fight against Bolshevism and gave orders to the Georgian forces to shoot the Abaza who were trying to flee from the combat-zone to safe areas. Haydar Bammat, on the other hand, conveyed to Kress that, if they insisted on being patrons to the Georgians in this way, Georgia's neighbours would not be able to be independent. Thus, Georgia would not be able to remain independent either.[38] Despite these warnings, the Georgian Mensheviks under German protection tried to capture Vladikavkaz at the end of July, but the detachment they sent could not get beyond Lars. [39] The Germans signed a complementary treaty with the Soviets on 27 August 1918, in Berlin. As per the agreement, Germany would prevent the Ottoman State from intervening in the Caucasus if it would be given a share of the Baku oil, and in return, Russia would recognise the independence of Georgia. Germans and Menshevik Georgians gave Bolsheviks a helping hand to facilitate their work in the Caucasus.[40] When the World War ended in the defeat of the Central Powers, all the balances had changed, and the British started to keep the Caucasus on a string as of November 1918. The Volunteer Army of General Denikin, under the auspices of the British, initially defeated the Bolsheviks, and from the beginning of 1919, rapidly began to occupy the lands of Southern Russia and the territory of the Republic of the Union of North Caucasian Mountaineers. The Abkhazian-Georgian issue and the Bolshevik-Menshevik fight fell off the agenda thereupon, and everyone focused on the fight against Denikin's Volunteer Army. The Georgian Mensheviks even released Nestor Lakoba and many prominent Abkhazian Bolsheviks they had detained in a Tbilisi prison. During this period, an interesting conversation took place in a cell in the Tbilisi prison between Valiko Dzhugheli and Nestor Lakoba, the Bolshevik leader of Abkhazia;

> Dzhugheli: "What would you do if I had become your prisoner?" To this Lakoba calmly replied: "We would shoot you, of course."[41]

Abkhazian nationalists sought to cooperate with Denikinist forces to change the balance in the pro-Georgian Abkhazian People's Council in order to seize power, but the Menshevik Georgians suppressed this attempt and arrested most of the Abkhazian nationalists. The Georgian Mensheviks were preparing to define a high autonomous status in order to retain occupied Abkhazia. The Foundation of the Commissariat of Abkhazia was announced in May, and the definition of the administrative unit named the "Sukhum Region" was renamed as "Abkhazia". In March 1919, a group of Abkhazian Social Democrats, including Mikhail Tarnava, broke away from the Georgian Mensheviks and united with the "Independents" (*nezavisemtsy*) to form the Faction of Social-Democratic Internationalists. This group, which parted company with the Georgian Mensheviks, made a statement and called on the Menshevik Georgians to end the "chauvinist policies" in Abkhazia.[42] Abkhazian Bolshevik leaders, who had been fighting against Denikin's army in the north since the beginning of 1919, returned to Abkhazia in the last quarter of the year. The Abkhazians who were under severe threat from the Menshevik Georgians, on the one hand, and the monarchist Denikin, on the other, were inclined towards the Bolsheviks. To find a compromise, the

Menshevik Georgian administration proposed a conference in Tbilisi with the participation of the representatives of the republics of the North Caucasus, Azerbaijan, and Armenia. Despite a fourteen-day meeting-schedule, the Congress could not continue after the first meeting on 14 November, due to border-disputes between the parties.[43]

Fleeing Denikin's forces, the Bolsheviks were secretly infiltrating Georgian lands and hiding in the mountains.[44] The Georgian Mensheviks very well understood how the North Caucasus was important as a defensive wall for them and could predict what would happen, if harmful elements such as Bolsheviks and monarchists were able to break through this wall. On the one hand, Denikin's boisterous attacks, and, on the other hand, the anarchy caused by the Bolsheviks in Georgian lands prompted the Georgian Menshevik leaders such as Evgeny Gegechkori and Grigol Lordkipanidze to seek help from the allies.[45]

Panicked Menshevik Georgians held a Conference in Tbilisi to discuss the measures to be taken against invasions by the Denikinist forces, under the chairmanship of North Caucasian politician Ahmet Tsalykkaty, and with the participation of Georgian, Azerbaijani, and North Caucasian delegates. Kapba Kazim Kap, a young officer of Abaza origin of the Ottoman army, was elected as the commander of the Caucasus Front on 10 August 1919, with 49 votes of the 52 delegates during this conference. The Georgian Government placed General Tasov and several Georgian officers of various ranks under the command of Kazim Bey, along with 49 wagons of weapons, ammunition, and provisions.[46] At the beginning of October, the Georgian government also supported an uprising in Daghestan, organised by Kapba Kazim Bey, and another ethnic Abaza Ottoman politician Mkanba Aziz Meker. The report prepared by Major E. De Nonancourt, the commander of the French Military Mission in the Caucasus, was composed of explicit statements about the role of the Menshevik Georgian administration in the events of the era in the Caucasus. The Menshevik Georgian administration considered the North Caucasus as a buffer-zone to secure their own independence, and both kept the enemy outside the Georgian territory and also wore out the enemy without being battered with the mess fabricated in the north. The fact that the Mountaineers' non-conflict environment with the Volunteer Army was disturbing the Georgian Mensheviks as much as the Bolsheviks.[47] As a matter of fact, after a year of intense clashes, the Union Assembly of the Caucasian Mountaineers functioning in Tbilisi and the national forces of the Defence Council stationed in Daghestan defeated Denikin's Volunteer Army. While Denikin's collaborators were fleeing the territory of the Republic of the North Caucasus, a Provisional Government of the Union of North Caucasian Mountaineers was established at the meeting held in Vladikavkaz in March 1920, and Haydar Bammat, who was in Tbilisi at that time, was elected head of the government in his absence.[48] Trying to avoid confronting the Bolshevik terror in the Georgian territory, the Mensheviks issued a decree on 6 April and decided, at the North Caucasus Defence Council's demand, that the members of the Volunteer Army detained in Georgia, who were of North Caucasian origin, be released and sent to the north to fight against the Bolsheviks. In line with this decision, a group of 100 individuals was released and sent from the Poti concentration camp to Daghestan as a result of the investigation conducted by Ismael Abaev, the representative of the North Caucasus Defence Council in Tbilisi.[49]

General Erdeli, who was appointed as the governor of the Caucasus by General Denikin, also accepted that the sole sovereign power in the North Caucasus was the Mountaineers' government until the planned meeting of the All-Russian constituent assembly.[50] Entente forces also realised that they were betting on the wrong horse by supporting Denikin, but somehow they could not take any concrete steps to help the Mountaineers' government. British High Commissioner Oliver Wardrop texted the Allied headquarters before the beginning of January 1920. He urged the Allies to recognise the North Caucasus and the Trans-Caucasian Republics immediately instead of supporting General Denikin, who retreated south while fleeing from the Bolsheviks in pursuit. He also warned London that, if effective measures would not be taken, the Mountaineers would have to come to terms with the Bolsheviks. [51] Menshevik Georgians, trying to prevent the Allies from aiding the Mountaineers directly, imposed their cause on the Allies by assuming a "facilitator" role. The British, who did not find the Menshevik Georgians convincing, consulted the information of the National Democrat Zurab Avalishvili, a member of the Georgian delegation at the Paris Peace Conference. Zurab Avalishvili's statements about Abkhazia were very striking. Avalishvili, who is known to be a very true and consistent politician, was giving clues to interesting facts about the Georgian presence in Abkhazia. Stating that in the second half of the 19th century, most of the indigenous population of Abkhazia were deported to Asia Minor and cleansed through the genocidal practices of the Russians, Avalishvili was revealing that the Abkhazians were the real owners of the country and the fact that the existence of the ethnic Georgian majority was purely derived from the demographic disaster that the Russians caused.[52] After a year had passed following the consultation of Avalishvili, other striking truths started to appear in the British intelligence reports on Abkhazia;

> *"The population of Abkhasia and Transcaucasia is wonderfully mixed. On a territory of 7.5 thousand square versts live Abkhasians, Russians, Mingrelians, Armenians, Turks, Greeks, Estonians, etc, who have mixed in a queer way. Despite that mixture of nations, there is a nation in Abkhasia that may and must be considered as the owners of the land, That nation is the Abkhasian one. No matter how far we peep into history, we shall always meet on the Abkhasian territory, the Aborigines of the land of the Abkhasians. Other nations come later, after intervals of centuries, and, without a doubt, are newcomers for the Abkhasians."[53]*

The Democratic Republic of Georgia under the leadership of the Menshevik leader Noë Zhordania approached, on the one hand, the allies, and the Soviets, on the other. Towards the end of April 1920, Grigol Uratadze, furnished with broad powers, was sent to Moscow for a secret mission. As per secret agreements made with the Soviets, on 5 May,

Lenin texted Sergo Ordzhonikidze, demanding that the Red Army units in Georgia be withdrawn to the border and prevented from attacking Georgian territory. Immediately afterwards, on 7 May, Lev Karahan and Grigol Uratadze signed a 16-point agreement in Moscow. According to the first article of the Treaty, Russia unconditionally recognised the independence of the Georgian State and renounced all Russia's claims of sovereignty over Georgian territory. While in the 5th article of the treaty, Georgia promised that it would not allow any formation on its territory that could pose a threat to Soviet Russia, with the 6th article, Soviet Russia made the same commitment to Georgia. The Mensheviks also promised to stop punishments against the supporters of the Soviets. As per the secret clause added to the treaty, the Georgian side would allow Communist organisations to broadcast propaganda in their territory and legalize the secret Georgian Communist Party as well.[54] The Georgian Mensheviks, who thought they had secured their land, were relieved. Thinking that the Bolsheviks would no longer pose a threat to them, they began to increase the pressure on the representatives of other Caucasian peoples who had gathered in Tbilisi for the anti-Bolshevik struggle. They immediately arrested the prominent nationalists and monarchists who tried to take refuge in Georgia and immediately deported the dissidents they caught to Turkey in order not to have problems with the Russian Bolsheviks.[55]

The Bolsheviks, on the other hand, had conquered the war-torn North Caucasus, which could not get any support from anywhere, without difficulty in only two months and were advancing towards the Georgian border like an avalanche. More than 60,000 people were trapped on the Georgian border of occupied Abkhazia.[56] Pro-independence Abkhazians boycotted the elections for the representatives to be selected for the Georgian Constituent Assembly. The Abkhazians, losing all their hopes for establishing a life together with their Georgian neighbours, were inclined towards the Soviets. *"The majority of the Abkhazians are hesitant and entirely do not support us, as if they are waiting for some-*

body," Valiko Dzhugheli wrote to the Central Committee of the Georgian Mensheviks in Tbilisi. Many members of the Abkhazian People's Council were arrested by the Georgian Mensheviks on the grounds of allegations they had ties to the Bolsheviks. The Bolsheviks were also incessantly strengthening their organisation in Abkhazia. The Georgian Communist Party, which became legitimate in Tbilisi, especially after the secret agreement between Uratadze and the Bolsheviks in Moscow, intensified underground activities in Abkhazia.[57]

The short-sighted attitude of the Entente towards supporting the Mountaineers and the chauvinistic policies of the Georgian Mensheviks were pushing Abkhazians into the Bolsheviks' trap. In the autumn of 1920, the Georgian Mensheviks also realised their fate when the Bolsheviks gained an absolute victory in the north.[58] Abel Chevalley, the French High Commissioner in Tbilisi, rose from the dead and text-ed Paris to send urgent and direct aid to the Mountaineers to stop the Bolsheviks.[59] Closing the stable door after the horse has bolted did not help anyone. The Georgian Mensheviks, who left the Mountaineers alone in the face of the Bolsheviks, believing that they would secure their independence, would watch bitterly as their country was trampled under Bolshevik boots. Although the Menshevik Georgians knew very well that they would never have Abkhazia, they pushed Abkhazians into the lap of the Russian Bolsheviks through their insatiable passions. The Entente, which first relied on the surviving monarchist Russians, then followed the Menshevik Georgians and blatantly handed over the Caucasus to the Bolshevik Russians. On the eve of the Bolshevik victory in Georgia, the Mountaineer-Azerbaijani Committee was organised in Tbilisi on 17 February 1921. The committee formed detachments of Mountaineer and Azerbaijani volunteers for the defence of Tbilisi, but they could not pre-vent the Bolsheviks from capturing the city on 25 February.[60] On the night of 24 to the 25 February , the Menshevik leader Noë Zhordania left Tbilisi by the last train while Mountaineer-Azerbaijani detachments were carrying on close combat against the Bolsheviks for the defence of Tbilisi.

A week later, Abkhazia would join the USSR with the status of a union republic. Abkhazia, which was one of the republics that formed the basic mortar of the USSR, was forced to sign a special union agreement with the Georgian Soviet Socialist Republic on 16 December 1921, united with Georgia and received the status of a "treaty" socialist republic. Even so, it was not an autonomy within Georgia, but a stakeholder of the republic which united with Georgia on equal rights.

The chauvinistic Georgian state-system tried to destroy Abkhazia with the conspiracies of the world-renowned Georgian tyrants of the USSR, Stalin and Beria, from 1931. With the collapse of the USSR in 1991, Abkhazia experienced a *deja vu* of the turbulent days from 1917 through 1921 once again. If Georgian chauvinists cannot learn from their mistakes in history, they must bear in mind that Abkhazia will not be losing its independence to them. Moreover, even if Abkhazia may lose its independence, it will not be only Abkhazia which will lose it...

The chauvinist Georgians' greed means they are cutting off their nose to spite their face...!

Endnotes

[1] Zaza Abzianidze-Niko Nikoladze, "The Architect of Future Georgia", Modi to Georgia, 2012, pp. 39-40

[2] Salavat Ishakov, *Pervaya Russkaya Revolyutsiya i Musul'mane Rossiyskoy İmperii*, Moscow, 2007, p.202

[3] Comité de bienfaisance des Émigrés Politiques de la Ciscaucasie en Turquie, *Aperçu historique sur les Ciscaucasiens pendant la Guerre Mondiale*, Istanbul, 1918, p.15

[4] Genelkurmay Askerî Tarih ve Stratejik Etüt ve Denetleme Başkanlığı Arşivi, (Hereafter ATASE) BDH Kol., Kls.1854, D.120, F.1-31, 32

[5] Haus-, Hof- und Staatsarchiv, Politisches Archiv (Hereafter HHStA, PA), I 947 Krieg 21 k Türkei: Georgisch-grusinischer Aufstand im Kaukasus 1914-18, Fol. 103-104, *Resolutions of the Caucasian Committee in the Ottoman Empire, to convey its President to Marshal Fuad Pasha, Gottlieb von Jagow, State Secretary, Ministry of Foreign Affairs of the German Empire of Constantinople*, 15 October 1915. L.91

[6] Georgy Chochiev, "Reclaiming the Homeland: The Caucasus-Oriented Activities of Ottoman Circassians during and after World War I", in *War and Collapse World War I and the Ottoman State* ed. by M. Hakan Yavuz and Faruz Ahmad, Utah, 2016, p.598

[7] Mustafa Çolak, *Alman İmparatorluğunun Doğu Siyaseti Çerçevesinde Kafkasya Politikası (1914-1918)*, Ankara, 2014, pp. 141-142

[8] Chochiev, Reclaiming the Homeland, p.601

[9] Jaeschke, "Poraboshennie Rossiey Narody na Lozanskom Kongresse 1916 goda", *Severny Kavkaz*, 42-43, 1937, pp.18-23

[10] L'Office centrale de l'Union des Nationalités, *Compte rendu de la 3'me Conférence des Nationalités réunie a Lausanne 27-29 juin 1916*, Lausanne, 1917, pp. 129-138

[11] Comité de bienfaisance des Emigrés Politiques de la Ciscaucasie en Turquie, *Compte-rendu des assemblées des peuples de la Ciscaucasie et de leurs travaux legislatifs*, Istanbul, 1918, p. 6

[12] Çolak, Alman İmparatorluğunun Doğu Siyaseti, p.163

[13] ibid. p.168

[14] Gacikurban Kakagasanov, Leyla Kaymarazova (Ed.), *Soyuz Obedineniy Gortsev Severnovo Kavkaza i Dagestana (1917-1918)*, 1994, Mahachkala, p.62

[15] Shalva Amiredzhibi, "Iz Nezakonchennogo Proshlogo", *Gortsy Kavkaza*, 4-5, 1929, pp. 5-7

[16] Muhammed Kadı Dibirov, *Istoriya Dagestana v gody Revolyutsii i Grazhdanskoy voyny*, Mahachkala, 1997, p.31

[17] Timur Muzaev, *Sojuz Gortsev, Russkaja Revolutsija I Narody Severnogo Kavkaza 1917 – Mart 1918 g.*, Nalchik, 2012, pp. 238-241

[18] Akdes Nimet Kurat, *Türkiye ve Rusya*, Ankara, 1990, pp.468-471

[19] Enis Şahin, *Trabzon ve Batum Konferansları ve Antlaşmaları (1917-1918)*, Ankara, 2002, pp.542-3

[20] Haydar Bammat, *The Caucasus Problem, Questions Concerning Circassia And Dagestan*, Bern, 1919, pp.30-31

[21] Kakagasanov, Kaymarazova (Ed.), Soyuz Obedineniy Gortsev, pp.122-123

[22] Institut istorii, arkheologii i etnografii Dagestanskogo federal'nogo issle-dovatel'skogo tsentra Rossijskoj akademii nauk (Hereafter IIAE), DSC RAS, F. 2. Op. 1. D. 60. L. IZ - 114. Fund for the History of the Civil War. Op. 4. D. 7. L. 95

[23] A. Ivanov, "Gorskaja kontrrevoljutsija i interventy", *Krasnyj Arhiv – Istoricheskij Zhurnal*, 68, 1935, pp.131-132

[24] Ruslan Gozhba, *Abkhazia – Dokumenti i Materiali (1917-1921g.)*, Sukhum, 2009, p.27; Zurab Papaskiri, *O Natsional'no-Gosudarstvennom Oblike Abkhazii/Gruzija S Drevnejshikh Vremen Do 1993g.*, Tbilisi, 2003, pp.53-54

[25] ibid. pp.41-43

[26] ibid. pp.33-35

[27] Vassan Girey Jabağı, *Kafkas-Rus Çatışması*, Istanbul, 1995, p.87

[28] Kakagasanov, Kajmarazova (Ed.), Sojuz Obedinenij Gortsev, p.132

[29] Tsentral'nyj gosudarstvennyj arkhiv Abkhazii (Hereafter TsGAA), F.-39, Op.1, D.6, L.49-50

[30] Gozhba, Abkhazia – Dokumenti i Materiali (1917-1921g.), p.110

[31] ATASE, BDH. Kls.1857, D.428-133.F.1-3

[32] Türkiye Cumhuriyeti Başbakanlık Osmanlı Arşivleri (Hereafter BOA), HR.SYS D.2455. G.9 F.1-2

[33] Ömer Turan, "Bolşevik İhtilalini Takip Eden Günlerde Kuzey Kafkasya'da Bağımsızlık Hareketleri ve Yusuf Ercan'ın Sohum Müfrezesi Hatıraları.", *Askeri Tarih Bülteni*, 21/40, 1996, pp.156-7

[34] BOA, *From General Mehmed Esad Pasha to Haydar Bammat*, HR.SYs. Dos.2293 G.8 F.023-024

[35] "Drug. Nachalo otchuzhdenija: Abkhazija 1917-1920 gg", *Gazeta Kavkazskij aktsent*, 3-4-5, 2000

[36] BOA, *From Simon Basaria to Haydar Bammat*, HR.SYs. Dos.2293. Göml.8. F.026-028

[37] Stanislav Lakoba, et al (Ed.), *Istorija Abkhazii*, Sukhum, 1991, p.300

[38] Werner Zürrer, "Deutshland und die Entwicklung Nordkaukasiens im Jahre 1918",*Jahrbücher für Geschichte Osteuropas*, 26,1978, p.41

[39] İsmail Hakkı Berkuk, "Büyük Harpte Şimali Kafkasya'daki Faaliyetlerimiz ve XV. Fırkanın Harekâtı ve Muharebeleri", *Askerî Mecmua*,35, 1934, pp.32-33

[40] IIAE DFITS RAN. *Ot Gajdara Bammatova do Tapy Chermoeva, 31 ijulja 1918 g.* F. 2. O. 1. D. 59. L.15

[41] Timothy Blauvelt, *Clientelism and Nationality in an Early Soviet Fiefdom, The Trials of Nestor Lakoba*, Tbilisi 2022, p.25

[42] Zurab Anchabadze, *Ocherki etnicheskji istorii Abkhazskogo naroda*, Sukhum, 1976, p. 110

[43] Firuz Kazemzadeh, *The Struggle for TransCaucasia (1917-1921)*, New York, 1951, pp.174-6

[44] Maria Kotlyarov, Viktor Kotljarov, *Betal Kalmıkov, geroj i palach*, Nalchik, 2018, pp.23-4

[45] Anita Burdett (Ed.), *Caucasian Boundaries*, London, 1996, pp.629-32

[46] Tarık Cemal Kutlu, "Kâzım Kap Unknown Commander of the Struggles in the North Caucasus Between 1918-1921", *Kafkasya Yazıları*, 7, 1999, p.39

[47] Archives Ministère des Affaires étrangères de la France, (Hereafter AMAEF), 637 A&B. Z.653/2,3,4. L.99-103

[48] "Provozglashenie Gorskogo Pravitel'stva", *Volny Gorets*, 36, 29.03.1920, p.2

[49] Hadji Murad Donogo, *Denikinskaja «avtonomija» v Dagestane. 1919–1920 gg.*, Makhachkala, 2018, p.140

[50] Haydar Bammat, *Le Caucase et la révolution russe*, Paris, 1929, pp.51-52

[51] Richard Ullman, *Anglo-Soviet Relations, 1917–1921, Vol.2*, London, 1968, p.322

[52] The National Archives (Hereafter TNA), Public Record Office, *Notes of conversation with Zourab Avaloff*, FO 371/3321, L.9

[53] ibid, *From Lord Curzon, Foreign Secretary, to General Officer in Command*, FO 608/84, L.2

[54] Grigory L. Bondarevsky, "Relations Between RSFSR and Georgia During Civil War and Intervention Years.", *World Affairs: The Journal of International Issues*, 3, 1991, pp.67–72

[55] AMAEF, 637 A&B. Z.653/2,3,4. L.104; Tsentral'nogo gosudarstvennogo istoricheskogo arkhiva Gruzii (Hereafter TSGIAG) F.1861. Op.2. D.17-18

[56] Ruslan Mashitlev, *Adygi Severo-Zapadnogo Kavkaza v revoljutsionnykh sobytijakh i grazhdanskoj vojne :1917-1920 gg*, Armavir, 2005, pp.133-134

[57] Blauvelt. Clientelism and Nationality. pp.29-30

[58] Cem Kumuk, *Düvel-i Muazzama'nın Kıskacında Kafkasya Dağlıları*, Istanbul, 2022, pp. 461-474

[59] AMAEF, 637 A&B. Z.653/2.L.150-151

[60] Bammat, Le Caucase et la révolution russe, pp.62-63

Thirty Years of Peace-negotiations

Charlotte Hille

Associate professor of international law and international relations at the Department of Political Science, University of Amsterdam. She worked at UNPO on the Georgian-Abkhazian conflict and at the Dutch Ministry of Justice and the Ministry of Foreign Affairs, among others as a Caucasus specialist. Her dissertation was on Statebuilding in the Transcaucasus Since 1917, followed in 2010 by a monograph entitled State Building and Conflict Resolution in the Caucasus. Dr Charlotte Hille is a mediator and was visiting scholar at the Minda de Gunzburg Center, Harvard University, in Spring 2007.

Abstract

With the outbreak of the Russian-Ukrainian war, the UN, OSCE and EU decided to postpone indefinitely the peace-negotiations between Abkhazia and Georgia, since the conflict might negatively affect the Geneva International Discussions, as the peace-process is called. However, the negotiations have been far longer in an impasse. It seems impossible to have a functioning Incidence Prevention and Response Mechanism, when no compromise can be reached on a non-use of violence declaration. All parties are worried about the militarisation of the region. Between 1992 and 2008 peace-negotiations between Georgia and Abkhazia also turned repetitive, resulting in a frozen conflict. Is there a way out of this impasse?

Introduction

On 14 August 2022, it will be 30 years since fighting broke out between Georgian troops and Abkhazians in Abkhazia. It will be 30 years ago that I went to the Dutch Ministry of Foreign Affairs with the Secretary-General of UNPO to ask the Ministry if the Netherlands could mediate in the conflict. A cease-fire was eventually signed on 3 October 1992, under the watchful eye of Russian President Boris Yeltsin.[1]

Peace-negotiations started in Geneva between the Georgian and the Abkhazian delegations. The UN Secretary-General appointed a Special Envoy for the Conflict, who shuttled between the parties when necessary, reported to the Secretary-General for the Security Council, and played a mediating role at the meetings in Geneva. For 16 years, talks took place with the UN acting as mediator.

In the period between 1992 and 2008, cease-fires were violated several times and renegotiated. The recurring breakdown-point was the status of Abkhazia, and the way in which Georgia could negotiate with Abkhazia without recognising it, while Abkhazia had problems with the impartiality of the UN, which had adopted resolutions underlining the territorial integrity of Georgia.

Peace-negotiations Between 1992 and 2008

State-building in Abkhazia

As a de facto independent state, Abkhazia strengthened itself when it adopted its own constitution, formulated in such a way that a solution to the conflict was textually possible both inside and outside of Georgia. This constitution was presented to the government in 1993, and after discussion in parliament and government, officially came into force on 24 November 1994, when President Ardzinba took the oath on the new constitution.[2] It is worth noting that this constitution was drafted earlier than the constitution of Georgia, which was not finalised until 1994 and came into force on 17 October 1995.[3]

After a declaration of sovereignty and a referendum on the question of acceptance of the constitution in 1999, the formal declaration of independence of Abkhazia followed on 12 November 1999, which made it more difficult to find a solution where all parties could be content.[4]

The situation changed again when, after the Five Day War between Georgia and the Russian Federation in August 2008, the Russian Federation recognised Abkhazia as a state *de jure*, changing the scope of negotiations between Georgia and Abkhazia.

UN Involvement in the Conflict

A *Declaration of Measures for a Political Settlement of the Georgian-Abkhaz Conflict* was adopted on 4 April 1994. The settlement included a *Quadripartite Agreement on Voluntary Return of Refugees and Displaced Persons*, which was followed a month later by an agreement on a cease-fire and a separation of forces.[5] This document also included a protocol with regard to the stationing of CIS peacekeeping forces. Apart from CIS peacekeepers, the UN deployed UN military observers who would patrol the border-area, the United Nations Observer Mission in Georgia (UNOMIG).[6]

The UN Security Council has adopted many resolutions, urging the parties to refrain from hostilities, and observe the cease-fire agreements of 1993. The negotiations following the 1994 resolutions mainly dealt with the return of refugees and internally displaced persons (IDPs) to Abkhazia, in addition to seeking a resolution to the conflict.

Early in the conflict, in 1993, a Special Envoy of the Secretary General was appointed to brief the Secretary General and the Security Council on the developments in the relation between Georgia and Abkhazia. The Special Envoy also played a role as mediator in the negotiation-process. Negotiations involved, apart from the parties to the conflict, the Special Envoy of the Secretary General to the UN, representatives of the Russian Federation as facilitators, the OSCE, the Group of Friends of the

Secretary General (consisting of the United States, Great Britain, France, Germany, and the Russian Federation).[7]

These met in a Coordinating Council. The Coordinating Council was set up on 18 December 1997 in Sukhum(i) and Tbilisi and met regularly, alternating its meetings in Sukhum(i) and Tbilisi.[8] The Coordinating Council divided its work into Working Groups, in which two representatives for each of the parties participated, as well as the UN Special Envoy as chair, Russia as facilitator, the OSCE, and the Group of Friends as observers. Working Group I dealt with issues related to a lasting non-resumption of hostilities and to security-problems; Working Group II discussed the issue of refugees and internally displaced persons; Working Group III was responsible for finding a resolution for economic and social problems.[9] From 16 to 18 October 1998, as part of the ongoing negotiation-process that took place in Geneva, a meeting was convened in Athens to discuss confidence-building measures. In addition to the expected participants, the Georgian and Abkhazian delegations included academics, businessmen, cultural figures, journalists and representatives of NGOs, in order to create a broad support for the process.[10] This process took place while exchanging information on the decisions taken by the Coordinating Council.

The Secretary General presented a draft-protocol, indicating which measures should be taken as part of the confidence-building measures. Refugees and IDPs should have the right of voluntary return to the places of their permanent residence; violations of the cease-fire and separation-of-forces agreement of 14 May 1994 should be investigated jointly by UNOMIG and the CIS peacekeeping force; the prosecutors should be supported by both sides in investigating criminal cases; support for the leaders of the military structures of the conflicting parties for rapid response in the conflict-zone should be given; de-mining programmes should be promoted; contracts in the fields of energy, trade, agriculture, and construction should be promoted; there should be active involvement in the investigation of cases involving persons missing during the hostilities and the handing over of the remains of the dead; and lastly donor countries should support the carrying out of psychological-social rehabilitation of post-trauma syndrome.[11]

This initiative resulted in another important meeting concerning confidence-building measures in June 1999 when a proposal was adopted in Istanbul to renew efforts to solve the problem of the refugees and IDPs from Abkhazia. Another topic at this meeting was the economic situation.[12]

The UN Security Council regularly extended the mandate of UNOMIG, which in turn participated in confidence-building measures. Apart from UNOMIG, a CIS peacekeeping force was established in the border-zone between Georgia and Abkhazia from 1993.[13]

Frozen Conflict

The status as a 'frozen conflict' also resulted from the tactics of the negotiators. As time went on, the momentum for a breakthrough was lost. There were spoilers both in and outside the delegations. People willing to compromise were replaced by hardliners, there was sporadic fighting along the borders of the conflicting parties, and inflammatory rhetoric was used as another means of continuing the fight. As time went on, and new Special Representatives of the UN Secretary General were appointed to report on the situation and mediate, parties had to build confidence in the new mediator, and the willingness to work towards a compromise potentially diminished. Parties dug themselves in, and the peace-proposals were often reformulations of earlier versions, to which the other party could only say "no".[14] Although protracted conflicts between the metropolitan state and the secessionist entity at some point may be called a 'frozen conflict', this may be misleading, since negotiations, sporadic fighting, and developments in international politics in the Georgian-Abkhazian conflict continued.[15]

In the end, the conflicts over the status of Abkhazia were not only 'frozen conflicts', but worse, 'forgotten conflicts', with little international attention.[16] The fighting in August 2008 did two things: the conflict became violent, and it placed the 'forgotten' conflict back on the international political agenda, thus creating new possibilities to negotiate a settlement. The role of Russia in this process changed from facilitator, and as provider of military for the peace-keeping force, to a party to the conflict.[17]

The Situation Just After the 2008 Cease-Fire Agreement

French president Nicolas Sarkozy on 12 August 2008 brokered a cease-fire. From the beginning it was clear that both parties, the Russian Federation and Georgia, interpreted this document differently. The Russians insisted on not using the term 'territorial integrity' with regard to the Georgian territory. Another point for the Russians was the removal of Georgian President Saakashvili from office. The Georgian party interpreted the cease-fire as indicating that Georgia's territorial integrity would be preserved.[18]

On 15 and 16 October 2008 a meeting hosted by the UN, OSCE and EU took place to discuss further the terms of the cease-fire agreement. Georgia stressed that it did not want Abkhazian delegates to be present, which can be regarded as a missed chance, since both Abkhazia and Russia considered it important that in order to come to a lasting solution of the conflict, the delegates of Abkhazia would also participate in the talks.[19]

During November 2008 a second round of negotiations started. The mediators found a way to incorporate the relevant parties in the process. Georgia allowed participation of delegations from the Abkhazian government and asked that delegations from the (Georgian) Abkhazian Government-in-exile also be present. Instead of official meetings, the different groups met informally in working groups.[20]

The topics that are of concern at the moment are also those at stake just after the 2008 cease-fire agreement. Georgia rebuilt its military with the support of the West, the USA and NATO, and Abkhazia worried about its safety and contained a Russian military base on its territory. The Incident Prevention and Response Mechanism was very much needed, and it was difficult to keep parties in the same room.

When in June 2010 the need of a commitment on the non-use of force was discussed, this led to such diverse positions that the talks ended in deadlock. The US considered that the 12 August 2008 ceasefire-agreement between Georgian President Saakashvili and Russian President Medvedev, mediated by French leader Sarkozy, *"already establishes the sides' commitment to the non-use of force". The US considered regular meetings of the Incident Prevention and Response Mechanism a good addition. Abkhazia and South Ossetia wanted more security-guarantees from Georgia. Their opinion was not taken into account, and subsequently they walked out of the hall. Russia considered the 12 August 2008 agreement not sufficient and wanted a non-aggression treaty between Georgia, South Ossetia and Abkhazia. Note that a treaty is signed between states, and though Russia had recognised Abkhazia as a state, this would force Georgia to do so as well. Subsequently, this option was not realistic.*

Abkhazia walked out of the talks several times in 2009 and 2010, because the co-moderators consistently failed to facilitate the talks in a constructive and impartial manner. *Obviously there was an issue with commitment that found its origin in the fact that the co-chairs seemed biased. The Abkhazians returned, but lowered the level of their participation.*

We now should move to the question as to who has been negotiating with whom since 2008. What are the challenges of the multi-party negotiations and multi-party mediation-team? What conclusion can we draw from 30 years of negotiations between Abkhazia and Georgia?

Who is Negotiating with Whom?

Since 2008 Abkhazia and Georgia have been negotiating with the Russian Federation and South Ossetia in a format that is called the Geneva International Discussions (GID). This name should take the angle out of the problem that Georgia has with Abkhazia and South Ossetia being present at the negotiations, since Georgia regards Abkhazia and South Ossetia as part of its territory and thus considers that it negotiates on their behalf in international negotiations. In international law, negotiating with a government of a territory that is not recognised does not result in a recognition of that territory, and so, in principle, there should not be a legal problem. However, from a political point there is a sensitivity.

According to Jaba [Dzhaba] Devdariani and Teona Giuashvili in their article *Geneva International Discussions. Negotiating the Possible*

> *"Georgia views the GID as a process of mediation with Russia, following the August 2008 war between the two countries. Russia, Abkhazia and South Ossetia consider the GID a part of the negotiations regarding the conflict between Georgia on the one hand, and Abkhazia and South Ossetia on the other."[21]*

This different view on the process can easily lead to misunderstandings as who should move and who is responsible.

The mediating parties in this conflict are the UN, OSCE and EU. According to Devdariani and Giuashvili the EU – legally and institutionally – gravitates towards primarily mediating the Georgia-Russia conflict, while the UN and OSCE are more engaged in Georgia-Abkhazia and Georgia-South Ossetia dynamics, respectively.[22] This is a historical development, since the UN mediated in the Georgian-Abkhazian conflict, the OSCE mediated in the Georgian-South Ossetian conflict, and the EU mediated in the 5 day war between Georgia and the Russian Federation. Joining efforts as mediators seemed a logical step, combining knowledge of the conflicts and underlining the importance of the international community to peace in the region.

A topic of concern is the fact that the mediating organisations can be manipulated by one or more states participating in the GID format. In the UN Security Council, the Russian Federation and the US have veto power. A possible obstacle in the OSCE is the fact that decision making takes place by consensus. Since Georgia and Russia are participating in the OSCE, this can slow down the decision-making process.

Replacement of Mediators

When analysing the reports on the negotiations in the Geneva format, it is striking that the mediators in this process in all three organisations, UN and EU have been replaced several times, and for the OSCE on a yearly basis.

Devdariani and Giuashvili explain why the OSCE mediators change regularly:

> "CiO Special Representative is fully dedicated to mediation tasks, but in contrast with the EU Special Representative (EUSR) and the UN Team, the OSCE CiO engagement in the GID is limited to a calendar year – corresponding to the term of a participating State's Chairmanship."[23]

Thus for the OSCE the reason lies in the fact that the position of mediator is connected to the chairmanship of the OSCE, which changes yearly. A mediator should gain the trust of the parties in order to be accepted and be effective. If a mediator changes regularly, and this also happened in the EU and UN mediation-team, this affects the trust that parties may have in the mediator and the process. Each time a change in the teams or mediators occurs, commitment has to be developed and restored again. For the parties, of which the negotiators have also changed in this period due to changes of Ministers of Foreign Affairs and their aides, the building of trust between mediators and negotiators from the other party can be difficult, which undoubtedly may have been a factor in slowing down of results due to a lack of mutual trust.[24] Given the fact that the negotiations take so long, this is logical but increases the risk that the conflict becomes and remains frozen.[25]

Peace-negotiations and the Conflict in Ukraine

Since March 2022 the Geneva International Discussions have been postponed indefinitely pending the war between Ukraine and the Russian Federation. This was done on the initiative of the three co-chairs of the UN, OSCE and EU. The reason for this step is the fear of the co-mediators that the conflict between Russia and Ukraine will negatively affect the discussions.

However, continuation of negotiations in this format is the more important, since the International Geneva Discussions are the only format in which the security in the Caucasus is discussed.[26]

After the indefinite postponement of the talks, the co-chairs held bilateral talks with parties. On 31 May 2022 Irakli Tuzhba, the Deputy Minister of Foreign Affairs of Abkhazia, declared in a conversation with the co-chairs that he is willing to continue discussions within the Geneva format. Three weeks later a statement was issued that Russia wanted the discussions to be moved to a neutral state, away from Geneva, at the headquarters of the UN. According to Russia, the negative attitude of the USA, the EU, OSCE and Switzerland stand in the way of constructive negotiations.

Russia underlined the need to sign a legally binding document on the non-use of violence against Abkhazia and South Ossetia by Georgia. [27] Georgia also wants to sign a non-use of violence document, after Russia has withdrawn its troops from Abkhazia and South Ossetia, which means that there seems little room for compromise.

In the next section we shall look at the security-issues that are discussed, and why they were and are in deadlock.

Pre-pandemic Negotiations

The question may be raised whether the negotiations before the lockdown went any better. In June 2018 the Abkhazian delegates state that they wish for more effectiveness in the Geneva International Discussions, of which a clearly formulated agenda is one step, as well as favourable conditions for dialogue. According to an Abkhazian statement, the Georgian delegation avoids a direct dialogue with the Abkhazians, and concentrates on its conflict with Russia. The Abkhazian delegation complains that Georgia is supporting resolutions in the UN, OSCE and the Council of Europe that contain accusations against Abkhazia, while Abkhazia has no voice in these organisations, nor has it voting power. Impartial language is also an issue for the Abkhazian delegation, and Minister of Foreign Affairs Daur Kove called on the co-chairs of the Geneva Discussions to take a more responsible attitude to the formulations and abbreviations that they use to formulate the reports. "There is no administrative border along the Ingur River. There is a state border". [28] This shows once again how little scope for manoeuvre there is in the talks.

In March 2018 the atmosphere during the discussions had also been rather tense, and the same topics and statements are made as before and after, as we can see in the following summary of outcomes:

> *"The main requirement of the Abkhaz side at the 43-rd round of the Geneva discussions was still the adoption of a joint oral statement on the parties' commitment to the non-use of force which would serve as an important step towards signing a legally binding agreement on the non-use of force between Georgia and Abkhazia and Georgia and South Ossetia. However, the oral statement of the parties was never accepted because this time the American formulation was unacceptable returning the old theses about the nature of events in August 2008. "In turn, the representatives of the Georgian delegation tried to shift the discussion of the main issue by putting the case of the death of the Georgian citizen A.Tatunashvili at the center of the discus-*

sion accusing him of not only South Ossetia, but also Russia[29]. And they also continued to insist in their rhetoric that Abkhazia is an 'occupied territory' and is not a party to the conflict and Russia should take the responsibility for the non-use of force."[30] The concern that Abkhazia does not have the possibility to address international fora at the UN, EU, Council of Europe, the Parliamentary Assembly of NATO and OSCE and therefore present its position was again raised in June 2017. Abkhazia also announced concerns about the cooperation between Georgia and NATO.[31]

Earlier during the negotiations, in October 2016 and March 2017 the Abkhazian, South Ossetian and Russian delegates left the meeting because the needs of Abkhazia and South Ossetia were not taken into account.[32]

Negotiations During Pandemic and Lockdown

On 10 and 11 December 2020 discussions were resumed after a one-year break due to COVID. The Georgian delegation was very concerned about a programme on the creation of a common socio-economic space between the Russian Federation and Abkhazia, fearing that this would result in a gradual integration of Abkhazia into the Russian space, as we shall see later... Earlier, the Georgian delegation was especially concerned about a meeting between the Russian and Abkhazian presidents held in Sochi on 12 November 2020, calling it a step in the direction of formal annexation. The Georgian delegation was worried that this is part of Russia's policy of forcibly changing sovereign borders in Europe in contravention of international law.[33]

Another worry of the Georgian delegation was the Russification of the population in Abkhazia, and the Georgian delegation underlined the need for education in the native language, in this case Georgian for the ethnic Georgians living in Abkhazia. The importance of the Incident Prevention and Response Mechanism was also underlined by the Georgian side.

In 2021 one of the issues on the agenda was the need to make the negotiation-process more efficient, since to everyone it was clear that several issues on the agenda were in deadlock.

On 3 March 2021, during talks in the Geneva format Irakli Tuzhba, the Deputy Minister of Foreign Affairs of Abkhazia, said that "the Abkhazian Foreign Ministry has been regularly issuing statements urging the international community to take measures to prevent militarisation of the region. At the same time, the appeals of the Abkhazian side remain unanswered by representatives of international structures".[34] Notwithstanding the EU policy of 'engagement without recognition', it seems that some parties are better heard than others.

During the 52nd round of the Geneva International Discussions that same month (March 2021) the co-chairs, UN, EU and OSCE, as well as participants from Georgia, Russia and the US, members of the exiled Georgian administrations of Abkhazia and South Ossetia and the authorities of Abkhazia and South Ossetia met in their personal capacities, as a report of the meeting states.[35] The question that this raises is, if the parties to these discussions are not representing their constituents and governments, how can they validly sign any agreement at the end of the day? Doesn't this in itself undermine the whole negotiation-process, even if it is called a 'discussion'?

Topics of Discussion

For years the negotiations on security-issues have been in deadlock. One of the topics on which the parties are not able to agree was a declaration on the non-use of force. The Abkhazian side complained that the Georgian side did not want to sign a document on international guarantees of the non-use of force. The Abkhazian side was willing to sign such a document, but the Georgians first wanted guarantees from Russia that they will not use force against Georgia before deciding on signing. A draft-document from the Georgians with support of the US in 2018 was unacceptable for the Abkhazian delegation, since it referred to the situation in 2008 where the Abkhazian and South Ossetian delegations were not accepted as formal parties to the conflict.[36]

On 19 and 20 June 2021, the US issued a statement during the 53rd round of the Geneva International Discussions, underlining that they want "withdrawal of Russian troops to pre-conflict positions as a key step towards full resolution of the conflict. The United States also underscored the importance of providing full access to conflict-affected areas for humanitarian organisations, in order to improve the lives of conflict-affected people."[37] This shows one of the issues on which parties do not get any closer, since the Russians are not willing to remove their military base in Abkhazia, nor do the Abkhazians feel safe enough without military protection from Russia, and the Abkhazians do not allow the EU Monitoring Mission access to Abkhazian territory.

The OSCE Ministerial Council meeting and the Group of Friends of Georgia on 4 December 2020 issued a joint-statement, which did not take into account the position of the Abkhazian side. The Abkhazian delegation to the Geneva Discussions complained that they are not heard, and that this discredits 'the very idea of an Organisation for Security and Cooperation in Europe'.[38] The statement led for Abkhazia to a breach of confidence in the Geneva International Discussions and the OSCE as co-chair:

> *"The Abkhazian side never had confidence in this regional structure and during the previous negotiation-process between Georgia and Abkhazia, which lasted from 1993 to 2008, the Abkhazian side categorically opposed the participation of OSCE representatives in it, as a result of which it was held under the auspices of the UN."[39]*

This breach in confidence should be remedied before discussions can continue. The Abkhazian side complains that it is denied the opportunity to speak at international venues, which adds to the one-sidedness of the information. The Abkhazian delegation stated:

"At this stage, it can be stated that the OSCE has completely exhausted its confidence in itself as an objective mediator in the negotiation-process and has become an accomplice in the policy pursued by Georgia. Taking into account the current situation, the Abkhazian side reserves the right to demand the exclusion of OSCE representatives from the Co-Chairs of the international Geneva Discussions on Stability and Security in Transcaucasia.

"In the event that the OSCE representatives change their extremely tendentious attitude towards the problem of resolving the Georgian-Abkhazian conflict and provide the representatives of Abkhazia with an opportunity to speak within the framework of the activities of the relevant OSCE committees, this measure will allow revising the approaches of the Abkhazian side to the activities of this organisation."[40]

Previously, Abkhazia had already stated in press-communiqués that Georgia in UN organs complains about Abkhazia, while Abkhazia, not represented and not having the right to raise its voice in these organisations, cannot defend itself and correct information. This has, as we saw above, resulted in the Abkhazian side claiming that the three co-chairs are not so impartial, and therefore, the co-chairs will have to do their utmost to gain the trust of the Abkhazian side and strengthen the commitment for the Abkhazians in this (for them) asymmetrical process.

Another topic that has been in deadlock for years is the unblocking of the Incident Prevention and Response Mechanism (IPRM) in the city of Gal(i). The Abkhazian side considers that the Georgian delegation is unwilling to negotiate, while the Georgian delegation demands the withdrawal of Russian troops from Abkhazia as a precondition. Therefore, no movement has been visible in this respect.

The question whether the situation in the border-region of Abkhazia is stable is another topic of disagreement. While the co-chairs, Russia and Abkhazia consider the situation stable, Georgia does not agree on this, again referring to the Russian troops that are stationed in Abkhazia and agreements between Abkhazia and Russia that increasingly inter-twine the economies of both republics.[41]

Finally, the Abkhazian delegation has been complaining that Georgia is receiving military aid and training from NATO and that a NATO facility is built in the city of Poti, not far from the Abkhazian border. This fuels fears that Georgia might consider using force against Abkhazia, if talks would close down. A similar development already emerged in 2020 in the conflict between Azerbaijan and Armenia over Nagorno Karabakh. The Georgian delegation is concerned about the Russian military base on Abkhazian territory and increasing military support for Abkhazia from Russia. The Abkhazian spokesman states that as long as Georgia wants to join NATO and is improving its military, the Abkhazian government has no other choice.[42]

The Effect of the 2008 and 2014 Agreement On the Relation Between Abkhazia and the Russian Federation

In 2008 the Russian Federation signed a "Friendship, Cooperation and Mutual Assistance" agreement with Abkhazia. The agreement included border-protection, and customs-, military and security- cooperation, but also topics like education and health.[43] In September 2014 this was followed by an agreement between Abkhazia and the Russian Federation on an "Alliance and Strategic Partnership".[44]

Many Abkhazian citizens acquired Russian citizenship next to their Abkhazian citizenship, which brings with it the possibility of obtaining a Russian pension. Russia is (with 90%) the main beneficiary of Abkhazian exports, while Abkhazia imports mainly from Russia.[45] Since 99% of foreign investment comes from Russia, the Abkhazian government has adopted legislation to make it more difficult to buy Abkhazian property with Russian investments in order to avoid the Russian Federation becoming too dominant in the Abkhazian economy.[46]

The 2014 agreement provides detailed provisions on security-matters, according to Ambriosio and Lange. The document includes a commitment to "cooperate closely with each other in the [mutual] protection of its sovereignty, territorial integrity and security".[47] Both parties agree to come to each other's help in case of a threat to peace or breakdown of peace in order to guarantee a joint-defence, peace and mutual security. Russia has the right to base its armed forces in Abkhazia in order to be able to guarantee this, based on a subsequent treaty.[48] Article 10 of the agreement guarantees that parties may protect the rights of its citizens in the territory in accordance with general principles of international law.[49] Since most Abkhazians also hold Russian citizenship, this means that the Russian Federation reserves the right to intervene in Abkhazia, which reminds us of the situation in South Ossetia in August 2008.

Russia takes responsibility for "the maintenance and functioning of the financial and banking system" in Abkhazia, while legislation on economic activity, civil and tax law, social protection and pensions is unified in line with article 15 of the 2014 agreement.[50] The worries about a creeping annexation are therefore grounded.

Is there a way out of this deadlock? Can the theory of normalisation play a role?

Normalisation

In 2012 Russia and Georgia normalised their relations when bilateral trade and travel resumed. Normalisation is aimed at bringing progress in practical matters that are not related to the core question of the conflict. On the topic of the status of Abkhazia and South Ossetia, there are no moves. Abkhazia, according to the International Crisis Group, comes closer and closer in the sphere of influence to Russia. The International Crisis Group states: "The *de facto* governments' relations with Russia are so close that they both have former Russian officials serving in senior roles, particularly at ministries responsible for security."[51]

Russia and Georgia decided to appoint envoys who would meet in person and talk by telephone. Those appointed knew each other well, having been former colleagues in the Soviet administration. These were the first steps in confidence-building measures. Where normalisation led to developments in mutual cooperation in certain sectors, the Geneva discussions very soon became repetitive, and therefore stalled the process on solving issues related to the 2008 conflict. The bottom line is that Georgia has problems with Russia's recognition of Abkhazia and South Ossetia, which violates international law, and worries about the stationing of Russian troops in these republics. Russia has little incentive to make bigger moves, according to the International Crisis Group, since it has a military presence in these republics, and strengthens ties with the republics.[52]

The Georgian delegation wants an end to the limitations that Abkhazia has installed on the movement of the European Union Monitoring Mission (EUMM), and secondly, Georgia wants guarantees that Russia will not use violence against Georgia. Russia takes the stand that, since it has recognised Abkhazia, the EUMM should not cross an international border. With regard to the guarantee on non-use of violence, Russia states that in the conflict between Georgia and Abkhazia, it is a mediator, and not a party. This may be what it is, but in the Geneva discussions the outcome of the 5-day war and its cease-fire between Georgia and Russia is discussed with the support of the co-chairs UN, OSCE and EU, and in that sense Russia is definitely a party. With its military presence in Abkhazia, the Russian Federation does not have to worry that Georgia will soon become a member of NATO, since a state with a conflict on its territory cannot join NATO. The risk of escalation and the activation of Article 5 of the NATO Treaty (an attack on one is an attack on all) frustrates this, especially if the potential conflict-party is the Russian Federation. Accession-discussions to the EU will also take many years.[53]

Within the Geneva Discussions the Incident Prevention and Response Mechanism (IPRM) has been developed to contact the other party when tension is rising in certain areas in order to avoid an outbreak of violence. This system has not been used since 2017, after an Abkhazian lower-rank officer killed a Georgian, and in South Ossetia it has not been used since 2019, when Georgia built a military outpost close to the border in order to avoid the South Ossetian border being moved further into Georgian territory. Although in 2020 contact resumed, the problems concerning these matters have not been solved.

According to the International Crisis Group the normalisation-process could be a way out of the deadlock in the Geneva International Dialogue, because it gives even Georgia and Abkhazia the opportunity to intensify trade, without recognition and without considering the status of Abkhazia.[54]

Since the negotiations on the bigger issues have been deadlocked for more than a decade, the parties tend to concentrate on smaller projects that may provide results. As Devdariani and Giuashvili state: "Precisely since the talks about 'overall objectives' are effectively deadlocked, the GID participants are tempted to use technical projects to (re)assert the notions of statehood, identity and sovereign control."[55]

Conclusion

The negotiations between Georgia, Abkhazia and Russia went into deadlock very soon after the talks started in 2008, because the issue of status cannot be addressed, and a lack of mutual confidence leading to militarisation of the region.

The militarisation in the South Caucasus region in combination with the lack of confidence and the lack of communication makes the ceasefire agreement vulnerable. It is very surprising that from the start all parties wanted something different and that a strong mediation-team formed of UN, OSCE and EU is not capable of addressing the issue of trust and the common need of peace in the region.

Is the situation between 2008 and 2022 different from the period of negotiations between 1992 and 2008? Not that much – cease-fire agreements were violated and signed, and Russia was present in Abkhazia as guarantor of the peace, with a military base and, until 2008, in the capacity of a UN peacekeeping force. Abkhazia developed its state-structure, declared unilateral independence, and sought recognition. In the meantime, it became more dependent on Russia as guarantor for safety and main trading partner. In the past years the peace-process has been in lockdown – or frozen, if you prefer – but actually, given the lack of mutual trust, this has been the case for the past 30 years. The only point of light may be the normalisation-process which provides chances to trade and discuss all matters not related to refugees and status.

Endnotes

[1] Part of the text on the peace-negotiations between 1992 and 2008 is based on, and was published earlier in, C.M.L. Hille, 2010, *State Building and Conflict Resolution in the Caucasus*, Brill, Leiden.

[2] C.M.L. Hille, 2010, *State Building and Conflict Resolution in the Caucasus*, Brill, Leiden, p. 230.

[3] C.M.L. Hille, 2010, *State Building and Conflict Resolution in the Caucasus*, Brill, Leiden, p. 246-247.

[4] C.M.L. Hille, 2010, *State Building and Conflict Resolution in the Caucasus*, Brill, Leiden, p. 230.

[5] C.M.L. Hille, *State Building and Conflict Resolution in the Caucasus*, Brill, 2010, Leiden, p. 232, Declaration on Measures for a Political Settlement of the Georgian/Abkhaz Conflict signed on 4 April 1994, in S/1994/379, Annex I and Quadriparite Agreement in Annex II of the said document. The Agreement on a Cease Fire and Separation of Forces of 14 May 1994 in S/1994/583, 17 May 1994.

[6] The number of UNOMIG observers was expanded pursuant UN Security Council Resolution 937 (21 July 1994).

[7] The aim of the Group of Friends of the Secretary General was to create a favourable situation for conflict-transformation and confidence-building measures.

[8] https://www.c-r.org/our-work/accord/georgia-abkhazia/keytext8.php, accessed 19 April 2009.

[9] Ibid.

[10] https://www.c-r.org/our-work/accord/georgia-abkhazia/keytext8.php, accessed 19 April 2009.

[11] Ibid.

[12] https://www.c-r.org/our-work/accord/georgia-abkhazia/keytext8.php, accessed 19 April 2009.

[13] S/1994/583, 17 May 1994, and S/RES.937 (1994), 21 July 1994, where the mandate of UNOMIG was expanded, including overseeing the activities of the CIS peacekeeping forces as well.

[14] Chester Crocker et al explain in *Taming Intractable Conflicts: Mediation in the Hardest Cases*, (Washington: United States Institute of Peace Press,

2004), how conflicts become intractable (a feature which applies to the Georgian-Abkhazian conflict).

[15] SC/6671, 7 May 1999.

[16] Crocker, C., Hampson, F.O., Aal, P. (eds), *Intractable Conflicts, Mediating in the Hardest Cases,* United States Institute of Peace Press, Washington, 2004, describe various forms of forgotten conflicts. *In casu* the Georgian-Abkhazian conflict could fall in the sub category 'neglected conflicts', p. 49-52.

[17] https://www.circassianworld.com/croniclewar.html, accessed 31 March 2009 and Crocker, C., ibid.

[18] C.M.L. Hille, 2010, *State Building and Conflict Resolution in the Caucasus,* Brill, Leiden, p. 236.

[19] https://www.rferl.org/content/Talks_Betwen_Moscow_And_Tbilisi_Break_Down/13300183.html, accessed 15 October 2008.

[20] C.M.L. Hille, 2010, *State Building and Conflict Resolution in the Caucasus,* Brill, Leiden, p. 237.

[21] Jaba Devdariani, Teona Giuashvili, "Geneva International Discussions. Negotiating the Possible", in *Security and Human Rights*, volume 26, 2016, p. 387. GID stands for Geneva International Discussions.

[22] Jaba Devdariani, Teona Giuashvili, "Geneva International Discussions. Negotiating the Possible", in *Security and Human Rights*, volume 26, 2016, p. 387.

[23] Jaba Devdariani, Teona Giuashvili, "Geneva International Discussions. Negotiating the Possible", in *Security and Human Rights*, volume 26 No 2016, p. 389.

[24] More on trust and commitment in C.M.L. Hille, B.E.E. van Sytzama, *Introductie (Internationale) Medation, Voor iedereen die mediation wil begrijpen en toepassen*, Boom Bestuurskunde, 2019, Amsterdam, pp. 40.

[25] More on frozen conflict in C.A. Crocker, F.O. Hampson, P. Aall, 2004, *Taming Intractable Conflicts. Mediation in the Hardest Cases*, Washington DC, US Institute of Peace.

[26] 31 May 2022, "During the conversation, the Abkhaz side expressed its readiness to continue working in the format of the International Geneva Discussions, which are the only international platform in which secu-

rity issues in the South Caucasus are discussed", On the Meeting with the Co-chairs of the International Geneva Discussions, http://mfaapsny. org/en/allnews/news/geneva-discussions/o-vstreche-s-sopredsately-ami-mezhdunarodnykh-zhenevskikh-diskussiy/, accessed 29 July 2022.

[27] On the Meeting with the Co-chairs of the International Geneva Discussions, http://mfaapsny.org/en/allnews/news/geneva-dis-cussions/o-vstreche-s-sopredsedatelyami-mezhdunarod-nykh-zhenevskikh-diskussiy/, accessed 29 July 2022.

[28] On the 43rd Round of Geneva Discussions, http://mfaapsny.org/en/allnews/news/geneva-discus-sions/o-43-m-raunde-zhenevskikh-diskussiy/, accessed 29 July 2022, On the 45th Round of the Geneva Discussions, http://mfaapsny.org/en/allnews/news/geneva-discussions/o-45-m-raun-de-zhenvskikh-diskussiy/, accessed 29 July 2022

[29] This is indeed the text from the MFA's website, but there is clearly an error. It should surely read: '...accusing not only South Ossetia but also Russia of it' [Ed.].

[30] On the 43rd round of the Geneva Discussions, http://mfaapsny.org/en/allnews/news/geneva-discussions/o-43-m-raun-de-zhenevskikh-diskussiy/, accessed 29 July 2022.

[31] On the 40th Round of the Geneva Discussions, http://mfaapsny.org/en/allnews/news/geneva-discussions/o-40-m-raun-de-zhenevskikh-diskussiy/, accessed 29 July 2022.

[32] On the 37th Round of the Geneva Discussions, http://mfaapsny.org/en/allnews/news/geneva-discussions/o-37-om-raun-de-zhenevskikh-diskussiy/, accessed 29 July 2022.

[33] Statement by the Ministry of Foreign Affairs on the 51st Round of the Geneva International Discussions, https://mfa.gov.ge/News/%E2%80%8Bsagareo-saqmeta-saministros-ganckhadeba-jenev-(3).aspx?CattID=5&lang=en-US, accessed 29 July 2022.

[34] "Irakli Tuzhba held a meeting with the Co-Chairmen of the Geneva International Discussions on Security and Stability in the Transcaucasia", in http://mfaapsny.org/en/allnews/news/geneva-discussions/irak-

liy-tuzhba-provel-vstrechu-s-sopredsedatelyami-mezhdunarod-nykh-zhenevskikh-diskussiy-po-bezopasn/, accessed 29 July 2022.

[35] "The GIDs are co-chaired by representatives of OSCE, EU, and UN, and involve participants from Georgia, Russia, and the U.S., as well as members of both the exiled Georgian administrations of Abkhazia and Tskhinvali Region/South Ossetia and the two regions' Russian-backed authorities, in their personal capacities. Sessions are held in two working groups, with the first group discussing peace and security matters, and the second – humanitarian concerns." 52nd round of the International Geneva Discussions on Security and Stability in the Transcaucasus, in http://mfaapsny.org/en/allnews/news/geneva-discussions/o-52-m-raunde-zhenevskikh-mezh-dunarodnykh-diskussiy-/, accessed 29 July 2022.

[36] September 17, 2020, On the Meeting of the Co-Chairs of the Geneva International Discussions, http://mfaapsny.org/en/allnews/news/gene-va-discussions/o-vstreche-s-sopredsedatelyami-zhenevskikh-mezhdun-arodnykh-diskussiy/, accessed 29 July 2022.

[37] Press Statement On the 53rd round of the Geneva Discussions, http://mfaapsny.org/en/allnews/news/geneva-discussions/o-53-m-raun-de-zhenevskikh-diskussiy-/, accessed 29 July 2022.

[38] December 4, 2020, Commentary of the Ministry of Foreign Affairs of Abkhazia on the Statement of the Group of Friends of Georgia at the OSCE, in http://mfaapsny.org/en/allnews/news/geneva-discussions/kommentar-iy-mid-abkhazii-v-svyazi-s-zayavleniem-gruppy-druzey-gruzii-v-obse/, accessed 29 July 2022.

[39] Commentary of the Ministry of Foreign Affairs of Abkhazia on the Statement of the Group of Friends of Georgia at the OSCE, in http://mfaapsny.org/en/allnews/news/geneva-discussions/kommentariy-mid-abkhazii-v-svya-zi-s-zayavleniem-gruppy-druzey-gruzii-v-obse/, accessed 29 July 2022.

[40] Commentary of the Ministry of Foreign Affairs of Abkhazia on the Statement of the Group of Friends of Georgia at the OSCE, in http://mfaapsny.org/en/allnews/news/geneva-discussions/kommentariy-mid-abkhazii-v-svya-zi-s-zayavleniem-gruppy-druzey-gruzii-v-obse/, accessed 29 July 2022.

[41] Inter alia in 52nd round of the International Geneva Discussions on Security and Stability in the Transcaucasus, http://mfaapsny.org/en/allnews/

news/geneva-discussions/o-52-m-raunde-zhenevskikh-mezhdunarod-nykh-diskussiy-/, accessed 29 July 2022.

[42] Inter alia in Press Statement On the 53rd round of the Geneva Discussions, http://mfaapsny.org/en/allnews/news/geneva-discussions/o-53-m-raunde-zhenevskikh-diskussiy-/, accessed 29 July 2022, 52nd round of the International Geneva Discussions on Security and Stability in the Transcaucasus, http://mfaapsny.org/en/allnews/news/geneva-discussions/o-52-m-raunde-zhenevskikh-mezhdunarodnykh-disk-ussiy-/, accessed 29 July 2022,

[43] Thomas Ambrosio, William Lange, "The Architecture of Annexation? Russia's Bilateral Agreements with Abkhazia and South Ossetia", in *Nationalities Papers* 2016, Vol. 44, No. 5, p. 674.

[44] Thomas Ambrosio, William Lange, "The Architecture of Annexation? Russia's Bilateral Agreements with Abkhazia and South Ossetia", in *Nationalities Papers* 2016, Vol. 44, No. 5, p. 674.

[45] Thomas Ambrosio, William Lange, "The Architecture of Annexation? Russia's Bilateral Agreements with Abkhazia and South Ossetia", in *Nationalities Papers* 2016, Vol. 44, No. 5, p. 677 and International Crisis Group, "Abkhazia, Deepening Dependence", *Europe Report*, #202, 2010, 6-7.

[46] Thomas Ambrosio, William Lange, "The Architecture of Annexation? Russia's Bilateral Agreements with Abkhazia and South Ossetia", in *Nationalities Papers* 2016, Vol. 44, No. 5, p. 677-678, T. German, 2012, "Security the South Caucasus: Military Aspects of Russian Policy Towards the Region Since 2008", *Europe-Asia Studies*, 64(9), p. 1657.

[47] Thomas Ambrosio, William Lange, "The Architecture of Annexation? Russia's Bilateral Agreements with Abkhazia and South Ossetia", in *Nationalities Papers* 2016, Vol. 44, No. 5, p. 679.

[48] Thomas Ambrosio, William Lange, "The Architecture of Annexation? Russia's Bilateral Agreements with Abkhazia and South Ossetia", in *Nationalities Papers* 2016, Vol. 44, No. 5, p. 679-680.

[49] Thomas Ambrosio, William Lange, "The Architecture of Annexation? Russia's Bilateral Agreements with Abkhazia and South Ossetia", in *Nationalities Papers* 2016, Vol. 44, No. 5, p. 680.

[50] Thomas Ambrosio, William Lange, "The Architecture of Annexation? Russia's Bilateral Agreements with Abkhazia and South Ossetia", in *Nationalities Papers* 2016, Vol. 44, No. 5, p. 680.

[51] International Crisis Group, *Georgia and Russia, Why and How to Save Normalisation*, Briefing No. 90, 26 October 2020, https://www.crisisgroup. org/europe-central-asia/caucasus/georgia/b90-georgia-and-russia-why-and-how-save-normalisation, accessed 29 July 2022.

[52] International Crisis Group, *Georgia and Russia, Why and How to Save Normalisation*, Briefing No. 90, 26 October 2020, https://www.crisisgroup. org/europe-central-asia/caucasus/georgia/b90-georgia-and-russia-why-and-how-save-normalisation, accessed 29 July 2022.

[53] International Crisis Group, *Georgia and Russia, Why and How to Save Normalisation*, Briefing No. 90, 26 October 2020, https://www.crisisgroup. org/europe-central-asia/caucasus/georgia/b90-georgia-and-russia-why-and-how-save-normalisation, accessed 29 July 2022.

[54] International Crisis Group, *Georgia and Russia, Why and How to Save Normalisation*, Briefing No. 90, 26 October 2020, https://www.crisisgroup. org/europe-central-asia/caucasus/georgia/b90-georgia-and-russia-why-and-how-save-normalisation, accessed 29 July 2022.

[55] Jaba Devdariani, Teona Giuashvili, "Geneva International Discussions. Negotiating the Possible", in *Security and Human Rights*, volume 26, 2016, p. 391.

A Reflection on Conflict, Consequence and Lessons

Christopher Langton

*Director of The Independent Conflict Research & Analysis (ICRA). He
spent thirty-two years in the British Army. During that time, he served
as the Deputy Commander of the UN Observer Mission in Georgia
(UNOMIG) as well as holding various attaché posts in Russia, the
South Caucasus, and Central Asia.*

It was early December 1995. I stood on the south bank of the Inguri
river waiting for the arrival of a newly appointed ambassador to
Tbilisi who wanted to be briefed on the situation in Abkhazia.

Looking across the river on that cold dark afternoon as the wind
came down from the mountains, I could almost see the village where
stood the remnants of a school I had visited a few days before.

I reflected on my visit to that place in the Gali region; a place that
had suffered the trauma of the war, and from which people were driven
from their homes. Many to perish as the fled into exile. Many more to remain in exile for the rest of their lives. The children of the conflict would
become the adults of the same conflict. Some I would see in Zugdidi after
the so-called 5-day war in 2008; still displaced; still unemployed; waiting for a future.

What did it all mean? War, displacement, refugees, broken homes,
casualties. Is this a necessary consequence of ethnic divide in humanity?

135

I have no answers. However, a glimmer of light in 2022 during the unnecessary and brutally dangerous war in Ukraine was to read that a group of Abkhaz called for an end to the fighting having suffered a long and brutal war themselves. Perhaps this is a consequence and lesson of war that can be used louder and more effectively to urge those who perpetuate conflict to see reason. The Abkhaz people being of the same region have that unique possibility to speak out based on their own brutal experience.[1]

But on that day in 1995 all I could do was to begin writing a poem that recalled my sadness on visiting the school in Gali region, but also the courage of those children.

Children of war[2]

> The school had few windows
> There was a partial roof
> Yet the children sat in perfect quiet
> As the teacher read the book.
>
> These the children of the dreadful war
> Children whose parents long lay dead
> Whose homes were burned and lives destroyed
> Sat quiet while the teacher read.
>
> The shell hole in the playground.
> A shell hole full of putrid water;
> Pock-marked walls now crumbling.
> The rain crying; the children playing.
> Unsmiling, wide-eyed childrens' faces.
> The faces of a thousand places.
> Where blow the winds of war.
>
> The pig trotted down the track
> Past the shell holes dark and black
> With fetid oily water
> Reminders of the genocidal slaughter
> Which took away in just one day

The parents of the children now at play
In the dirty filthy water black.
Parents who would not be coming back.

Then down the track; the aged man
On the donkey cart began
To chant an old Mingrelian rhyme
Reminding of a time
When, as a child, he had played
In peace in the scented shade
Of the towering protective trees;
Eucalyptus, their scented cool
Long since burned for heat
In the broken childrens' broken school.

Endnotes

[1] https://abkhazworld.com/aw/current-affairs/1978-call-of-inhabitants-of-abkhazia-to-stop-the-bloodshed-in-ukraine

[2] Published under the pen name of Roland Christopher in *"Wild Blue Geraniums" ©Christopher Langton*

Abkhazia's Relationship with the Environment since Independence – Its Successes and Challenges in the Face of International Isolation

Clayton Payne

Researcher on environmental governance in Abkhazia and South Ossetia. SOAS, University of London. UK.

Independence for Abkhazia has been as far as a country could get from an easy transition, with a complete lack of recognition by U.N. member states pre-2008 to only a handful post-2008. As a country lacking international recognition, it has been excluded from environmental governance systems and access to wider initiatives. Consultation on projects influencing their natural resources has been denied to the nation on the basis that, in the international community's eyes, they have no legitimacy to manage and preserve their own land's ecosystems and natural resources and therefore require no consultation on projects affecting it. It would therefore be a legitimate and understandable position to take in believing that Abkhazia's government and people, due to the economic constraints that have hampered them, resulting from their international exclusion, would have caused vast environmental damage as their natural resources were over-exploited out of economic necessity. In fact, this was a position that was often voiced to me by many Georgian NGOs and academics about Abkhazia as I was conducting research. There is much environmental lore in Georgia pertaining to Abkhazia most of which Is easily disproven, some of which has reasonable though not totally satisfactory explanations, but all of which sounded logical against the political and economic backdrop.

Being cut-off from international systems has led to more than one negative consequence which I shall also look at openly and honestly, but which must be viewed within the context of international isolation and the lack of international cooperation and resources that result from this.

Preservation of Abkhazia's forestry, endemic species and water

Two of the most vocalised objections I had heard whilst researching in Georgia pertaining to Abkhazian environmentalism were linked to Forestry – the first being stories of vast logging in the 1990s being sold to 'black flag' Turkish ships looking to exploit economically Abkhazia's economic isolation and subsequent loss of tourism-revenue; the second being that, during the construction period of the Sochi Olympics, Abkhazia's forests were again logged heavily, clearing swathes of intact forest to sell to Russia for lower prices than their domestic wood. From a logical standpoint, given the economic turmoil the country suffered from its isolation, these seemed like reasonable and understandable claims. However, they were both easily debunked. Abkhazia's tree-cover is not only important for its high level of carbon sink but sitting in a Marine subtropical humid temperature banding, high levels of deforestation would led to increased landslips and mud-flows as a result of soil-erosion and changes in rainfall-pattern which would destroy ecosystems and endanger existing settlements. This in turn would endanger endemic species populations, creating a habitat-loss that would be irreversible. However, in the last 20 years less than 0.2% of tree-cover in Abkhazia has been lost, a figure in line with loss of cover due to forest-fires and tree-disease. Satellite imaging showed after the construction-period of the Sochi Olympics that there had been a 3,000-hectare loss of forestry on the Russian side and none on the side of Abkhazia, disproving the belief that logging had occurred within Abkhazia. While any loss of forest-cover is less than ideal, the current loss of tree-cover in Abkhazia is still higher than would be optimal. International recognition would help greatly with this and offer the country access to cross-border cooperation on management of tree-disease and early-warning technology of forest-fire, which would mitigate these losses, reducing them to an even lower level.

Political isolation has not only rendered Abkhazia unable to control the usage of shared waterways, such as the vitally important Ingur river but has also left it excluded from transnational cooperation on the protection of its coastline. Abkhazia's energy-security has been over reliant on the Ingur hydropower-plant since independence, which is now suffering from reduced water-flow. This could be exacerbated further by the proposed hydropower-plants in Georgia at Nenskra and Khudoni, which are being financed by the EBRD and other foreign investors. Were these plants to go ahead, not only would there be a further reduction in the water-flow of the Ingur river but there would also be loss of habitat for endemic species as well as further landslips and natural disasters. While these plants would affect Svan communities the most, the fallout from this would extend into Abkhazia, further increasing deforestation and loss of species-habitat, with Abkhazia being denied any consultation on this.

The Abkhazian Black Sea coast has also been excluded from schemes due to Abkhazia's political isolation. Despite the wetlands and Black Sea coast being home to IUCN red-list birds which are close to extinction, transnational cooperation such as the Commission on the Protection of the Black Sea from pollution and the UNEP (United Nations' Environment Programme) do not work on these projects with Abkhazia, thereby neglecting the coastline, a result of which has seen coastal erosion to the entrance to the Ingur river to the extent that 'Hungry Coast' (viz. where sediment is stripped from the river-bed allowing erosion of the coast) has become obvious. This damage has been allowed to happen only a short distance from the UNESCO-protected Kolkheti wetlands-site, preserved due to its important ecosystems and endemic species.

Abkhazia's energy-security crisis

In Abkhazia today there is probably no bigger question than that of energy-security. In recent years there have been blackouts and 'brownouts' plus a wave of miners of Bitcoin taking advantage of Abkhazia's low energy-costs. Abkhazia now has difficulty in effectively expelling the miners with as a consequence both a vast increase in energy-usage and impending energy price-rises on the horizon resulting from this shortage and global price-increases for energy.

Energy-prices were set low after independence to help counterbalance the economic plight of Abkhazia's citizens. However, the ongoing international isolation of the country has never led to a natural increase of these prices. These low prices have resulted in years of neglect of internal infrastructure in the power-grid affecting power-lines, transformers and causing burnout of the electrical system. Alternative forms of electricity to the Ingur dam hydropower-plant have not received investment (due to the necessarily high costs involved), whilst Georgia's reliance on the power from the dam has waned as it has received funds from EBRD and private companies to expand its power-network. The Ingur dam has needed increasing maintenance due to build-up of silt, seepage and decreasing water-levels. Its location on a seismic area is also cause for long-term concern as natural disaster could in the future render it ineffective. This has led to a single point of failure for Abkhazia's energy-security, low retail prices combined with a hydropower-plant that is ageing in an over-used river, no investment in infrastructure due to a lack of profits and no external investment in alternative long-term, affordable power-sources. While the low prices were honourable if not economically essential for people, this was in effect a policy with a short shelf-life that has now been operating for thirty years and has come to a head as the country faces excessive usage and global inflation in energy.

Other environmental issues

The other pressing environmental issue in independent Abkhazia is that of ecotourism and waste. Tourism has been, since Soviet times, a key economic industry in Abkhazia, but political isolation combined with increased high-quality tourism-infrastructure in Sochi has led to Abkhazia becoming a budget tourist-destination for more or less exclusively Russian tourists. Abkhazia's current positioning in the tourism-market has stopped it fully exploiting higher-cost ecotourism, which could help it develop more environmentally sustainable tourism with higher profits. Abkhazia's current isolation politically, combined with the difficulty faced by nationals of countries which do not recognise Abkhazia's independence in obtaining a visa, means this is unlikely to change and the necessary investment is unlikely to be forthcoming. This, over time, will likely see a high-traffic, low-profit industry gradually degrade the infrastructure that is there without the needed income to build new sustainable infrastructure and projects for ecotourism that can work in equalibrium with the environment.

Waste-management has also been an acute problem in Abkhazia. Since the filling of the refuse-site in Sukhum, there has been no viable alternative, and waste has been dumped improperly in Gal as a result of there being no other viable option. While this is a deeply problematic issue, it is also an issue which could be solved relatively quickly with international cooperation or investment in infrastructure.

Conclusion and thoughts

In my opinion, despite the economic and geopolitical difficulties that Abkhazia has faced during its first thirty years of independence, environmentally Abkhazia has performed better than could have been realistically expected. It would be easy to point an accusing finger at the relative failures of the country on issues such as energy-security and waste-management, but these are problems that demand vast investment, and very few countries perform successfully without external investment and co-operation. Where Abkhazia has truly performed admirably is its preservation of its forestry, a key environmental feature of the country, when it might have been expected of a country suffering hardship to exploit what is an enormous economic resource.

Going forward, what is truly needed to secure areas where Abkhazia has been struggling most and to improve on some of Abkhazia's good work is recognition by the international community. Even if this was only in a 'soft' form, where international cooperation and investment would (a) allow the necessary help that the country needs to protect its coast, (b) permit debate on shared resources, (c) create a thriving eco-tourism-industry, (d) help with waste-management and (e) provide investment on alternative sources of low-cost energy.

Despite the good work done in Abkhazia, continued lack of recognition will only exacerbate environmental issues over the long term, and resolutions should be made to bring Abkhazia into the fold on International environmental issues, as the country is exceptionally important in the region for endemic species, carbon-sink by forestry and coastal integrity, all of which will undoubtedly be negatively affected long-term by continued isolation. Without Investment in the environmental infrastructure of the country, the problems faced will continue to spiral, just as they have with energy-security.

Environmental protection should not be a matter to be politicised, and, hopefully, there will be a change whereby International cooperation can help turn the tide on the most pressing issues and cross-border dialogue can begin. Shared resources should be the starting-point of any dialogue, since damage to them affects everyone in the region, not just Abkhazians.

References and sources available in the 2021 environmental report: "Environmental effects of Frozen conflict in Georgia" (October 2021) at: https://www.researchgate.net/publication/355680031_Environmental_ effects_of_Frozen_conflict_in_Georgia

Negotiating a UN Peace-deal Between the Abkhazians and the Georgians – the Failed Initiative of 2001/2

Dieter Boden

Ambassador (ret) Former Special Representative of the UNSG in Georgia (1999 - 2002). Germany.

I t may sound utopian today but there have indeed been efforts in the past to help solve the Abkhazian-Georgian conflict in a comprehensive deal. One of these efforts dates back to the years 2001/2003. It was then that in my capacity as Special Representative of the UN Secretary-General and Head of the UNOMIG Mission in Georgia I was authorised to launch a document on the "Distribution of Competences between Tbilisi and Sukhumi" worked out by my Mission in Tbilisi. In substance, this was an attempt to have the Abkhazian and the Georgian sides to the conflict sit down at the negotiating table and elaborate modalities for a peaceful-settlement within the framework of certain principles laid down in the Document.

The settlement of the ethno-territorial conflict between Georgia and Abkhazia was at the core of my UN mandate when I served in Georgia from 1999 to 2002. From my very arrival in Georgia I was encouraged by well-intentioned people from both sides not to give up hope of engagement in what they called a basically hopeless matter. Soon I realised that this was indeed going to be a Sisyphean task – due to, in the first place, the devastating war of 1992/93 between Abkhazians and Georgians which led to Abkhazia's secession and had left the population on both sides deeply traumatised. Positions seemed irreconcilable with the Abkhazians insisting on independence and the Georgians on the return of Abkhazia into the Georgian state. There was zero readiness to compromise as I soon learned in meetings with the main protagonists, President Shevardnadze in Tbilisi and President Ardzinba in Sukhum/i.

During the long history of their being close neighbours, the relationship between Abkhazians and Georgians was characterised over the centuries by both peaceful co-existence and also by controversy. The demise of the Soviet Union resulted in an abrupt worsening of relations and finally in war. The document which I was supposed to submit to both sides had one particularly sensitive key-clause in Article 2: "Abkhazia is a sovereign entity, based on the rule of law, within the State of Georgia".

In 2001 the overall political climate around Georgia seemed to be conducive to this new initiative. Incidents on the cease-fire lines were on the decline, with the exception of the Upper Kodor(i) valley where units of the Georgian armed forces were introduced in violation of existing agreements. There were also indications of some greater flexibility on behalf of Russia, which up to this point had been rather reluctant to back any fresh moves on key aspects of the conflict, particularly the so-called status issue. The terrorist attacks in New York of 11 September gave an additional boost to efforts to reset US-Russian relations on a range of hitherto contentious matters, including conflicts in Georgia.

For a short while, a window of opportunity opened up which seemed to allow for conflict-settlement between Abkhazia and Georgia on the much-disputed basis of Georgia's territorial integrity, a position held at that time by all members of the United Nations, including Russia.

It was obvious that for any successful initiative on the Georgian/Abkhazian conflict Russia as a key player had to be on board. From spring

2001 I received signals from high-ranking Russian officials that a new ne-gotiating proposal to the two conflict sides might be of use provided such a proposal was "equally unacceptable to both of them". Following up on this hint I circulated a draft paper to the representatives of the "Friends of the UN Secretary-General" in Tbilisi, i.e. the accredited Ambassadors of France, Germany, Russia, the US and the United Kingdom. After a meeting which I had with the then-Permanent Representative of Russia to the UN, Sergej Lavrov, on 31.10.2001 in New York I got the impression that a breakthrough was possible. The "Friends" subsequently gave the green light to the submission of the Document to the two conflict sides. President Shevardnadze, whom I had kept informed, equally signalled agreement.

On 7 December 2001, I was mandated by the UN Secretary-General to submit the Document to the two sides to the conflict with a view to initiating meaningful negotiations.

It became clear immediately that the Abkhazian side was taken aback by this course of events, despite the fact that I had, in a general way, informed it that a new initiative for conflict settlement might be forth-coming. Obviously, Abkhazian consultation with Russia on the matter had left something to be desired. Sukhum/i was facing a delicate choice: how to deal with a negotiating proposal approved by its closest ally? In Sukhum/i Prime Minister Anri Dzhergenia was acting for Ardzinba, who had fallen seriously ill. He chose the tactic of delay. When I finally met him mid-January 2002 Dzhergenia was visibly embarrassed and refused to receive the Document. His comments implied hidden criticism of Russia. Shortly after our meeting, Dzhergenia went to Moscow. After his return, the tone of Abkhazian reactions changed drastically. In a press conference Dzhergenia rejected the Document in strong terms, still us-ing language which indicated doubts about the reliability of the Russian partner ("As far as I have been informed...").

As for Tbilisi, I counted on affirmative reactions. But, to my astonishment, the Georgian political leadership avoided expressing approval of the Document, for some time adopting instead a position of "wait and see". The support for the initiative turned out to be deplorably weak. President Shevardnadze cancelled a meeting which I was supposed to have with him before my departure for a brief Christmas holiday. To add to my bewilderment, a media campaign unfolded against UNOMIG and me personally on the basis of leaked text excerpts from the Document. Offence was mainly taken at the formulation which defined Abkhazia as a "sovereign entity". This was interpreted as a plea in support of independence, and I was accused of high treason, with some members of the Georgian Parliament demanding my expulsion. My reference to the constitutional practice in Switzerland – where some of the cantonal constitutions claim "sovereignty" as a basis while remaining fully loyal members of the Federation – was ignored.

By that time, I had come to realise that the UN were at risk of being drawn into a controversy of domestic Georgian policy. Very obviously assurances had been given to the so-called "Abkhazian Government in Exile", led by Tamaz Nadareishvili, that the Document would pass only with their express consent. I met with their representatives, trying to convince them that the interests of Georgia were fully safeguarded in the Document. At the invitation of the Chairwoman of the Foreign Affairs Committee of the Georgian Parliament, Mrs. Burdzhanadze, I went to argue in its favour in a session of the Committee which took place in a heated and agitated atmosphere. Valuable time was lost before the Georgian political leadership reconsidered the matter and finally came out with clear support for the UN initiative.

Meanwhile, the Abkhazians had seized their chance and realigned powerful allies in Moscow to their cause. Although the next UN Resolution on Abkhazia adopted by the Security Council on 31.1.2002 carried a strong appeal to the Abkhazian side to receive the Document, no action followed. At Russian request a clause had been added to the text stipulating that nothing should be "imposed" on the conflict sides. The Abkhazians readily took this up in order to sidestep any commitment. There was another factor which worked in their favour, namely an increasingly tense situation in the Kodor(i) valley. Unfortunately, the Georgian side had missed undertaking steps for a de-escalation during the crucial days when the Document was at stake.

The Document remained high on the agenda before my UN assignment in Georgia came to an end in early June 2002. But by then the window of opportunity was closing. The Abkhazians' resistance to the Document stiffened despite numerous efforts to explain to them the advantages that it could also offer for their cause. During a visit to Moscow in mid-May, I urged my Russian counterparts, among them Foreign Minister Ivanov, to take this matter up again with the Abkhazians with a view to persuading them to commit. The answers were evasive; I was given to understand that priority now belonged to the Kodor(i) issue. The following UN Resolutions on Abkhazia until 2006 continued to appeal to the Abkhazians to reconsider their position, but they all remained a dead letter. Afterwards, reference to the Document was dropped. Relations between Russia and Georgia had meanwhile reached a new low and were soon to end up in the 2008 war.

Repeatedly there have been misinterpretations of the 2001 UN Document: it does not offer ready-made solutions for the conflict but invites parties to engage in a negotiating process leading up to such solutions. The UN clearly appears in the role of mediator, whereas the main responsibility for action lies with the Abkhazians and the Georgians as sides to the conflict. In those days neither of them was ready to seize the opportunity, apparently due to a lack of political will and an unwillingness to engage in compromise. The Abkhazians were adamant in their rejection of any solution "within the State of Georgia"; any search for alternatives was equally ruled out. The Georgians ignored the fact that, for the Document to be successful, a serious cooperative effort on their behalf would have been needed; they were all too reliant in the belief that time would anyway work in their favour. Today at least the Georgian side is realising that an opportunity has been wasted – possibly the last opportunity to solve the Abkhazian conflict on the basis of Georgia's territorial integrity.

Re-activating the Document today in its original shape will make no real sense. The August 2008 war in Georgia has dramatically upset the political coordinates. With the subsequent recognition of an independent Abkhazia by Russia the very basis on which the 2001 Document rests has been shaken. However, it is an established fact that one-sided actions can never solve conflicts. As long as there is no negotiated agreement which involves all sides concerned in the Georgian/Abkhazian conflict instability will linger on in the South Caucasus infesting the region, including also neighbouring EU countries. The war in the Ukraine has additionally complicated matters. But all this should in no way detract from efforts to keep the issue on the agenda, albeit in the light of changed geopolitical circumstances. The experience over the failed initiative of 2001/2 may then serve as a useful lesson.

Kodor Corridor Adventures

Dodge Billingsley

Director, Combat Films & Research and Global QRF. Editor and Contributor: OE Watch (FMSO), Author: Fangs of the Lone Wolf: Chechen Tactics in the Russian Chechen Wars 1994-2009. UK. November 1997.

B ack in Abkhazia, again staying at the United Nations Observer Mission in Georgia (UNOMIG) compound. This was my fourth trip to greater Georgia since 1993 and my second to Abkhazia specifically. I first arrived in Sukhum during summer 1995 via an overnight boat from Turkey. The boat departed Trabzon once a week arriving in Sukhum the next morning. One of the first things that struck me about Abkhazia, even before getting there, was the variety of nationalities present in the aspiring breakaway republic. The collapse of the Soviet Union and relative ease with which one could move around the region in the early to mid-1990s led members of the diaspora to return to Abkhazia, while others, now free to leave, moved away from the post-Soviet bloc likely never to return. The ship's passengers were a microcosm of these movements of people. Prior to departure I sneaked a look at the ship's manifest. There were nearly 100 people on board. More than half were of Abkhazian or Circassian lineage but from the Middle East: Syria and Jordan primarily. On board, an Abkhazian doctor, who resided in Sukhum and had been in Turkey to buy essentials, befriended me, and I was grateful. At one point during the overnight voyage some of the Syrian men seemed agitated with my presence. They confronted me although the language barrier precluded me from truly understanding what the problem was. It crossed my mind that they might throw me overboard. My new, and first, Abkhazian friend had a few harsh words for them and made me bunk with him and his family. He watched over me the rest of the night.

I lost track of the doctor during disembarkation the next morning. I looked around, but he was gone. He was my first positive impression of Abkhazia, and I hadn't even stepped onto Abkhazian soil. I hoped I would see him again, but I never did A moment later, I met up with my contacts in the Foreign Ministry, who were waiting for me next to the "customs" table Russian soldiers had set up—next to a tripod-mounted machine-gun—lest any of the arriving passengers posed a threat. Standing nearby, Satenik, who would become my second Abkhazian friend, called my name. I raised my hand and identified myself, she waved back, and a few minutes later we were on our way to the Foreign Ministry building in the centre of town, past the Red Bridge, with which I would become familiar as my Abkhazian hosts told me the story of the war with Georgia.

Sukhum was in a pretty rough condition, and it was recommended I stay at the UNOMIG compound south of the city centre and the Red Bridge. A few days later during the heat of the day a German soldier and I walked across the M27 highway from the UNOMIG compound to take a swim in the Black Sea. The beach and shoreline were still scarred from war, but the water was cool, and it was a much needed break. At one point a Russian soldier, in half uniform, came riding up on a horse shouting: "I will show these Abkhazians how to ride a horse!" I'm not sure why he felt the need to tell us that, but he stopped, looked us over critically as if to ask "What are you doing here?" but more as a declaration rather than a question, and kicked his horse into a fast trot down the beach.

I was very interested in Abkhazia's bid for independence and met numerous Abkhazians who had been combatants during the war. A former militiaman named Tetra took me to the heights around the city and pointed out the village of Shroma. He explained the final battle pushing the Georgians out of the capital. Later he took me up into the Kodor Corridor to a place where they set up watch-positions to observe the final exodus of Georgian civilians and combatants out of Sukhum and into Svanetia, or the Svan Valley in early fall 1993. I was intrigued by the narrow Kodor Valley, the River Kelasur and its mined riverbank. It was a potential back door in and out of Abkhazia, and Georgia at the time was full of gossip about a pending offensive to retake lost territories. I determined then to explore this on my next trip, and now I would get my chance.

I arrived a few days ago, this time via car across the River Ingur and the *de facto* border with Georgia. Actually two cars. A Georgian friend dropped me off at the border-area. I walked through what amounted to a demilitarized zone and was met by Abkhazian friends, who took me into Sukhum—again to the UNOMIG compound. The faces had changed but the Mission was the same. A few days into my trip I connected with UNOMIG for a patrol up the Kodor Corridor led by a British Royal Marine named Chris. Chris was the deputy team-leader of the Kodor Valley Patrol. Our party consisted of two vehicles, three UNOMIG personnel, two Abkhazian translators, my colleague Rod and myself. We turned south out of the compound onto the M27, and left again a few miles south, due east towards Svanetia. The wide valley narrowed quickly. According to Chris, the Kodor Corridor was "potentially a route that could be used for an attack on the Abkhazians or for the Abkhazians to attack the Georgians... so we are here to monitor and make sure there is no military movement up and down this road." At the end of the Kodor Corridor lay Svanetia, the Svan Valley, occupied by Svans, whose ethnic connection to Georgians was in dispute depending whether you were talking to Abkhazians, Georgians or Svans themselves.

Reflecting back, 1997 seemed far enough removed from the war that ended in the fall of 1993, but there were still multiple military checkpoints in the Kodor. Ostensibly, the checkpoints were there to protect the integrity of the national boundary, but according to the UN personnel, the real purpose was to monitor traffic, because the "Abkhazians don't want the Georgians re-supplying the Svans and we don't want anyone resupplying the Abkhazians via this east-west main supply-route." I don't know how serious this threat was, but I heard it numerous times while in Abkhazia. Eventually we came across the last Abkhazian military checkpoint in the corridor. There were four Abkhazian soldiers manning the checkpoint, but it didn't seem as though they had a lot to do. They were gutting a fish they had just caught in the River Kelasur below. They reminded us to stay on the road before we left—don't walk to the river!—there were mines everywhere.

We continued up the narrow valley until we reached a Russian military checkpoint near the village of Lata. The Russian commander was used to the semi-regular UNOMIG patrols, but there was some interest in the Americans accompanying the patrol. They let us proceed up the canyon as they knew we had to pass by them on the way back. The road became impassable a couple miles upstream—washed out by high water on the river. According to Chris: "There are currently six areas where a vehicle can't pass due to raging water coming off the high ground. It is part of our monitoring job to know the condition of the road. We hired a contractor to make the road passable but it doesn't get done. We're pretty sure the Abkhazians don't want the road passable."

We turned around and went back to the Russian checkpoint. The company commander and members of his staff came out to talk. Eventually the discussion turned to me and my colleague. It was unusual to see Americans up in the valley. There had been at least one American soldier on the UNOMIG mission, but he was of Russian heritage and told me that he was always considered a spy by the Russian peacekeepers in Abkhazia. We were invited to come inside for a sit down and a drink from the homemade still operating just outside the back door of the command post, otherwise known as a "*chacha ambush*". Satenik and others had warned me about the homemade-alcohol being served around Abkhazia, but the commander's strongly suggested invite was more of an order.

The building was in pretty rough shape and appeared to double as the barracks and command-post. The building had been the centre of at least one previous firefight. It was pockmarked by bullet and RPG fire, and burn-scars stained the walls black above the exterior windows. Many of the windows were boarded up against the cold. Bits of smoke billowed out from some of the window openings. Inside two soldiers played ping-pong on a table in the centre of the main room. Light from the partially boarded up windows streaked across the floor and table and cut into the smoky haze that permeated the entire room. The source of the smoke, a stove in the corner provided heat—but it wasn't enough. We followed the Russian commander down a hall and into a smaller room adjacent to what looked to be an operations room. By now there were three or four Russians in addition to the captain. Within minutes a jug of *chacha* was brought in. Instead of a tiny shot glass, full pint tumblers were put in front of each of us and filled to the brim. I am not a drinker and knew there was no way I could pass this test. I was stressed and wondered how I would get out of this. Thankfully, the floorboards were roughly assembled and the cracks between planks were a half-inch or more. One toast led to another and after bringing the glass to my lips I would lower it to my side hold it near my ankles and pour it down between the floorboards so my glass would empty like all the others. Unfortunately, I became impatient and was the first to empty my glass to which there were some looks of surprise and a refill. The Russian sergeant sitting across from me raised his glass and proclaimed: "The American shows us the way." Everyone laughed, but this was a terrible turn of events. The jug came out again, the glasses filled, and the drinking accelerated. This time I faked my drinking more slowly.

By now Rod was drunk, the Russians were drunk, the UNOMIG personnel were less so, while our vigilant patrol leader Chris and his translator had abstained. I still don't recall how it was decided we should go to the *banja*, but, before I knew it, Chris had split off to talk to the Russian captain, and Rod and I were undressed and in a very hot steam room. I was sure it was too hot to have been of any health benefit. Rod and I talked about how we had to get out of there, but, before we could hatch a good excuse, a sturdy Russian sergeant entered the sauna wearing flip flops, a skull cap and gloves—nothing else. He also held a branch and proceeded to beat us with it to bring the blood to the surface. It was so hot, and now this guy was beating us with a branch for some dubious health benefit. I had to get out of there. Thankfully the light bulb broke—I am sure due to the excessive heat. I stepped out the door to find a towel or something with which to cover myself when a young Russian soldier threw a bucket of ice water on me. I nearly jumped back into the steam room. They laughed and maybe apologized for not having a cold pool nearby. They pointed to the river and suggested we could run across the minefield to jump in the frigid water but were afraid we would step off the trail and get blown up. Instead these junior enlisted guys were ordered to bring water up and douse us as we came out of the sauna. I put on a towel and had Rod take a polaroid to commemorate the strange afternoon, although it wasn't over yet...

Before leaving, the Russian captain insisted that we, mainly he and the British Royal Marine Chris, have a marksmanship challenge. Normally this would be okay but half the group was still fall-down drunk. Rod complained he couldn't feel his lips and worried he might have alcohol poisoning. I thought it served him right for drinking so much. I also thought one of us is going to get shot by accident. Chris was also not excited about the situation and was doing his best to be accommodating while figuring out how to get us safely on our way back to UNIOMIG HQ in Sukhum. He clearly shot better than anyone else, and that only made the Russians try harder. We all took turns shooting at targets on the fence in front of the minefield. All of a sudden in-coming tracer rounds originating from our right hit the target. We all jumped, some of us scrambled for safety. I crouched down by the rear bumper of one of the UN vehicles. A jeep with a mounted crew-served weapon pulled up packed with Abkhazian soldiers we had met at their checkpoint previously. They had heard the shooting from their position and came to investigate. Seeing it was just friendly target-practice they decided to join the fun and announced their arrival by going full automatic on our targets.

The Russians were angry. There were multiple arguments going on at the same time between the Russians and Abkhazians. One of the drunk sergeants lunged out at the Abkhazians who easily moved to avoid his inebriated punches. "Let's go, let's go!" Chris saw his chance to get us out of there and quietly ordered all of us back into the vehicles quickly while the Russians and Abkhazians were sorting out their differences. I looked in the rearview-mirror as we drove away. We had left abruptly, and I saw one of the Russians say something to the company commander and point to us. We raced ahead. The road was winding and up and down, we sped up over one more hill and were beyond line of sight. There was a mutual sigh of relief, and we sped a little faster than we probably should towards the M27. Chris turned to us all and stated somewhat dictatorially: "We will not be discussing this part of the patrol in the debriefing." A few days later I was preparing to leave Abkhazia. One of the translators I had been with came in with some sad news. One of the Abkhazian militiamen I talked to at the checkpoint, who had warned us not to leave the road, had stepped on a mine and lost his leg.

To Resolve the Georgian-Abkhazian Conflict, One Must First Acknowledge It

Professor of Politics at the School of Law and Government, Dublin City University (DCU) where he lectures on post-Soviet politics, unrecognised states, Irish studies, and foreign policy. Ireland.

Firstly, I should like to commend the herculean efforts of Metin Sönmez who, more than anyone else I can think of, has brought the Abkhazian people to a global audience. Unfortunately, I have not visited Abkhazia since August 2014 and so my in-person recollections are somewhat fossilised. My last trip took place during a time of upheaval[1] that led to Alexander Ankvab fleeing Abkhazia, only to be replaced by Raul Khadjimba following a dubious election.[2]

During the intervening years I have published several academic articles devoted to Abkhazia, based on my field research there. These have included articles focussing on elections[3], nation-building[4], attempts to attain recognition from UN member states[5], and the Georgian-Abkhaz conflict.[6] I have also used Abkhazia as a case in works devoted to unrecognised states both in professional peer-reviewed journals[7] and in the popular media.[8]

The Georgian-Abkhazian conflict comes to Ireland

While I have not been to Abkhazia in recent times, Abkhazia has in a way come to me via the Georgian embassy here in Dublin. In March last year, the Georgian ambassador wrote a letter to the president of my university complaining that students taking a module I teach devoted to post-Soviet politics were being forcibly indoctrinated. The letter called on the president to act and was copied to other leaders within the university, as well as senior figures in Ireland's Department of Foreign Affairs.

The ambassadorial communication said, *inter alia*, that "presenting Russia-Georgia war as if it were ethnical [*sic*] conflicts between Georgians, Abkhazians and Ossetians" was "nothing but an attempt to brainwash students through imposing false views that totally correspond to Russian narratives to justify its unlawful actions." It continued:

"The fact is that the conflict in Abkhazia and Tskhinvali regions of Georgia is not an internal rebellion or a civil war but coordinated attack [*sic*] fomented, planned and carried out by the Russian Federation. As a result of Russian military aggression against sovereign Georgia illegal, proxy regimes were created by Russia in both Abkhazia and Tskhinvali regions of Georgia."

It could not be said that my students had been deprived of a Georgian perspective. Over the course of recent semesters, I had facilitated 13 hours of guest lectures from Georgian professors, including a former ambassador, minister, and MFA director. In fact, the only sitting ambassador ever invited to my classroom was the current one from Georgia, who had written the letter. This was never, therefore, a question of students not being exposed to the Georgian perspective; the problem for the embassy was that the Georgian perspective was not presented as an unchallengeable truth. In this the ambassador confused the role of an embassy, which is to promote the interests of the state it represents, and a university, which is to foster critical thinking not least by exposing students to multiple viewpoints.

The Georgian ambassador's intervention provoked strong criticism and was rightly characterised as an unacceptable attack on academic freedom in Ireland by the representative of a foreign government. Throughout the academic community and civil society more generally there was an outpouring of indignation. On national radio the Minister for Higher Education characterised the attempt to interfere with academic freedom as "most unwelcome". The matter was raised[9] in both houses of Irish parliament and addressed by the Minister for Foreign Affairs.[10] As one governing party MP emphasised "academic freedom and independence are central parts of our universities and democracy [that] can't be censored to suit political or commercial sensitivities". In a letter[11] to the Georgian ambassador the largest trade union in Ireland described "such political interference and suggested threats" as "unacceptable to our members, as it is to civil society across Ireland". The union repeated calls on the ambassador to withdraw his letter. Despite the substantial and universal condemnation, the Georgian ambassador declined invitations to defend his position before the Irish media.

Conflicting narratives

The case affirmed a central feature of how successive Georgian governments have presented the conflict to the outside world. Abkhazian resistance to Georgia is de-emphasised in favour of a narrative that suggests that there is in fact no quarrel between Georgians and Abkhazians. According to this view, it was Russia that attacked Georgians in 1992 and Abkhazians want to be part of Georgia but are held back by the Kremlin. Usually, Abkhazians are not referred to at all in these presentations but their home is simply referred to as Georgian territory occupied by Russia.

This narrative is impossible to reconcile with the intense and bitter war launched in August 1992 by Georgian military forces controlled by Tengiz Kitovani and Jaba Ioseliani, and under the titular leadership of Eduard Shevardnadze. Abkhazians believed their struggle at this time was for nothing less than survival. These fears were reinforced by statements made by the Commander-in-chief of Georgian troops in Abkhazia, General Giorgi Karkarashvili, and Georgian Minister for Abkhazia in Tbilisi, Giorgi Khaindrava, both of whom publicly threatened genocide. During the 13-month war Georgians killed approximately 4 percent of the Abkhazian population. As is well known to all those familiar with the subject, the invasion had far-reaching effects on Georgian-Abkhazian relations and has left a legacy of bitterness.

It is not only Abkhazians that harbour resentment. During the war terrible atrocities were committed against Georgians, 250,000 of whom fled in terror. The vast majority never returned. Although tens of thousands (many of them Mingrelians) have since resettled in Gal/i they have consistently been denied basic rights. The inter-communal bitterness is reflected in the monuments Georgians and Abkhazians have erected to commemorate the war. Each side only remembers their own dead; the names of their ethnic adversaries are pointedly omitted. These kinds of exclusions chime with Abkhazian presentations of Georgia as an enemy state but sit less well with the oft-proclaimed position in Tbilisi that Georgians and Abkhazians are kindred peoples destined to live under the same jurisdiction.

It is difficult to envisage any resolution to the dispute between Georgians and Abkhazians given the mutually exclusive features of their respective nation-building projects. Although the Georgian official narrative portrays the conflict as being one between Georgia and Russia, the clash is at heart an intra-Caucasian one between two different nationalities that have polar-opposite views. Georgians still speak of "territorial integrity" and of absorbing Abkhazia, whereas Abkhazians – separated from Georgia for three decades – say they would fight again rather than be governed from Tbilisi. Certainly, the prospects for reconciliation are remote if the official position of Georgia's representatives is to deny there is any conflict with Abkhazians, only with Russia.

Endnotes

[1] https://theglobalobservatory.org/2014/06/what-happens-when-unrecognized-country-experiences-revolution/

[2] https://theglobalobservatory.org/2014/09/dubious-election-divisive-new-president-abkhazia/

[3] https://www.academia.edu/17533377/Elections_without_recognition_presidential_and_parliamentary_contests_in_Abkhazia_and_Nagorny_Karabakh

[4] https://www.academia.edu/25922055/Elections_and_Nation_Building_in_Abkhazia

[5] http://publications.tlu.ee/index.php/stss/article/download/761/631

[6] https://link.springer.com/referenceworkentry/10.1007/978-3-030-11795-5_48-1

[7] https://www.academia.edu/25391304/The_secret_lives_of_unrecognised_states_Internal_dynamics_external_relations_and_counter_recognition_strategies

[8] https://www.rte.ie/brainstorm/2017/1204/925056-dont-look-for-it-on-the-map/

[9] https://twitter.com/malcolmbyrne/status/1386696343276638208

[10] https://www.oireachtas.ie/en/debates/question/2021-05-05/337/

[11] https://twitter.com/DonnachaDCU/status/1384855828990205952/photo/1

Russia, Georgia, and Abkhazia

Edward Mihalkanin

Associate Professor in the Department of Political Science at Texas State University. U.S.A.

Russia's[i] relations with Georgia and Abkhazia since the breakup of the Soviet Union and a reflection of Russia's consistent strategies and tactical foreign policy goals towards the post-Soviet space, the near abroad the former Soviet socialist Republics (SSRs)[ii] dating to the earliest years of the Boris Yeltsin presidency. The changes in Russia's actions towards Georgia and Abkhazia during Vladimir Putin's second presidential term are due to changes in Russia's capabilities, the international environment (especially in Europe and MENA), and the actions of the former SSRs themselves. What follows will be a review of Russian policy toward the former SSRs generally; Abkhazia-Georgia relations from the twilight of the Soviet Union to 2008; the Russo-Georgian War of August 2008 and the consequences of that brief but intense war, and concludes with observations on Russia, Georgia, and Abkhazia.

Russia and the Near Abroad

Even when the Russian government was weakest in 1992-1993 and again in 1998-1999, Moscow has wanted the former SSRs to be seen by the

West and by the former republics themselves as existing within a Russian sphere of influence. What that meant in practice is that the successive Russian governments have wanted the former SSRs to be *protectorates* of Russia and for their protectorate status to be recognized by the world, especially Europe and the USA. Although the Russian government itself had used the phrase "sphere of influence" to denote its interest in being the dominant state in the former SSRs, protectorate is a better term for what Russia actually has wanted and expected in its relations with the former SSRs.[iii]

Historically, a protectorate is an independent country whose foreign and defence policy are determined by a stronger country. Usually, the protectorate country grants a military base, that many times include a fuel depot or fuel storage facility, to the "protecting" country. Laws dealing with domestic issues and in, usually, purview of the protectorate's government.[iv]

Russia has wanted to determine or guide the defence and foreign policies of the former SSRs, and as part of these preferred relationships, has wanted states, especially The USA and Europe, and international organizations to grant Russia authority to act to maintain peace and stability in the former SSRs. Some have called this preference Russia's Monroe Doctrine (Stent, 2019: 35) but it is closest to the Roosevelt Corollary to the Monroe Doctrine than to the Doctrine itself.[v]

The importance of the former SSRs has been stressed in a number of Russian government documents and by a range of Russian officials. Alexei Arbatov, then a member of the Russian State Duma, explained "Consistent policymaking should be envisioned as the maximum desirable goal, economic integration and close political cooperation with some of the principal republics. The minimal vital goal should be good neighbourly relations with them and *the prevention of an emergence of a coalition of republics hostile to Russia, supported by major powers.*" (emphasis added) (Arbatov, 1994; 14). The first speaker of The Duma flatly asserted that the Commonwealth of Independent States (CIS) is "the zone of Russia's interests… where Russia must say: Gentlemen, keep out of here, it will be bad for you if you don't." (Drezner, 1997: 75).

A Russian Foreign Ministry document in December 1992 states that Russia needed to be the defender of stability in the former SSRs (Porter and Savietz, 1994: 88) (Toal, 2017: 83). The CIS Treaty on Collective Security appeared on 15 May 1992. Article One said "The participating states will not enter into military alliances or participate in any groupings of states, nor in actions directed against another participating state." (Rivera, 2003; 92).

President Yeltsin on 28 February 1993, asked the international community to acknowledge that Russia has a right of intervention in the former SSRs. Specifically, Yeltsin said "Stopping all armed conflicts on the territory of the former USSR is Russia's vital interest. The world community sees more and more clearly Russia's special responsibility in this difficult undertaking." (Toal, 2017: 83,84) Later that year, foreign minister Andrei Kozyrev declared that if Russia did not intervene in the former SSRs, then Russia would face "losing geographical positions that took centuries to build." (Toal, 2017: 83,84)

President Dmitry Medvedev in September 2008 reiterated the interests of Russia in the former SSRs: "There are regions in which Russia has privileged interests. These regions are home to countries with which we share special historical relations." For Medvedev, Russia's "traditional sphere of interests" includes the countries of the near abroad." (Allison, 2008: 1167). Former Soviet president Mikhail Gorbachev defended Russia's war against Georgia in terms of Russia's interest in The Caucasus, but his statement can be applied to all of the former SSRs (except possibly The Baltic States):

> "By declaring The Caucasus, a region that is thousands of miles from The American continent, a sphere of its 'national interest,' The United States made a serious blunder… It is simply common sense to recognize

that Russia is rooted there by common geography and centuries of histo-
ry. Russia is not seeking territorial expansion, but it has legitimate inter-
ests in this region." (Mankoff, 2014: 66; Gorbachev, 2008: A13)

Russian President Vladimir Putin's opposition to additional former SSRs joining NATO is a reflection of Russian national security interests since the beginning of the Yeltsin presidency. Putin was very clear in the Spring of 2008: "We view the appearance of a powerful military bloc on our borders...as a direct threat to the security of our country. The claim that this process is not directed against Russia will not suffice. National security is not based on promises." (Toal, 2017: 125)

Different Russian governments have been so insistent and consistent in their assertion of Russia's special interest in the former SSRs because there has been a consensus view that Russia's security border does not lie at the borders of Russia but instead lie on the external borders of the former Soviet Union. Yeltsin in 1995 described Russia as "the leading power in the formation of a new system of interstate political and economic relations over the territory of the post-Soviet expanse" (Drezner, 1997: 75). Earlier in January 1992, Vice President Alexander Rutskoi wrote that "The historical conscoiusness of Russians will not permit anyone to mechanically bring the borders of Russia in line with [the borders of] the Russian Federation." Later that year in April, Evgenii Ambartsumov, chair of the parliament's Committee on International Affairs stated that "Russia is something larger than the Russian Federation in its present borders. Therefore, one must see its geopolitical interests much more broadly than what is currently defined by the map. Precisely from this starting point do we intend to develop our formulation of mutual relations with the near abroad." (Rivera, 2003: 87).

Gorbachev's comment that Russia's interest in the former SSRs is "rooted" in "centuries of history" points us to the obvious reason for Russia's concern about the near abroad. As Stent noted, "the USSR was larger than any previous Russian state" in 1945 while the dismantling of the Soviet Union "reduced Russia to the smallest size it has been since 1654." (2019: 142-143). In less than three score and ten years, the gains of centuries disappeared. Not to put too fine a point on it, "There was no precedent in Russian history for accepting the loss of territory." (Stent, 2019: 17).

Russia throughout its history expanded and contracted territorially. From the Imperial Russian rulers' point of view, Russia could be safe only if it conquered neighbouring territory, following what Stent has described as "defensive expansion." Russia has faced invasions from the West repeatedly: Poland in the 1500-1600s; Sweden in the 1600s-early 1700s; Napoleon in 1812, Imperial Germany in 1914-1919, and Nazi Germany in 1941-1945. Only by securing greater and greater territory could Russia absorb the assaults and protect its heartland and launch counterassaults and new expansions. From Russia's perspective, having friendly neighbouring states is not a luxury, it is a national security necessity. (Kotkin. 2016: 4).

It's through this context of Russian history and the positions of the post-Soviet governments that Russia's interest in having friendly neighbours must be understood. After the Kuchma government of Ukraine signed a NATO partnership agreement in 1997, then Russian Foreign Minister Yevgeny Primakov said that from the Russian point of view, "The geopolitical situation will deteriorate" if NATO were to "engulf that territory of the Warsaw Pact." Primakov expressed the concern that "should NATO advance to new staging grounds, the Russian Federation's major cities would be within striking range of not only strategic missiles, but also tactical aircraft." (Gotz, 2016: 308-309; Toal, 2017:125).

Ukraine announced in 2006 that NATO's annual Sea Breeze exercises as part of NATO's Partnership for Peace Program would be held in Crimea. Ukraine ignored the resulting Russian protests. Putin and other Russian officials repeatedly and publicly had clearly stated that Ukraine and Georgia being brought into NATO was a "red line" and it would be opposed by Russia. (Asmus, 2010: 127). President Putin could not be more direct: "We view the appearance of a powerful military bloc on our borders... as a direct threat to the security of our country. The claim that this process is not directed against Russia will not suffice. National Security is not based on promises." (Gotz, 2016; 311)

As Darden has demonstrated clearly, the international environment from 1991 to 2008, if not until 2016, would appear very threatening to Russia. U.S. military spending increased from $415 billion to $610 billion from 2000 to 2005, while NATO expanded with the Czech Republic, Hungary, and Poland in 1999, and with Bulgaria, Estonia, Latvia, Lithuania, Romania, Slovakia, and Slovenia in 2004. Further, as already mentioned, NATO announced in 2008 that Georgia and Ukraine "will become members." If these actions were not enough, the U.S. government announced that foreign democratization was a new international security interest. To sum up: "If the perception of threat derives from a combination of capability and intent, one would have to be strongly committed to the idea of the benevolence of American power and influence to not find the United States threatening [to Russia] in the post-Cold War period. (Darden, 2017: 131).

Russia's specific demands/interest have been consistent across both time and geographic place as it has attempted to turn the former SSRs into Russian protectorates. In the former SSRs, Russia has demanded control over strategic Soviet assets (and is willing to achieve this by long term base contracts), right to military bases and stationing their troops there, protection of Russians outside and control (ownership) of energy deposits and infrastructure (what Cooley calls "National Security Infrastructure") (2000-2001: 113) (willing to reach agreement by debt-equity swaps). Continued control of military bases by Russia would permit it to continue intelligence gathering, realize cost savings since housing would not need to be built for the soldiers in Russia and would give Russia foreign policy leverage (Drezner, 1997: 75-79).

Russia was particularly interested in Georgia due to its geographical location, its energy infrastructure and resources and because Transcaucasia, like Ukraine, appears to be part of the geographic image that Russians have of Russia, their "affective geopolitical" understanding of their country. (Nation, 2015: 2-6; Toal, 2017: 44-49).

It is difficult to discuss Russian foreign policy in the early 1990s towards Georgia because of the disarray at the very top of the Russian government and the resulting lack of control of Soviet then Russian officials on the ground in Georgia. Also, it is not possible to explain Georgian-Russian relations without at least mentioning actions that people took in Abkhazia. Hopf flatly asserts that "There was no Russian state for most of 1992." The foreign ministry was fighting a losing battle for control of foreign policy against the Supreme Soviet and the Presidential Administration while more of the Federal government bodies controlled the local Russian military forces. (Hopf, 2005: 226). Even when Russian state government bodies were cohering in 1993, Yeltsin was in a ferocious struggle with the national legislature and needed the support of the defence minister Pavel Grachev to win that struggle, and Grachev supported Abkhazia. (Hopf, 2005: 231).

The Abkhaz Supreme Soviet passed a resolution on the State Sovereignty of The Soviet Socialist Republic of Abkhazia which the Georgian legislature declared null and void (Mihalkanin, 2004: 147). Georgia held a national referendum to decide on Georgia independence on 31 March 1991. Although non-Georgians boycotted the election, 98 percent of the voters supported "the restoration of independence of Georgia'' based on Georgia's declaration of independence of 26 May 1918. At the urging of Zviad Gamsakhurdia, Georgia's ruler, the Georgian Supreme Soviet declared Georgia independent on 9 April 1991 by a unanimous vote (D'Encausse, 1993: 262; Anchabadze, 1998: 137; Barner-Barry and Hody, 1995: 215).

Georgia refused to join the Commonwealth of Independent States (CIS) formed at the time of the dissolution of the Soviet Union in December 1991. The Russian government had multiple goals concerning Georgia based on their competing government bodies with the result that they contradicted each other. The Ministry of Defence and the Russian military wanted a military base, access to the Turkish border, and control of Soviet military facilities. The Duma and regional leaders supported Abkhazia. The Foreign Affairs Ministry wanted to reduce Georgia's importance in Transcaucasia. Yeltsin supported Georgia so that it would join the CIS and generally cooperate with Russia. The local Russian military forces in the region supported Abkhazia backed by their superiors in Moscow (Filippov, 2009: 1831; Hopf, 2005: 228-230).

Russia's competing interests and goals were played out in the glare of the Abkhazian-Georgian War of 1992-1993 as the new Georgian President Eduard Shevardnadze attempted to win the war he had initiated and protect his government from the forces of Gamsakhurdia, the Zviadists, who had launched a major attack to win back control of the country.

In the face of losing his war against Abkhazia and the threat that the Zviadists posed to his government, Shevardnadze agreed to Georgia joining the C.I.S. and that body's Collective Security Treaty. Georgia also agreed to leasing Russia four military bases for 25 years. Russia promised to protect all the borders of Georgia and to help it defeat the Zviadists forces. Russia secured the rail line from Poti to Tbilisi and Russian naval forces secured Poti. Russia and Georgia signed a Treaty of Friendship, Neighbourliness and Cooperation on 4 February 1994 and in July of that year, Russia sent 3,000 peacekeepers to Abkhazia (Mihalkanin, 2004: 150; Hopf, 2005: 229; Porter and Saivetz, 1994: 85, Glenny, 1994: 47; Barner-Barry and Hody, 1995: 270).

Although the Yeltsin government wanted excellent relations with Georgia and other SSRs, his government consistently used "economic coercion to extract concessions" from them to maintain Russian influence (Drezner, 1997: 65). Hedenskog and Larssen identified at least fifty-five incidents since 1991 in which Russia used cutting of gas shipments, threats to cut off gas supplies, even bombing of pipelines on Russian soil, and substantially increased gas prices when Georgia refused to sell its pipeline networks to Russian companies (Cameron and Orenstien, 2012: 29-30). Russia also offered debt for equity swaps as a carrot.[vi]

Although Georgian-Russian relations were good, in part by Russian actions that impoverished Abkhazia, Shevardnadze chafed at Georgia's subordination to Russia. In 1999, the Georgian government began to express an openly pro-Western orientation. In February 1999, the Parliamentary Committee on Defence and Security formally requested that NATO "protect Georgia's Security and independence" (Feinberg, 1999: 18). Shevardnadze echoed the request in April 1999 and promised in October 1999 that Georgia "will knock vigorously at NATO's door" in 2005 (Fuller, 2001: 4,6).

Russia's concern about NATO crystallized in 1999. In addition to the statements of the Georgia government about NATO, NATO actions themselves exacerbated Russia's concerns. The Czech Republic, Hungary, and Poland joined NATO and less than a week later, NATO bombed Belgrade in March 1999. Yeltsin angrily asked, "Wasn't it obvious that each missile directed against Yugoslavia was an indirect strike against Russia?" (Stent, 2019: 120-123).

Putin, Prime Minister in August 1999 and then President in 2000, was initially open to exploring a positive relationship between Russia and NATO, but Putin did protest against the substantial enlargement in 2004 when seven Eastern European states joined. However, his protests did not register with the U.S.A. despite Putin's unprecedented cooperation with the U.S.A. in its war on terrorism.

Putin increased pressure on Georgia, starting in 2000. Russia repeatedly cut off natural gas supplies to Georgia in the winter of 2000. In

December of that year, Russia required Georgians to have visas to travel to Russia. Foreign Minister Igor Ivanov accused Georgia of not fighting terrorism sufficiently while Sergei Ivanov referred to Georgia as a "nest of terrorists" (Filippov, 2009: 1833).

In response, Georgia sent troops to the Pankisi Gorge in late August 2002 and announced the next month that it had 2,500 troops patrolling the Gorge. Moving the goalposts, Putin stated that Georgian territory had been used by terrorists who attacked the U.S.A. on 9/11 and Russia in 1999. Under pressure, Shevardnadze agreed to a number of concessions including the establishment of joint Georgian-Russian border patrols. Shevardnadze's domestic opponents condemned the concession (Filippov, 2009: 1833-1834).

The Russian position hardened in response to the terrorist attack on a school in Beslan in September 2004, which affected Russia as 9/11 affected the United States. The Russian government was convinced the terrorists had outside help and even as the school siege was unfolding, Russian officials suspected Georgian help. These suspicions were another burden on Georgian-Russian relations after Mikheil Saakashvili took the presidential oath in January 2004, after peacefully overthrowing Shevardnadze in The Peace Revolution of November 2003. Saakashvili wanted Georgia to join both the E.U. and NATO and ingratiate himself with U.S. President George W. Bush (Filippov, 2009: 1835; Toal, 2017: 146-147, 151).

Saakashvili's diplomatic and military statecraft faced a Russia increasingly opposed to his government. Saakashvili seems to have believed that he would be able to restore Georgian territorial integrity, while also leading his country into NATO and the E.U., in the face of serious Georgian dependency on Russia. Georgia received 88% of its natural gas from Russia in 2006. At the start of that year, Russia cut off gas shipments to Georgia (and Ukraine). Coordinated bomb explosions on Russian territory damaged two gas pipelines to Georgia in January 2006 while Russia cut electric lines to Georgia. Russia forced Georgia to accept gas price increases from $63 per TCM in 2005 to $110 TCM in 2006, and $235 TCM in 2007 (Newnham, 2011: 137, 140-142).

Furthermore, in the spring of 2006, Russia banned the importation of Georgian wine and mineral water which were the two largest Georgian exports to Russia. Russia suspended all transportation and postal services to and from Georgia in October 2006. The Russian action was taken in retaliation for Georgia arresting four Russian officers on espionage charges, even though Georgia quickly released them. Russia increased the deportation of thousands of Georgians from Russia in 2006 and 2007, causing the guest-workers substantial hardship. The Russian actions were retaliation for Georgia sending troops to Iraq and continuing to express its desire to join NATO. Russian Foreign Minister Sergei Ivanov stated publicly that Georgia (and Ukraine) joining NATO "is unacceptable to Russia" (Lapidus, 2007: 152-154; Newnham, 2011: 142; Karagiannis, 2013: 79; Toal, 2017: 152-153).

Abkhazian-Georgian Relations

From all the evidence, the Abkhazian people have been in "continuous occupation of the land over the last three millennia". Christianity was introduced into Abkhazia during Justinian's reign. Abkhazia was forged into a nation from wars against Arabs, Byzantium, and Persia from the sixth through the eighth centuries (Benet, 1974: 6-7; Bgazhba, 1998: 59-60). Leon II established the Kingdom of Abkhazia after decisively defeating an Arab army in the late eight century. The Kingdom of Abkhazia included what is today's western Georgia and it lasted for roughly 200 years. Bagrat III (c. 960-1014) was the King of Abkhazia (as Bagrat II) and the King of Georgia (as Bagrat III) from 1008 until his death. For the 200 years of the Abkhazian Kingdom's existence, the term "Abkhazia" referred ambiguously either to Abkhazia proper or to the whole of today's western Georgia. Bagrat inherited from his Abkhazian mother, Gurandukht', the Abkhazian Kingdom in 978. He was the first king to unite Abkhazia with all Kartvelian-speaking lands after inheriting most Georgian provinces from his father Gurgen in 1008. Mediaeval Georgia reached its zenith during the reign of Queen Tamar (1184-1213) (Bgazhba, 1998: 60; Hewitt, 2009: 184).

Georgia could not withstand the overwhelming force of the Mongol invasions and broke apart into many kingdoms and principalities. Abkhazia developed into a separate princedom and became a protectorate of Russia in 1810, running its domestic affairs until the 1860s. Most Abkhazians left their homeland for the Ottoman Empire after the Abkhazia revolts of 1866 and 1877-1878, the latter allied to the Turks in the Russo-Turkish War. Due to Russian expulsions and Abkhazian fears of Russian retaliation, between 120,000 to 200,000 Abkhazians left Abkhazia for Turkey. The Abkhazians refer to those migrations as the Great Exile, *Makhadzhirstvo* (Lak'oba, 1998: 78, 80; Hewitt, 2009: 185).

In some ways, the hostility between Abkhazia and Georgia (from the late 1970s until today) can be traced to the years of upheaval in Russia from 1917 to 1921. Abkhazia joined The Union of United Mountain Peoples of the Caucasus after the first Russian Revolution of 1917. In November of that year, an Abkhazian assembly established the Abkhazian People's Council, This new council approved a declaration calling for the "self-determination of the Abkhazian people '' on 9 November 1917. The Union of United Mountain Peoples was reorganized into the North Caucasian Republic on 11 May 1918 with Abkhazia being one of its constituent territories. Georgia declared its independence on 26 May 1918 and signed a treaty with Abkhazia on 11 June (Lak'oba, 1998: 89, 186, 89-90; Hewitt, 2009: 185-186).

Yet, in late June 1918, Georgia invaded Abkhazia. Georgia's military rule of Abkhazia ironically facilitated the establishment of Soviet rule on 4 March 1921 and the Abkhazian Soviet Socialist Republic (SSR) was proclaimed officially on 31 March 1921. Abkhazia, with full republic status, became a member of the Transcaucasian Federation. This federation was an original part of the Union of Soviet Socialist Republics (USSR) formed on 30 December 1922. Abkhazia adopted a constitution in 1925. This constitution codified both Abkhazia's treaty relationship with Georgia and its union republic status - Nest'or Lak'oba, an Abkhazian, led the Abkhazian government from 1922 to 1936. Lak'oba resisted introducing collectivization to Abkhazia in 1930 and 1931. Joseph Stalin agreed not to force collectivization if Lak'oba agreed to reduce Abkhazia's status to an autonomous republic within Georgia. The status change went into effect in February 1931 (Chervonnauya, 1994: 22-27; Lak'oba, 1998: 90-93; Ozgan, 1998: 188; Hewitt, 2009: 186).

Lavrenti Beria became head of the Georgian Communist Party in 1931 and the head of the whole of Transcaucasia in 1932 with Lak'oba's support. Beria presented Lak'oba with a plan to resettle Georgian peasants to Abkhazia. Lak'oba purportedly said "over my dead body." The next day on 16 December 1936, Lak'oba was murdered, some allege by Beria. Stalin, a Georgian, and Beria, a Mingrelian, led the terror with forced relocation and exile and executions in Abkhazia. Beria supervised the forced resettlement from 1937 to 1953 and purged the Abkhazian government. Beria's policies resulted in a further reduction in the ethnic Abkhazian proportion of the population in Abkhazia from 28 percent in 1926, 18 percent in 1939, and 13.3 percent in 1950 and 1955 (Lak'oba, 1998: 24, 94, 95; Hewitt, 1995: 186, Lak'oba, 1990: 17, 29; Slider, 1985: 52-53; Hewitt, 2009: 186).

Beria oversaw a frontal assault on Abkhazian culture which worsened after World War II. The new Beria-installed Abkhazian government introduced a new Abkhaz alphabet and script based on Georgian. According to Slider, "The period after World War II until Stalin's (and Beria's) death in 1953, was an especially harsh one for the Abkhaz, as Beria launched a campaign apparently designed to obliterate the Abkhaz as a cultural entity." The Abkhazian government forced all schools to close that used Abkhaz as the language of instruction and made the Georgian language mandatory in all Abkhaz schools. The government stopped all Abkhaz journals, Abkhaz language radio broadcasts and Abkhaz newspapers. The Soviet government gave the best land to the new Georgian settlers and increased access to higher education for them to the detriment of Abkhazians. The Soviet government was drawing up plans after World War II to relocate all Abkhazians to Kazakhstan or Siberia (Slider, 1985: 53-54; Lak'oba, 1998: 17,95; Chervonnya, 1974: 29-31; Hewitt, 1995: 203-4).

The most overt anti-Abkhazian policies ended with the deaths of Stalin and Beria in 1953. Abkhaz schools reopened using a new alphabet for the Abkhaz language and Abkhaz language journals, newspapers and radio broadcasts began again, but the Stalin-Beria oppression created a fundamental mindset towards the Georgians in the Abkhazians. In 1957, 1964, 1967,1978, and 1989, Abkhazians organized many meetings demanding Abkhazia be detached from the Georgia SSR. Although the Soviet government did not agree to these requests, the USSR did respond - the number of Abkhazian schools increased from 39 in 1966 to 91 in 1978; the number of Abkhazians in office as district- and city- secretaries increased from 4 percent in 1949 to 37 percent in 1978 and as party department heads, from 29 percent in 1949 to 45 percent in 1978 (Ozgan, 1998: 187; Lak'oba, 1998: 96-97: Slides, 1978: 53-54).

The Abkhazians still had grievances. The only official language in Georgia was Georgian, but according to the 1979 Soviet census, only 1.4 percent of the Abkhazians spoke it. University entrance exams were in Georgian. Finally, the government budget for Abkhazia was 40 percent lower on a *per capita* basis than Georgia's while capital investment for Georgians increased 39.2 percent, whereas in Abkhazia the increase was only 21 percent. There were only 34 Abkhazian graduate students in all of the USSR in 1975 (Slider, 1985: 54, 57, 57; Lak'oba, 1998:96).

As a result of the demonstrations and mass-meetings in 1978, the Sukhumi Pedagogical Institute was transformed into the Abkhazian State University, which resulted in a substantial increase in the size of the student body. Further, two new Abkhaz art and education journals began publishing while Abkhaz television started to broadcast in the Abkhaz language in November 1978. Finally, new capital investment brought new roads, airports, hospitals, and schools. As a result, there "was Georgian disquiet, an Abkhazian demand for even greater reforms and a deterioration in relations with Abkhaz and Georgian nationals within Abkhazia" (Slider, 1985: 60-64; Hewitt, 1995: 205; Lak'oba, 1998: 98; Mihalkanin, 2004: 146).

As a result of Abkhazian advances, in 1978 Georgia restarted a policy of resettling Georgians in Abkhazia in order to decrease the Abkhazian percentage of the population in Abkhazia. This was achieved by granting students in the Georgian language sector of the Abkhazian State University, who had come from outside Abkhazia, residency rights in Abkhazia after graduation. The Abkhazians knew what was happening, so "the daily lot of members of both adversarial communities were humiliation and violence." As the 1980s wore on, "muffled hostility" mutated into "overt hatred" (D'Encausse, 1993: 76).

A group of Abkhazian intellectuals requested that Abkhazia should become part of the Russian Soviet Federative Socialist Republic (RSFSR) on 17 July 1988. Several thousand Georgians protested against the proposal and the treatment of Georgians in Abkhazia on 18 February 1989 in Tbilisi. The National Forum of Abkhazia - Ajdgylara in the Abkhaz language - organized an Abkhazian national assembly in Lykhny on 18 March 1989. This assembly adopted a resolution (the Lykhny Declaration), which asked the Central Committee of the Communist Party of the Soviet Union (CPSU), the Supreme Soviet, and the Council of Ministers of the USSR to make Abkhazia a Union Republic again (D'Encausse, 1993: 77-78; Chervonnaya, 1994: 57; Nahaylo and Swoboda, 1990: 319; Ozgan, 1998: 188; Anchabadze, 1998: 132; Hewitt, 1995: 205).

In protest of the Abkhazian request, thousands of Georgians protested in Gali, Sukhumi, Leselidze and many other towns in late March and early April culminating in a multi-day rally by tens of thousands of Georgians in Tbilisi, the capital of the Georgian SSR. On 9 April 1989, Soviet Interior troops attacked the rally in Lenin Square in front of Government House, with shells and poison gas, killing at least twenty and injuring hundreds. Secretary General Mikhail Gorbachev tried to distance himself from the Politburo decision and he had both the head of the party and government officials in Georgia removed from office. Yet the April Tragedy "radicalized political life in the republic" and changed a civil rights movement into on demanding Georgian independence (Chervonnaya, 1994: 60; *New York Times*, 1989: 1; Russel, 1991: 2). As Fuller observed, the Abkhazians' demand that Abkhazia should be granted the Union- republican status, which it had until 1931, fueled the Georgian demonstrators and "Georgia's nascent chauvinism towards the non-Georgian population of the republic" (Fuller, 1989: 18).

The Georgian Supreme Soviet claimed Georgia's sovereignty and its right to secede on 18 November 1989. The Abkhazian Supreme Soviet approved a declaration on the Soviet Socialist Republic of Abkhazia's State Sovereignty on 25 August 1990. Georgia promptly declared that act null and void. Zviad Gamsakhurdia's Free Georgia Round Table coalition won an overwhelming majority of the seats in the Georgian Supreme Soviet with the slogan 'Georgia for the Georgians' in the October of 1990 legislative elections (Nahaylo and Swoboda, 1990: 340; Shane, 1989; Barner-Barry and Hody, 1995: 230, 214-215; Anchabadze, 1998: 135-137; D'Encausse, 1993: 241, 262).

Vladislav Ardzinba was elected chair of the Supreme Soviet of Abkhazia on 4 December 1990. Gorbachev called a referendum on the reformation of the USSR which was held on 17 March 1991. Though Georgia boycotted the election, of the 318,317 registered voters in Abkhazia, 52.3 percent participated and of these 164,231 (98.6 %) voted in favour (Volkhonskij, et al, 2008: 118). It follows from these figures that an absolute majority of those eligible to vote elected to stay part of a reformed Union. Given the ethnic mix and balance of Abkhazia's population, this means that Gorbachev's proposal must have commanded support from all of the region's communities (including Kartvelian (aka Georgian/ Mingrelian/Svan) voters. To no one's surprise, when Georgia held a referendum on Georgian independence on 31 March 1991, non-Georgians boycotted it. Reportedly, 90 percent of the registered voters cast ballots, and 98 percent of them voted for "the restoration of the independence of Georgia". As previously noted in this essay, Gamsakhurdia convinced the Georgian Supreme Soviet to pass a declaration of independence on 9 April 1991 (Anchabadze, 1998: 136-137; Hewitt, 1995: 213; D'Encausse, 1993: 262; Barner-Barry and Hody, 1995: 215).

Gorbachev publicized a treaty to replace the Union Treaty of 1992 on 18 June in an attempt to shore up the USSR. His plan backfired. Temur Koridze, Georgia's Minister of Education threatened Abkhazia that "rivers of blood would flow" if Abkhazia signed the treaty. Further, top members of the CPSU staged an anti-Gorbachev coup on 19 August 1991. The heads of the governments of the Union Republics were the strongest defenders of Gorbachev's government. When the USSR ceased to exist in December 1991, Abkhazia was no longer a part of the USSR because of Georgia's unilateral declaration of independence. Georgia rejected all parts of the Soviet Constitution of 1936 except the part that made Abkhazia a part of Georgia (Hewitt, 1995: 215).

Gamsakhurdia became increasingly autocratic and xenophobic, arresting political opponents, imposing media censorship, and "blaming Moscow for any manifestation of dissent". His government rejected non-Georgians participation in Georgian politics and government. Paramilitary groups arose in Georgia in the 1980s. The most important such force was the *Mkhedroni* (Horsemen), led by Jaba Ioseliani, a convicted bank robber. After months of armed clashes between anti- and pro-Gamsakhurdia groups, the extremist *Mkhedroni* and others overthrew Gamsakhurdia and he left Georgia on 6 January 1992 (Fuller, 1993: 2, 43; Woff, 1993: 30; Theisen, 1998: 144; Hewitt, 1998: 216; Anchabadze, 1998: 138).

The ruling junta, in a brilliant political move, asked Eduard Shevardnadze to lead the new State Council. As the former Soviet foreign minister, Shevardnadze had instant international credibility. Less than a week later, the United Kingdom, the E.U. and the U.S. recognized the new Georgian government and established diplomatic relations with it. Georgia also was made a member of the IMF, the World Bank, and the UN, all before the October elections in Georgia that would legalize Shevardnadze's government (Hewitt, 2009: 188-189).

To strengthen the independence that the Abkhazians proclaimed on 25 August 1990, they reinstated the 1925 Abkhazian Constitution on 23 July 1992. Georgia invaded Abkhazia on the morning of 14 August 1992, weeks after Georgia was admitted into the UN. Georgia quickly gained control of the Sukhumi airport and entered the Abkhazian capital city the same day. Georgia's amphibious landing near Gagra was successful and they took that city by August. Only Gudauta and its surrounding communities remained under Abkhaz control (Human Rights Watch, 1995: 17-19; Amchabadze, 1998: 140; Hewitt, 1998: 222, Hewitt, 2009: 189).

The Abkhazian Defence Minister, Tengiz Kitovani declared the situation to be dire, and the Abkhazian government drafted all Abkhazian males between the ages of 18 and 40. The Russian Supreme Soviet passed a resolution condemning Georgia for starting the war on 25 August 1992. Abkhazians regained Gagra on 2 and 3 October 1992 which freed them from a two front war and secured the ports and border to their northwest, thereby ensuring supplies and volunteers to sustain the war effort. Abkhazia was on the offensive for the rest of the war (Human Rights Watch, 1995: 17-20; Anchabadze, 1998: 140-141, Hewitt, 1998: 222; Hewitt, 1995: 219).

Yeltsin stated official Russian policy on 27 August 1992 when he affirmed that Russia would uphold Georgia territorial integrity and promised that Russia would not allow armed volunteers from entering

Abkhazia from Russia. The Russian military did transfer weapons to Georgia yet failed to stop the stream of men and material from Russia to Abkhazia. It is estimated that in fall 1992, between four to seven thousand volunteers from the Confederation of the Mountain Peoples of the Caucasus (CMPC) entered Abkhazia to fight Georgia. Further, the Russian army base in Gudauta gave the Abkhazian forces air cover, heavy artillery, and missile launchers. Georgia alleges that Russian Su-27 fighters waged a terror campaign against Georgian civilians to push them out of Abkhazia. There is evidence the Russian military bombed Georgian army positions, gave ammunition to Abkhazian forces and sent Russian soldiers to fight alongside the Abkhazians (Hopf, 2005: 229, 230, 231; Cooley, 2000-2001: 122; Rivera, 2003: 95).

In late October 1992, Georgian forces plundered, vandalized, and torched the Abkhazian University, Museum, State Archive, Resource Institute for Language, Institute of Physics and the Institute of Experiential Pathology. The wanton destruction of the artifacts of Abkhazian culture reflected the Georgian disdain and contempt for what they see as pretensions of Abkhazians to independent statehood. Illogically, the Georgians view the Abkhazians as indistinguishable from themselves and yet also as "guests" who are allowed to exist on the sufferance of Georgia. This attempted annihilation of Abkhazian culture and history is more disturbing given the genocidal comments of two important Georgians (Hewitt, 1995: 2019; Anchabadze, 1998: 141).

Gia Q'arq'arashvili publicly said that he would accept the deaths of 100,000 Georgians in order to kill all 97,000 Abkhazians in order to preserve the territorial integrity of Georgia. Giorgi Khaindrava, then Minister for Minorities, wrote that if ten to fifteen thousand young Abkhazians were killed, it would annihilate the gene pool. He wrote "we are perfectly capable of doing this." The Abkhazians realize the threat from the Georgians to their culture. The Director of the Abkhazian State Library has said "It is absolutely natural that people are killed in a war... However, what our people could not understand was why the Georgians destroyed our libraries and monuments. That was the moment when real hatred broke out" (Hewitt, 2009: 195, footnote 14; Harzl, 2001: 71-72).

The Abkhazians made three unsuccessful offensives to retake Sukhumi, the capital of Abkhazia, on 5 January, 16 March with support of seventy Russian tanks, and 1 July 1993. It was at this time that a Russian tilt in favour of Abkhazia became explicit, especially after Georgia shot down a Russian helicopter in Abkhazia in December 1992. It was February 1993 when Yeltsin publicly asked the UN to "grant Russia special powers as a guarantor of peace and stability in the region of the former union". Under Russian pressure, Georgia signed a ceasefire agreement with Abkhazia that obliged Georgia to remove all its heavy artillery from Sukhumi. Georgia, by failing to withdraw its heavy weaponry violated the ceasefire and the Abkhazians duly attacked the city and captured it and the airport on 27 September 1993. The attack was led by volunteers from the Northern Caucasus and Russian troops did nothing to stop the attack (Crow, 1993; Goltz, 1993: 107-108; Porter and Savietz, 1994: 85; Hopf, 2005: 229).

Georgian troops retreated in confusion, along with their president, so that Abkhazians were able by 30 September to secure their border to the River Ingur, the *de facto* Abkhaz-Georgian border. The war was effectively over by 1 December 1993. Shevardnadze agreed to Georgia becoming a member of the CIS in October and the Georgian parliament agreed to the stationing of Russian troops in Poti in November (Hewitt, 1995: 220; Schmemann, 1993; Hewitt, 1998: 223).

The stalemate between Abkhazia and Georgia was inevitable given the irreconcilable sentiments of the two sides. The Georgian Minister of State Vazha Lortkpanidze said: "The Abkhaz conflict is a military and political conflict started in order to preserve the Soviet Union, and it is the Russian government who is responsible for it". Abkhazian Foreign Minister said "we have no intention of giving up our independence. Under the alternative scenario, there exists a real threat of annihilation for the

Abkhazian race." Abkhazia lost 4 percent of its population because of the war. Overall, 20,000 lives were lost, and 250,000 Georgians were displaced from their homes in Abkhazia. The Georgian view about Abkhazia is described by Harzl as "extraordinarily strange." The Georgians view all ethnic minorities as "Russian Trojan horses." The late Georgian historian Marik'a Lordkipanidze flatly asserts that "The existence of Abkhazian autonomy in any form within the boundaries in which it took shape under Soviet rule is absolutely unjustified" (quotation in Harzl, 2011: 72), while Mikhail Saakashvili explains the Abkhazian desire for independence this way: "When one day Russian generals woke up and discovered that their dachas were suddenly part of a foreign country and realized that they lost property, they started to bomb Georgia" (Fuller, 1998: 44; Shamba, 1997; Harzl, 2011: 72-73).

As stated earlier, Georgian weakness led to increased Georgian-Russian cooperation. Georgia signed a collective security agreement with Russia on 25 October. As a result, Russian troops protected the railroad from Poti to Tbilisi and Russia secured Poti. As part of the agreement, Georgia leased four military bases to Russia, the one in Abkhazia was for 25 years; Georgia gave Russia the authority to protect the international land- and maritime- borders of Georgia while Russia would train and equip the armed forces of Georgia (Porter and Saivetz, 1994: 85; Glenny, 1994: 47; Barner-Barry and Hody, 1995: 270; Feinberg, 1999: 17; Fuller, 1993: 203).

Abkhazia and Georgia began negotiations on 1 December 1993. In the resulting Declaration of Understanding, the parties agreed to a cease-fire, prisoner exchange, and to continue the negotiations. In an attendant joint communiqué, the two parties agreed that CIS peacekeeping forces (CISPKF) would monitor the cease-fire. In practice, these peacekeeping forces were troops of the Russian armed forces (Human Rights Watch, 1995: 39).

The parties signed the Moscow Agreement on 4 April 1994 by which the parties committed themselves to the cease-fire and to the "non-use of force or threat of the use of force" and they "reaffirmed their request for a peacekeeping force" that included Russian troops. As part of the agreement, Abkhazia would have "state symbols such as an anthem, emblem, and flag" and its own constitution. Further, Georgia made even greater concessions when it agreed to "powers for joint action" that included "foreign policy; border guards and customs; energy; communication and transport; and protection of human and civil rights" (Hewitt, 1998: 266-267; Chirikba, 1996: 209, 212, 215).

The parties also signed on 4 April a Quadripartite Agreement on Voluntary Return of Refugees and Displaced Persons (Annex II) signed by Abkhazia, Georgia, Russia, and the United Nations High Commissioner for Refugees (UNHCR). The agreement has not facilitated the return of displaced persons because the right of return was not applicable to persons who had committed "war crimes and crimes against humanity," nor to people "who have previously taken part in hostilities" or who "are currently serving in armed formations" preparing to fight in Abkhazia (Hewitt, 1998: 267-271; Chirikba, 1996: 215). As part of its new status, Abkhazia approved a new constitution on 26 November 1995 (Hewitt, 1998: 202; Ozgan, 1998: 197).

Surviving his severe domestic political crisis, Yeltsin began to assert more control over Russian foreign policy in the Caucasus. Russia closed its border with Abkhazia on 19 September 1994. On 19 December it closed the Abkhazian border along the River Psou. Abkhazia's major port, Sukhumi, was closed to Abkhazian shipping on 30 August 1995. Russia then ordered Sukhumi closed to all shipping on 5 January 1996. Earlier Abkhazian passports were declared invalid outside of the CIS. Russia also interrupted electricity to Abkhazia and closed Sukhumi Airport. All CIS states, except Belarus, agreed to negative sanctions against Abkhazia (Hopf, 2005: 229-230, 231).

The Russian region of Kransnodar ignored the Russian sanctions against Abkhazia imposed in 1993-1994. Further, Tatarstan and Bashkortostan signed Treaties of Friendship and Cooperation with Abkhazia in August 1994 (Hopf, 2005: 232).

Georgia, feeling emboldened by the Russian actions, repeatedly threatened violence when discussing Abkhazia in violation of the Moscow Agreement – in August 1994, February 1995, September 1996, and July 1996. Under pressure, Georgia agreed to establish a Coordinating Council where negotiations would take place in November 1997 (Chirikba, 1996; Hewitt, 1998: 209, 212, 215; Fuller, 1999: 18).

In complete defiance of multiple agreements entered into, Georgians formed two paramilitary groups, the White Legion and the Forest Brothers, who "systematically targeted" CIS peacekeepers and Abkhaz forces in the Gali region of Abkhazia in 1997 and 1998. The guerrillas launched a six-day war, 19 to 25 May 1998, by attacking an Abkhaz guard-post that killed 17 Abkhazian police officers. In retaliation, 1,500 Abkhazian militiamen launched a successful counter-offensive against the guerrillas. An estimated 30,000 to 40,000 Georgians fled the region during this short war. By the Gudauta ceasefire- agreement of 24 May 1998, Abkhazian and Georgian forces had to withdraw their forces from the Gali District and Georgia had to prevent any future guerrilla activities in Gali (Feinberg, 1999: 34; Fuller, 1998: 13). The two sides reached agreement on two documents. The first tried to make the ceasefires of 1994 and 1998 permanent and the second tried to resolve issues of Georgian displaced persons (Fuller, 2001: 5).

The Georgian government felt stronger, and so it articulated a more pro-Western position starting in 1999. The Georgian Parliamentary Committee on Defence and Security made a formal request to NATO to protect Georgian "security and independence" in February 1999. In April of that year, Shevardnadze stated that Georgia wanted to join NATO and emphasized that preference the next month when he said Georgia "will knock vigourously on NATO's door in 2005". Georgia also ratified the Statute of the Council of Europe on 27 April 1999, the European Convention on Human Rights (ECHR) on 20 May 1999, and the European Convention for the Prevention of Torture (ECPT) on 20 June 2000. As of May 2003, Georgia ratified 192 Council of Europe treaties (Feinberg, 1999: 18; Fuller, 2001: 6; Bowring, 2003: 253-254).

Under its Constitution of 1994, Abkhazia held a referendum on Abkhazian independence on 3 October 1999. On election day, 87.6 percent of the registered voters took part and 97.7 percent of the voters approved the constitution, thereby approving Abkhazian independence. President Ardzinba and the People's Assembly proclaimed Abkhazian independence on 12 October 1999. President Ardzinba also ran for and won re-election to a second five-year term in October 1999 (Chirikba, 1999; Fuller, 1999: 48).

The Russian government, weathering an economic crisis in 1998 and 1999, started to exhibit the disorganization that characterized it in 1992 and 1993. In September 1999, Russia reopened its border with Abkhazia and in general eased its isolation. Georgia and Abkhazia signed a protocol on 11 July 2000 whereby each side promised to reduce the number of armed forces along the *de facto* border; to create joint organizations to fight crime and smuggling; continue renunciation of the use of force; and to work on repatriation of Georgian displaced persons to Abkhazia (Fuller, 1999: 48; Fuller, 2001).

Georgia violated the new protocol when Georgian and Chechen guerillas attacked a village in eastern Abkhazia on 4 October 2001 and then pushed their offensive deeper into Abkhazia. The guerillas shot down a UN helicopter on 8 October killing all nine people on board. When the paramilitaries neared Sukhumi, Abkhazia responded by bombing the guerillas in the Kodori gorge. In response to this unprovoked military assault, Abkhazian Prime Minister Anri Dzhergenia announced that

Abkhazia would seek "associate status" with the Russian Federation (Diamond, 2001).

Abkhazia rejected a UN draft agreement concerning Abkhazia as a part of Georgia on 5 February 2002. Georgia accused Abkhazia of being a "haven for international terrorists". For Russia, these actions signified that Georgia was preparing a new military offensive against Abkhazia. In retaliation, Russia, in June 2002, provided 150,000 Abkhazians with Russian passports. The Abkhazian government viewed the passports as insurance against a new Georgian invasion of their country (MacKinnon, 2002).

Abkhazian P.M. Dzhergenia and South Ossetian President Eduard Kokoiti reached an agreement on a mutual defence treaty to protect their countries from Georgian "aggression". Further, Russia opened a rail line between itself and Abkhazia in late 2002. When a Georgian official denounced the new line, the Russian Foreign Ministry was nonplussed over Georgia's "insistence on draconian measures to isolate Abkhazia" (Devdariani, 2002; Blagou, 2003).

The Georgian-Russian War of 2008

The war of 2008 was not inevitable no matter how much the new Georgian President Mikheil Saakashvili, elected in 2004, rubbed Putin the wrong way. The Russian leader was willing to work with Georgia but events in Russia, Georgian actions, and U.S. actions convinced Putin that what some might see as isolated events with their own specific origins actually were connected as part of a plan to undermine Russian national security and even the Russian government itself.

The seizure of a school in Beslan in September 2004 by Chechen terrorists had the same effect on Russia as 9/11 had on the USA. Hundreds of children were killed, and Putin blamed the West. This terrorist attack resulted in a hardening of Russian domestic politics and foreign relations both. The terrorist attack along with the Colour Revolutions, especially the Orange Revolution, and the incipient revolutionary activity within Russia, led Putin to construct his authoritarian model, dubbed "sovereign democracy", for Russia and adopt a more revanchist foreign policy.

At a news conference, General Leonid Ivashov stated that there were terrorist groups in the Pankisi Gorge where the terrorists holding the school children had trained. Russian government officials refused to exclude the possibility that Georgia was involved with Beslan, and that Russia would launch pre-emptive strikes outside of Russian territory. Putin used the terrorist threat to push for greater centralization of authority in the presidency and greater restrictions on civil society (Filippov, 2009: 1835-1836).

A range of Russian political groups took encouragement from the Ukrainian Orange Revolution (November 2004 - January 2005) to demand change in the Russian government. These demands were a shock to the Russian government which was still recovering from the "political earthquake" that the fall of the Kuchma government and its replacement by a pro-western government in Ukraine represented. Mass protests broke out in Russia while the *Rodina* Party defected from the parliamentary bloc supporting Putin and tried to lead the protests. Putin's government responded by cutting the Duma's internet connections; hacked the *Rodina* party's website; created a pro-Putin national youth organization; imposed new legal restrictions on NGOs; and changed election law; further court decisions kept parties off the ballot; the mass media refused to cover opposition groups and parties; there were violent attacks on non-Putin parties and organizations; and new laws limiting election monitoring, all in the name of "sovereign democracy" (Horvath, 2011: 6-12, 15-20; Funkel and Brundy, 2012: 15-26; Kryshtanovskaya & White, 2009: 285-293; Wilson, 2010: 22-25).

Relations between Russia and Georgia deteriorated from 2004 on. Putin tried to work with Saakashvili even when the Georgian president made it plain that he wanted his country to join both NATO and the EU. Saakashvili made a great effort to ingratiate himself with US President George W. Bush while referring to Putin as "Lilli-Putin". What appears to have tipped Russia against Georgia for good was when the Georgian government arrested Russian diplomats assumed to be spies and then expelled them from the country in 2006 (Stent, 2019: 161).

Russia used a range of policies to pressure Georgia to change its foreign policy preferences. Russia increased the cost of natural gas to Georgia from $110 TCM in 2006 to $235 TCM in 2007 (Newnham, 2011: 140-142). In the Spring of 2006, Russia barred the importation of Georgia wine and mineral water (Georgia's two largest exports to Russia). Russia suspended all transportation and postal services to and from Georgia in October 2006. Russia increased the deportation of thousands of Georgians from Russia in 2006 and 2007, causing the guest-workers substantial hardship. The Russian actions were also retaliation for Georgia sending troops to Iraq and continuing to express desire to join NATO. Russian Foreign Minister Sergei Lavrov stated publicly that Georgia (and Ukraine) joining NATO "is unacceptable to Russia" (Lapidus, 2007: 152-154; Newnham, 2011: 142; Karagiannis, 2013: 79; Toal, 2017: 152-153).

While Russia did remove its troops from some bases in Georgia in November 2007, it violated Georgia airspace and permitted Abkhazian and South Ossetian skirmishes against Georgian forces in 2007 and early 2008. In 2007, Russian helicopters shelled Georgian administrative buildings in the Kodori Gorge and in August of that year, Russian aircraft attacked a Georgian radar station near South Ossetia. In late April 2008, a Russian plane shot down an unarmed and unmanned vehicle over Abkhazia. The USA and Georgia took part in joint military exercises in July 2008 while Russia conducted its own military exercises in the region at the same time. The US troops left the area while Russian troops stayed (Cornell, 2008: 310; Toal, 2017: 156; Karagiannis, 2013: 79).

Specifically, the Russian 58th Army had just completed military exercises yet many of its units stayed near South Ossetia and Abkhazia. It is estimated that 12,000 Russian soldiers were deployed at the northern end of the Roki Tunnel (a major transportation artery on the border between South Ossetia and North Ossetia in Russia) by the evening of 5 August. By early August 2008, Russia had sent military aircraft to a South Ossetian air base. At least part of a Russian armed regiment entered South Ossetian territory on 7 August 2008 (Asmus, 2010: 21-23; Allison, 2008: 1148-1149). Furthermore, Russia deployed a Black Sea naval task-force near Georgia and airlifted the 76th Air Assault Division to Tskhinvali, the capital of South Ossetia. Finally, a battalion of Russian railroad troops repaired 54 kilometers of a major Abkhazian railroad in June and July 2008. Russia was able to move Russian troops through Abkhazia and into western Georgia thanks to that strategic rail-line (Allison, 2008: 1151).

Events accelerated in the spring and summer of 2008. With Western encouragement, Kosovo declared its independence on 17 February 2008. The USA and twenty-two of the then EU states immediately recognized Kosovo. Putin denounced the "Kosovo precedent" saying "This is a harmful and dangerous precedent. You can't observe one set of rules for Kosovo and another for Abkhazia and South Ossetia." At a meeting with Saakashvili on 22 February 2008, Putin warned him that "we have to answer the West on Kosovo. And we are very sorry, but you are going to be part of that answer" according to the Georgian record of the meeting (Asmus, 2010: 105, 106; Toal, 2017: 154-155; Stent, 2019: 124).

To add insult to injury, from Russia's point of view, NATO members at the Bucharest summit approved a communique on 3 April 2008 that stated, "we agree today that Georgia and Ukraine will become members of NATO." Although Putin fulfilled his promise to Bush that he would be moderate in his speech to NATO the next day, the Bucharest Declaration completely ignored Putin's warning to Secretary of State Condoleezza Rice and Secretary of Defense Robert Gates that Georgia being a part of

NATO was a "red line" for Russia (Stent, 2019: 129- 131; Toal, 2017: 7; Asmus, 2010: 134-135, 127).

If one is to judge a diplomatic initiative by its consequences, then the Bucharest Summit was a disaster. It did nothing to reassure Georgia and Ukraine and it alienated Russia. NATO did not extend a MAP to Ukraine and Georgia, exposing NATO divisions at Bucharest, but a virtual promise was made to offer one at NATO's next meeting in December 2008. Saakashvili was angry at the results of the NATO Summit since the statement of future NATO membership lacked a commitment to assistance of Georgia before NATO membership was a reality. For Russia, the Bucharest conference showed that Georgia and Ukraine becoming NATO member states was very real, and so it led to Russia increasing its efforts to dominate the Transcaucasus (Stent, 2019: 130-131; Asmus, 2010: 138-139; Toal, 2017: 7-8).

Russia rescinded a CIS weapons embargo on Abkhazia and South Ossetia and began to arm them in March 2008. The Duma passed a resolution on 21 March recommending that Russia should recognize Abkhazia and South Ossetia and protect Russian citizens there (Toal, 2017: 155). Putin signed a decree on 16 April 2008, ordering Russian government departments to open direct trade and transportation to Abkhazia and South Ossetia (Cornell, 2008: 310).

Abkhazia claimed that Georgia was increasing its troops near the Kodori Gorge on 18 April but a United Nations Observer Mission in Georgia (UNOMIG) found no evidence of that. Russia made a similar claim about Georgian forces and said it was adding 400 more paratroopers to support its peacekeepers in Abkhazia. In May, Russia announced that its troop-strength in Abkhazia was 2,500 while Georgian intelligence said the soldiers numbered close to 4,000. In the same month, the Russian air force publicly asked for military helicopter pilots with experience flying in mountains regions (Asmus, 2010: 148).

The USA and the EU were increasingly concerned about the probability of war in the Caucasus and began different diplomatic initiatives but neither the US nor the EU warned Russia of the negative consequences for Russian military action against Georgia. Germany also attempted to reach a diplomatic agreement, but the German effort was hampered due to Germany and Georgia distrusting each other and Germany negotiating the proposals with Russia before presenting them to Georgia (Asmus, 2010: 152-156).

A major problem for diplomacy was that the NATO members were divided on a range of issues. The USA trusted Georgia more than Europeans did. The Europeans did not want the EU to have the largest presence in the Caucasus while the USA refused to play a dominate role there as well. Furthermore, Russia undermined the regulations (Asmus, 2010: 157-158). Saakashvili also tried negotiating directly with Medvedev in June presenting the new Russian president with some specific proposals, but by early July, these initiatives proved to be futile (Asmus, 2010: 159-161).

From April to August 2008, Saakashvili repeatedly said that if Russia recognized Abkhazia and South Ossetia and/or Russian troops were built up there leading to *de facto* annexation of these regions, then Georgia would have to use military force or risk being turned out of office. Europe and the USA repeatedly warned Georgia not to go to war against Russia because it would fight alone if it did so (Asmus, 2010: 146-147; Stent, 2019: 161).

Violence increased in South Ossetia in July and August. Leaders of the Georgians and South Ossetians were targeted while South Ossetian military shelled Georgian villages and peacekeepers. "Volunteers" arrived in South Ossetia and were quickly integrated into its interior military forces. Georgia protested Russia allowing "mercenaries" and their weapons into South Ossetia. Russia criticized Georgia for moving troops and armour so near to the South Ossetian border (Allison, 2008: 1147; Asmus, 2010: 165; Toal, 2017: 157-158).

South Ossetia and Georgian forces shelled each other's positions on 7 August and a Georgian military vehicle was hit, killing two Georgian soldiers. President Saakashvili ordered a Georgian military offensive against South Ossetia late the same day with the goal of quickly capturing Tskhinvali (Allison, 2008: 1148; Toal, 2017: 158, 161; Asmus, 2010: 19).

The rapidity of Russia's military counter offensive against Georgia betrays a substantial amount of planning and training, not only for Russian troops moving through South Ossetia into Georgia, but also for Russian troop deployments by land and sea into Abkhazia and then into western Georgia (Allison, 2008: 1149-1151; Asmus, 2010: 165-168; Toal, 2017: 164, 171-173).

Russian forces were able to drive Georgian forces from South Ossetia by the early afternoon of 10 August. Russian military aircraft began bombing sites in Georgia on 8 August, when they attacked the Russian military base in Gori. Russia increased its air operations against Georgia in August, bombing Georgian airports and military bases and the port of Poti. Russia began its invasion of Georgia on 10 August from both Abkhazia and South Ossetia. By 12 August, it occupied western Georgia, occupying Zugdidi, Poti, and Senaki. Russian tanks were only two hours from Tbilisi, the Georgian capital. On the same day, Georgia concentrated its forces at Mtskheta, in anticipation of making a final stand there to protect the capital (Allison, 2008: 1149, 1151; Asmus, 2010: 180-183; Toal, 2017: 170-173).

President Bush was in Beijing for the Olympics when the war broke out and did not return to Washington D.C. until 13 August. By that time, Bush had decided that the USA would not support Georgia militarily, nor would it take the lead diplomatically to try to end the war. Unsurprisingly, that decision was agreed to in a principal's meeting Bush created to discuss the issues. The attendees included the Secretaries of State and

Defense and the National Security Advisor, among others (Asmus, 2010: 189-191; Stent, 2019: 132).

The unenviable task of ending the war fell to French President Nicolas Sarkozy due to France holding the rotating chair of the European Union (EU) presidency. Sarkozy wanted the war to end as soon as possible because he was convinced that Putin wanted to crush Georgia leading to regime-change at least, or Russian annexation of Georgia at worst. Sarkozy contacted the Russian government and promised he would travel to Moscow to negotiate a cease-fire agreement if Russia implemented a cease-fire unilaterally and halted the advance of its troops towards Tbilisi. Russia agreed. Sarkozy arrived in Moscow on 12 August. Russia had declared a cease-fire and had stopped its advance on Tbilisi, although some Russian ground-forces were advancing in other parts of Georgia (Asmus, 2010: 191-194, 197-198; Toal, 2017: 173).

On behalf of the EU, Sarkozy negotiated a cease-fire with Medvedev the same day. The agreement included a non-use of force pledge, all hostilities would cease, humanitarian assistance would not be hindered, Georgian armed forces were required to withdraw to "their permanent positions", Russian armed forces "must withdraw to the line where they were standing prior to the beginning of hostilities", and there would be an international meeting on the status of Abkhazia and South Ossetia (Asmus, 2010: 201; Toal, 2017: 173). Saakashvili and Medvedev signed the agreement.

Russia used the clause in the cease-fire of 12 August that allowed Russian peacekeepers to take "additional security measures" to establish at least eight military stations in uncontested Georgian territory, expand the Abkhazian buffer zone to the edge of Semaki, and at times, Russian peacekeepers patrolled Poti. The vagueness of some of the cease-fire language and the cost to the Georgian economy from the Russian army check-points often near ports and highways lead to a second set of negotiations between Medvedev and Sarkozy, joined by two EU officials, on 8 September 2008 (Toal, 2017: 174-175; Asmus, 2010: 201-212).

The new EU-Russian agreement reduced some of the advantages Russia received from the 12 August agreement. Russia promised to remove all of its check points on Georgian soil in a week, removed its armed forces from the Abkhazian-Georgian and South Ossetian-Georgian buffer-zones in a month, allow a large EU observer-mission to monitor the cease-fire, and begin international negotiations on Abkhazia and South Ossetia (Toal, 2017: 174; Asmus, 2010: 212-214).

The Georgian government reports that 413 persons died during the August War with the wounded numbering over two thousand. It is estimated that twenty thousand Georgians were displaced from their residences, most from South Ossetia and Abkhazia. The South Ossetian government reports 365 persons died during the war with the wounded numbering more than two hundred. The Russian government reports 67 persons dead with 283 wounded, all soldiers (Toal, 2017: 195-196).

In between the two agreements, Russia unexpectedly acted and extended diplomatic negotiation to both Abkhazia and South Ossetia, recognizing their independence on 26 August 2008.

Medvedev defended Russia's recognition of the two *de facto* states by saying it was necessary to save the two countries from Georgian genocide and pointed to earlier examples of Georgian ethnic cleansing and cited what the Russian government refers to as the Kosovo precedent. Medvedev stated, "We have taken the same course of action as other countries took with regard to Kosovo" (Stent, 2019:162-163) As of today only Russia, Nicaragua, Venezuela, and Nauru also have recognized them.

Asmus has made a good point that everyone was a loser from the Russian-Georgian War of 2008. Georgia obviously lost the war that it should not have started. "Saakashvili began a war his allies had warned him not to start, a war that they would not support, and a war he could not win... The armed forces of Georgia sent into battle were neither trained nor equipped to confront the Russian army." Furthermore, of Georgia's live brigades, one was a training brigade, and one was in Iraq. Georgia would have all three brigades engaged in South Ossetia if it pulled a brigade away from the border with Abkhazia. A few weeks before the war, the Georgian army released roughly half of its soldiers while sending a number of its tanks to the capital to be modernized. The Georgians launched the war with a new plan that had never been tested with troops that lacked the required training. As a result of the war, Georgia's loss of Abkhazia and South Ossetia was consolidated, while tens of thousands of Georgians either left or were driven from their homes in those regions (Asmus, 2010: 172-174, 219).

Abkhazia and South Ossetia are recognized by only a handful of countries and are heavily subsidized and protected by Russia. Many important positions in their government are held by Russians. Their economies are shadows of what they had been in 1990 and very constrained (Asmus, 2010: 218-219).

Russia won the war but lost the peace. Georgia is deeply embittered toward it. Western capital left Russia as a result of the August War and the Russian economy was further damaged by the financial meltdown of the autumn of 2008. The EU's Tagliavini Report disagreed with Russia's claim of genocide and rejects its assertion that Russia's military invasion was a humanitarian intervention. Russia, in some ways, became an international outcast, no longer trusted the way it had been before (Asmus, 2010: 220-221).

The West also was a loser from the war. The USA and the EU refused to provide real peacekeepers to Georgia, Abkhazia, and South Ossetia who may have kept the peace in 2008. They also failed to anticipate the fallout from their recognition of Kosovo and their compromise statement on future NATO membership. The USA insisting that Russia would not damage Georgia did not constitute contingency planning. Bush insisted on some statement of support for NATO membership for Georgia and Ukraine in the face of a badly divided NATO, the opposition of his senior advisors, and at relatively the last minute. During the August crisis, the USA was AWOL (Asmus, 2010: 221-222) or proved to be, in a Texas phrase, "all hat and no cattle".

Some Concluding Observations

John Foster Dulles, Secretary of State (1953-1959) during the presidency of Dwight D. Eisenhower, would regularly talk about the "good Russian state" and the "good Russian national interest" opposing then to the "bad Communist Party" (Holsti, 196: 247). Yet, over the years of a post-Soviet Russia, The United States did very little to help that country during the economic upheavals of the 1990s. These included substantial unemployment, decline in natural income, recessions, and massive shortages. To add insult to injury, the USA and the EU refused to acknowledge Russia's claim to having legitimate security interest when it came to the former SSRs. Even without giving a blank cheque to any country, there is a general understandability that a country does have legitimate interests when it comes to bordering states.

During that same time, NATO and EU added multiple members to their organization. Focusing on NATO, the security alliance added the Czech Republic, Poland, and Hungary in 1999, Estonia, Latvia, Lithuania, Slovakia, Romania and Bulgaria in 2004, brushing aside the concerns of the Russian government as irrelevant.

Post-Soviet Russia refrained from using military force against any of the former SSRs from December 1991 to July 2008; instead using diplomatic and economic strength (including negative and positive sanctions) to try to achieve its foreign policy goals. When Russia did use military force against Georgia in August 2008 in response to a Georgian invasion of South Ossetia, it was roundly denounced as a country caught in, at best, a nineteenth century time warp, an anachronism.

The USA has an extensive history of using military force and covert action against Latin American countries, all in the name of protecting US national interests, and yet it was not made a pariah by the international community. Just referencing the post-World War II history, the USA has quite a record in Latin America. In 1954, a CIA operation overthrew the democratically elected Jacobo Árbenz government. In 1961, the CIA trained Cuban paramilitaries who attacked Cuba at the Bay of Pigs and were totally routed by Cuba troops. President Lyndon B. Johnson ordered the invasion of The Dominican Republic in 1965. President Ronal Reagan ordered the invasion of Grenada 1983 and created and funded the Contras, a paramilitary group designed to overthrow the Sandinista government in Nicaragua throughout his presidency. His successor, George H.W. Bush, invaded Panama in 1998, while Clinton invaded Haiti in 1994.

At no time did the USSR try to lead an international coalition against the USA to ostracize and isolate it in the international community. In fact, when then Soviet leader Gorbachev visited the USA in June 1990 and met with the Congressional leadership, he brought up the US invasion of Panama. Gorbachev asked why the USA took issue with Soviet action towards Lithuania, then still a part of the USSR, after the USA had invaded Panama. He asked, "Why that double standard?" (*Los Angeles Times*, June 2, 1990).

The only incident where the Soviet Union ignored US dominance in the western hemisphere was when Soviet Premier Nikita Khrushchev sent Soviet nuclear missiles to Cuba in 1961. The response of the US government is well known, but that of McNamara's not so much. Secretary of Defense Robert S. McNamara initially argued that the US need not react because Soviet missiles in Cuba did not significantly affect the overall nuclear balance between the USA and the USSR (Allison, Graham, 1971: 195-196). At the end of the first day of the ExCom meetings, McNamara repeated his position saying, "I don't believe it's primarily a military problem." McNamara identified the real issue: "The missiles were principally a political problem" (Allison and Zelikow, 1999: 341, 340).

The reason the US government reacted to the installation of Soviet missiles in Cuba was not because it negatively affected US global dominance in nuclear weapons. It was because President John F. Kennedy, and most of his advisors, realized that a lack of US military response would destroy Kennedy's presidency and the credibility, prestige, and power of the USA in the eyes of the international community. The missiles in Cuba would do that because of their geographic proximity to the USA. If the USA could not protect itself from nuclear weapons in Cuba, how could it protect itself and other countries from more distant weapons? (Allison, 1971: 194; Allison and Zelikow: 339-340).

Except for the Cuban crisis, the Soviet Union, and later, post-Soviet Russia respected US interests in the western hemisphere. Yet, during the George W. Bush administration, the USA ignored legitimate security interests of Russia in the former SSRs. Bush visited Georgia in May 2005 and on 10 May participated in a rally with Georgian president Saakashvili.

During the rally, Bush addressed the people in the central square in Tbilisi and lauded Georgia's Rose Revolution.

> *Your courage is inspiring democratic reformers and sending a message that echoes across the world: freedom will be the future of every nation and people on Earth... Now across the Caucasus, in Central Asia and the broader Middle East, we see the same desire for liberty burning in the hearts of young people... They are demanding their freedom and they will have it. As free nations, the United States and Georgia have great responsibility and together we will do our duty (Toal, 2017: 122-123).*

Bush had been pushing for a fast-track process for Georgia to join NATO.

As Meyer has conjectured "Imagine Washington's response had Brezhnev himself taken part in a rally in Nicaragua to announce that Nicaragua would be welcomed as a new member of the Warsaw Pact, and then offered the equivalent of a billion dollars to stiffen Sandinista resolve" (Meyer, 2008: 121).

Bush's warm embrace of Georgia in becoming a member of NATO and the EU furthered Russia's perception of a US threat arising from Washington's new national security doctrine announced in Bush's Second Inaugural Address. The then new U.S. doctrine defined foreign democratization and human rights as a primary national security interest. On 20 January 2005, President Bush said "It is the policy to seek and support the growth in every nation and culture, the growth of democratic movements and institutions with the ultimate goal of ending tyranny in our world" (Darden, 2017: 134). For Russia, the external and internal security threats were merging and NATO expansion to include Georgia and Ukraine was all of a piece with the US interfering in the domestic affairs of countries in the name of democratization.

If the USA is so against Russia's interests being recognized in the former SSRs because it views such articulated interest as anachronistic, then it may want to consider returning Guantanamo Bay to Cuba. As Toal observed, "Given this history of intervention... it is difficult for U.S. leaders to frame Russian interventions in its 'backyard' as anachronistic and reprehensible 'sphere of influence' behaviour without generating countercharges of hypocrisy and double standards" (2017: 288-289).

Kotkin correctly described the nub of the problem of Russia wanting acknowledgement from the West of Russia's security interests in the former SSRs. That is "the real challenge today boils down to Moscow's desire for Western recognition of a Russian sphere of influence in the former Soviet space (with the exception of the Baltic states)." That recognition the West will not grant. Yet, at the same time, "Neither is the West really able to protect the territorial integrity of the states inside Moscow's desired sphere of influence" (2016: 8-9).

Russia's decision to invade Georgia can be seen to mark the end of the unipolarity that emerged from the disintegration of the former Soviet Union. It can also be seen as a change of tactics by Russia towards the West given that the USA, from Russia's point of view, has ignored

Russia's legitimate national security concerns by taking the following actions: nullification of the ABM treaty (2002), US invasion of Iraq (2003), instituting a Train and Equip Programme with Georgia (2002), favouring of Georgia quickly joining NATO (2004-2008), Bush visiting Tbilisi and taking part in a rally showing strong support for the Georgian president, and the US recognition of Kosovo (2008) (Meyer, 2008: 121; Stent, 2019: 306). It is due to such actions by the West that led John Mearsheimer to assert that the West was to blame for the Ukraine Crisis (Mearsheimer, 2014: *passim*).

The lack of diplomatic creativity in the West coupled with the increasingly suspicious and distrustful Russian government that believed correctly the West would never recognize what it considered its legitimate security interests led to the Russian invasion of Georgia in 2008 and Ukraine in 2022. Another factor in the latter invasion was the US insistence that both countries were going to be NATO member without taking one practical action to enhance the security of those states.

It is not an accident that the only two former SSRs that Russia has invaded border the Black Sea. When Ukraine and Georgia became independent, Russia lost more than half of its southern seacoast and its most important ice-free ports. The old Russian Black Sea littoral has a place in the Russian national imagination which its lands washed by the icy waters of the Baltic Sea and the Gulf of Finland do not. Even without the "affective geopolitics" (Toal, 2017: 217, 231) of Southern Russia, the Black Sea territories lost by Russia were and are very important. Imagine by analogy, that the states of Texas and Florida became independent countries and expressed interest in joining a Russian- backed collective security organization. Instantly, the USA would lose more than half of its sea-coast on the Gulf of Mexico and lose the NASA facilities at Cape Canaveral and Houston. It is doubtful that the USA would raise no objection to the expressed goal of Texas and Florida joining a new Warsaw Pact.

One final point needs to be addressed, concerning the West's relations with Russia. Due to today's debased political discourse in the USA, many may not realize now different comments made by Western, especially US, leaders have done real damage to international peace and security. Saakashvili referring to the Russian leader as "Lilli-Putin" and Obama describing Putin as "the bored kid in the back of the classroom" and Russia as a "regional power," helped convince Putin that the only thing the West was sincere about was to turn practically every former European SSR into a member state of NATO (Asmus, 2017: 71; Stent, 2019: 310).

Bartmann made a strong case almost twenty years ago that Abkhazia and many other *de facto* states have legitimate claims to become recognized as sovereign independent states by the existing of the international community. He argued that a substantial number of "would- be states... would seem to demonstrate more convincing and more promising conditions of long-term capacity and viability than a number of the smallest states" in the General Assembly (Bartmann, 2004: 17).

Bartmann also raised the issue of the newer norms that the international community has used to recognize states as full-fledged members of the international community since the 1960s. Bartmann points out, correctly, "the nearly four-dozen micro-states that sit in the General Assembly have not undermined the authority and effectiveness of United Nations bodies. Nor have they compromised conventional conditions of statehood" (Bartmann, 2004: 17-21).

According to the UNDP, thirty-two member states of the United Nations have less territory than Abkhazia. The UN estimated the population of Abkhazia in 2020 to have been 244,926. Twenty-one member states of the UN have less of a population than Abkhazia. Why has the international community, except for Russia, Syria, Nicaragua, Venezuela and Nauru, not extended diplomatic recognition to Abkhazia even though smaller states have received such recognition? Many would say that it is because Abkhazia is not economically viable, that it would not exist without Russian financial and military support.

Some would argue that Abkhazia is not economically self-sufficient and relies over much on Russian aid to pay Abkhazian government expenses, thereby making Abkhazia not truly independent. The Abkhazian economy is weak, but most Abkhazians blame their economic isolation and relative poverty on the refusal of the USA and the EU countries to grant their country diplomatic recognition in the name of upholding Georgian territorial integrity which does not exist (Hoch, 2018: 404). Further, Russia has funded the Abkhazian government budget from 2009 to 2018 in the amount of approximately 40 billion roubles. Russia also provides Abkhazians their pensions. It's estimated that the Russian contribution represents more than half of the Abkhazian state budget (Kolstø, 2020: 141, 153).

If such a contribution undermines the legitimacy for internationally recognized statehood, then the USA and Europe should have refused to grant diplomatic recognition to the post-Shevardnadze governments because the United States sent millions of dollars to pay Georgian pensions and government salaries after he was overthrown (Toal, 2017: 112-113).

Abkhazia has repeatedly shown its independence from Russia. Abkhazia re-wrote a treaty drafted by Russia that substantially eliminated or reduced the advantages received from the treaty. Although Russia provides almost 99 percent of all foreign investment and the overwhelming majority of foreign tourists, Abkhazia refuses to enact legislation allowing non-Abkhazian nationals to buy real-estate (Kolstø, 2020: 144-145, 146, 149).

The Abkhazian people see themselves as a nation and are tenacious to protect their independence. A huge part of Abkhazian memory is the catastrophe of the expulsions of hundreds of thousands of Abkhazians from their national homeland during the 19th century. Since independence in 1993, Abkhazians have increased in number and "they see their survival as a nation as linked to having their own state" (Kolstø, 2020: 151).

An entire generation of Abkhazians have no knowledge of the Georgian language. The Abkhazians link the preservation of their identity with never again existing within a Georgian state (Hoch, 2018: 392). Abkhazian Foreign Minister Daur Kove insisted "We have existed for centuries and will not disappear" (Kolstø, 2020: 149). Abkhazia has established a "foreign policy of social moves" that show "its dedication to the development of its youth, the preservation of its culture and language, and the rebuilding of its tourism-based economy" (Smith, 2018: 202).

Ethiopia's territorial integrity was ignored with the recognized independence of Eritrea. Sudan's territorial integrity was ignored with the recognition of the independence of South Sudan. Yugoslavia's territorial integrity was violated with the recognized independence of Slovenia, Croatia, Bosnia, Macedonia, Kosovo, and Montenegro. Yet the "non-existent territorial integrity" (Coley and Mitchell, 2010: 74) of Georgia appear to be sacrosanct and at the expense of a people whose very existence remains under threat – the Abkhazians.

The author wishes to thank Metin Sönmez for inviting me to be a part of his publication and to George Hewitt for reviewing my manuscript draft and making me aware of and providing a translation of a citation from the publication of Volkhonskij, Zakharov, and Silaev.

Endnotes

[i]   The author will be using the term "Russia" for the "Russian Federation" throughout this article.

[ii] There is no agreed upon term for the countries that had been a part of the Union of Soviet Socialist Republics (USSR) and are now independent of the USSR's successor state, Russia. Some have used the term "post-Soviet space" (Stent, 2019). Russia and many scholars use the term "near abroad" which Toal has described as the consensus translation of the Russian term that is literally translated as "near beyond border," or *blizhenye zarubezhye* (Toal, 2017: 3). Cooly uses the term "former Soviet Union" (FSU) (200-2001: 101). This essay will use the term "former-SSRs" to denote the countries other than Russia that had a part of the former Soviet Union.

[iii] Roy Allison is the only scholar the author has found who has used the term "protectorate" but Allison applied that term only to Abkhazia and South Ossetia (Allison, 2008: 1162-1163).

[iv] Cuba was an excellent example of a U.S. protectorate based on the Cuban-US treaty of May 22, 1903. Others include the Dominican Republic, Haiti, Hawaii, and Panama.

[v]   The Roosevelt Corollary to the Monroe Doctrine (RCMD) was the last extension or application of the M.D. and was enunciated by President Theodore Roosevelt (1901-1909) and his Secretary of State Elihu Root, in 1904. Specifically, Roosevelt claimed that the USA had the authority to enforce international laws, to "exercise an international police power," in the Western Hemisphere in his annual message to Congress on 6 December 1904. Please refer to Serge Ricard, "The Roosevelt Corollary," *Presidential Studies Quarterly, XXXVI* (March 2006).

[vi] On the Russian use of both positive and negative sanctions, see Randall Newnham "Oil, Carrots and Sticks: Russia's Energy Resources as a Foreign Policy Tool," Journal of Eurasian Studies, 2 (2011) 134-143. For a more general analysis of economic sanctions, please see David Baldwin, Economic Statecraft (985).

Bibliography

Allison, Graham and Philip Zelikov, *Essence of Decision: Explaining the Cuban Missile Crisis, Second Edition,* New York: Addison Wesley Longman IMC, 1999.

Allison, Graham *Essence of Decision: Explaining the Cuban Missile Crisis,* Boston: Little, Brown and Company, 1971.

Allison, Roy. "Russia resurgent?: Moscow's Campaign to 'Coerce Georgia to Peace'." *International Affairs* 84: No. 6 (2008) 1145-1171.

Anchabadze, Jurii, "History: The Modern Period." in Georgie Hewitt (ed.) *The Abkhazians: A Handbook* (New York: St Martin›s Press, 1998.

Arbatou, Alexei, "Russian Foreign Policy Priorities for the 1990s." in Steven E. Miller and Teresa Pelton Johnson eds. *Russian Security After the Cold War: Seven Views from Moscow,* CSIA Studies in International Security no. 3 (Washington, DC: Brassey's 1994).

Asmus, Ronald D. *A Little War That Shook the World,* New York: St. Martin's Press, 2010.

Baldwin, David A., *Economic Statecraft, new edition,* Princeton; Princeton University Press, 2020.

Barner-Barry, Carol and Cynthia A. Hody, *The Politics of Change: The Transformation of the Former Soviet Union,* New York: St. Martin's Press, 1995.

Bartmann, Barry, "Political realities and legal anomalies: Revisiting the politics of international recognition." in Togun Bahcheli, Barry Bartmann and Henry Srebrnik, eds. *De Facto States: The quest for sovereignty.* London: Routledge, 2004.

Bgazhba, Oleq. "History: First 18 Centuries." in George Hewitt, ed. *The Abkhazians: A Handbook.* New York: St. Martin's Press, 1998.

Blagou, Segei, "Military Issues Block Russia-Georgia Detent." *Eurasia Insight,* 6 January 2003, at *eurasianet*.org/departments/insight/articles

Bowring, Bill, "Postcolonial Transitions on the Southern Border of the Former Soviet Union." *Griffith Law Review,* Volume 12, No. 2, (2003) 238-262.

Cameron, David R. & Mitchell A. Orenstein, "Post-Soviet Authoritarianism: The Influence of Russia in Its 'Near Abroad'." *Post-Soviet Affairs,* Volume 23:1, 1-44.

Chervonnaya, Svetlana. *Conflict in the Caucasus: Georgia, Abkhazia and the Russian Shadow*, translator Ariane Chanturio. Somerest, UK: Gothic Image Publications, 1994.

Chirikba, Vlacheslav, "Republic of Abkhazia (aspny) Review of the Events of the Year 1996." at *apsny.org/review*

Cooley, Alexander and Lincoln Mitchell, "Abkhazia on Three Wheels." *World Policy Institute,* Summer 2010, 73-81.

Cooley, Alexander. "Imperial Wreckage: Property Rights, Sovereignty, and Security in the Post-Soviet Space." *International Security* 25, No. 3 (Winter 2000-2001): 100-127.

Crow, Suzanne, "Russia Seeks Leadership in Regional Peacekeeping." *RFE/RL Research Report*, 15 (1993).

D'Enausse, Hélène Carrère, *The End of the Soviet Empire: The Triumph of the Nations*, Trans. Franklin Philip (New York: HarperCollins Publishers, 1993.

Darden, Keith A., "Russian Revanche: External Threats & Regional Reactions." *Daedalus,* Volume 46, No.2, Spring 2017, 128-137.

Devdariani, Jaba, "Fresh UN Resolution on Abkhazia Fails to Generate Optimism." *Eurasia Insight*, 7 February 2002, at *eurasianet*.org/ departments/insight/articles

Diamond, Todd, "UN Secretary-General Reports on Abkhazia, as Georgia Unravels." *Eurasia Insight* 1 November 2001 at *eurasianet.org/departments/ insight/articles*

Drezner, Daniel. "Allies, Adversaries, and Economic Coercion: Russian Foreign Policy Since 1991." *Security Studies,* 6: No.3, 65-111.

Feinberg, Jared, *The Armed Forces of Georgia,* Washington D.C.: Center for Defense Information (1999).

Filippou, Mikhail, "Diversionary Role of the Georgia-Russia Conflict: International Constraints and Domestic Appeal." *Europe-Asia Studies,* 16, No. 10, December 2009, 1825-1847.

Finkel, Eugeny & Yitzhak M. Brudny, "Russia and the Colour Revolutions", *Demo cratization,* Volume 19, No. 1, (February 2012), 15-36.

Fuller, Elizabeth, "Abkhaz Deadline Expires." *RFE/RL Caucasus Report*, (1999).

Fuller, Elizabeth, "Edward Sehvardnadze's Via Dolorosa." *RFE/RL Research Report,*

Fuller, Elizabeth, "Georgia Appears to Backtrack on Abkhaz Accords." *RFE/RL Caucasus Report* 4, 5 (2001).

Fuller, Elizabeth, "Georgia, U.N. to Draft New Abkhaz Peace Plan?" *RFE/RL Caucasus Report*, 4, 17 (2001).

Fuller, Elizabeth, "Quotations of the Week." *RFE/RL Caucasus Report*, 1, 44 (1998).

Fuller, Elizabeth, "What are the Meskhetians' Chances of Returning to Georgia." *Report on the USSR*, 1, 26, (1989).

Fuller, Liz, "Georgian President Hints at Concession to Russia." *RFE/RL Caucasus Report* 4,6 (2001).

Glenny, Misha. "The Bear in the Caucasus." *Harper's Magazine,* 288, 1726. (1994).

Goltz, Thomas, "Letter from Eurasia: The Hidden Russian Hand." *Foreign Policy* 92 (1993).

Gorbachev, Mikhail, "A Path to Peace in the Caucasus." *Washington Post*, August 12, 2008, A13.

Gorbachev, Mikhail, "We Are Not Asking for a Free Ride", *Los Angeles Times. A. Times* Archives, June 2, 1990.

Götz, Elias, "Neorealism and Russia's Ukraine Policy, 1991-Present." *Contemporary Politics*, Vol. 22, No, 3, 301-323

Harzl, Benedikt C, "Nationalism and Politics of the Past: The Cases of Kosovo and Abkhazia." *Review of the Central and East European Law*, 36 (2001), 53-77.

Hewitt, George. "Abkhazia and Georgia: Time for a Reassessment." *Brown Journal of World Affairs*, Volume XU, Issue II, Spring/Summer 2009.

Hewitt, George. "Abkhazia: A Problem of Identity and Ownership" in J. Wrights, S. Goldenburg and R. Schofield eds. *Transcaucasia Boundaries*, New York: St. Martin's Press, 1995.

Hoch, Tomáš, "Legitimization of Statehood and its Impact on Foreign Policy in De Facto States: A Case Study of Abkhazia." *Iran and the Caucasus*, Vol. 22, 2018, 382-407.

Holsti, Ole, "The Belief System and National Images: A Case Study." *Conflict Resolution*. Volume III, Number 3, 19 pp. 244-242

Hopf, Ted, "Identity, Legitimacy and the Use of Military Forces: Russia's Great Power Identities and Military Intervention in Abkhazia." *Review of International Studies*, Volume 31, (December 2005), 225-243.

Horvath, Robert. "Putin's 'Preventive Counter-Revolution': Post Soviet

Authoritarianism and the Spectre of Velvet Revolution", *Europe-Asia Studies*, Volume 63, Number 1, (January 2011), 1-25.

Human Rights Watch Arms Project & Human Rights Watch, Helinski, *Georgia/ Abkhazia: Violations of the Law of War and Russia's Role in the Conflict* (New York: Human Rights Watch) 1995.

Karagiannis, Emmanuel. "The 2008 Russian-Georgian War via the Lens of Offensive Realism"." *European Security*, 22:1, 74-93.

Kolstø, Pål, "Biting the hand the feeds them? Abkhazia-Russia client-patron relations." *Post-Soviet Affairs*, (2020) Vol. 36, No. 2, 140-158.

Kotkin, Stephen. "Russia's Perpetual Geopolitics: Putin Returns to the Historical Pattern." *Foreign Affairs*, Vol. 95, No. 3 (May/June 2016), 2-9.

Lak'oba, Stanìslav. "History: 18th Century-1917" in George Hewitt, ed. *The Abkhazians: A Handbook*. New York: St. Martin's Press, 1998.

Lak'oba, Stanìslav. "History: 1917-1989" in George Hewitt, ed. *The Abkhazians: A Handbook*. New York: St. Martin's Press, 1998.

Lakóba, Stanislav. "On the Political Problems of Abkhazia." *Central Asia and Caucasus Chronicle,* 9, 1 (1990).

Lapidus, Gail W. "Between Assertiveness and Insecurity: Russian Elite Attitudes and The Russia-Georgia Crisis." *Post-Soviet Affairs* 23:2, (2007), 138-155.

Mackinnon, Mark, "Russian passports anger Georgia", *Toronto Globe and Mail*, 2 July 2002.

Mankoff, Jeffrey. "Russia's Latest Land Grab", *Foreign Affairs*, Volume 93, Issue 3, (May 2014) 60-68.

Mearsheimer, John J., "Why the Ukraine Crisis is the West's Fault: The Liberal Delusions That Provoked Putin", *Foreign Affairs* September/October 2014, pp.1-12.

Meyer, Karl E., "After Georgia: Back to the Future." *World Policy Institute*, Fall 2008, pp. 119-124.

Mihalkanin, Edward, "The Abkhazians: A National Minority in Their Own Homeland" in Tozun Bahcheli, Barry Bartmann and Henry Srebrnik, eds. *De Facto States: The quest for sovereignty*. London: Routledge, 2004.

Nahaylo, Bohdan and Victor Swoboda, *Soviet Disunion: A History of the Nationalities Problems in the USSR*. (New York: The Free Press, 1990).

Nation, R. Craig. "Russia and The Caucasus." *Connections*, Vol. 14, No.2 (Spring 2015), 1-12.

Newnham, Randall. "Oil, Carrots and Sticks: Russia's Energy Resources as a Foreign Policy Tool." *Journal of Eurasian Studies,* 2 (2011) 134-143.

New York Times, "Soldiers Patrolling Soviet Georgia Amid Wave of Nationalist Protests", *New York Times,* 8 April 1989.

Ozgan, Konstantin. "Abkhazia- Problems and the Paths to their Resolutions" In Ole Hoiris and Sefa Martin Yürükél eds. *Contrasts and Solutions in the Caucasus* (Aarhus, Denmark: Aarhus University Press, 1998.

Porter, Bruce D. and Carol R. Saivetz, "The Once and Future Empire: Russia and the 'Near Abroad'." *The Washington Quarterly* 17: No. 3, 75-90.

Rivera, David W. "Engagement Containment, and the International Politics of Eurasia." *Political Science Quarterly* Volume 118 Number 1, 2003, 81-106

Russell, John. "The Georgians." *Minority Rights Group Sovet Update.* London: The Minority Rights Group, 1991.

Schmemann, Serge, "Georgia Truce Collapses in Secessionist Attack on Black Sea Port." *New York Times,* 19 September 1993.

Schmemann, Serge, "In Crushing Blows to Georgia, City Falls to Secessionists." *New York Times,* 28 September 1993.

Shamba, Sergei, "Interview with Abkhazian Foreign Minister" Sergie Shamba with Nikolaus VonTwickel, correspondent of Mittel Deutscher Zeitung Kolner Stadt Anzeiger, 26 September 1997 at *apsny.org/shamba19970926*

Slider, Darrell. "Crisis and Response in Soviet Nationality: The Case of Abkhazia." *Central Asian Survey,* 4, 4 (1985).

Smith, Mary Elizabeth, "De Facto State Foreign Policy 'Social Moves' in Abkhazia and South Ossetia." *Iran and the Caucasus,* 22 (2018), 181-205.

Stent, Angela. *Putin's World: Russia Against the West and with the Rest.* New York: Hachette Book Group, 2019.

Theisen, Soren, "Mountaineers, Racketeers, and the Ideals of Modernity-State Building and Elite Competition in Caucasia" in Ole Hoiris and Sefa Martin Yürükél eds. *Contrasts and Solutions in the Caucasus,* Aarhus, Denmark: Aarhus University Press, 1998.

Toal, Gerard. *Near Abroad: Putin, The West, and The Contest Over Ukraine and The Caucasus.* Oxford: Oxford University Press, 2017.

Volkhonskij, M.A., and V.A. Zakharov, and N. Ju. Silaev, (eds), *Konflikty v abxazii juzhnoj osetii..Dokumenty 1989-2006 gg. Prilozhenie k " Kavkazskomu*

Sborniku". Vypusk No.1 (The Conflicts in Abkhazia and South Ossetia. Documents 1989-2006. Supplement to "Caucasian Collection", Issue No. 1). Moscow: Russjaja Panorama, (2008).

Wilson, Jeanne L. "The Legacy of the Color Revolutions for Russian Politics and Foreign Policy." *Problems of Post-Communism*. 57, No. 2. March/April 2010.

Woff, Richard. "The Armed Forces of Georgia." *Jane's Intelligence Review,* (1993).

The State-building Process of Abkhazia

Elçin Başol

Lecturer at Aydin Adnan Menderes University, PhD Candidate at Kadir Has University, International Relations Department. Turkey.

As an academic researching Abkhazia, I have always thought that being an Abkhazian is my biggest advantage and disadvantage at the same time. On the one hand, Abkhazia, is the lost fairy-tale land of my childhood, whilst, on the other, it is a frozen conflict-area stuck between political and legal theories...

Every study I have done related to Abkhazia without removing the lens of objectivity has brought me one step closer to this fairy-tale land and its people. At the point we have reached today, there have been great changes over the years both in my personal history and for Abkhazian history in general. The 30 years since the war has reconnected Abkhazia with its diaspora and witnessed many international gains. In these 30 years, Abkhazia has produced successful statesmen, bureaucrats, and diplomats. However, despite the steps taken in terms of international recognition, it is very sad to see the world turn a blind eye to Abkhazia over and over again.

The state-dimension of independence and recognition is also within my area of research. But I would like to touch more on international organisations' issues. Non-governmental organisations or similar organisations operating in many parts of the world with such challenging goals as peace, stability, and sustainability, suddenly forget all their basic values when it comes to Abkhazia. Also they are caught in the wind of the global political climate. This means that all these organisations are liable to be questioned for their legitimacy. I experienced the most visible event in this regard during my book-study with an international foundation on Syrian Refugees. In this study, the chapter on Syrian Refugees who went to Abkhazia was removed from the book, using the "legal status of Abkhazia" as an excuse, and my name was removed from the book. Censorship, which is applied under the pretext of "Abkhazia's legal status", even in such an organisation with "freedom"-based discourses, is actually the best example of the political bias towards Abkhazia.

Despite all the negative repercussions arising out of this global political climate over the past 30 years, when we look at Abkhazia's state-building process, we encounter a more positive picture. It is possible to see that many large or small-scale steps have been taken on Security, Democracy, Internal Legitimacy, Economy, Infrastructure, and Welfare. It would be appropriate to say that the Abkhazian State, which suffered great destruction from the war and then lived under an embargo for many years, has carried out its state-building process quite successfully. In terms of internal legitimacy, the change that the Abkhazian police-force has undergone over the years is undeniable. With the devoted work of Abkhazian National Bank President Beslan Baratelia, great progress has been made regarding the currency *Apsar*, which is one of the most fundamental elements of domestic legitimacy. However, it should be noted that there are many problems and deficiencies regarding relations and return-policies regarding the diaspora. Even so, in the wake of war and embargo, it is appropriate to assert that Abkhazia today maintains its internal legitimacy quite successfully.

I dream of a world where all the hospitable and pure-hearted people of Abkhazia, whose life is at one with nature, will live in a more peaceful, secure atmosphere without having to worry about the future and free from international discrimination. May the coming decades bring peace to the Abkhazian people and to all peoples the whole world over!

Is Russia Shadowing Abkhazia's Independent Future?

Fehim Taştekin

Turkish journalist and a columnist for Turkey Pulse who previously wrote for Radikal and Hurriyet. Tastekin specializes in Turkish foreign policy and Caucasus, the Middle East, and EU affairs. France.

Abkhazia's distant and recent strategic history tells us that it is not a good "geographical destiny" to be on the borders of rival power-balances located against each other.

Why hasn't Abkhazia been successful in "international recognition" over the course of the 30 years since it embarked along the path of independence? Or, to put it another way, why has Abkhazia been recognised by far fewer countries than those who recognise Kosovo, even though they share the parameters imposed by similar power-equations?

The leading driver in Kosovo was the USA, and in Abkhazia it was Russia. The US is more successful in forcing its allies to act according to its own preferences. Russia's relationship with its allies or friends does not produce political dependence. Maybe that is why even the The Commonwealth of Independent States' (CIS) members, whose patron is Russia, did not feel the need to follow in Moscow's footsteps. But is there not some other craftiness here? Moscow left its relations with the "de facto" independent republics to their own devices until it faced rehearsals for the "colour revolution" against Russian influence in the former Soviet geographical space. Moreover, it did not mind keeping Abkhazia under the CIS embargo until sensing that Georgia's Turkey-linked NATO intervention into Russian spheres of influence had turned Abkhazia into a Trojan Horse. Never mind Abkhazia's distinctive position, Moscow has ignored South Ossetia's request to unite with North Ossetia and join the Russian Federation.

Changing conditions and Russia's new regional policy

While Russia gradually ended the embargoes imposed on Abkhazia after the "Rose Revolution" in 2003 in Georgia, it started to strengthen its hand by means of the distribution of passports, in the face of the developments surrounding this tiny country by Georgia and its partnerships with the west targeting Russian influence in the region.

When Russia recognised Abkhazia and South Ossetia, the trigger was the bombardment of Tskhinval in August 2008 by the Georgian army, which had gained confidence from the "Train-Equip" plan carried out by the United States in close cooperation with Turkey. The Abkhazians opened a second front in solidarity with the Ossetians and took back the Upper Kodor Valley and the area where the hydro-electric power plant on the River Ingur is located and which they lost to Georgia in 1993. The step that really changed the course of history was the decision of Russia to recognise Abkhazia and South Ossetia following this war. Moscow thus took its revenge on the Western front, which recognised Kosovo's unilateral declaration of independence. But the strategic imagination was far beyond revenge. Repelling Georgia's attempted invasion, Russia recognised two "de facto" independent republics and secured its immediate surroundings as a buffer-zone.

The factors determining the direction of politics in Abkhazia changed after 2008 in parallel with the establishment of partnership-relations with Russia. In 2008, the slogan "together with Russia", which caused the loss of the election by Raul Khadzhimba, the ambitious candidate of the 2004 election, made certain a win for Sergej Bagash. But there was also a pride instilled in the Abkhazians: "Together with Russia, two equal countries, two equal leaders."

There are reasons to open a speculative thread on the sustainability of this equation. The critical question is: did recognition by Russia bring South Ossetia and Abkhazia to the status of 'equal states'? The relationship of economic and financial dependence overshadows the goal of political and territorial domination. The fact that the relations with Georgia do not show any softening from hostility to interstate relations creates a constant perception of threat, whilst the conviction in military security from Russia becomes permanent. Of course, Abkhazian pride in historical references says otherwise. Maintaining independence is an important claim, and it is impossible to erase it from the basic codes within Abkhazian society. But the main doubt is about Russia's intentions and plans, not Abkhazia's will. If it is said that Russia is disrespectful to this will, it may be difficult to enumerate the evidence and documents to justify it. The discourse on the importance and inevitability of relations with Russia generally comes from Abkhazian circles; it is fair to say that Russians often avoid rhetoric with any 'expansionist' intentions.

Growing doubts after the Ukraine war: Is annexation an option?

Despite Moscow's careful rhetoric, the allegations that Russia keeps the possibility of incorporating Abkhazia and South Ossetia into the Federation in the future, when conditions permit, cannot be ignored.

The first doubt as to whether this scenario would come to fruition arose with the annexation of the Crimea into the Russian Federation in 2014. But Russia had no intention of opening a new front until the reaction from the West was over. By being involved in the Syrian war, Russia shifted attention from the fight in the Black Sea basin to the Middle East.

The second source of skepticism manifested itself even more troublingly with the invasion of the Ukraine in February 2022. The fact that Russia bases its interest in the former Soviet geographical space with the motive of protecting ethnic Russians or peoples who have acquired Russian citizenship inevitably leads to questions about the future of Abkhazia. Of course, Abkhazia is a country which is friends with Russia. While both the government and the opposition embrace the alliance with Russia in Abkhazia, there are divergences over the dependence on Moscow, which the Russians do not need to worry about. While the doors of a world other than Russia have not been opened for Abkhazia, there does not seem to be a reason to force Moscow to take further steps in domestic political dynamics. However, when the plan to transfer to Russia a 185-hectare paradise-like region in Pitsunda, where Soviet leaders used to spend their holidays, came to the fore at a time when the war in the Ukraine was still in train, discussions about the future of sovereignty also flared up. However, the liveliness of the debates in society and politics confirms that there is a remarkable sensitivity about the transfer of sovereign rights.

Being under the auspices of Russia provides protection against Georgia's interventionist approach, which it keeps alive with the claim of preserving "territorial integrity". This is an important foothold. However, this situation exhausts the possibility of Abkhazia being recognised especially in the Western camp. In fact, the Abkhazians' expectations of recognition and an international presence are quite modest in the face of geostrategic realities. The emphasis we heard many times during our conversations with political and intellectual circles in Sukhum was: "If Russia and Turkey recognised us, it would be enough."

Turkey and Russia are enough, but how?

The course of a small geography in the international arena depends to a great extent on the changes in the political fault-lines outside of it. In this slice of history, Abkhazia considers reliance on Russia as an existential issue. Turkey can be constructed as an alternative area to balance Russia. The dynamics of expectations from Turkey, offering an alternative economic area, being a corridor extending to Europe, and the intersection of motherland and diaspora in the historical background make Abkhazia's interest in this country inevitable. The fact that the Abkhazian population in the diaspora is 5-6 times greater than in the homeland inevitably brings Turkey to the fore. However, the opposition to Turkey's international alliance with Russia has not allowed relations between Sukhum and Ankara until now. Turkey's establishment of the equation in the South Caucasus (Transcaucasus) through Georgia has completely taken hostage Ankara's policy regarding Abkhazia.

It is possible to say that efforts to establish relations with Turkey were met with a "disreputable" response, and although the Abkhazians took offence, hopes that this situation will change one day are preserved. The historical background very well explains the difficulties of cooperating with Turkey:

- After the Bolshevik revolution taking the opportunity of the clashes between the White Army and the Red Army, the first country on whose doors the Caucasian peoples knocked when they founded the North Caucasus Republic on 11 May 1918 was the Ottoman state. On 8 June 1918, Istanbul had recognised the independence of only this Caucasian republic and signed a friendship- and aid-agreement. But this republic, which was/is the symbol of Caucasian unity, did not survive long enough even to see the end of the Ottoman Empire.
- The President of the Abkhazian Soviet Socialist Republic, Nestor Lakoba, negotiated with Mustafa Kemal Atatürk and Rauf Orbay during his three visits to Turkey in the 1920s both bilateral relations and the return of the diaspora to the homeland. Lakoba named his son Rauf because of his friendship with Orbay, who was originally Abkhazian.

- After the collapse of the Soviet Union, the leader of Abkhazia, Vladislav Ardzinba, first knocked on Turkey's door. Ardzinba had gone to Istanbul, not Moscow, the day after the Abkhazian Parliament decided to cancel the 1978 Constitution and pass the 1925 Constitution, that is, to remove its constitutional ties with Georgia and embark on the path of independence on 22 July 1992. However, the Prime Minister of the Republic of Turkey at the time, Süleyman Demirel, not only rejected Ardzinba, but also prevented him meeting with the opposition and the media. While the leader of Abkhazia was waiting for an appointment in his hotel-room, Demirel flew to Tbilisi with Foreign Minister Hikmet Çetin on 30 July 1992 and signed six agreements with Eduard Shevardnadze, which confirmed the territorial integrity of Georgia on the map, which, of course, had been the product of Soviet administrative engineering. Georgia, with the strength of the agreements with Turkey, brought troops into Abkhazia on 14 August 1992.

- The policy that sacrificed Abkhazia to Georgia repeated itself in 2007. The President of Abkhazia, Sergej Bagapsh, wanted to visit Turkey, thinking that the international climate, which inclined to recognise Kosovo's unilateral declaration of independence in 2007, might also be of some benefit Abkhazia. Ankara stated that it would only allow Bagapsh's visit if he accompanied Georgian President Mikhail Saakashvili. It was a condition that Sukhum could not accept. Thereupon, Bagapsh forgot official contacts and requested permission for a special trip to embrace the diaspora. Although Turkey accepted the proposal, but the green light turned red when Tbilisi stepped in.

- After the 2008 war, while Turkey started a new initiative within the framework of the "Caucasus Stability and Cooperation Platform", in order to influence the conflict between Abkhazia and Georgia in favour of Tbilisi, it decided to take Sukhum to the close but there was no concrete development.

- Following the crisis that broke out when Georgia seized Turkish ships trading with Abkhazia in open waters of the Black Sea, Ankara sent Deputy Undersecretary of Foreign Affairs Ünal Çeviköz to Sukhum on 8 September 2009. According to Abkhazians, this visit could be considered a milestone in terms of Turkey-Abkhazia relations. But the way and method of starting relations contained elements that were unacceptable for Abkhazia. The Turkish government thought that building a mosque in Sukhum would be a good start. However, the plan was made conditional on obtaining approval from Tbilisi and working in coordination with the Georgian authorities. Since Sukhum did not approve of the method followed, this novel diplomatic manoeuvre had failed.
- Bagapsh's desire to meet Abkhazians in Turkey became possible through an informal visit in 2011. Official institutions did their best not to address Bagapsh. The bitterness of the diaspora only grew.

There has always been an expectation that, if Turkey normalises relations with Armenia, the importance it attaches to Georgia in the Caucasus will decrease, and this will positively affect the approach to Abkhazia. Stanislav Lakoba, the historian and father of the Lykhny Declaration of March 1989, expressed this expectation while answering my questions in Sukhum in 2009.

Possible effects of Turkish-Russian rapprochement

With a similar logic, there are evaluations that this will have positive repercussions on Abkhazia, while expanding strategic relations with Russia in parallel with the tensions Turkey has with the West. Here, as much as the potential change in Turkey's preferences, the extent to which Russia will allow the Turks to assume a role in the Caucasus is also important. It is obvious that the Caucasus has historically been a Turkish-Russian area of competition; Russia won this fight, and the Russians will not easily yield their strategic superiority.

Stanislav Lakoba, in his capacity as Chairman of the Committee on Foreign Affairs and Inter-Parliamentary Relations of the Supreme Soviet of the Republic of Abkhazia, at the conference on the *North Caucasus in Our Age*, held in London on 23 April 1993, when Abkhazia was under the occupation of Georgian troops, said: "Today, some are saying 'Abkhazia is Russia', some are saying 'Abkhazia is Georgia,' but 'Abkhazia is Abkhazia'. And at the end of the A 20th century we want to preserve our own identity, our own face for the simple reason that it is ours, even if somebody else may not find it appealing."

How long will Lakoba's words remain valid in the future of Abkhazia, as the repercussions of the Ukrainian war reinforce the perception that Russia has started to retrace its footsteps to empire? Time will tell...

Abkhazia: Experiences of Fieldwork, from Professional to Personal

Giulia Prelz Oltramonti

Assistant Professor in International Relations at ESPOL, Université Catholique de Lille, France. She has written on the political economies of conflict in the Caucasus and on informality in eastern Europe and the former Soviet Union. France.

I take this opportunity to reflect on the research-process that I undertook years ago (starting in 2009) and that led me all the way to Sukhum/i, a small city of which much of the world has never heard but which became one of the critical centres of my mental map. When pondering this process, I find myself navigating between two different sets of experiences, a professional one and a personal one. Of course, these experiences often overlap, but often the former overshadows the latter, at least more publicly. A lot of the research that is carried out on Abkhazia focuses on trends and common behaviour of large groups of people, but the field-research experience is made up of individual stories and individual perspectives. Here, I want briefly to explore this dynamic and focus on the personal and human dimension of working in and on Abkhazia.

As social science researchers, we try to understand determinants of, *inter alia*, historical events, political allegiances, institutional mechanisms, common identities, and systems of power and exploitation. We look for the commonalities among people's behaviour, observing smaller or larger groups. I, for one, went to Abkhazia in 2012 to study the political economy that characterised it before the Russo-Georgian War. In 2015, the research-project that financed my trip centred on the perceptions of the EU in Abkhazia.

As part of our work, we (social scientists) focus on the social and cultural aspects of human behaviour but very rarely on the downright human aspect, and even more rarely on the individual aspect – unless the individual is a notable figure, or a key or representative respondent. But Abkhazia has a fraught history that has engendered such different emotions by so many different people; it has determined personal trajectories in such dramatic fashion that there is no understanding of the currents of thought and behaviour without grasping the intensity of the individual stories.

I – and many others – would have had no access to Abkhazia, its history and its present, if not for the individuals (both in various parts of Abkhazia and outside of it) who shared with me/us their stories, their experiences, their 'personal' Abkhazia. I am convinced that our work does not (cannot?) properly convey the extensive and complex path of discovery that eventually leads to the more tangible output of our research – publications, reports, etc... I write 'we' and 'our' having shared some of these considerations with colleagues and friends, but I shall now zoom in on what this means for me.

My experience of field-research in and on Abkhazia has acquired a personal significance that goes far beyond what transpires from the resulting publications. I have met exceptional people thanks to the work that I carried out on Abkhazia; I lived through some unforgettable experiences (mostly positive, but not exclusively), which led to enduring memories; and, most importantly, I laid the foundations of many long-lasting friendships that make my life richer in so many ways.

These encounters and experiences have constructively challenged what I understand as resilience and how I relate to memory. Resilience is a cornerstone of living with, or relating to, Abkhazia. This is the result of Abkhazia finding itself on a geopolitical fault-line, but also of navigating a scenario for which the international system does not really make space. As for memory, every trip to Abkhazia entails an incursion into the past. It is a difficult and complex past and, at the same time, a very present one. As everyone remembers and interprets such a past in widely different ways, I have had to reflect at length about how memories are created, by whom, and their influence.

I was guided through these voyages of discovery by interviewees, friends, colleagues, and random acquaintances and, thanks to them, working in and on Abkhazia has been such a defining feature of both my professional life and my personal life. I am not listing names, but many of those people will recognise themselves in this short text; as for the others, I hope that our encounters left them with something positive as they did for me. These are all people who have a strong attachment to Abkhazia; I am grateful to them for sharing it with me.

In the New Realities Georgia and Abkhazia Need Peace

Inal Khashig

Journalist, editor of JAMnews. Abkhazia.

A s we approach mid-summer, we have to admit that no end is in sight to the war in Ukraine. Although its millstones continue to grind up thousands of lives day by day, in terms of number of parties involved and other parameters the war has reached its limit. The stalemate on the battlefront, alas, has brought peace no closer. It has not compelled the warring sides to sit down at the negotiating table. On the contrary, they are raising the stakes in their game. Either Ukraine, with the full support of a united West, will bring Russia to its knees, or Russia will reduce Ukraine to a condition that satisfies the Kremlin.

Against the current background of politicians furiously competing to see who can pour yet more fuel onto the fire, Georgian prime minister Irakli Garibashvili looks almost like a 'white crow.'[1]

Of course, the idea of spiting Russia by 'opening a second front' and thereby solving the 'Abkhaz' and 'South Ossetian' problems once and for all, as the aroused masses wish, appears quite 'timely' but in reality is absolutely irresponsible.

Whatever labels may be attached to him,[2] Garibashvili's rejection of this idea makes perfect sense. For the opening of such a 'second front' might cost Georgia not only a second 'Mariupol' – as the Georgian prime minister warns – but its very statehood.

Georgia, whatever forces might back and support it, will not survive a new military adventure. Third-party forces will return home, but Georgia may cease to exist as a sovereign state.

However, the same is true of Abkhazia.

In this contest between big players – Russia and the united West – it makes more sense for us little countries to keep our powder dry. Or, better yet, forget that we have any.

For the war between Georgia and Abkhazia that took place thirty years ago, despite the large number of casualties, was nonetheless a local conflict. And for this reason Georgians and Abkhaz were able to influence its course and outcome. But in a new war the decision-making centers will be not in Tbilisi and Sukhum but in Washington, Brussels, and Moscow. For a new Georgian-Abkhaz war will be a small fragment of a big war – that is, a small pawn in a big game. And in such games pawns are, as a rule, sacrificed without undue regret.

In general, now it makes more sense to direct all our accumulated negative energy into a creative channel. Otherwise we shall not survive.

So in this difficult time for the world Georgia and Abkhazia – and not they alone, but the whole region of the Southern Caucasus – will survive not by 'opening second fronts' but by creating a regional oasis of peace and stable development.

It is clear that in neither the short nor the long term are Tbilisi, Sukhum, and Tskhinval going to find a common language regarding the status of territories, but in all other areas cooperation is quite possible.

In the current situation of global crisis, moreover, the unblocking of transportation corridors, the creation of new logistical centers, and the establishment of all sorts of economic and humanitarian interaction look quite promising as anti-crisis measures.

From this point of view, the global crisis around Ukraine is not only a big knot of problems and challenges but also a small window of opportunity. At least for Georgia and Abkhazia there has emerged a chance to shift their frozen conflict onto another, more constructive plane.

And we must make use of this opportunity. Otherwise, when everything around us is on fire there will always be those who want to 'open a second front.'

Endnotes

[1] Garibashvili has adopted a very cautious stance with regard to the war in Ukraine. While he has criticized the invasion of Ukraine, he has decided that Georgia will not join economic sanctions against Russia, he has prevented Georgian volunteers from flying to Ukraine to fight on the Ukrainian side, and he has rejected the proposal that Georgia 'open a second front' against Russia by attacking Abkhazia and South Ossetia (https://civil.ge/archives/476348).

[2] Domestic opponents have denounced Garibashvili as a 'traitor.'

Gender, Diaspora, Homeland

Jade Cemre Erciyes

Post-Doctoral Associate, Sussex Centre for Migration Research, University of Sussex. Editor of the Journal of Caucasian Studies (JOCAS). Turkey.

As a woman who settled in Abkhazia on the 15th year of the start of the conflict, my understanding of this political, male dominated reality was barely a vague history of what I remembered from my childhood when my grandfather supported the region with medical supplies and what I had learnt from reading academic articles as a scholar of the post-Soviet world. Of course, theres were also the stories told in various North Caucasian associations and in the coffee-houses where the returning migrants gathered that added to my knowledge of the realities of 1992-93, but one could never knew how much of it was real...

Hence on 14 August 2007, 6 months after my arrival, everything changed. In Abkhazia, young people were commemorating the start of the conflict by walking from the three borders of Abkhazia (the River Ingur, the River Psou and the mountain-pass where "the Adyghe brothers" had arrived after the start of the conflict), to the Red Bridge that is known as the place "it all started". The march with historical flags and crowds coming out to meet them in each town/village on the road, was a way to claim "homeland" Abkhazia by the new generation growing up after the "war". It was a time when remains of "war" were disappearing and houses were being built, bullet-holes in the buildings were being covered, new cafés and restaurants were opening all around... So the march helped to claim the space with its history, language, culture, symbols, and to construct the country as a *place of memory*[1], borrowing the word from Pierre Nora[2]. On that day, the distinction between Abkhazians and other ethnic peoples of Abkhazia, between the diaspora and the homeland, between women and men, elderly and youth disappeared. There was the memory of a conflict that defined this land, each person living on it, each building that still existed as well as everything that had disapeared.

On that day, I, as a non-Abkhazian diaspora-scholar, wanted to say a few words in Abkhaz on the state-television about how important it was to hear and understand one another for all of us. The next day, I found a whole new world of Abkhazian women opening their hearts, their lives and their stories of 1992-1993 to me in Abkhazian, which they would say I could only learn better by listening and speaking more. In the market-place, women would tell me they saw me on TV and in the streets, women would stop me, hug me, pray for me by turning their hands in a circle around my head, and tell me about their losses in the "war" and how valuable it was for the diaspora to return to the homeland so that the homeland, the culture, the language would live on, and the losses would not be in vain.

***

With the possibility to travel developing in the region, while doing research for my Ph.D, I started to go back and forth between Abkhazia, the North Caucasus, Turkey and beyond which captured the attention of many in the Caucasus. I was not the first woman to "return" to the Caucasus, but in their eyes I was a lone female "return" migrant/diasporan who was always mobile, who was always on the road, constantly making the "long and hard journey"[3]. The journey defined the homeland-belonging in the eyes of the diasporans, and non-belonging in the eyes of the locals. In this regard understanding the gendered journey to the homeland is crucial.

In case of the North Caucasus, the first woman whose story of her return-journey to the homeland is set against a discussion of the pre-histories of globalisation, is narrated by Prof. Dr. Setenay Shami, an internationally renowned Circassian female scholar from the diaspora. In her article Shami relates a woman return-migrant's story to that of a Circassian slave's journey in the 1850s, while questioning the gendered experiences of migration and mobility[4]. She states:

> *Yet the possibilities offered by the transnational encounters of the present can be explored in light of different pasts, such as pasts that foreground interconnections, histories of movement that complicate notions of home and exile, of self and other. (Shami 2007, p. 191)*

It must be understood that in the case of Abkhazia, whose history is primarily defined by the 1992-1993 conflict, for the younger generation of return-migrants who were neither part of the things happening in the diaspora nor came to the homeland, the notion of home, self and other is complicated. Besides, for a diasporic identity, knowledge and memory of exile is at the core, and with the journey to the homeland this core is challenged by a new type of victimisation of which they do not feel part. For women, as they were not expected to come to fight in Abkhazia, the situation may seem easier. In the article *We left our skirts to men as we went to the front*[5] is told the rare stories of women who came to their homeland in 1992-1993 because of the conflict. Written by Assoc. Prof. Dr. Setenay Nil Doğan, a Circassian female scholar from Turkey, this is the first and one-of-its-kind piece about the gendered experiences of the diaspora in relation to the 1992-1993 conflict. In her article she focuses on the story of Birgul – a woman who made jam and war through her children's narratives, of Yesim – a woman who worked as a nurse during the war, and of the women whose stories were told in the Turkish media as war-heroines. Doğan concludes her piece about these women who came to Abkhazia at the time with the following words:

> *Although all the women remember the 1992–1993 war in Abkhazia as a rightful and just war fought for self-defense, nevertheless their memories of the war are loaded with guilt, silences and apologies for penetrating into the war zone, "a male zone." Those penetrations of women were transformed into different militarized images of women in war: an apologetic mother, a silent nurse-sister and rebellious but patriotic girls. (Doğan 2016, p. 158)*

The guilt, silences and apologies are also observed among the newly returning migrant-women who can communicate with the local women. As for the women of Abkhazia, who have lost their children, partners, lovers, siblings, classmates, colleagues, neighbours and many others they cared for in 1992 and 1993, their connection to the homeland and everything on it is defined by this loss... For the diaspora, it is a hard to relate to this feeling and this feeling of not-belonging fully is reflected in the narrative of a young female return-migrant that I quote in an article on Gendered Experiences of Return[6]:

> *Those who want to return choose a very small, long path. [...] A majority of the girls went back (to Turkey). Those we thought can never stay, stayed. [...] (I remind myself) it is your choice. Today people go in every direction. Human being is no more a constant. [...] I live in the devil's triangle. You are dispersed bodily, one half there, one half here... [Gupse, Female, in her 20s] (Erciyes forthcoming)*

✳✳✳

In a land, where you feel a historical belonging (your ancestors being exiled so you are originally from there) but not a historical connection to the core historical event there (you have not lived the 1992-1993 Conflict or its effects like others) belonging is questioned every day. For me 2007, was the year I was accepted by the women of Abkhazia as someone who cared and who had to know more, understand more, so that more could be felt. I learnt Abkhaz, I got to know a multitude of people living in

Sukhum, and I felt a belonging. That year, a good friend of mine told me how she and her little sisters luckily survived an unfortunate event in 1993. If you have watched the 2015 movie *Hunger Games, Mockingjay Part II*, you may remember how people were tricked into believing something nice was going to come from the small parachutes which were actually carrying bombs... That scene was real for my friend. Three girls survived such an attack, with some scars in their legs, and a cow was killed protecting them from the blast... While I was telling this story at work and how it pained me, my colleague aged 21 at the time revealed her shoulder and showed me her scar, telling me that she wasn't so lucky as not to get hurt... I had heard before of a female war-veteran who was telling with a laugh how she was no more a woman as she had been wounded in her private parts in the war, but these young women, who were kids at the time should notionally not have been part of this. They could tell me how their elderly relatives were killed, how their fathers fought at the front, but it was not their place to be suffer, they were just kids, playing in the fields and lands...

***

Reflecting in 2022 on Abkhazia in relation to 1992 may seem easy at first glance. All these interconnected and unrelated narratives of the diaspora, return, homeland, identity, belonging and conflict through the gendered lens that I shared shows that it is not easy at all. I cannot watch either an action-movie or news of wars without thinking about the women who have suffered greatly in times of conflict. Many in the homeland decided to stay in black mourning garb till Abkhazia's recognition in 2008 as an independent state. 2008 was the year when those of us in Abkhazia lived a "war" and the days that led to recognition, a more recent key-event in Abkhazia's history.

Now people want to look forward, to a future they want to build for future generations. Women are seeking their independence from traditional values that limit their existence as equal human beings in the society. They are questioning male-dominated life that limits them to the roles of mothers, sisters, daughters, carers, servants. Still it remains the case that the land is defined as a place of memory, "freed" by sons, brothers, fathers, heroes of war.

Endnotes

[1] Nora, Pierre, "Between Memory and History: Les Lieux de Mémoire", Representations, Spring, 1989, No. 26, Special Issue: Memory and Counter Memory (Spring, 1989), pp. 7-24

[2] Nora states "Our interest in *lieux de memoire* where memory crystallizes and secretes itself has occurred at a particular historical moment, a turning point where consciousness of a break with the past is bound up with the sense that memory has been torn – but torn in such a way as to pose the problem of the embodiment of memory in certain sites where a sense of historical continuity persists. There are *lieux de memoire*, sites of memory, because there are no longer *milieux de memoire*, real environments of memory." (Nora 1989, p. 7)

[3] In my Ph.D thesis I discuss how the ancestral homeland in the Caucasus is still seen as "far away" by many in the diaspora, and the journey itself is seen as hard with so many unknowns – languages, routes and peoples. See Erciyes, Jade Cemre, Return Migration to the Caucasus: The Adyge-Abkhaz Diaspora(s), Transnationalism and Life after Return, University of Sussex, 2014.

[4] Shami, Seteney. "Prehistories of Globalization: Circassian Identity in Motion." Caucasus Paradigms: Anthropologies, Histories, and the Making of a World Area. Ed. Bruce Grant and Lale Yalcin-Heckmann. Berlin: Lit, pp. 191–218. Duke Press, 2007.

[5] Doğan, Setenay Nil. "" We Left Our Skirts to Men as We Went to the Front": The Participation of Abkhazian Women from Turkey in the Abkhazian War." In *Gendered Wars, Gendered Memories*, pp. 145-158. Routledge, 2016.

[6] Erciyes, Jade Cemre (Forthcoming) The Gendered Experiences of Return to Adygeya and Abkhazia: Dual Transnationalism Between the Caucasus and Turkey.

Where East Is Past

Karlos Zurutuza

Freelance correspondent specializing in the Caucasus and the Middle East regions. He has reported for numerous publications including Al Jazeera, IPS, Vice, Deutsche Welle, and The Diplomat. Basque Country.

It is often argued that Abkhazia is a one road country. It is 200 kilometres along the coastal road between the Ingur and the Psou rivers; between Georgia and the border with Russia. Sukhum lies just half-way along that road. The Abkhazian capital remains sleepy for most of the year and it is only in summer when it gets busy with Russian tourists aching for the sun and the warm waters of the Black Sea. Although a majority of them will stay in Gagra or Pitsunda —two summer resort-towns further west along the coast close to the Russian border—, Sukhum is always good for a day trip.

But these days hardly any of the Russian visitors venture east from Sukhum. Places like Ochamchira have slipped below the visitors' horizons. It's a ghost town which was popular in the days of the Soviet Union. At Ochamchira's derelict train station, blue paint peels off the walls of the once smart waiting rooms. It is difficult to believe that trains would regularly arrive here from Moscow in the 1980s, each one laden with Russians coming south to recharge their sun-starved batteries.

Ochamchira was especially popular as an autumn-break destination for a pre-winter dose of sun, vodka and tangerines.

Those getting off the trains from Russia stretched on the platform while they were ambushed by a legion of *babushkas* armed with *gherkins* and *khachapuri* — the local cheesecake — or ice cream and soft drinks for the kids. On the platform, it was easy to distinguish between visitors who had just arrived and those who were about to leave. The latter always took their tan back home. Suddenly, there was a roar as the coal-train from Tkvarchal rumbled through the station. It was transporting thousands of tons of high-quality coal on its back, down to the quayside in Ochamchira whence it would be shipped to Sevastopol or Odessa. Children covered their ears as the train passed and then sooty faces broke into smiles. But that was three decades ago. Today, the cheesecake-vendors are long gone, the railway tracks are rusting and it's many a year since any coal was exported through Ochamchira.

Ochamchira is Очамчыра in Abkhaz and Очамчира in Russian. For Mingrelians it's not the way a name is written that matters for, despite attempts to establish Mingrelian as a literary language going right back to late-tsarist and early Soviet times, this is a language where the spoken word is everything. They have their own language, culture and identity, but they have never asserted rights to statehood, and neither Georgia nor Abkhazia is much inclined to give space to these inhabitants of the border-zone.

Today, Mingrelians are few and far between in Ochamchira. There is the dramatic poignancy of silence, the unspoken, unwritten name of a community that was once home to one of Europe's rare minorities.

Andrei, we're told, is a Mingrelian. He wanders aimlessly through the ruins of the station. "Please do not record me," he says, even before we introduce ourselves. This blue-eyed man in his early 60s used to be a mechanic: he worked here at the station for almost 20 years. "Over there, in that booth," he says. He quit when they needed someone to take care of the Ferris wheel in the city centre. "It's down there, just one kilometre from here, close to the beach."

Andrei says tourists would queue for an hour to enjoy the panoramic view over the sea to port, and the imposing Caucasus peaks to starboard. He remembers everything, even the Syrians. "They often stayed in that big hotel," he says, pointing to the shell of a 14-storey building. "That's where the élite of Damascus came on holiday." Apparently, the Syrians who rode the Ferris wheel always gave generous tips. "Everything was very cheap for them here." Andrei just had to make sure that the wheel kept turning. It only stopped when the queue vanished. Then the four engines of the Ferris wheel were ripped out.

"You cannot possibly imagine how beautiful all this was," he recalls nostalgically. It's the third time he has used those same words in our all-too-brief conversation. With each repetition of the litany, his voice becomes ever sadder. "I'm sorry, I have to leave because I have many things to do," he says abruptly, as if the Ferris wheel was about to crank back into action after decades of silence.

Protracted Conflict Syndrome – a Comfort Zone?

Ketevan Murusidze

Peace Researcher and Practitioner. Georgia.

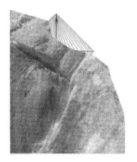 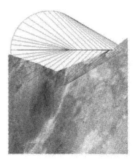

© Mareh Gorgiladze

Illustration by Mareh Gorgiladze: In search of Self-Similarity two circles in perpendicular planes are linked to each other creating a unified object - the Oloid. As a small scale of the universe, the object consists of primeval point of flow where voices follow the curves of the shape in order to be caught, felt, reflected and afterwards sent back to the beginning.

"Isolation and fear paralyze the capacity to imagine the web of interdependent relationships."

— John Paul Lederach, The Moral Imagination

249

Adjusting to the protracted conflict context has been a struggle for both Georgian and Abkhazian societies since the '90s. The complexity of the conflict(s), where Georgian-Abkhazian, Georgian-Russian and geopolitical dimensions are intertwined, reinforces its protracted nature. While simplifying this complex setting to a single dimension (only a Georgian-Russian or Georgian-Abkhazian dimension) requires significant diplomatic resources from conflicting actors, persisting issues related to basic human needs, security and identity on both sides of the conflict-divide remain unaddressed and sometimes neglected in political discussions.

Protracted Conflict syndrome - a condition when "all parties have come to expect that their conflict will not be resolved for the foreseeable future, and they have adapted to that expectation"- OSCE, Protracted Conflicts in the OSCE Area.

Although signs of Protracted Conflict Syndrome, as OSCE[1] named "the collective acceptance of the intractableness of the conflict", are sorely familiar to the people living on different sides of the Engur/i river, it cannot alleviate the implications of the unresolved conflict on the everyday peace of conflict-torn societies. In fact, the intractable conflict(s) penetrate every aspect of life. However, in the context of incompatible aspirations for a political settlement of the conflict, radicalised narratives shape an exclusive perception of how the unresolved conflict affects the Georgian and Abkhazian societies with a vivid tendency to monopolise an image of the victim. It further creates solid societal support for political decision-makers to address the issues concerning only in-group interests (either Georgian or Abkhazian), disregarding the perspectives of the outer-group (the "other side"). In addition, Protracted Conflict Syndrome creates a ground for declaring a moratorium on any issue primarily concerning even in-group society, if it requires engagement with the "other side". This can be considered one of the main obstacles hindering the conflict transformation process that has the potential for reducing human suffering caused by the conflict in the absence of a comprehensive conflict resolution.

While there is a range of areas where the conflict imposes distinct restrictions on the Georgian and Abkhazian societies, there are less discussed but striking similarities in how conflict-divided societies experience the implications of the protracted conflict. For example, Everyday Peace Indicators (EPIs)[2] elicited from the local communities during June-December 2021 demonstrate a similar linkage between perceptions of a safe home and the peace-and-security nexus in conflict-torn societies:

Peace is, when...

- there are no bullet marks on houses; houses are not destroyed and burnt [Sukhum/i]
- houses are not struck by bullets [Gori]
- when your house survives the war undamaged [Akhalgori]
- for IDPs, peace is being safe at home [Tbilisi]
- having your own roof (house) [IDPs, Zugdidi]

Preserving local voices and how people framed these everyday peace indicators further illustrates stubborn similarities in the way local communities speak about insecurity, instability and fear of war:

Peace is, when...

- you are not afraid that at some point somebody decides that this is the best moment for a war [Sukhum/i]
- you do not hold back building a house due to fear of the breaking out of a war [Gori]
- there is no fear that tomorrow the occupier will come, kick you out from your house and take away everything you worked for [Zugdidi]
- you can plan for the future assured that a war will not change your plans. [Akhalgori]

The common struggle deriving from the intractable conflict and heavy cost that both Georgian and Abkhazian societies consciously or unconsciously pay on a daily basis are often left unrecognised or swept under the status-related disputes. In this context, the Protracted Conflict Syndrome provides a sort of comfort zone, relieving the pressure and responsibility on duty-bearers to address pressing issues related to access to healthcare and quality-education, freedom of movement, essential security and stability – a range of areas affected by the protracted and unpredictable conflict setting. Importantly, a justification for inaction provided by the protractedness of the conflict is not only exploited by ruling parties/figures but neither opposition nor civil society actors and society at large question this practice, on either side of the Engur/i river.

The time-tested method of disregarding one's own duty while placing full responsibility on "the other side" is still effective. However, tragic incidents, such as the drowning of a family in the Engur/i river, lives lost due to delayed medical assistance, and detentions at the Administrative Boundary Lines, to name a few, are sporadic but a continuous reminder of the human suffering caused by the protracted and untransformed conflict.

For many years, the established practice of overlooking the consequences of the protracted conflict has relied on the patience of so-called ordinary people who have been given no other choice but continuously to compromise in every aspect of their life. Therefore, in a truly complicated context, where Moscow has effective control over the local dynamics with overt annexation tendencies, the drastic geopolitical changes caused by Russia's invasion of Ukraine, and, at the same time, Georgian and Abkhazian diverging positions on the issue of status, it is still important to ask – what else can be done to find common ground between the Georgian and Abkhazian societies to improve living conditions of people living on different sides of the dividing line?

Endnotes

[1] https://osce-network.net/file-OSCE-Network/documents/Protracted_
     Conflicts_OSCE_WEB.pdf

[2] https://www.pmcresearch.org/policypapers_show/94/
     Everyday-Peace-Indicators-in-Conflict-Affected-Communities

The Night Abkhazia Won the World Cup

Kieran Pender

*Australian writer, lawyer and academic. He served on the board of
CONIFA from January 2017 to January 2020.*

As a writer, I have been fortunate to witness many incredible sporting moments. I have covered some of the biggest sporting events in the world: The *Tour de France*, the men's World Cup, the women's World Cup, the Olympics. But nothing will ever compare to the night, in June 2016, when Abkhazia won the Confederation of Independent Football Associations (CONIFA) World Football Cup, and I was standing pitch-side.

I remember it like it was yesterday, even though sometimes it feels like it was a dream. A surreal, week and a half long international football tournament for the forgotten, the excluded, the neglected – nations, territories and minority groups that were not part of the formal international sporting framework. Instead, they found a home in CONIFA and a host in Abkhazia, wedged between the Black Sea and the imposing Caucasus mountains.

What a tournament it was. The Abkhazians were welcoming hosts, the tournament ran relatively smoothly (well, as smoothly as could be expected of a major event convened by a volunteer-run international NGO), and the football was largely entertaining. But nothing could prepare observers for the exhilarating final, as the home-side took on Panjab (representing an ethnic group from India and Pakistan).

The atmosphere was electric. The stadium in central Sukhum/i was heaving with cheering fans, their faces painted in the national colours. Indeed, the stadium was so far over capacity I had safety concerns – about 10,000 people had crammed in to a 5,000-seater stadium, such was their desperation to watch the Abkhazian team play on this international stage.

But by the 86th minute of the final, the deafening noise had subsided. Concern grew – Panjab was up 1-0. Then suddenly Abkhazia were on the break. A cross came in from the right, and Abkhazia's striker sent it past the Panjab goalkeeper. Pandemonium. The World Football Cup would be determined on penalties.

The tension in the stadium rose. Abkhazia missed consecutive spot-kicks, gifting Panjab two opportunities to secure the trophy. But somehow, remarkably, the home-team's goalkeeper saved both and the game was level once more.

Panjab scored. Abkhazia scored. Panjab missed – and Abkhazia scored.

It was like nothing I have ever seen, before or since. Instantaneously fans ran towards the centre circle, mobbing the players, celebrating, holding the Abkhazian flag aloft. They chanted: 'Apsny [Abkhazia], Apsny, Apsny'. The voice of then-President, Raul Khadzhimba, came over the stadium's loudspeaker system, announcing that the following day would be a public holiday. Jubilation. Scenes.

Abkhazia has a complex past, present and future (which are canvassed by others in this collection). I'm not for a moment suggesting that a sporting tournament can resolve these challenges. But in its own way, sport is powerful. On that incredible night, the people of Abkhazia saw their nation reflected on the football pitch. That was no small thing.

The theme for this collection of contributions is "Reflections on Abkhazia: 1992-2022." My visit to Abkhazia for the 2016 CONIFA World Football Cup was my first; I have been back several times on reporting trips. But that first visit will always be my abiding memory of Abkhazia, culminating as it did with the greatest sporting moment I have ever witnessed. The night Abkhazia won the world cup.

Georgian-Abkhazian Direct Dialogue: Necessity or Danger?

Marina Elbakidze

Project Coordinator at the Caucasus Institute for Peace, Democracy and Development and coordinator of the 'Memory Project' in Tbilisi. She is a lecturer in psychology at the Department of Organisational Psychology, Tbilisi State University. Since 1997 she has participated in a range of peacebuilding activities and has played a key role in Georgian-Abkhaz dialogue processes. Georgia.

3 0 years have passed since the start of the Georgian-Abkhazian conflict (1992-93) and, regardless of the efforts of the subjects to the conflict (official Tbilisi and Sokhumi) to realise their political positions, neither side has fully achieved its desired results, and relations between them have not been substantially resolved. To date, the parties have not been ready to cross the so-called *red lines* they have established and take essential compromise steps to regulate the relationship.

Fundamental positional differences

Basically the following political issues are defined by the so-called *red lines* that are insurmountable by official Tbilisi and Sokhumi: the status of Abkhazia; the issue of occupation and relevant legislation; the return of displaced persons; the recognition of Abkhazia as a party to

259

the conflict; and a *peace-treaty*. Arising from the noted issues, there are also other problems which are equally important, but also equally difficult on which to reach agreement. More than once political leaders have made public declarations concerning the red lines significant for the sides, and the mutually exclusive positions have similarly been analysed by experts.[1]

The status of Abkhazia represents the essential issue with regard to which the parties hold mutually exclusive positions: official Tbilisi considers the territory of Abkhazia to be an integral part of the Georgian state, whilst official Sokhumi states that Abkhazia is an independent state. But it is important to assess how far the parties have each achieved the result of their firmly stated position after 30 years. It should be noted that the Georgia's government defends its sovereignty on all international platforms and the territorial integrity of Georgia is recognised by international law. This in itself is an important political result for the country, but Georgia cannot actually exercise control over its territories of Abkhazia and the Tskhinvali Region/South Ossetia. In 2008, Abkhazia received recognition of independence by Russia and several other countries[2]; But this is not real independence – the recognition of several countries cannot make it a subject of international law and a part of the international community. Accordingly, it can be said that the positional declaration of both subjects about status has been only partially put into effect.

It should also be noted that despite the incompatible positional views on status, at different periods the parties have not rejected certain types of cooperation or support in relation to individual issues; for example, the joint-management of the Engur HPP, or acceptance of Georgian health-services by the population of Abkhazia. These positive examples give hope that even in the conditions of an unresolved conflict, the parties can take agreed decisions to solve other problems as well, and as a result to improve the living standards of a population harmed by the conflict.

Russian occupation is similarly an issue on which the views of the parties are mutually exclusive: according to the official position of Tbilisi, Russia has occupied 20% of the territory of Georgia (Abkhazia and South Ossetia/Tskhinvali Region), while official Sokhumi and Tskhinvali consider Russia not as an occupier, but as the guarantor of security (although it is possible for us to assume that in both Abkhazian and Ossetian societies there is a part that perceives Russia as an occupier or a threat to their sovereignty. It is also possible that there is a small part in Georgian society that does not consider Russia an occupier or an essential threat). Departing from positions on this issue, along with other barriers, creates additional difficulties as regards the implementation of the announced strategy for the de-occupation of Georgia. It is difficult for one to work for the liberation of a society that does not consider itself occupied. The probability of lessening this difficulty depends significantly on the attitudes in Abkhazian society, and for changing their attitudes, it is important to have active direct communication with the Abkhazian society and political leaders, and to offer them real support in solving current problems, which have become especially acute against the background of the Russo-Ukrainian war.

The peace-treaty is another cause of tension between the visions of official Tbilisi and Sokhumi. According to the official position of Georgia, mainly after the war of August 2008, the conflicts of Georgia are mainly discussed in terms of the Russo-Georgian conflict, and Georgia and Russia are deemed to be the main parties to the conflict; accordingly, if one is talking about concluding an agreement, according to official Tbilisi, it is logical that it should be concluded between Russia and Georgia. However, in reality, all parties are aware that there equally also exists a conflict between Tbilisi and Sokhumi, as well as between Tbilisi and Tskhinvali. In addition, the political leaders of Georgia have repeatedly stated publicly that they recognise only a peaceful way of settling conflicts; this position was repeatedly voiced also after the start of the Ukrainian-Russian war. In the vision of the State Minister for Reconciliation and Civil Equality

Madam Thea Akhvlediani, the peace policy of Georgia is clearly established, and it includes 8 tasks. The first task involves precisely the protection and guaranteeing of peace.[3]

We have to suppose that the representatives of the Abkhazian society positively evaluate this position, although, as it seems, merely a declaration from the Georgian side is not enough for them. Over the years, official Sokhumi has been openly declaring that it is important for it to conclude a definite peace-agreement with Tbilisi in order to obtain a guarantee of security. Georgia's position on this issue is well-known – it has a conflict with Russia, therefore the peace-treaty too should be concluded with Russia. In addition, according to official Tbilisi, concluding such an agreement with Abkhazia represents for it a kind of danger, because it can strengthen the legitimacy of Abkhazia's independence and also undermine the international recognition of Russia's occupation of Georgian territories. The question arises: if the conclusion of this agreement is very important for the Abkhazians and its conclusion will contribute to the restoration of trust between Abkhazian and Georgian societies, is it possible to formulate this document in such a way that the red lines important for Georgia are not violated, its interests are not harmed, the status of Russia as a party to the conflict is not lost, and at the same time the fears of Sokhumi are answered? To obtain an answer to this question it is important that the text of this possible agreement be discussed within the format of a direct dialogue between the representatives of Tbilisi and Sokhumi. However, in order to overcome the fears of both parties, it can be said as an offer that the different vision of the subjects regarding the status of Abkhazia, as well as the legal situation of the status of Abkhazia, should be clearly recorded in such an agreement, and it should be stated that this document does not imply any change of the existing status in favour of any of the parties. In addition, in order to preserve the status of Russia as a party to the conflict, it should be noted in the text that the agreement will come into force only after the withdrawal of Russian military forces from the territory of Abkhazia. By itself, the conclusion of a similar agreement between Tbilisi and Sokhumi does not completely exclude the need for a peace-agreement between Georgia and Russia, and it may even strengthen the importance of signing an agreement with Russia for Tbilisi and Sokhumi due to the clause of the "Tbilisi-Sokhumi Agreement" that mentions the withdrawal of Russian troops. At the same time, the parties should accept the fact that Georgia's conflicts are multi-level, and if Abkhazia is the subject of the conflict for Georgia on one level, Russia is on the other level.

Regardless of different political positions on certain issues, the main thing is that both sides have a common interest – **peace and security**; this is precisely why they should find a form of agreement which will be the guarantee of ensuring their shared interest.

The return of IDPs is another issue on which the subjects of the conflict have different views and evaluations. Every year, the UN resolution steadily affirms the right of the IDPs from Abkhazia and South Ossetia/ Tskhinvali Region to return safely and with dignity, and this should be considered unequivocally as a political achievement of Georgia in this field. However, it should be noted that the resolution only recognises the right of IDPs, it but does not in reality increase the chances of their return over the years. For its part, Sokhumi expresses dissatisfaction with the fact that ethnic Georgians living in the Gali Region (Abkhazia) are not recognised by the Georgian side as returnees, and they still officially keep the status of an IDP (and also Georgian citizenship). It is clear to everyone that, even if the parties agreed on the return, the mass-return of the IDPs is a very difficult political and psycho-social process, the implementation of which is not realistic today, because neither party is ready for it. Furthermore, Sokhumi sees the danger of demographic imbalance in the return of ethnic Georgians, which, from Sukhumi's point of view, may pose a political threat to independence. But it is also well-known that in the struggle between the parties' positions and political interests, it is precisely the interests of the population of Gali that suffer the most.

It would be more beneficial for the parties if the issue of the Georgian population of Gali becomes an object of cooperation rather than a cause of confrontation. At this stage, a conversation might start on safeguarding the rights of the population of Abkhazia as a whole and equally of Gali in various spheres (freedom of movement, education, economic relations, etc.), based on certain compromises. For example, in case of recognition by the Georgian side of the population of Gali as returnees, Sokhumi might in response recognise them as its fully-fledged citizens and at the same time officially allow those who wish to retain Georgian citizenship, especially against the background where Abkhazia allows dual citizenship – of Abkhazia and Russia.[4] In response, Georgia should promote the free movement of the population of Abkhazia to other countries, the obtaining of education for young people abroad, their participation in various international sports and cultural events, etc. Obviously, it would be better if the official Tbilisi and Sokhumi took care over the protection of the rights of Abkhazia's population without preconditions, but to begin with, protecting human rights based on a rational deal/agreement would also be advantageous for people affected by the unresolved conflict.

Space for compromise and cooperation

It is difficult to give an unequivocal answer to the question – is the need for compromises and cooperation on the part of both entities recognised together with the willingness to take appropriate steps? It can be said that the need real does exist, but as to the extent to which the parties are ready – the answer is not unequivalent, to judge by their declarations and activity.

Again if we rely on the vision of Madam Thea Akhvlediani, Minister of State for Reconciliation and Civil Equality, Tbilisi is ready to take certain steps in this direction.[5] This is evidenced also by the initiative "Step towards a better future" developed within the framework of the Policy of Reconciliation and Engagement, which involves cooperation with the subjects of the conflict in certain areas to improve the living standards of precisely the population of Abkhazia and South Ossetia/Tskhinvali Region.[6] As is well known, a small part of the population of Abkhazia took advantage of the offerings announced within the framework of this initiative, but their number is smaller than would be desirable. It is clear that the adoption of opportunities created within the framework of such initiatives will not be massive in the short time, but at the same time we must analyse the reasons that prevent individuals from accepting similar offers. One imagines this is the fear that in this form Georgia is trying to return Abkhazia to within the composition of Georgia or that they will be condemned, considered traitors by their fellow citizens or the government. It is precisely to overcome similar fears among ordinary citizens that coordination is essential with relevant official bodies of the second side.

A readiness for direct dialogue with the Georgian authorities in different formats has more than once also been publicly voiced by Abkhazian leaders at different times. This has been announced by Mr. Aslan Bzhania, Sergej Shamba, and Alexander Ankvab.[7] In December 2020, Abkhazia's leader Aslan Bzhania approved a "Concept of Abkhazia's Foreign Policy", the second chapter of which deals with the regulations of Georgian-Abkhazian relations; Obviously, both in Georgian documents and likewise in this Abkhazian document the red lines are respected and Abkhazia is considered a sovereign state, although in the second chapter there was a statement about readiness for dialogue with Georgia in different format[8]; But a few months later, in May 2021, thanks to pressure from Abkhazia's opposition, which virtually considered this step to be a betrayal on Bzhania's part, this clause was removed from the Concept.[9] It should be noted that the aforementioned point met with a critical evaluation not only from the Abkhazian opposition but also from part of the Georgian political élite and society, even though this step was fundamentally ignored by the Abkhazian side. If the Abkhazian opposition considered the aforementioned point as a step by a pro-Georgian

Bzhania, on the Georgian side some politicians and experts considered it a pro-Abkhazian plan, an attempt by the Abkhazian side to become an equal party to the conflict in the negotiations, instead of Russia, which would have strengthened its legitimacy. A number of coarse and critical statements against Georgian-Abkhazian dialogue and cooperation were made by Inal Ardzinba following his appointment as Minister of Foreign Affairs of Abkhazia (November 2021). However, some of the representatives of Abkhazia's civil society, as well as some officials, believe that dialogue with Georgia is essential.[10]

It can be said that in relation to direct dialogue and cooperation both the Georgian side and likewise the Abkhazian side have ambivalent attitudes. On the other hand, the parties do not trust each other, accusing each other of dishonourable, hidden motives (of a desire to cross the red lines), whilst, on the other hand, they consider direct dialogue to be necessary in order to achieve their goals. Such an ambivalent attitude is created by the parties' attempts to protect their political positions. But the starting point for direct dialogue should not be for the subjects of the conflict the proving of their personal "political truth" and playing a mutual blame-game but rather the desire to solve or mitigate the unresolved problems of ordinary people caused by the conflict. In addition, should there be the desire, in the format of a direct dialogue issues which are politically significant for them (personal doubts and fears) can likewise be examined.

The described ambivalent political picture, in the conditions of unresolved conflict, can be considered as one of the main reasons that societies divided by a line of conflict have problems in several areas. Therefore, it is necessary to analyse these problems and such find ways to solve them which will be mutually beneficial for both subjects, or even for one party, which implies indirect benefits at least, in terms of restoring trust. And this is possible only in the form of direct dialogue, the resources for which the parties really do have, despite certain difficulties.

Based on the results of various expert analyses and studies and likewise on the experience of Georgian-Abkhazian civil dialogue[11], it can be said that it is necessary and possible to cooperate via the path of compromises in almost all areas; but against the background of the ongoing war in the Ukraine, joint-work on the following issues can be considered particularly relevant:

- Freedom of movement / Travel-document
- Transport- (transit-)communications: land, railway, sea, air
- Safeguarding banking/financial operations
- Alternative communication networks
- Economy/ Legalisation of trade
- Education
- Healthcare

Obviously, this list is not a complete list of needs that are important to one or the other party. Nor does their relevance mean that they are more easily solved. On the contrary, work on such issues will be more of an object of criticism, arising out of the external and internal political situation. But

It is necessary to start working on these issues so that, in case of creating a favourable environment, there should already exist a concrete plan for solving them.

Why direct dialogue?

It is logical to ask the question, what is needed to create a new dialogue-format to solve the above-mentioned issues, when several are already operating: the Geneva International Negotiations (GID)[12], the Incident Prevention and Response Mechanism (IPRM)[13] and the so-called "Karasin-Abashidze" format. Moreover, there is a fear and critical view of face-to-face dialogue on both sides:

- The fear on the part of the Abkhazians: consent to a direct dialogue will be understood as capitulation, moving towards integration in Georgia, recognition of the desperate situation.
- The fear on the part of the Georgian side: consent to a direct dialogue will be understood by the Abkhazian side as the legitimisation of their independence, etc.

In response to this it should first of all be noted that the already existing formats have their own specific mandate and cannot cover all the issues mentioned in the article. This apart, GID is the format of Georgian-Russian negotiations, just as it is for the "Karasin-Abashidze" process, whilst IPRM has been temporarily suspended since June 2018 with respect to Abkhazia.

In addition to the above, the following arguments can likewise be stated in support of a Georgian-Abkhazian direct dialogue:

- As already mentioned, both sides have at different times expressed their readiness for direct dialogue in a certain form. In addition, as already mentioned, the Georgian side has recognised the format of direct dialogue as an important mechanism within the framework of a peace-policy[14].
- Albeit in order to achieve their own political goals (in the case of Georgia – the reintegration of Abkhazia, and in the case of Abkhazia – recognition of independence), the parties need direct communication; it is not enough just to invest hope in foreign, powerful partner. In particular, if Georgia desires to regain the goodwill of the Abkhazian people, it should talk face to face with the representatives of this community; and the same applies to Abkhazia.
- Both subjects likewise look for a guarantee of security and peace among powerful allies, but without mutual trust and direct dialogue, and agreement the two communities will be unable to live in peace.
- Both societies need to reach agreement through direct dialogue with regard to confronting common threats.

In order to eradicate the specific problems caused by the unresolved conflict and improve the living standards of the people on both sides of the dividing line, direct communication is needed not only at the level of political leaders, but also at the level of specific agencies.

In conclusion it can be said that the current geo-political situation is quite difficult for making decisions about the above-mentioned issues, and, at the same time, the taking of these steps does not depend only on official Tbilisi and Sokhumi. But, at the same time, it is precisely the urgency of these difficulties and issues that creates space for compromise-steps, which can only be achieved through direct dialogue between the parties. For a start, the parties should agree that there are issues on which they will not be able to reach agreement in the near future – for example, the status of Abkhazia. But at the same time, they should agree that, despite the existing red lines, there is a space within which it is possible to solve a range of issues that will be beneficial for both or directly at least one or other of the parties. Even in such a case, both parties will win, because satisfying the interest of one or other of the parties will facilitate the strengthening of trust, and thus it will be indirectly beneficial for both. The parties should begin today to develop a plan to resolve the issues so that they are ready to start acting when the time is propitious.

It should be noted right here that for the implementation of issues agreed upon in the process of direct dialogue it is important to make use of the support and expertise of authoritative international organisations acceptable to both sides, to receive guarantees from their side, as well as likewise to involve Russia at a certain stage and receive certain guarantees from its side too.

Endnotes

[1] Ivlian Khaindrave "On the 'Red Lines' and Not Only". 2020.

[2] Abkhazia is recognised by 5 UN member-states: the Russian Federation (26 August 2008), Nicaragua (5 September 2008), Venezuela (10 September 2008), Nauru (15 December 2008), and Syria (29 May 2018), as well as by other equally partly recognised or unrecognised countries.

[3] https://smr.gov.ge/en/page/35/ministris-xedva

[4] https://tass.ru/mezhdunarodnaya-panorama/14101273utm_source=-google.com&utm_medium=organic&utm_campaign=google.com&utm_referrer=google.com
http://www.emb-abkhazia.ru/konsulskie_voprosy/zakon_j/
https://hikeit.ru/abhaziya/apsny-citizenship

[5] https://smr.gov.ge/en/page/35/ministris-xedva

[6] https://smr.gov.ge/en/page/40/nabiji-uketesi-momavlisken

[7] https://sova.news/2020/08/20/sergej-shamba-dialog-s-tbilisi-neobhodim/
https://sova.news/2021/01/31/shamba-prizval-k-dialogu-s-tbilisi-zaya-viv-o-vnutrennih-a-ne-o-vneshnih-ugrozah/
https://1tv.ge/lang/ru/news/sergej-shamba-nastalo-vremja-nachat-dia-log-s-gruziej/
https://www.ekhokavkaza.com/a/30380405.html

[8] "The Republic of Abkhazia admits the possibility of creating conditions for the formation of an additional format of multi-level negotiations between Georgia and the Republic of Abkhazia, within which the opportunity to discuss with the Georgian side issues of mutual interest, a decision on which is not possible within the framework of the International Geneva Discussions" (In Russian).

[9] http://presidentofabkhazia.org/upload/iblock/e3b/KONTSEPTSIYA-Vneshey-politiki.pdf

[10] https://www.ekhokavkaza.com/a/31661584.html
https://sputnik-abkhazia.ru/20220427/ardzinba-gruziya-vedet-gibrid-nuyu-voynu-protiv-abkhazii-1038836238.html , https://sputnik-abkhazia.ru/20220720/otnosheniya-s-gruziey-i-sotrudnichestvo-s-rossiey-obsudi-li-v-mid-abkhazii-1040388362.html

[11] https://geabconflict.jam-news.net/ru/%d0%bf%d1%80%d0
%b5%d0%b4%d0%bb%d0%be%d0%b6%d0%b5%d0%bd%d0%
b8%d1%8f%d1%83%d1%87%d0%b0%d1%81%d1%82%d0%
bd%d0%b8%d0%ba%d0%be%d0%b2%d0%bd%d0%b5%
d1%84%d0%be%d1%80%d0%bc%d0%b0%d0%bb%d1%8c%d0%b-
d%d0%be%d0%b3/
[12] https://smr.gov.ge/en/page/26/jenevis-saertashoriso-
molaparakebebi
[13] https://smr.gov.ge/en/page/27/incidentebis-prevenciisa-
da-matze-reagirebis-meqanizmi
[14] https://smr.gov.ge/en/page/35/ministris-xedva

"Good Neighbourhood"

Maxim Gvindzhia

Former Minister of Foreign Affairs of Abkhazia.

S peaking of my country, many people often refer to its past. Usually, researchers write about Soviet times, about decades of struggle for self-determination and rights. The history and aspects of the Georgian-Abkhazian conflict have become the subject of study by many prominent researchers, politicians and scholars, as well as propagandists and liars. Despite its small size, my country has always remained where it is. We have been part of many great and already vanished empires. I often think about what gives us the opportunity to survive for many centuries. We have always suffered when the giants clashed and may have been able to develop immunity to the challenges of the time.

However, returning to the history of Abkhazia, I always noticed special moments that today can be called "advanced" or progressive thinking. At a time when many peoples remained pagans, Christianity was already adopted in Abkhazia. When the slave-trade flourished in the western hemisphere, representatives of other races became equal members of our society. Abkhazia often became the homeland for representatives of different peoples who came here as a result of persecution, famine, and wars.

In other words, Abkhazia, even in the Middle Ages, was much more democratic than those who have usurped the concept of "democracy" today.

Looking back at the past, one can imagine what challenges await us in the future, because the cyclical nature of history is obvious.

But, has Abkhazia retained this hidden potential to accept the new demands of the time? How ready are we for the "advanced" approach? The blows of the past are deeply embedded in our consciousness, and we are often afraid of everything new, we are afraid of dissolving and disappearing. But it is this fear that can help us take a step into the future. Let us move to "advanced" development.

From the point of view of futurology, extrapolating modern technical and social trends in the world and global processes, we can say that the future of the world-economy and social life belongs to mega-cities and small countries. A kind of return to ancient times, when big cities and small states became centres of trade and knowledge-exchange. However, "tomorrow" is no longer the same as in antiquity. In our time, the word "tomorrow" has acquired the meaning of the present, something that is happening today or has already happened.

I suggest that we look together into the future of Abkhazia for at least 50 years:

A favourable climate and nature are an integral part of the culture and lifestyle of the Abkhazians. Consequently, the "green" direction of the development of our state is the same priority of national security as the preservation of our identity. In 50 years, almost all road transport in Abkhazia will be electric. The abundance of hydro-resources and new technologies will allow us to use green energy at 100%. Humid subtropical climate, soft laws, and easy-going life will attract more and more immigrants, both permanent and temporary. It is possible that a large number of pensioners from Europe will choose Abkhazia as a place for permanent residence, which will create a new labour market and attract more guest workers not only from Central but also Southeast Asia. The Western financial system is no longer reliable – your money can be confiscated merely because of holding the citizenship of a particular country. Perhaps immigrants from other countries will also want to keep their money closer, and Abkhazia will become a financial resort. All these factors will contribute to the development of the state and the growth of living standards. The development of regional infrastructure will open up new opportunities and jobs. Close and active trade-ties in the region will be the basis for stability. People will be able to travel freely, get an education and simply LIVE.

Such a prospect for Abkhazia is impossible without sustainable peace in the region. Not only a peace-agreement between Abkhazia and Georgia, but also between Armenia and Azerbaijan is the key to such a future. Strong friendship and cooperation between Russia and Turkey is a platform on which to build long-term prospects. Iran plays an equally significant role here. The future of successful economic development for the Caucasus will depend on access to the Middle East and Asia.

The perspectives described above are reminiscent of John Lennon's utopian song "Imagine". However, is it possible to imagine that anyone in the Caucasus would oppose this? The Caucasus is very large, despite its small size. The Caucasus is Abkhazia, and Azerbaijan, and Armenia, and Georgia, and Karabakh, and the Russian Federation, and Turkey, and South Ossetia.

As mentioned earlier, tomorrow is now. The time has come to put real flesh on the bones of aspirations to achieve a peaceful Caucasus. This idea can be realised through the adoption of a multilateral declaration to commit to a "Peaceful Neighbourhood". The place of signing of such a Declaration could be Tehran. The text could look something like this: "We, the representatives of the peoples of the Caucasus, despite the existing disagreements and unresolved disputes between us, express our commitment to the peaceful resolution of existing conflicts based on the principles and concepts of a peaceful neighbourhood".

The Declaration of such a "Peaceful Neighbourhood" should be prepared without intermediaries. We ourselves, the participants in its signing, will agree on all the terms and details.

I understand the smile on your face, but in order to break the cycle of history, such bold decisions are needed. Such are the "advanced" decisions that proved to be life-changing for our states many centuries ago.

Freedom Paid For With Blood

Natella Akaba

Historian, Chairperson of the board of the 'Association of Women of Abkhazia'.

This is how this world is: to some countries, freedom and independence are presented as a gift from above, while others have to get them at the cost of huge sacrifices and trials. It is no coincidence that the residents of Abkhazia style the 30th September 1993 either 'Victory Day' or 'Independence Day'. It is clear that, if there had not been a victory over the Georgian aggressors, Abkhazia would not have become an independent country. The attack was as sudden as it was treacherous for the Abkhazian side: literally, on the eve of the invasion, i.e. on 13 August 1992, the Chairman of the State Council of Georgia, Eduard Shevardnadze, in a telephone-conversation with the Chairman of the Supreme Council of Abkhazia, Vladislav Ardzinba, announced that Georgian troops would not be sent to Abkhazia. However, it soon became clear that, since 11 August, preparations for *Operation Sword*, aimed at the lightning takeover of Abkhazia, had been in full swing in Georgia, and on 14 August the invasion took place.

The city of Ochamchira was the first to suffer the blow and was occupied by Georgian armed forces in literally a matter of hours. Since ethnic

Georgians [or Mingrelians] were the majority in the city itself, and as the attack for the non-Georgian population was sudden, it was not difficult to "conquer" Ochamchira. Ethnic Abkhazians, Armenians and Russians, who found themselves in the territories occupied by Georgian troops, had to choose: either to get out of the city or village by secret paths to ensure their safety, or to join the partisan-struggle against the enemy. However, among the non-Georgian population of the Ochamchira district there were those who remained at home. Mostly they were elderly people and mothers with young children who were counting on the humanity of the Georgian military or on help from their Georgian neighbours.

However, these illusions vanished in the very first days after the invasion. This is not surprising, if we keep in mind that the Georgian armed formations brought into Abkhazia on 14 August hardly at all re-sembled a regular army – they were hastily put together and untrained detachments. As it became known later, in the course of preparations for the invasion of Abkhazia, those who were able to hold weapons in their hands were released from prisons and psychiatric hospitals in Georgia. As a result, sophisticated criminals, sadists and drug-addicts came to Abkhazia. Nevertheless, many local Georgians greeted these Georgian detachments with champagne and joyfully shouted: "Our people have come!" Some Georgian women threw fresh flowers at the tanks and ar-moured personnel carriers.

In those days, something unimaginable began in Ochamchira: in a city where people of different nationalities had lived side by side for dec-ades, had helped each other, had sat at common wedding or memorial tables, and had shared their most intimate stories, brutal murders and robberies along ethnic lines suddenly began to occur. Moreover, among the Ochamchira Georgians there were also those who informed the Georgian security-forces about their Abkhazian, Russian and Armenian neighbours. However, sometimes, albeit infrequently, there still were such cases when Abkhazians, Armenians and Russians were protected by their Georgian friends and neighbours.

Starting the war, the Tbilisi "strategists" led by the well-known political intriguer Shevardnadze and his criminal associates Kitovani and Ioseliani could not foresee that the Armenians and Russians living in Abkhazia would stand shoulder to shoulder with the Abkhazians. An even greater surprise for them was that immediately after the beginning of the war, North-West Caucasian related to the Abkhazians (viz. Abazins, Adyghes, Kabardians, Cherkess), as well as Chechens, Ingush, Ossetians, Russians, Cossacks and other residents of the North Caucasus and South Russia came to the defence of Abkhazia.

The fact that during the war armed people kill each other and try to inflict as much damage as possible on the enemy's troops is, unfortunately, a common phenomenon. However, when armed groups crack down on helpless old men, women and children, it is already difficult to explain from the point of view of military tactics or strategy. It is rather a manifestation of aggressive chauvinism. Moreover, all this took place immediately after the invasion of Georgian military-criminal groups into Abkhazia in 1992. The massacres of civilians of non-Georgian nationality shocked by reason of their cruelty, and it is hardly necessary to mention robberies. If the cruelty of the semi-gangster formations that invaded Abkhazia can be explained, though with difficulty, then it is much more difficult to understand why hatred for the Abkhazians and the Russian-speaking residents of our republic suddenly spread among many of the local Georgian community.

Abkhazia suffered irreparable losses during the Patriotic War of 1992-93. In November 1992, Georgian armed formations that invaded the territory of Abkhazia burned down the Abkhazian Scientific Research Institute with all its historical archives, archaeological and ethnographic materials, as well as the Central State Archive of Abkhazia. The Sukhum Local History Museum, libraries, and some schools were also destroyed. All this was the done by 20th-century vandals, headed by the "great democrat" and favourite of Western leaders, E. Shevardnadze. It is clear that the destruction of monuments of Abkhazian history and culture was aimed at destroying the Abkhazian national identity and spiritual heritage.

As is known, according to the norms of international humanitarian law, in the course of hostilities, citizens who do not participate in an armed struggle as well as objects of cultural and spiritual heritage are liable to protection. However, all these norms were grossly violated by the Georgian armed formations. These facts largely clarify the official Abkhazian position regarding the ways of resolving the Georgian-Abkhazian conflict and the possibility of returning Georgian refugees to Abkhazia, with the exception of the territory of the border Gal District, where ethnic Georgians [mostly Mingrelians] previously lived compactly and continue to live after the war.

Particularly significant is one of the episodes of this war, which largely predetermined its outcome. The Sochi Agreement, concluded on 27 July 1993, mediated by Russia, provided for a ceasefire from 28 July as well as the immediate start of a phased demilitarisation of the conflict-zone and the return of the legitimate Government and the Supreme Council to Sukhum. The idea was to effect this process under the control of international observers.

The Chairman of the Supreme Council of Abkhazia Vladislav Ardzinba instructed the representatives of the legislative and executive authorities who were in the city of Gudauta for the duration of the war to begin preparations for returning to the capital Sukhum. However, these plans were not destined to be realised, because in the territories of Abkhazia occupied by Georgia, including Sukhum, local Georgians began to hold mass-rallies, the participants of which carried posters with the such slogans as: "We will not allow the return of the Abkhazians!", "We do not want to live next to the Abkhazians!" etc. Moreover, all these actions were widely covered by Georgian TV-channels and print-media and were plainly authorised by the authorities. It is clear that this caused extreme indignation among the Abkhazian, Armenian and Russian deputies, members of the government, the general public and combatants. Such rallies are seen as confirmation that in the future the joint-existence of Abkhazians and Georgians in one state is not possible.

As a result, this war did not last several days, as the Georgian aggressors planned, with the subsequent suppression of "Abkhazian separatism", but lasted more than 13 months and ended with the defeat of Georgia. The defeat in the Georgian-Abkhazian war was a complete surprise for Georgia, since the initiators of the invasion – the Shevardnadze-Kitovani-Ioseliani triumvirate that was operating at that time – counted on a successful *blitzkrieg*. For many citizens of Georgia, this became a cause for disappointment, and the loss of Abkhazia (and South Ossetia) debunked the idea of a single, indivisible, unitary Georgia, which many previously perceived as a "mini-empire". This led to the beginning of the formation of the two independent republics of Abkhazia and South Ossetia.

As is well-known, in 2003, because of the Rose Revolution, Shevardnadze was removed from power by the opposition, and Mikheil Saakashvili became the leader of Georgia, who in 2008 decided to unfreeze the "frozen conflicts" in South Ossetia and Abkhazia. In response to the attack on South Ossetia, the Russian leadership brought armed forces into the conflict-zone in order to launch an operation to force Georgia to make peace. Within five days, Russian troops, together with the South Ossetian armed formations, ousted the Georgian armed detachments from South Ossetia, and also, in cooperation with the Abkhazian forces, from the Upper Kodor Gorge in Abkhazia.

In response to Georgia's aggressive actions, on 26 August 2008, Russia officially recognised South Ossetia and Abkhazia as independent states. In response, Georgia broke off diplomatic relations with Russia, and on the initiative of Mikheil Saakashvili, official Tbilisi stopped considering Abkhazia and South Ossetia as parties to the conflict. To this day, Georgian leaders are still trying in every possible way to convince the world-community that Abkhazia and South Ossetia are Georgian territories occupied by Russia. They stubbornly promote this myth at the Geneva negotiations.

The fact that a significant part of Georgian society is still under the influence of such myths may indicate an inability or unwillingness to analyse objectively and rethink the past of their country. Consequently, the repetition of the tragic mistakes made in the past cannot be ruled out, which is an obstacle to building a sustainable world.

In addition, to this day, the citizens of independent Abkhazia live under the conviction that there exists a very biased attitude towards them on the part of international organisations. For example, the Parliamentary Assembly of the Council of Europe (PACE) has repeatedly adopted resolutions in which Abkhazia appears as a territory of Georgia occupied by Russia, thereby denying the people of Abkhazia the right to determine their own destiny. In addition, the demands to revoke the recognition of the independence of Abkhazia and South Ossetia that are periodically and ritualistically presented to Russia by some international organisations cause a very negative reaction.

The Radioactive Decay of Russian Imperialism

Paata Zakareishvili

Former State Minister for Reconciliation and Civic Equality from 2012 until 2016. Georgia.

The main result of the current stage of the war in Ukraine is that Russia made a mistake in all its calculations. Moscow was planning for a long time before invading, but from the very first hours something went wrong. The "special operation", as Russia called its actions on the territory of another state, quickly turned into a war, no matter how the Kremlin avoided this word. Where did Russia go wrong? In that she considered Ukraine as weak and indecisive as in 2014, when Kyiv, and the whole world, swallowed the annexation of Crimea, Moscow did not expect that Ukraine would fight better than eight years ago in Donetsk and Luhansk. Then Russia managed to take control of parts of the Luhansk and Donetsk regions. Russian arrest of ships in the Sea of Azov[1], threats from the Kremlin, which did not like the fact that a British warship sailed off the coast of Crimea... [2] Seeing that the world turned a blind eye to these episodes, Moscow decided that it was possible to act even more brazenly – the world would not react even now. Russia convinced itself of its omnipotence and was sure that it would easily achieve its plans in Ukraine, but this time the world did not give in. Moscow has lost control of the situation – now it is the situation that is dictating the terms.

The coronavirus pandemic has also played a cruel joke. Already suspicious, Russian President Vladimir Putin has become even more withdrawn into himself. Strict observance of physical distance at long tables during meetings with foreign guests and other comic scenes that have spread on social networks indicate that V. Putin shuns and avoids contact with people. As one can see, he has distanced himself from his inner circle. Putin's "lecture" on the history of Ukraine, which he gave on 21 February, showed that the Russian president deliberately distances himself from reality. He lives more comfortably in the myths he has created, and his entourage helps him to believe in them. Belief in these myths led Russia to invade Ukraine, thereby taking a step into the abyss. The war is not over yet, but the main conclusion can already be drawn – with one action, Russia is overthrowing itself and creating Ukraine.

What is happening now is what should have happened after the First World War, as a result of which Prussia, the Ottoman and Austro-Hungarian empires ceased to exist. Only Russia survived – at first it was saved by Bolshevism, then the idea of imperialism continued to smoulder thanks to the CIS [Commonwealth of Independent States]. The tragedy of Putin is that he wanted to recreate something quasi-imperial, but in the end he cannot even keep what he inherited from Yeltsin. Wishing to strengthen the "Russian world", he has destroyed the Slavic one. Having seized power from Yeltsin in due time, Putin believed that he was saving Russia, but it turned out that he was ruining it. Yeltsin, having signed the Belovezhskaja Accords on 8 December 1991 (with the heads of Belarus S. Shushkevich and Ukraine L. Kravchuk), in the ruins of the collapsing Soviet Union, preserved the smouldering embers of Russian imperialism, from which a fire broke out during Putin's rule. It was thanks to Yeltsin that the three Slavic republics broke away from the USSR and established the foundation of the CIS. Ukraine, Belarus and Russia became the core, around which Central Asia and other countries were later "built up" (Georgia was the last to join the CIS and the first to leave). So, Putin has transformed this core from a semi-decayed state into final disintegration. With this released energy, the Slavs today are at war with each other. And as one can see, the end of Russian imperialism will be brought about not by the Americans and not by the Chinese, but by the Ukrainians. The Angel of Death for Russian imperialism was Kyiv – "Mother of Russian cities."[3] This is very symbolic. I think for Putin the scene of the arrival of the Angel of Death in the shape of Ukraine looks very impressive.

Ukraine and Russia: Today and Tomorrow

By invading Ukraine, Putin not only destroyed Russian imperialism, but also completed the creation of the Ukrainian nation. Today Ukraine is an established nation. She is finally freed from paternalistic attitudes. If in a certain part of Ukrainian society there were doubts about the importance of the connection with Russia, then after the start of the war, they completely evaporated. In the modern history of Ukraine, Russia will take the same role that fascist Germany plays in it. The only difference is that the memory of the current war will be stronger, because today, in the age of the Internet, all events are carefully documented. Terrible pictures from Bucha and other cities will always stand before one's eyes. The Ukrainians will have two big victories over the enemies of humanity in the 20th and 21st centuries – a victory over German fascism and a victory over Russian imperialism. Both phenomena were a global threat, the Ukrainian people were able to resist both.

How will events develop further? One of the likely scenarios is that Kyiv and Moscow will agree (most likely on Ukraine's terms), the troops will disperse and negotiations will begin. The Crimea, Donetsk, Luhansk will remain in the basket of negotiations. The most acceptable concession that Kyiv can make is neutrality and refusal to aspire to NATO. Given the huge sacrifices that the country is making, such a decision must be respected. In the end, one can always return to this topic, depending on how Russia will change in terms of democratisation. For Ukraine, the main challenge today is not to slip into a military democracy. History shows that the shadows of the First and Second World Wars often haunted the victors. In the victorious countries, generals were easily tempted by the authorities – Charles de Gaulle in France, D. Eisenhower in the USA, L. Brezhnev and N. Khrushchev in the USSR. But a good warrior does not mean a "good politician". The question "Where were you during the war?" should not be heard in the new Ukraine. If the country avoids this, it will be trusted, and it will be easier for Western democracies to support it.

I believe that the biggest changes after the signing of a peace-treaty between Kyiv and Moscow will take place in Russia. As long as Putin is in power, the international community should not lift economic sanctions. The removal of Putin from governing the country should become a public or at least an unspoken condition for the lifting of sanctions. The President of the Russian Federation cannot go unpunished, but the punishment will not be in the style of Saddam Hussein or Adolf Hitler – he must be ousted from power, as Khrushchev or Yeltsin were ousted in their time. Putin's place should be taken by another politician, most likely also not a democrat, but one who will determine a new course. The new Russia, as during the "thaw" of Khrushchev, will have to purge itself of its international "sins" – it will withdraw its troops from Ukraine (including the Crimea), Moldova and Georgia. These will be Russia's obligations not only to Ukraine, but also to itself and the world=community. If Russia abandons its imperial ambitions and starts reforms, the world-community will support it and lift sanctions. Contrary to the myths of the Russian authorities, no-one wants the collapse of Russia, the world is interested in its integrity and democratisation.

How the war in Ukraine will affect the South Caucasus region?

The domino-principle has been set in motion. The weakening of Russia will definitely affect the processes in Belarus, Moldova, Georgia,

Armenia, Azerbaijan, and the countries of Central Asia. Russia does not have enough resources to monitor all fronts simultaneously. Existential challenges are coming for the countries of the post-Soviet space. The peoples who want to get rid of, or reduce, dependence on Russia have a chance. They can use it, or they can, once again, miss out.

Turkey

After the events in Nagorno-Karabakh in the autumn of 2020, Turkey strengthened its position in the South Caucasus.[4] Having shown itself to be a decisive player in the confrontation over Nagorno-Karabakh, Turkey also resolutely appeared in Russo-Ukrainian relations. Against the backdrop of a weakening Russia, Turkey is expanding its spheres of influence. Ankara has closed the skies to Russian aircraft flying to Syria, restricted the access of Russian warships to the Black Sea, supports Ukraine and sells weapons to it (Turkish-made drones bomb Russian troops). However, Moscow does not criticise Ankara. On the contrary, the press-secretary of the President of the Russian Federation Dmitry Peskov said that Russia and Turkey have "excellent relations in which partnership based on mutual benefit prevails". By agreeing to negotiate with Kyiv on Turkish territory, Moscow shows that it takes Ankara's interests into account and accepts the new reality.

Turkey can be styled the ruler of the Black Sea: it is a member of NATO, the keeper of the keys of the Bosphorus, the initiator of a new sea-route bypassing the Bosphorus (Istanbul Canal). Among the international interests of Ankara, there are three areas that are relevant for the Caucasus region: firstly, there is Turkey's clear interest in the South Caucasus; secondly, there is its expanding influence in the Black Sea; and, thirdly, there are the prospects for access to Central Asia. Regarding the first area, there is the Georgia-Azerbaijan-Turkey: the countries conduct military exercises together, implement joint energy-projects, and synchronise common interests in the geopolitical context. Of all the countries of the South Caucasus, only Armenia remains on the sidelines so far, but the negotiations that have begun between Erevan and Ankara are encouraging. I think it is within Turkey's power to convince Armenia that nothing threatens its sovereignty and that a worthy presence of Armenia in the region can contribute. In addition, Ilham Aliev and Nikol Pashinjan have already met twice in Brussels. They outlined the contours of a peace-treaty. The meeting took place without the mediation of Russia. This suggests that Erevan and Baku can agree on their own. If Erevan, on the one hand, and Baku-Ankara, on the other, find a common language, the South Caucasus will change dramatically. A new common context will emerge with which Russia will have to reckon.

As for the second area, Turkey seeks to be strengthening its influence in the Black Sea. Turkey should not benefit from the expansion of Russian influence in the Black Sea region. Georgia can have its say here. If an Azerbaijan-Georgia-Turkey bloc is possible in the South Caucasian context, why can't a Ukraine-Georgia-Turkey bloc be possible in the Black Sea context? Such an alliance could strengthen Turkey. Tbilisi should support Ankara in this endeavour. Moreover, Turkey has always pursued a consistent policy towards Georgia – it respected its territorial integrity and never took ambiguous actions. This is the only neighbouring state with which Georgia has coordinated borders.

Turkey is also strengthening in other areas. The situation in Syria attracts attention. Given the fact that Russia has to pay more and more attention to Ukraine, conditions are being created for Ankara to expand its involvement in Syria. Against the backdrop of a general weakening of Russia, Iran and Turkey can claim their places in Syria. However, strengthening of Iran in the region does not suit either the West or Israel. It can be expected that Europe, the US and Israel will allow Turkey's strengthening rather than Iran's. Most likely, the balance of power in Syria will change in favour of Turkey.

Georgia

In the new realities, Georgia has a chance to find its exclusive place. At the beginning of the war in Ukraine, the Georgian authorities took a neutral position. However, the cautious policy of not irritating the northern neighbour did not bring results. On the contrary, the *de facto* president of South Ossetia, Anatoly Bibilov, in defiance of Georgian-Russian relations, proposed holding a referendum on South Ossetia joining Russia, and deputies of the Russian Duma and senators of the Federation Council welcomed this initiative. Georgia has an opportunity to use Bibilov's voluntarism and adjust its policy towards Russia. The world should be proactively reminded that Georgia is just as much a victim of Russian imperialism as Ukraine. Especially since the first victim of Moscow's new aggressive policy, which Putin announced in Munich in 2007, was precisely Georgia. On 12 August 2008, after a five-day war, Russia signed a six-point "Ceasefire-plan", under which it committed to withdraw its troops to the position of 7 August 2008. This document is "live", all its provisions are being implemented. On its basis, the "Geneva talks" and the UN Observer Mission (EUMM) are conducted, and they are still operating today. Only one point is not being fulfilled, the fifth – Russia is not withdrawing its troops in accordance with the obligations it undertook. Tbilisi has been constantly raising this topic, but now, after 23 February, it has stopped doing so. Although, right now is the most opportune moment, by supporting Ukraine, as the world is doing, to insist on Russia fulfilling its obligations under the "six-point ceasefire-plan".

Instead of "reviving" the Georgian case in the international arena, Georgia is pursuing a strange policy: on the one hand, at the UN General Assembly, it votes for the exclusion of Russia from the Human Rights Council, and in The Hague it supports a lawsuit against Russia, but, on the other hand, it does not join international sanctions and does not insist on the Kremlin withdrawing its troops. Such a strange approach may be explained by the fact that Georgia is easily involved in a collective "chorus", where its voice is drowned out among others, but where it is necessary to sing solo with one voice, Tbilisi remains silent, thereby strengthening Moscow's positions, freeing it from the status of an aggressor and in respect of another state too. The main thing in the Ukrainian crisis is not Ukraine, but Russian imperialism. Ukraine did not annoy anyone, there was no provoked aggression on its part. Despite this, Russia attacked her.

Today, the ruling Georgian Dream Party has a chance to correct the mistake, which, in its opinion, was made in 2008 by the government of the United National Movement. Now is not the time to turn the Ukrainian topic into an internal political showdown – we need to use this unique opportunity and move the country's interests forward in the implementation of the "six-point ceasefire-plan". When the world starts lifting sanctions on Russia, the international community must be reminded that Russia has not yet fulfilled its obligations to Georgia. By this, Georgia will strengthen its commitment to resolve the Georgian-Abkhazian and Georgian-Ossetian conflicts by exclusively peaceful means.

The probable withdrawal of Russian troops from the territory of Georgia may create additional challenges for Georgia. The Abkhazian and South Ossetian societies are concerned about the issue of security. Their fears stem from the fact that, when Russian troops leave the territories of Abkhazia and South Ossetia, no-one will protect them. Sukhumi and Tskhinvali fear being left face to face with Tbilisi. Therefore, Tbilisi must constantly send clear messages to the Abkhazian and South Ossetian sides in the conflicts. Georgia must convince them that it will never, under any circumstances, resolve the Abkhazian and South Ossetian conflicts by military means. Such a way of resolving the conflict is excluded, as is laid down in the "six-point ceasefire-plan". Georgia has signed agreements on the inadmissibility of a military solution to the conflict with 27 EU countries – with each separately. Even if such a short-sighted idea comes into someone's head, then Georgia will violate not one, but as many as 27 treaties – and then the country can forever forget about its European aspirations.

In this context, it should be borne in mind that the observers of the European Union Mission (EUMM) are working along the 'line-of-contact' on the basis, again, of the "six-point ceasefire-plan". By the way, the EUMM in Georgia is the most suitable structure that can replace the Russian troops, which are perceived by the Abkhazians and Ossetians as guarantors of their security. When Russia withdraws its troops, there will be no need to invent anything new – it is enough to expand and supplement the powers of European observers, turning them into EU peace-keeping forces. This possibility is not ruled out by their mandate. This is a unique chance, real and quite feasible, of which Georgia can take advantage at this stage. In the context of the weakening of Russia's position, it will be difficult for the Abkhazian and South Ossetian societies to refuse such an opportunity to replace their security system from Russian to European.

There is one more point to which attention is worth paying. Sukhumi and Tskhinvali are constantly demanding to sign some kind of agreement on the non-use of force. Georgia constantly refuses to discuss this issue. Until now, the position of official Tbilisi (both of the former government of the United National Movement, and of the current ruling Georgian Dream party) is as follows: as long as Russian armed forces are stationed on the territory of Abkhazia and South Ossetia, it makes no sense to sign an agreement with Sukhumi and Tskhinvali as parties to the conflict on the non-use of force, since they cannot ensure that a commitment is made in the presence of Russian armed forces. In the new realities, this becomes possible. The possible withdrawal of Russian forces allows us to return to this issue.

After the withdrawal of Russian troops from the territory of Georgia, Georgian-Russian relations may develop in a different direction. The new, post-Putin Russia will find it beneficial to cooperate with Georgia – for example, on the topic of the North Caucasus. Georgia could help Russia support sustainable peace and democratisation in the North Caucasian republics.

Endnotes

[1] https://en.wikipedia.org/wiki/Kerch_Strait_incident

[2] https://www.bbc.com/russian/news-57582958

[3] And Oleg, the Prince in Kiev, sat down and said: "Behold the mother of Russian cities." And she has Slovenes and Varangians and others, nick-named Rus.

[4] Turkish Rubicon – Karabakh, Russia – Netgazeti.ge
https://lenta.ru/news/2022/04/02/partn/

Western Media Coverage of Abkhazia Has Become the Pattern Thirty Years Later

Patrick Armstrong

Political analyst. He was an analyst in the Canadian Department of National Defence specialising in the USSR/Russia from 1984 and a Counsellor in the Canadian Embassy in Moscow in 1993-1996. Canada.

T he Georgia-Abkhazia war gave us a first glimpse of the model the Western media use to cover events in the former USSR territories. It was not fully developed in 1992 – circumstances were very new – and therefore the model did not operate as smoothly as we see today with the Ukraine situation; but the general lineaments may be discerned.

First, complete ignorance of the background. The Abkhazians and Georgians are ancient peoples who have interacted for at least 1,700 years and, because they may be the descendants of the first humans to inhabit the territory, probably for much longer. Ancient resentments and claims, frozen for years, re-appeared when the USSR collapsed just as buried issues fuelled conflicts elsewhere. But Western reporters – and governments – were ignorant of these backgrounds. In Abkhazia specifi- cally, even the most superficial knowledge of the interactions of Lakoba, Beria and Stalin would have shown outsiders how complicated the situ- ation really was. But, when they know nothing about background-conditions, observers cannot even see things that are right in front of their noses. A simple story is easier to tell and sells better, and so there was neither consideration of the Abkhazian point of view nor attempt to find it.

Second, rather than taking the trouble to see the issue whole, the Western commentators took sides. The picking of the "good side" was, at this time, complicated by a genuine policy-confusion – did the West support the unity of these post-Soviet entities or did it support further breaking up? Why could Georgia, with its Stalin-designed boundaries, leave the USSR but Abkhazia, put in the Georgian SSR by Stalin and Beria, not leave Georgia? Why was one of Stalin's cartographical choices sacrosanct and the other not? But even to ask the question required a minimal acquaintance with the background, and that was lacking or ignored in media- and government-circles. It's easier to pick a "good guy" and tell a simple story of admirable ideals opposed by bad people. Eduard Shevardnadze was popular in the West from his time as USSR Foreign Minister (probably why the warlords actually running Georgia had brought him in in the first place) and he could easily be painted as the "good guy". Therefore, the Western media called the Abkhazians "rebels" or "separatists" or applied other epithets less pleasing than "freedom-fighters". The tendency to pick one side and essentially act as its propaganda-organ – "Between 800 and 1,000 people, mostly Georgian civilians, were killed by Abkhazian separatists... Georgian officials were quoted" – has grown much stronger and, by the August War of 2008, was very strongly entrenched and is even more so today.

The third principle of Western coverage is to blame Russia as much as possible. Visible in the coverage of the 1992 fighting was a sense of wonder that the small number of Abkhazians could defeat the larger number of Georgians. This argument – "100,000 Abkhazians against four million Georgians" – was a foundation for *The Economist*'s assertion that the Abkhazians must have been backed by Russia. But determined fighters have often seen off larger forces – Vietnam and Afghanistan then and now – and the Georgian forces were divided and disorganised, and their leaders soon turned against each other. The Abkhazian fighters benefited from another post-Soviet daydream: the re-establishment of the Caucasian Mountaineer Federation. It became universally assumed that Moscow must be permitting the fighters to cross the mountains into Abkhazia as if Moscow, in its equally disorganised and chaotic situation after the collapse of the USSR, could have done anything much to stop them. Gradually the story hardened – Moscow was helping the Abkhazians against Georgia, and by 2001 the Abkhazians had been written out, and the story was simply: Russia vs Georgia. After 2008, Abkhazia (and South Ossetia) had become only passive entities "annexed" by an expansionist Moscow.

Thirty years later, the three principles – stay ignorant, pick a side, blame Russia – glimpsed in their infancy in the Western coverage of Abkhazia three decades ago, have grown into a mighty dogma indeed. Questioning the official story is grandly dismissed as "disinformation" or worse: "If you doubt [our] credibility... and want to find solace in the information the Russians are putting out, that is for you to do".

Lessons Learned in Long-Term Peacebuilding

Paula Garb

Ph.D. Anthropology, is a Senior Fellow at the Center for Peacemaking Practice at George Mason University. Since the early 1990s, Dr. Garb has facilitated citizen dialogues and taught peaceful problem-solving skills in conflict zones in the South Caucasus, Middle East, and gang neighbourhood of Southern California. She also taught mediation and conflict resolution at the University of California, Irvine (UCI) for twenty-five years. She serves on the board of UCI's Center for Citizen Peacebuilding which she co-founded and co-directed for twenty years.

A Brief History of the University of California, Irvine Peacebuilding Program

In the summer of 1994, when I began discussing with Abkhazian and Georgian nongovernmental leaders the desirability and feasibility of dialogue, their communities had recently been at war, from August 1992 to September 1993. The conflict had begun before the Soviet Union collapsed in 1991 because the two ethnic groups disagreed about governance of the Abkhazian autonomous republic within Soviet Georgia. After the Soviet Union broke up and Georgia became an independent country, the dispute escalated into violence between Georgians and Abkhazians on the territory of the Abkhazian autonomous republic. The war ended with an Abkhazian military victory and the territory's *de facto* independence from Georgia. No country recognized Abkhazia, including Russia, which enforced a blockade. The war resulted in tens of thousands of dead, hundreds of thousands of displaced persons, and survivors suffering psychological trauma. Although a ceasefire agreement was signed in May 1994, it was periodically broken when violence erupted on both sides of the Ingur/i River, the boundary between the former autonomous republic of Abkhazia and the rest of former Soviet Georgia.

When my Abkhazian and Georgian colleagues decided to pursue unofficial dialogue across this bloody divide, we knew from established research that a bottom-up peace process can enhance the top-down official process. We agreed that outside facilitation was necessary because of obstacles to travel to each other's cities, and that I would organize a U.S. based team to facilitate these conversations outside the conflict zone. The entity that sought funding for the program was the Center for Citizen Peacebuilding, housed at the University of California, Irvine (UCI), where I taught conflict resolution courses.

Our first initiative, from 1994 to 1998, brought together Abkhazian and Georgian environmental experts who shared similar concerns about the degradation of the Black Sea and surrounding environment. Our local partners included 12-16 civil society actors, sociologists, Black Sea environmentalists and scientists. The biggest challenge was that political leaders concerned about security issues eventually discouraged participants from conducting research together, or sharing sensitive information obtained by one side or the other about conditions on their side of the ceasefire line along the Ingur/i River.

That is why in 1998, I initiated a successor project resulting in a series of conferences with local participants who were mid-career professionals in their thirties and forties. These Georgian and Abkhazian academics and leaders of nongovernmental organizations conducted research on various topics, including policy options for overcoming obstacles to peace and preventing resumption of military action. Research conducted separately was discussed at the conferences. We hoped that eventually our efforts would foster a strong constituency for peace in both communities that would assist the official negotiators to reach a mutually satisfactory peaceful resolution and sustain peace. The 16 conferences resulted in 15 fully transcribed proceedings called Aspects of the Georgian-Abkhaz Conflict. My original facilitation team was comprised of Susan Allen (George Mason University), Jay Rothman (ARIA Group), and Amra Stafford (UCI). Later I co-hosted the conferences with Conciliation Resources and the Heinrich Boll Foundation.

The conferences provided a safe space for dialogue between civil society activists, academics, journalists, and policy makers from the two communities, even when negotiations stalled at the official level. Our activities during those periods were even more important because they kept some channels of communication open. At the latter conferences we involved counterparts from Russia and various international organizations. Because of the project's dedication to full transparency, the conferences engaged many more people in the dialogues through the publications and post conference meetings held in each community. Due to lack of funding for hosting in person conferences, our last conference was in 2009. See all publications at https://www.peacebuilding.uci.edu/research/reports/pb_cs_abkhaz_pub.php

From 2011-2016, I organized through UCI's Center for Citizen Peacebuilding, our Distance Learning and Dialogue Project. Our partners included 6 university faculty and 95 university students and young professionals located in Georgia/Abkhazia/South Ossetia. The purpose was to build relationships between university students and young professionals through online courses and in-person conferences. They would also interact with around 225 UCI students in 6 distance learning courses (2011-2016) and 2 in-person conferences at UCI (2014 and 2015). The courses were designed to provide all students with knowledge, skills, and abilities to analyze causes and consequences of conflict over territory and sovereignty; generate a problem and solution analysis of case studies; write a policy paper convincingly arguing a policy position based on data analysis, write, and present a briefing memo, and mediate between different parties of a conflict. The goal was to build a foundation of trust among the South Caucasus and U.S. students so that they could learn from each other about their societies and conflicts and connect with each other in positive ways. Another goal was to give students practice in discussing their conflicts with an international audience unfamiliar with their communities and the conflicts.

Our major achievement is that most of the local participants in the UCI programs who began this difficult journey together in the 1990s are still interacting with each other, with the UCI facilitation team, and most of the other outside facilitators with whom we coordinated our projects from their earliest stages. We never wanted to control the outcomes of the top-down official negotiation processes. What we controlled completely was our bottom-up processes and our enduring commitment to long-term programs working for a mutually acceptable peace agreement.

For an independent assessment of the UCI based South Caucasus program, and those of other organizations we partnered with, please see – *"Analysis of 30+ Years of Working with Conflict in the Georgian-Abkhaz-South Ossetian Contexts"* (Indie Peace).

What follows are the most important lessons I've learned about peacebuilding by working with these extraordinary individuals who are committed to the peaceful resolution of conflicts.

Lessons Learned

- **Building relationships across a conflict divide takes much effort and patience after entire communities are traumatized by violence, especially when sporadic violence continues for months and years.**

It took our UCI team two years of shuttle diplomacy before participants agreed to meet in person. During this long preparatory period, I organized and recorded parallel dialogues. This enabled each side to hear presentations by the other side. With patient and appropriate facilitation that creates a safe space for in-person dialogue, I learned that in the early meetings one can expect participants to accept the humanity of the other side and to understand their perspective without agreement. All this leads to mutually respectful and trusting relationships.

- **Sustaining trusting relationships requires even more effort, patience, and long-term commitment as the political context changes, and people become better acquainted, thus experiencing each other's flaws as well as assets.**

The core participants generally liked each other when they first met because we created a safe space to get acquainted and deliberately avoided talking about opposing perspectives regarding the war. Instead, we focused on shared concerns about how to prevent a resumption of violence and other topics of common interest that side-stepped controversy. It took several such in-person conferences during two years for participants to feel comfortable enough to discuss their opposing perspectives and grievances. What helped to sustain the relationships despite the challenges going forward was the core participants' high level of commitment to the process, the goal of preventing further violence, and our UCI program's funding that enabled us to hold meetings every few months. This momentum allowed for more nuanced communication for a few days, each time increasing everyone's insights about the other and offering opportunities to clear up misunderstandings, develop more trust, and sustain it. As we added new people to the process from both communities, most of them contributed to a constructive exchange of perspectives and remained in the process, while a few from each side did not and eventually dropped out.

- **Third-party intervenors experience transformation as the process develops**

At the outset of our dialogue program, I had long-standing colle-gial relationships and close friendships with Abkhazians from the pre-vious decade before the war, while I was conducting anthropological research on long-living populations in the region. I had no such ties with Georgians. Early in the process my asset was my ability to persuade Abkhazians to engage with me in dialogue with Georgians at a time when Abkhazians were turning down other facilitators. Abkhazians were more reluctant to meet with Georgians than the other way around because so many people in Abkhazia spoke out against such encounters, arguing that Georgians were the aggressor and were preventing the internation-al community from recognizing their new state. In these circumstances my Abkhazian colleagues trusted that I would not manipulate them into a process that might hurt them or their community. Even though I had experienced the trauma of the conflict from the Abkhazian perspective and grieved with my Abkhazian friends the deaths of their loved ones and my friends, I had no stake in the outcome of the conflict. My life in California would not be affected. I genuinely wanted to help the sides reach a mutually acceptable agreement, offering no solutions of my own. The Georgian participants seemed to trust me as a fair mediator even though I had no pre-war contact with them and they were aware of my close ties with Abkhazia.

After facilitating several in-person dialogues, spending equal time with Abkhazians and Georgians in their respective communities, I not only started to comprehend the Georgian perspectives, but also began to feel their deep trauma, especially that of Georgian refugees and other Georgians grieving the loss of Abkhazia and the loss of their loved ones in war. I observed similar transformations in international officials and facilitators who seemed to be more understanding of one side over the other before spending more time with all parties.

- **The dialogue is more likely to move forward when the parties choose the topics to discuss, facilitate the meetings, and decide what information to make public.**

At first the participants preferred that I and other outsiders facilitate the meetings. It was a familiar format used by other third-party organizers, and therefore it felt more comfortable to them while they were still getting to know one another. After the first few meetings, individuals from each community agreed to co-facilitate (one Georgian and one Abkhazian). Occasionally it was necessary for a member of our facilitation team to step in and run the meeting because the local co-facilitators wanted to engage in the conversation rather than mediate.

- **Collaboration with fellow third-party intervenors creates opportunities to share information, resources, and fill gaps in the dialogue process.**

Early in our process we reached out to other third-party organizations working on the conflict. The goal we agreed on was to prevent destructive competition and promote collaborative efforts to meet the interests of the outside facilitators as well as the local participants. We organized periodic meetings of third-party individuals and organizations, including local participants. We discussed the general context of the conflict and explored how we could support each other's work and encourage complementarity of our multiple efforts, including funding opportunities. We updated each other on project developments and co-ordinated plans; devised ways to combine our resources to fund local peacebuilding and democracy building activities; shared analysis of our productive and unproductive activities in the peace process; discussed options for how to continue this kind of coordination--whether as simple information sharing, resource sharing, joint strategy development, joint projects, or as a consortium. We also generated research together on the efficacy of our coordinating actions. These collegial relationships among third party facilitators have continued to this day.

- **It is necessary to engage younger participants in dialogue program at the outset and promote peace education as soon as possible.**

I should have included college age students in our dialogue process much earlier, which was around 2007. This was a decade after we had begun working mainly with mid-career professionals who at the outset, as mentioned above, were in their late thirties and forties. I realized too late that a younger generation was growing up with no prewar or post-war contact with people on the other side of the conflict. Had we included younger people earlier in our dialogues we would have developed many more opinion shapers for peaceful problem solving.

- **Prevention. Prevention. Violent conflicts can be prevented by officials who must continue to negotiate conflict issues however difficult and lengthy the process. Once blood is shed, it takes decades to reconcile the communities.**

Despite all efforts at top-down and bottom-up peacebuilding, twenty-eight years after the 1994 ceasefire, we have no peace agreement, and we still have large numbers of people on both sides, officials and everyday people who do not want to meet with anybody from the other side. We had underestimated the depth of trauma most people experienced in war, and the resulting resistance to, and even fear of, dialogue. Our local project leaders from both societies have faced negative public commentary and even threats which have also hampered widespread dissemination of dialogue results. This experience has shown me that war not only does not solve the intended problem(s) but adds many new problems that take decades to resolve and cause suffering to more than one generation.

Based on my personal experience, war casualty statistics do not begin to reflect the full impact of war on ordinary citizens trapped in war zones, combatants, medics, war correspondents, humanitarian aid workers, and political leaders. Most people survive wars, often without experiencing physical harm, but not without serious psychological damage. No one keeps track of these statistics, but many may die slow and torturous deaths caused by serious mental health issues that also impact their families. I came to understand this when I lost my son (a war cameraman) to the mental health issues that haunted him until he died at the age of forty-four. How many more daughters and sons are dying slow, torturous deaths like my son from their war experiences that happened thirty years ago? How many more will die from this hard to cure psychological trauma, breaking the hearts of loved ones? All the costs of war are so much greater than any gains some individuals might justify.

- **When violent conflicts occur, the international community must generously fund trauma healing, all forms of peacebuilding, including citizen/bottom-up peacebuilding, and peace education**

Funding for citizen peacebuilding and trauma healing after a ceasefire or a peace agreement is a tiny fraction of the millions and billions of dollars that countries and the international community spend on war. Since 2014, when the conflict turned violent between Ukraine and Russia, the minuscule funding for peacebuilding in the South Caucasus, including the Georgian-Abkhazian conflict, has become even more scarce. This must change, or we will continue, at best, to have permanently frozen conflicts and – worst case – resumption of violence. This is true for all the South Caucasus conflicts, for the Ukraine-Russia conflict, and all other war zones around the world.

Conclusion

In a world torn apart in so many places today by conflict and war, this is my hope for achieving peace locally and globally:

- May our political leaders who negotiate and sign peace agreements feel obligated to the people they represent to always keep channels of communication and diplomacy open at official and unofficial levels in the interests of peace.

- Let us teach peace literacy to our children, from pre-school through the university. Literacy in peaceful problem solving in the modern world is just as important as reading, writing and arithmetic.
- Be kind to ourselves and to others. Forgive ourselves and everyone else everything.

I know. This may sound detached from understanding the realities that make us feel powerless against the forces for militarism. For instance: (1) vested business interests in war and the related weapons industry fed by war; (2) politicians who maintain positions of power by distracting people from domestic failures with nationalistic calls for war and endless bloodshed.

I offer peace literacy as something all people of goodwill can do for a safer world, even when our politicians don't seem to be working in our interests. We can add peaceful problem solving in everyday life to the practice of recycling/reducing/reusing, what every person can do for peace and climate action.

I conclude with a few resources to consider for teaching and practicing peaceful problem solving from pre-school through the university:

The Holistic Educator: https://theholisticeducator.net
Peace Literacy Institute: https://www.peaceliteracy.org
Education for Global Peace: https://educationforglobalpeace.org
Valarie Kaur, Author of *See No Stranger*: https://valariekaur.com
The ARIA Group: https://ariagroup.com
One Humanity Institute: https://onehumanity.institute
Euphrates Institute: https://www.euphrates.org
Conciliation Resources: https://www.c-r.org
Indie Peace: https://indiepeace.org
UC Irvine's Center for Citizen Peacebuilding: https://peacebuilding.uci.edu
George Mason University's Center for Peacemaking Practice: https://carter-school.gmu.edu/research-impact/centers/center-peacemaking-practice

Citizenship Politics in Abkhazia

Ramesh Ganohariti

Ph.D. Researcher, Dublin City University. Ireland

National identity and citizenship are complex phenomena, influenced by a multitude of conditions. One way to explore the phenomenon of their inter-relationship is to adopt a politico-legal approach and study the citizenship legislation of a state. This piece explores how the development of citizenship legislation over the last three decades reflects the national identity of the Abkhazian state. The reflections are based on an analysis of citizenship legislation/literature and interviews with Abkhazian officials and citizens.

Citizenship legislation is a tool used to include desirable populations and exclude undesirable groups. Following the collapse of the Soviet Union, the newly independent republics had to define their citizenry. Most states followed the "new state model" which granted citizenship to all those permanently residing in the state. Further, states generally have citizenship laws that are either ethno-culturally selective (*jus sanguinis*), territorially selective (*jus solis*) or a mixture of the two.

Present-day Abkhazia is a young republic, but it has a century-long history that has influenced its national identity. Similarly, Abkhazia's citizenship legislation is heavily influenced by preceding Soviet poli-

307

cy. In 1993 with the adoption of its first citizenship law, Abkhazia followed a more ethno-culturally selective approach, which did not fit the "new state model" approach. Accordingly, all persons whose parents or grandparents were born on the territory were recognised as citizens. Furthermore, the ethnic Abkhazian diaspora was recognised as having the right to Abkhazian citizenship.

The ethno-culturally selective character became further strengthened following the passing of a citizenship law in 2005, which retroactively changes citizenship-eligibility criteria by differentiating ethnic Abkhazians from other ethnic groups. Thus, the first group consists of ethnic Abkhazians (both in Abkhazia and outside of it) who are automatically entitled to citizenship. The second category consists of all other ethnic groups who had to prove their eligibility, such as by showing that they continuously resided in Abkhazia between 1994 and 1999.

Furthermore, Abkhazia is restrictive in relation to dual citizenship since non-ethnic Abkhazians can maintain dual citizenship only with Russia. While most ethnic and non-ethnic Abkhazians living in Abkhazia (except for ethnic Georgians) have Russian citizenship, this policy targets the ethnic Abkhazian diaspora. The aim of granting preferential access to citizenship for the Abkhazian diaspora is to correct the historical injustice faced by those who were persecuted and forced to flee the Caucasus in the second half of the 19th century. Since members of the Abkhazian diaspora are automatically recognised as Abkhazian citizens, all they must do is to file a request to confirm their citizenship and obtain a passport.

One group disproportionately affected by Abkhazian policy are ethnic Georgians (including Mingrelians) living in eastern Abkhazia. In the period 2008-2013, many ethnic Georgians were issued Abkhazian passports (and thus by extension were recognised as citizens). However, in 2013 the Parliament decreed that these passports were issued in contravention of the law, since most ethnic Georgians possessed Georgian citizenship/passports. The question of ethnic Georgians is not just a politically sensitive topic but also highly securitised. Due to the unresolved nature of the Abkhazian-Georgian conflict, it is inconceivable to maintain the citizenship of two conflicting states. For example, in the case of another military confrontation, the question of military obligations arises. Thus, by certain parts of the Abkhazian population, this group is seen as a 'fifth column'.

Several factors can explain the above. The first relates to demographics. Following the expulsion of the Abkhazians by Tsarist Russia and the resettlements that occurred during the Soviet Union, the Abkhazians became a minority in their own land. Thus, both the people and the state are very sensitive to any potential demographic changes, and all attempts are made to ensure that the ethnic balance does not change to the detriment of the ethnic Abkhazians. That is why, for example, there is a policy granting diasporan Abkhazians citizenship, and a Committee on Repatriation has been established which works with Abkhazian communities across the Middle East. Similarly, naturalisation is quite restrictive, since persons need to have lived in the republic continuously for 10 years (or 5 years if married to a citizen). Abkhazians are even hesitant to allow Russian citizens simplified access to Abkhazian citizenship. A second factor influencing citizenship policy is the unresolved conflict with Georgia. Prohibiting dual citizenship with Georgia and restricting access to citizenship for ethnic Georgians addresses concerns of both security and demography. Thus, until the conflict is resolved, the inclusion of ethnic Georgians into the *demos* will remain a highly sensitive topic.

Abkhazia: Six Enduring Reflections from the 1990s

Rick Fawn

Professor of International Relations. University of St Andrews. United Kingdom.

I had the privilege as a young academic to travel to Abkhazia first in 1999, through the tremendous initiative of the UK-based NGO Conciliation Resources.

Doing so at any time is momentous; but that initial visit in 1999 was just after NATO had bombed Serbia-Kosovo/a for 78 days, and that in the name of human rights and of preventing genocide. To very fresh war-related feelings in Abkhazia were added new and necessarily contradictory ones that came from applying parallels to Abkhazia of NATO's intervention: on one hand, intense hope that international force could be remobilised for a small group's needs and interests, and, on the other, dread at the same, and its seemingly arbitrary application. And the many implications from 1999 and the NATO actions continue to reverberate widely ever since, including in official Russian military-security thinking.

So in this highly-charged context in Abkhazia we ran classes over two intensive weeks on International Relations, including on topics like (forcible) humanitarian intervention, international organisations, European integration, and nationalism. What amusement and surprise from outsiders that those who engaged in the practice of nationalism would partake in academic sessions on the myriad theories of the same! On that, and much more, we worked and reflected.

And from that time at least six observations remain.

A first, really a vignette, emerged even before entering Abkhazia. As a student in the late 1980s during what became the very end of the Cold War, our thinking and exposure was to an image of an omnipotent, global-reaching Soviet armed forces. The West, we felt then, cowered in fear. So I remember still the astonishment of this first interaction with a Soviet military successor when the lead soldier of an armed, Russian peacekeeping force stopped our UN-marked vehicle outside Zugdidi, as we headed towards the Inguri River. Rather than fearsome, the bedraggled and at that point also rain-drenched young solider asked nothing of our route or purpose (perhaps UN designations obviated that), but regardless, asked for cigarettes.

Once inside Abkhazia, the second reflection, alongside the many hours of our study-sessions, came the readily-familiar observation to veteran visitors: the warm hospitality that is offered, but which was made ever more meaningful in the situation of obvious privations from the conflict and also Abkhazia's beleaguered isolation. After all, in the 1990s Russia and allied post-Soviet states had imposed an embargo on Abkhazia: remarkably-sounding now, because those actions were ostensibly in support of Georgia and its territorial integrity.

In those circumstances, the lavish working lunches would impress anyone. I was told that all of their fruit and vegetables, luscious as they were, were organic, and that at a time when "organic" had not yet acquired its *caché*. This 'organic' was virtue-out-of-necessity because of the lack of chemical fertiliser and pesticides.

The hospitality extended also to efforts, made at the briefest mention, to satisfy a visitor's own interests. That included scuba diving. Efforts to source equipment immediately began, but we had more than

312

enough otherwise to work on and to see. And, alas, some warned too that the very many mines which had been laid and which had continued to maim and kill both people and prized livestock, might also have washed into the inviting coastal waters of the Black Sea. Scuba waited.

But alongside the daily interactions with the Abkhazians were those also with UN personnel, making for a third reflection. That included some contradistinctions of living and eating in the first and last parts of each day with the personnel of the UN Observer Mission in Georgia (UNOMIG). All students of IR wonder at the UN's workings, and of its myriad agencies and missions. Here was the opportunity to glimpse operations at one site – or rather three, of UNOMIG's bases in Sukhum/i, Gal/i and Zugdidi.

These first images of the UN from 1999 remained in my mind once the UN was effectively forced out after the 2008 Russian-Georgian war, when Russia vetoed UNOMIG's "technical role-over" because it was "built on old realities", – Abkhazia no longer after 26 August 2008 being recognised by itself and Russia as being 'in Georgia' [Ed.] – as Russia's UN Ambassador framed the this next postwar situation. Nevertheless, in later trips, the distinctive UN blue painted on the perimeter walls of UNOMIG's Gal/i UN base remained unadultered. Such was a reminder of that international initiative, even as the grounds within were converted into and remained a Russian FSB facility.

The third reflection on the UN extended also to residing in the UN compound in Sukhum/i and to engaging with it, for these in themselves were enlightening experiences for a young researcher of matters international. UN peacekeeping is always a major part of that, albeit abstractly, but also possibly in idealised ways to the outsider. And the UN had greater attention then for its non-performances in the face of mass-murders under its watch in Rwanda and Bosnia, just five and four years before.

UNOMIG's presence was as per its name – strictly observation and not intervention, and with a cohort small (not exceeding 150 across its three bases) and all the while unarmed. Some of the UN personnel were clearly fearful; others indifferent to, or dismissive of, risks (and that despite an explosion at the perimeter of their headquarters days before my arrival). It seemed like antithetical worlds when I would see some of the same UN staff, always in at least tandems of vehicles, driving through the same streets through which we casually walked.

Perhaps that was very understandable, considering that the Russian, but nominally multilateral from the Commonwealth of Independent States, peacekeeping forces outnumbered the UN probably twenty to one, and benefited from not only what seemed to be body armour and plenty of personal weapons, but even large assets including artillery, in clear evidence in their urban base in Sukhum/i. However, relations, between the Russian/CIS forces and UNOMIG, were, I was frequently told, good.

The various UN personnel, drawn from dozens of countries, had engaging personalities and many shared views over daily meals with them. Those probably fit into three sets. One was, perhaps calculatedly, of indifference to the conflict and to the parties. That perspective could translate into "it's a job", and with a necessary element of maintaining detachment from the conflict-parties. A second was clear scorn towards the Abkhazians, sometimes with vivid derogatory statements. A third, including by older reservists, was of genuine concern for human frailties in the conflict-scenario.

A fourth observation concerns the essential and often-unsung work of international NGOs. True, I declare a personal and professional bias. On this, so be it. This is work of the most tremendous individual and integral kind, creating essential links across dividing lines that we all need. As much as I had, and still do, read about INGOs and utilise their reports, to see and experience some of their painstaking, long-term work make real the importance of this under-stated group.

A fifth observation, one enduring across all of Abkhazia's political events since the early 1990s as much as the hospitality, was the Abkhazian determination to construct and run their own affairs, and to have a plurality of views in those processes. Probably every national group has far-reaching aspirations, as far-reaching as they are challenging to achieve. But the Abkhazians whom I met, including some of mixed parentage and multiple identities, were committed then and continue to be to that nation- and state-building project. That project was accompanied in discussions with multiplicities of views and ideas.

A sixth observation, bearing in mind that this first working visit was primarily to Sukhum/i and with those who were either part of, or working closely with, the Abkhazians, was that so many others who had lived there were now absent. One can read of accounts and contemplate the vast numbers, but these remain arid statistics that cannot reflect adequately the personal experiences and losses of displaced Georgians and Mingrelians. But to travel, and always through the Ingur/i crossing, to see now many times the expanse of abandoned homes is a reminder, if inanimate, of the vast and enduring societal costs deriving from what took place decades ago. Those countless forsaken structures are a ghostly testament to the high standard of living that this region achieved and enjoyed in Soviet times, where families could have a two-storey private family dwelling, and their own land, in contradistinction to the Khrushchev-era mass-apartment buildings that uniformly stretched from East Berlin to Vladivostok, housing millions in duplicate, cramped accommodation.

Later engagements, albeit in modest ways alongside the deeply impressive efforts of others, have been with the Georgian and Mingrelian communities in Gal/i and their immensely committed and capable members, working with Abkhazian authorities to improve local conditions. A multi-ethnic region is one to be cherished.

No frivolity is meant by this closing comment: rather, it is said with the deep hope that the routine, the 'everyday' that others take for granted in peaceable places may be re-shared in this potential land of paradise and plenty. And that is that the wonderful feasting and offerings, organic or not, and scuba diving along these Black Sea coasts can be shared in future with an undivided, internationalised, community.

East and West: Between Hammer and Anvil

Stanislav Lakoba

Professor in Archeology, Ethnology and History at the Abkhazian State University. From 2005 to 2009 and again from 2011 to 2013 he served as Secretary of the Security Council. Abkhazia

War Prediction

More than 30 years after the publication of the article "East and West: between the hammer and the anvil" (newspaper *Republic of Abkhazia* 29 February 1992, No. 33; editor V.Z. Chamagua), much has changed in the world.

In those very disturbing times, being a deputy of the newly elected parliament – viz. the Supreme Council of Abkhazia (headed by V.G. Ardzinba) – and feeling the breath of approaching war with Georgia (provoked by the collapse of the USSR), I had the idea of highlighting the new state of Abkhazia and Georgia against the backdrop of rapid global changes. It was a naive hope to warn, to influence people and society, and to save them from the impending catastrophe.

The article was the first attempt in Abkhazia to consider its difficult situation in the context of geopolitics. I remember that many then perceived the proposed world-alignment as a fantasy and did not believe in its reality. One of the deputies once said: "It's funny, do you imagine our little Abkhazia is becoming part of world-politics...?" About a year and a half passed, and already after the war with Georgia, in the autumn of 1993, the same person grumbled: "You turned out to be right."

The article appeared at a time when the National Guard of Georgia, headed by G. Karkarashvili (the future Minister of Defence of Georgia), entered the territory of Abkhazia for the first time (February 1992) under the pretext of fighting the "Zviadists" (supporters of the President of Georgia Zviad Gamsakhurdia who had been deposed on 5 January 1992). However, unexpectedly for Tbilisi and the Military Council of Georgia (consisting of Dzhaba Ioseliani, Tengiz Kitovani, and Tengiz Sigua), the Abkhazian and Georgian deputies in the Abkhazian parliament jointly demanded that the guardsmen immediately leave the territory of Abkhazia, which they did. Unfortunately, there was no such unity in the parliament on the eve of the outbreak of war on 14 August 1992...

Of course, not everything in my article came true, but much continues to be relevant for today's international politics. In this regard, literally in the form of abstracts, I will cite some excerpts from that publication, because at that time many people (not only in Abkhazia and Georgia) did not yet realise that the USSR had collapsed and that tectonic shifts had taken place in the world-order. The paradoxical nature of our situation lay in the very name of the country, which continued to be called a Soviet Socialist Autonomous Republic (although the USSR no longer existed after December 1991) until its renaming and the adoption of a new constitution, coat of arms and flag on 23 July 1992.

I will focus only on the most striking excerpts and provisions from the article:

- In order better to understand the political processes taking place in Georgia and Abkhazia, it is necessary to go beyond these countries and realise that you are a part of the rapid global upheavals. Only then will it become clear to us that both we and you are only hostages of a cruel geopolitical game. The main director of this world-spectacle is the United States, which is opposed by China and Islamic fundamentalists led by Iran.

- Turkey's claims to the Crimea, which Russia and the Ukraine, being on the verge of a collision, cannot divide in any way, could not be more clearly manifested.
- The strengthening of, let's say, Iranian influence in Nagorno-Karabakh will hinder Turkey's access to Azerbaijan, and most importantly, to Central Asia.
- Turkey openly supports Azerbaijan in the affairs of Nagorno-Karabakh.
- [On the visit of Secretary of State James Baker to Baku, despite the violation of human rights]: Only the extreme interest of the United States in the Caspian 'key' forced its administration to deviate from the general rule, because the Azerbaijani 'key' can open the doors to Central Asia.
- Fearing fundamentalist tendencies... which may develop into a wave, the US is trying to reorientate Azerbaijan and the Central Asian Turkic peoples towards Turkey and free these "independent" republics from the influence of primarily Iranian policy.
- [About the Kurdish issue in Turkey, Syria, Iraq, Iran]: The Kurdish issue, as one knows, is one of the most painful for these countries and can lead to disintegration. These may be examples of a chain-reaction of global political changes on the map of the East.
- If Iran and Turkey (in alliance with the United States) do not deal with spheres of influence in Central Asia in the near future, then China will come forward with claims to this richest space.
- In all likelihood, the US administration is not interested now in the final collapse of the Russian Federation, it is only interested in a weakened Russia.
- Only the Russian army can serve as a guarantor of "united and indivisible" Georgia. A small empire can only exist under the double-headed eagle wing.

- The "Chechen Syndrome" made allies of Russia and the Provisional Government of Georgia.
- The Abkhazians looked upon the "democratic" opposition's coming to power in Tbilisi with a certain hope and wished to see in the new Georgian leadership a positive force set on a course towards a peaceful settlement of political problems in Abkhazia and South Ossetia.

However, at the very end of the article, it was said about the possible military intervention of Georgia under the pretext of fighting the "Zviadists" in Abkhazia, with the alleged aim of "restoring the normal rhythm on the railway" for then, they argue, "the West will understand" the validity of this action.

And that is how it all happened. Less than six months later, on 14 August 1992, the war began. The State Council of Georgia invaded Abkhazia under the pretext of guarding the railway. The possible scenario of the outbreak of hostilities, expressed in the article, became reality.

On the eve of the war, a series of my publications came out. Many then called to mind the small note "Hour X" (newspaper *XXI century*, July 1992), written on 22 June 1992. It ended with the phrase "*We'll live until August...*". The editor of this youth newspaper, a well-known lawyer and participant in the war, Tamaz Ketsba, then asked: "How did you know that there would be a war in August ?!"

These articles and notes were repeatedly published, commented on in various publications (See the article by Yuri Anchabadze in the newspaper *Abkhazskij Vestnik*; in the journal *Civil Society., No. 12.* pp. 12-13, Sukhum, 2001; *Pages of the Georgian-Abkhazian information-war, Vol.2*, pp. 432-439, compiled by T. A. Achugba, D. T. Achugba. Sukhum, 2015.; V. Z. Chamagua *Essays on the History of Abkhazian Journalism: Epoch, Events, Personalities. (Second Half of the 19th-Beginning of the 21st Centuries)*, pp. 445-446, Sukhum, 2021. See also the site *apsnyteka.org* and others).

Such then, perhaps, is a brief history of those publications and significant events. I can hardly even believe that thirty years have passed...

31 July 2022, Sukhum

East and West: between Hammer and Anvil

*This article has been published in Russian on **29 February 1992**.*

Much of what I once had a chance to write about in subjective notes (*Republic of Abkhazia*, 5 October 1991) has become a reality today. In order better to understand the political processes taking place in Georgia and Abkhazia, it is necessary to go beyond these countries and realise that one is a part of rapid global upheavals. Only then will it become clear to us that both we and you are only hostages of a cruel geopolitical game.

The republics that were formed out of the ruins of the Soviet state, including the Russian Federation, are assigned only a secondary, and sometimes even a tertiary, role in this game. The main director of this world-spectacle is the United States, which is opposed by China and Islamic fundamentalists, led by Iran. Shi'ite Iran is essentially a theocratic state, while Turkey has long established a secular form of government, and Sunni Islam is separated from state-structures. It is necessary to note the following fundamental differences of an ideological nature. After Ayatollah Khomeini came to power, Iran led the pan-Islamic religious and political movement for the unification of Muslims around the world into a single Muslim polity. Turkey, on the other hand, stands for pan-Turkism and has now come close to the practical solution of this strategic doctrine, which preaches the unification under its rule of all Turkic-speaking peoples, who live mainly within the former USSR. The great Turkic state, according to the plans of the pan-Turkists, should be located over vast expanses from Turkey in the west to Siberia in the east and unite the following peoples and languages: Turkish, Chuvash, Azerbaijani, Turkmen, Salar, Tatar, Karachaj-Balkar, Bashkir, Kazakh, Kyrgyz, Karakalpak, Kumyk, Nogai, Karaite, Uzbek, Uighur, Yakut, Dolgan, Altai, Khakass, Tuva and others. As for the Iranian-speaking group, its area of distribution is significantly inferior to the Turks and covers the

321

following languages: Tajik, Kurdish, Farsi, Pashto, Ossetian, Tat, Talysh and others.

In addition, Turkey's claims to the Crimea, which Russia and the Ukraine, being on the verge of a collision, cannot divide in any way, could not be more clearly manifested. Meanwhile, several million Turks declared themselves Crimean Tatars and expressed a desire to return to their homeland. A detachment of warships from Turkey recently visited Sevastopol on a friendship-visit.

In actively pursuing its interests in the Transcaucasus and Central Asia, the United States actively uses, first of all, Turkey and Russia, and tries to counter pan-Islamism with pan-Turkism. This position is quite clearly manifested in relation to Azerbaijan, because of which there is a clear rivalry between Ankara and Tehran. The latter has already *de facto* annexed the Nakhichevan Republic. The Azerbaijani-Iranian border is also becoming more and more conditional. Apparently, in the near future, a small part of the territory of Azerbaijan on the shore of the Caspian Sea (Massali, Lankaran, Astar and Lerik regions), inhabited by Talysh, a small Iranian-speaking people, will go to Iran in the near future.

The energetic actions of the Iranians worry the United States and its ally Turkey, which hastened to recognise the independence of Turkic-speaking Azerbaijan and establish contacts with Mutalibov. At the same time, Iran is not averse to establishing relations with Mutalibov, but on a completely different basis – not recognising the independence of this Caucasian republic. The leadership of Iran considers it an integral part of itself (Northern Azerbaijan), along with South Azerbaijan (as part of Iran), which cannot but cause concern for the President of Azerbaijan.

A different position is taken by the spiritual leader of the Muslims of Transcaucasia and Azerbaijan, Sheikh-ul-Islam Pashazade (resident in Baku), who is closely associated with Islamic fundamentalists. Thus, Azerbaijan recently joined the Organisation of the Islamic Conference (OIC), and at a meeting in Dakar, as reported in the press, the Baku delegation was included in the Iranian one and expressed its solidarity with the Libyan leader Muammar Gaddafi. It is also known that Iranian helicopters and militants took part in the battles in Nagorno-Karabakh (*Megapolis-Express* No. 51 p. 13 1992), and Iranian Foreign Minister Velayati addressed the students of Baku University and called on them to "unite under a single green banner". Repeatedly, Minister Velayati proposed to Azerbaijan and Armenia to act as a mediator in the settlement of the conflict in Nagorno-Karabakh.

In Nagorno-Karabakh, it was not only the interests of the Muslim and Christian worlds, East and West, that clashed. Here, first of all, Iran and Turkey, pan-Islamists and pan-Turkists, clashed, because the strengthening in Karabakh of, say, Iranian influence will hinder Turkey's access to Azerbaijan, and most importantly, to Central Asia.

Armenia, apparently, is more satisfied with the Iranian position than the Turkish one, but the fact is that behind Ankara is the US administration, which has just opened its embassy in Erevan. Armenia simply cannot ignore such an important circumstance... On the other hand, Turkey openly supports Azerbaijan in the affairs of Nagorno-Karabakh.

The complexity of the situation, the pressure of fundamentalists and the fear of being swallowed up by Iran, as happened with South Azerbaijan, forced Mutalibov temporarily to join the CIS [Commonwealth of Independent States].

The ambiguous situation in Baku and the extremely important military-strategic position of this republic led to the US administration abruptly changing its tone and going for rapprochement with Azerbaijan, so as not to throw its desperate leadership into the arms of Tehran. This is evidenced primarily by the recent visit to Baku by Secretary of State J. Baker, which nevertheless took place despite the suppression of national minorities and the violation of human rights in this republic. Only the extreme interest of the United States in the Caspian "key" forced its administration to deviate from the general rule, because the Azerbaijani "key" can open the doors to Central Asia.

In order to stake out their presence (and therefore influence) in a number of former Soviet republics, the Americans, unlike Russia, hastily open their embassies. Thus, there is a rapid narrowing of Russian geopolitical interests in the Transcaucasus and Central Asia.

Fearing the strengthening of fundamentalist tendencies, which may grow into a wave, the US is trying to re-orientate Azerbaijan and the Central Asian Turkic peoples towards Turkey and free these "independent" republics from the influence primarily of Iranian policy. Pakistan is also active in the position of fundamentalism, recently proposing the creation of a confederation of 42 Islamic states with the participation of the former Soviet Central Asian republics. As one can see, a new redistribution of the world is taking place under the conditions of a limited world war.

A significant confrontation between Iran and Turkey and their plans in the Transcaucasus and Central Asia in the near future may lead these two countries to a military clash. In connection with the escalation of tensions, the United States urgently transferred $12 billion to its ally in Ankara. In the event of a war between these countries, Afghanistan, Pakistan, Iraq and others will be involved in the conflict, which will certainly once again raise the many millions of Kurds (who live in Turkey, Iraq, Syria, Iran) to fight for the creation of their own state of Kurdistan. The Kurdish issue, as we know, is one of the most painful for these countries and can lead to their collapse. These may be examples of a chain reaction of global political changes on the map of the East.

If Iran and Turkey, in alliance with the United States, do not deal with spheres of influence in Central Asia in the near future, then China will come forward with claims to this richest of spaces. The Caucasus will play an important role in the new alignment of forces. The commander-in-chief of the CIS forces, Shaposhnikov, having apparently lost

Azerbaijan, finally decided to stake on Christian Armenia and Georgia. Russia's position on Nagorno-Karabakh has also become more definite.

As a result of the military coup in Georgia and the coming to power of the Provisional Government, there was a sharp turn and rapprochement between the Georgian authorities and the army of the "non-existent state." The first duty was to cancel the decision of the Georgian Armed Forces on the occupational nature of the Russian army located on the territory of the republic. This, perhaps, was the main issue on which both sides immediately found a common language. As a sign of gratitude, the CIS army handed over part of its weapons to Georgia to strengthen the position of the new leadership, and to intimidate and suppress various national minorities.

Suffice it to recall here the recent transfer of three infantry fighting vehicles (light tanks) to Sukhum by the CIS air assault battalion for the needs of the National Guard of Georgia, about which Marshal Shaposhnikov knew nothing. The equipment was handed over by order of the command of the ZakVO (Transcaucasian Military District).

Standing behind the scenes of these events is prominent Soviet diplomat [sc. the Georgian Eduard Shevardnadze – Trans.] who, just like two hundred years ago, again chose the northern master, having firmly learnt the old truth. Only the Russian army can serve as a guarantor of "united and indivisible" Georgia. A 'small empire'[1] can exist only under the eagle wing of two-headed Russia.

Russia is quite satisfied with this situation, that is, "independent" Georgia still remains in the orbit of its military and geopolitical interests. Moreover, the strengthening of Russian positions in Georgia blocks movement in the North Caucasus, and primarily in Chechenia, isolating it from direct external contacts. All this is being done with the only hope of slowing down the further disintegration of the Russian Federation and cooling ardours in Tatarstan, Bashkiria, and so on.

In all likelihood, the US administration is not interested now in the final collapse of Russia – it is only interested in a weakened Russia. At the same time, the Russian Federation is a nuclear state, and the Americans cannot but reckon with its interests, just as they cannot but reckon with the interests of Turkey. However, the US apparently supports pan-Turkist plans only in the Azerbaijani-Central Asian direction. As for Armenia, Georgia and the North Caucasus, here they are interested in strengthening the common Christian zone of influence, the guarantor of which can only be Russia. But if "democratic" Russia does not cope with the processes, and national patriots come to power in it in the near future (remember the "Russian Legion" introduced into South Ossetia, which did not obey the Russian government and consisted of militants of patriotic parties and movements – tomorrow such legions maybe hundreds), then the US will probably play the Turkish card here.

Strange as it may seem, President Gamsakhurdia's policy objectively led to an "independent" Georgia within the composition of Turkey or Iran and strengthened pro-Turkish influence in the North Caucasus. One fine day, the ZakVO troops would leave not only Tbilisi, Kutaisi, but would also leave the Georgian-Turkish border, depriving it of protection. One can imagine what would follow these actions. Suffice it to recall the years 1917-1921. Where would Adzharia [in Georgian Ach'ara – Trans.] have ended up, which, by the way, under the agreement of 16 March 1921 between Turkey and the RSFSR, would have ended up with Russia, and not Georgia? What would happen to the areas densely populated by Azerbaijanis near Tbilisi, and what kind of ultimatum would be presented in connection with the Meskhetians?

The West solved this problem in a different way. Through Russia and Shevardnadze, with the sole purpose of preventing an excessive increase of the influence of its ally Turkey in Armenia, Georgia, on the Black Sea coast of the Caucasus.

The "Chechen Syndrome" made allies of Russia and the Provisional Government of Georgia, which jointly, as in the 19th century, began to suppress the liberation-movements in the North Caucasus and Abkhazia. We are once again caught between a rock and a hard place. Their plans for the Confederation of the Mountain Peoples of the Caucasus, the foundations of which were laid in Sukhum, are especially disturbing. The confederation, in turn, is presented to the West as an Islamic union of the highlanders, which has access to the Black Sea through Abkhazia.

In order to lock the key on Abkhazia, the new leadership of Georgia is trying to strengthen its presence here with the direct support of the CIS military machine. Just the other day, the Provisional Government of Georgia enlisted all-round economic assistance from Russia on preferential terms from the CIS, using the provided assistance as a means of economic and political pressure on the Republic of Abkhazia – on Abkhazia, which Russia has been pushing away from itself since 1989, and on the people, who since 1810 have found themselves under its "protection".

As is well-known, the Abkhazians looked upon the "democratic" opposition's coming to power in Tbilisi with a certain hope and wished to see in the new Georgian leadership a positive force set on a course towards a peaceful settlement of political problems in Abkhazia and South Ossetia.

However, the direction of recent events is beginning to convince us otherwise. Governments in Georgia come and go, but their course towards the Abkhazians and other peoples remains invariably imperial and traditionally harsh. The Georgian leadership prefers to speak with these peoples through force. This is also evidenced by the entry into the territory of Abkhazia of elements of the National Guard of Georgia under the pretext of fighting Gamsakhurdia's supporters. The organisers of, and participants in, rallies and strikes on the railroad and at Sukhum airport were persons of Georgian nationality who constantly stirred up political passions in the capital of Abkhazia and played the role of a "Trojan horse" for the introduction of Georgian military force into our republic. And only at the request of the Supreme Council of Abkhazia was the National Guard of Georgia withdrawn from our territory.

At present, it can be assumed that the Georgian government, in collusion with some supporters of President Gamsakhurdia, is inspiring various actions on the railways in Abkhazia, preventing the delivery of bread and food in order to cause a social explosion among the multinational population and use destabilisation as a pretext for repeated armed intervention, dissolution of the Supreme Council of Abkhazia (the legally elected leadership which they find objectionable), and the introduction of a state of emergency here by the forces of Georgia, as happened in October 1918 during the dissolution of the Abkhazian People's Council. Tbilisi still needs only an Abkhazian government that is obedient.

As for the economic boycott and the suffocation of our republic with famine, it frankly echoes Stalin's methods in the autumn of 1921, when the leader did his best to strangle independent Abkhazia financially and economically. It is sad that the new Georgian democrats chose this simple but dubious path and did not follow one of federative and confederate ties with Abkhazia. To what such a policy could lead, were it applied today, is not difficult to imagine ...

At the same time, the new government of Georgia, I think, is not indifferent to the light in which it can appear before the whole world, especially since the one who is primarily responsible for today's events in Georgia and Abkhazia is the comrade who will shorlty be celebrating the 20th anniversary of the resolution adopted in 1972 by the Central Committee of the CPSU on the Tbilisi City Party Committee...[2]

The Abkhazian people boycotted the election of President Gamsakhurdia and did not rally to his defence. But, apparently, it is very beneficial for the new authorities to locate the stronghold of the Zviadists precisely in Abkhazia and, under the pretext of fighting them with the alleged aim of restoring the normal rhythm on the railway (for in that case the West will understand such "noble" motives), to carry out in Abkhazia its own business infringing the political rights of our republic and its multinational people. But, paraphrasing a well-known saying, I want to remind you: Don't hammer, and you'll remain unhammered!

Endnotes

[1] In Andrej Sakharov's famous description of Soviet Georgia – Translator.

[2] Eduard Shevardnadze became First Secretary of the Communist Party of Georgia on 29 September 1972 – Translator.

On the 30th Anniversary of the Georgian-Abkhaz Conflict

Stephen Shenfield

*Specialist on politics and society in Russia and the post-Soviet region.
For several years he produced the Research and Analytical Supplement
to Johnson's Russia List. USA.*

I s it 30 years already? Perhaps it does not seem as long as that because the conflict is frozen, as though it persists in some eternal realm outside the flow of time. The positions of the two sides remain irreconcilable. The main change followed in the wake of the Russian-Georgian war of 2008, when Russia and a handful of its allies – Syria, Nicaragua, Venezuela, and the Pacific island of Nauru – recognised Abkhazia and South Ossetia as independent states. This change, however, made a diplomatic resolution of the conflict even more distant: now Abkhazia and South Ossetia are even less likely to surrender their statehood, while Tbilisi is as adamant as ever in asserting its territorial integrity within the borders of Soviet Georgia.

Of course, time flows on. There have been many important changes in the world situation in the course of these 30 years – changes that cannot but affect the Caucasus in general and Georgia and Abkhazia in particular. In no sphere is this truer than in that of climate change.

Global warming is very much in evidence both in Georgia and in Abkhazia. A farmer on Shiraki Plain in eastern Georgia (Kakheti) reports a temperature of 18 degrees Centigrade in January 2019 – a time of year when 'its normally below freezing'.[1] One result is more crop diseases. Meanwhile, the average year-round temperature in Abkhazia has increased by 1.8 degrees Centigrade in recent years.[2]

While both eastern Georgia and Abkhazia are getting warmer, precipitation has changed in opposite directions in the two regions. The farmer on Shiraki Plain notes a sharp decline in rainfall and consequently in the level of groundwater. 'There was no snow at all this year,' he reports. Drought, exacerbated by 'strong dry winds that erode fields and scatter seeds,' has put paid to the traditionally high soil fertility of the area.

In the Abkhazian capital of Sukhum, by contrast, the amount of rainfall has roughly doubled since the turn of the century, when it was already at a high level – a meter and a half (1,500 millimeters) per year. 'The water level is rising in rivers, eroding the banks and destroying the surrounding infrastructure... We see that long-term rainfall creates serious problems for agriculture [in Abkhazia].' Presumably the section of the Black Sea littoral to the south that belongs to western Georgia faces the same problem.

So eastern Georgia endures drought while Abkhazia and western Georgia face flooding -- consistent with the worldwide pattern of increasing spatial concentration of precipitation. Is there some way to channel excess rainfall from west to east, across the rugged terrain in between?

Much worse is certainly to come in the next 30 years. Expanding areas of the earth's surface will turn into uninhabitable deserts and swampland. Low-lying coastal cities will be inundated. Extreme weather events will become ever more extreme and ever more pervasive.

Given the rising threat of climate chaos, what sense does it make to continue to waste our attention on trivia like 'territorial integrity' and the location of state borders? Let's decide territorial disputes by arbitration – if the sides can agree on an arbiter – or by wrestling matches between champions, or just by tossing a coin. We might even dismantle existing states and set up a world administration. Then we can focus single-mindedly on the real problems facing our species and our planet.

Endnotes

[1]   See the website of the UN Environment Program: https://www.unep.org/news-and-stories/story/restoring-fortune-fields-georgia

[2]   Talk by Roman Dbar, director of the Institute of Ecology of Abkhazia, at the Discussion Club of the World Abaza Congress, February 28, 2020. See: https://abaza.org/en/global-climate-change-and-the-role-of-abkhazia-in-these-processes-were-discussed-at-the-wac-club

On Memory, Loss and Mental Divisions: Reflections on Abkhazia, 1992-2022

Thomas de Waal

Senior fellow with Carnegie Europe, specializing in Eastern Europe and the Caucasus region. United Kingdom.

What is Abkhazia? It's a basic question but one that eludes an answer.

I have written a lot about the politics and history of Abkhazia and Georgia and will not do so here. Reflecting on the sad anniversary of 30 years of conflict I want to note here how that politics has reduced the rich identity of Abkhazia to dry politicised husks of stereotype and slogan.

This was once a special cosmopolitan place of many nationalities and multiple identities. Conflict and historical trauma always lurked in the background, but had history taken a different turn—had Tengiz Kitovani perhaps not sent in his marauding army in August 1992—Abkhazia could have had quite a different story.

What do I mean? Go to Google Maps and you see a region where an unbroken black line, the border, defines it as a region of Georgia, whose towns are written in the Georgian script, as well as English. The people for whom Abkhazia is named, the Abkhazians, are erased. Go to the place itself, or look at Russian maps, and you see only the Abkhazian and Russian identity of the place – it is Georgians who are erased or forgotten. Neither of these stories is a true one. People from Abkhazia, who know its past, know better but are powerless to do anything about it.

Since the unlucky tragedy of August 1992 blighted Abkhazia and all its people—and continues to do so—these two conceptions of the place have diverged even further.

In the last 30 years, scholars and peace-practitioners have developed a whole new field of study, researching the role of memory and trauma in conflict, as phenomena that perpetuate conflict in people's minds and continue to sow division and injustice if not properly confronted. Marianne Hirsch gives the useful name "Postmemory"[1] to the phenomenon whereby unresolved trauma and painful memories are handed down to subsequent generations, who did not experience them directly. The concept of "transitional justice" has been developed to help societies come to terms with injustices in the past.

Abkhazia, a place of multiple and diverging memories, of buried trauma, of a depressingly long litany of grievances, badly needs the creative power of these ideas.

In October 1992 Abkhazia's collective memory was gravely wounded when Georgian paramilitary soldiers deliberately burned down the republic's archive and more than 90 percent of the precious records inside were destroyed. It is a story[2] to which I have a personal connection, as I came to know the archivist Nikolai Ioannidi, who rescued what he could of the archive, after it was burned, and preserved it. I counted him as a friend and a model of decency and professionalism in time of war.

Before that, at the height of the Stalinist era, another attempt was made to erase and falsify Abkhazian culture and history in the 1930s. This fear of genocide lies behind the Abkhazian national movement of the 1980s.

On the other side, there are still more than 200,000 Georgians who also feel written out of history. They were born in Abkhazia, were forced to flee in 1993 and are still unable to return. They must endure the unhealed trauma of still being separated from their homes and homeland.

Kamila Kuc's film *What We Shared*[3], released in 2021 is the best work I have seen or read on Abkhazia in recent years. Kuc spent many months in Abkhazia thanks to a residency at the Sklad arts-centre. As an artistic project she had the idea of asking local people to tell her dreams—intuitively sensing that there was another reality behind the one she saw every day and that dreams might reveal a different Abkhazia.

What Kuc did not anticipate was how memories of the war of 1992-3, of loss and tragedy, are still the main stuff of dreams in Abkhazia, and are the background to everything that happens there. The dreams people tell in her film are both non-fiction and fiction, told by both real people and actors. They ache with loss and nostalgia. Beautiful images of empty houses and of the sea (the medium of submerging and sublimation) permeate the film. It is a profound evocation of the beautiful, mysterious, often surreal place that is Abkhazia.

I know that, if Abkhazia has a decent future (and I still hope it eventually will find one), it will be as a place that respects all these stories and the people who tell them. What is for sure is that the political labels that currently apply are all inadequate and a different kind of thinking is required.

Endnotes

[1] https://cup.columbia.edu/author-interviews/hirsch-generation-postmemory

[2] https://www.opendemocracy.net/en/abkhazia_archive_4018jsp/

[3] https://www.kamilakuc.com/wws

Nestor Lakoba and the Menshevik

Timothy K. Blauvelt

Professor of Soviet and Post-Soviet Studies at Ilia State University in Tbilisi. Georgia.

The *N. A. Lakoba Papers* collection at the Hoover Institution – a remarkable set and immensely valuable set of documents not only for the study of Abkhazian history but for the history of the USSR as a whole – contains a long and thoughtful letter sent to Nestor Lakoba in June 1926 by a former Menshevik activist named Artem Fillipovich Pantsulaia.[1] A near contemporary of Lakoba born in the Senaki district of Georgia in 1895, Pantsulaia had been a member of the Russian Social Democratic Labor Party since 1912, and prior to the 1924 August Uprising had been the chairman of the underground Menshevik district committee (Obkom) in Abkhazia. According to a later indictment, despite entreaties from the Menshevik Central Committee to Pantsulaia opposed the formation of a military organization in Abkhazia because of the ethnic diversity there.[2] He was among those put on trial for participation in the "Parity Committee" during the uprising, but was released by a decree from the Supreme Court of Soviet Georgia in 1925. It is not clear what became of Pantsulaia, he does not seem to figure in the Troika protocols from the period of the Great Terror at the end of the 1930s, the fate that befell so many of the former Mensheviks who remained in Soviet Georgia.

In October of 1925, the congress of a working committee of representatives of the former Menshevik Party of Georgia was held in Tiflis in order to liquidated itself, following which a special department was created in the Central Committee of the Georgian Bolshevik party "for working among Mensheviks." In January 1926 the newspaper *Sovetskaia Abkhaziia* published a "conversation" with Pantsulaia about this commission, in which he (though it is difficult to discern here what are direct quotations from Pantsulaia and what is framing by the editors) emphasized the need, in the wake of the failed uprising, for the former Mensheviks and the population of Georgia to make their peace with the Bolshevik regime. At the same time, Pantsulaia threw some pointed barbs at the Bolsheviks: the Georgian Mensheviks had the "most experienced workers, peasants and intellectuals in the revolutionary struggle" he said, implying that the Georgian Bolsheviks were none of these. Therefore, according to Pantsulaia, making peace with the Mensheviks and involving them in "Soviet construction" would "make use of this valuable *aktiv* for the good of the toilers of Georgia and of the entire USSR." Criticism of the existing regime on the part of the Menshevik working committee, Pantsulaia asserted, "had greatly assisted the [Bolshevik] leadership center in giving due deserts to those provincial thugs (*derzhimordy*) who, wrapping themselves in the flag of the Communist Party, poisoned the life of the population with their satrap-like dealings," referring to local Bolshevik officials censured after the uprising. While observing that "it is no longer in the interests of the Georgian people to look to the West in expectation of salvation from occupation," and that "the Soviet Constitution sufficiently guarantees the rights of the nationalities," Pantsulaia saw Menshevik cooperation with the Bolshevik regime as a two-way street: the Bolshevik committee for working with the Mensheviks "will turn into a fiction and a self-delusion if they do not cease speaking with the former Mensheviks, who still feel themselves uneasy among the ranks of the builders of the Soviet state, in the language of the punitive organs." This phrase seems to have particularly enraged the Abkhazian Party Obkom Chairman Giorgi Sturua, who published his angry response in the same issue (both articles were framed under a single headline, "A Conversation with Com. Pantsulaia and Response of Com. G. Sturua"). Nevertheless, Panstulaia concluded his "conversation" by asserting that the process of "drawing together" (*sblizheni-ye*) was working out better in Abkhazia then elsewhere in Georgia, as here there were comparatively more Mensheviks transitioning to the Bolshevik party. What was more, he hinted, the Mensheviks in Abkhazia were less radical than others: "I can bravely and with pleasure declare that since I returned to Abkhazia after the August events I have not met a single madman who would retain his old views, I am deeply convinced that there is not a single well-known Menshevik in Abkhazia who would dream of recreating the Menshevik organization." This was facilitated in part, Patsulaia stated, "because all the responsible local comrades attempt to implement cooperation with the former Mensheviks in the same spirit as in Georgia." Pantsulaia was particularly positive towards the Bolshevik leadership in Abkhazia: "I was underground in Abkhazia for about three years [prior to the 1924 uprising], and I will admit that I had not been aware of all of the achievements of Soviet power; I state without exaggeration that it has brought much that is good to Abkhazia, and I will be genuinely glad if I will be able to do my bit for the construction of a new life for the toiling masses of Abkhazia."

It was in the wake of this public discussion that Pantsulaia addressed his letter to Nestor Lakoba, dated June 10, 1926, and marked "between us." Writing in Russian and using the formal "*vy*", Pantsulaia framed the correspondence as the continuation of their last conversation in which "my esteemed Nestor Apollonovich" had brought up "the most burning question of our day," the national question in Abkhazia, "or more simply put, the interrelations between the Abkhaz and Georgians," and during which neither had been able to fully express their thoughts. Since "a conversation would take more time than reading a letter," Pantsulaia decided to lay out his views in written form.

Pantsulaia began with this with a discussion of the dominating influence of Russia in the region, as a "young, large nation" inevitably expanding and representing to "small nations" the dual dangers of either physical destruction or "spiritual degradation and assimilation." Had Europe not intervened, Pantsulaia held, "there would now be no Persia, no Turkey, or even a number of Balkan states, there would be one united, undivided Mother Russia 'from the north pole to the Arabian sea' – no other nation can so threaten small nations in our region as Russia." In the case of Abkhazia, in Pantsulaia's view, "Russia came here as a 'liberator' from the Turkish yoke, and nearly 'liberated' Abkhazia from the Abkhaz; until the arrival of Russia there was not, and could not be, Mukhajirs," referring to the mass deportations of Abkhaz in the 1860s and 1870s.

Georgia, in Pantsulaia's view, as a small "but not young" nations, was "nearly wiped from the face of the earth, but having avoided physical destruction it faced the danger of spiritual degradation." It was only Georgia's "own rich literature and culture of the past" that prevented Russia from assimilating it ("from imposing upon it 'the Russian soul'"), "at least to that measure which it was able to do so in Abkhazia." Yet Pantsulaia felt that Georgia had become so weak and degraded "as a nation and as a social organism" that it could not itself present a threat to smaller nations: "Georgia cannot 'swallow' anybody, it is weak and continues to restore itself, to gather its discarded strengths and transform itself into a healthy organism." Yet Russia obstructed this, as Georgia's restoration "is not beneficial to Russia itself, since Georgia is the most imperative nation in the Caucasus for it." If not forever, Pantsulaia thought, then "at least for a very long time Georgia will be in the defensive role (as will be the other nations of the Caucasus), while Russia will be in the offensive one."

Pantulaia then moved on to speak about "policy in Abkhazia," by which he seems to refer to Georgian policy towards Abkhazia. He became by saying that he "had to argue a lot about this with my colleagues [presumably his fellow Mensheviks], who finally agreed with me in Metekhi Prison [presumably while incarcerated following the failed 1924 uprising]". "Many of them then and probably still now," he added, "are certain that ministerial posts still await them." The correct policy for Georgia, in his view, was at the same time the healthy policy towards Abkhazia. "Sometimes medics give diagnoses, and if I may, as a 'medic in politics,' go a little further," he elaborated, "I am deeply convinced that the Abkhaz themselves, as soon as their cultural level increases, will support without any kind of dictate from Tiflis, truly, and better than any true believing' Georgian, that very same Abkhazian policy in Abkhazia." But what does this policy comprise? Pantsulaia continues rather obliquely: "Many political officials, since they want to 'create' policy around Abkhazia," should familiarize themselves more closely and dispassionately with Abkhazia and its particular history of interrelations with Georgia from the distant past. "It seems to me that we – socialists of one sort or another – turned out to be poor inheritors of our ancestors who enabled peaceful co-habitation and mutual coexistence of the Georgians and the Abkhaz." At the same time, Pantsulaia seemed critical of what he described as the Menshevik policy towards Abkhazia, presumably referring to that of the Georgian Democratic Republic in 1918-1921: "When I glace backwards at the policy of the Mensheviks in Abkhazia, I feel shame for my comrades and many others; here we encounter empty philosophizing." The Georgian Menshevik policy, he seems to admit, lacked focus and specific goals: "Those who desire to serve the nation should work out ahead of time, created a comprehensive and clear program that will not need to be altered, say, on a yearly basis; they must have a range of vision, a sweep, they must clarify ahead of time where the paths of positive development lead for the nation that they serve, understanding who is its friend and enemy." The Georgian and Abkhazian peoples were always linked, "and there is no reason to think that this will not be the case in the future." Those Georgians who are particularly concerned for Georgian interests in Abkhazia, he asserted, "should yearn to improve the cultural and economic wellbeing of the Abkhaz, directly in the Abkhazian spirit." To the great misfortune of both the Georgians and the Abkhaz, Pantsulaia surmised without offering specific details, "many political officials approach this question armed with bile and demagoguery, attempting to capitalize on this accursed issue for political gain, it is such a pity." Later in his letter Pantsulaia returned to the topic of the earlier Menshevik approach to Abkhazia: "I don't know what the former Mensheviks think 'when they're all alone,' but I know that genuine Mensheviks, mainly during the recent 'underground' period, looked at Abkhazian policy in the same way as I do, as I've briefly laid out here; I am also aware that almost all of the last Menshevik underground Central Committee (up to 1924) spoke negatively of the policy of the Mensheviks in Abkhazia in the past."

In the next section of his letter, Pantsulaia addressed an issue that had been a main focus of politics in Abkhazia over the previous year, that of official languages.[3] Under pressure from different quarters either to fully implement the local indigenization element of Soviet nationality policy making Abkhazian a genuinely administrative language on the one hand or to accept greater use of the Georgian language, the Abkhazian leadership under Lakoba maintained a cautious middle road, preferring Russian as a functional *lingua franca*. Pantsulaia instead urged Lakoba to give priority to developing the Abkhazian language: "In so far as they (or the Abkhaz themselves) want to turn the Abkhaz into a healthy nation, all measures should be taken to make Abkhazian into the state language; before all else the Abkhaz themselves must treat their language and their newly born literature with respect – how else can they demand that others learn the Abkhazian language?" He was directly critical of the *de facto* preference for Russian in Abkhazia, holding that "the assertion that Russian should be preferred over others because it is the language of the October Revolution, the language of Lenin, has nothing in common with the real framing of the issue, and only naïve idealists could reason in this way." Russian had been imposed on the region, and as he had argued earlier, carried the risk of assimilation and degradation. Caution was required in this issue, Pantsulaia warned Lakoba, but also insisted that "one should not refuse to be decisive: the logic of things demands the expunging of Russian from here, but how?" During the three-year existence of the Georgian Democratic Republic they "were not able to nationalize even all the institutions in their own capital." In Abkhazia there were even more obstacles, though he added obliquely that these "cannot be spoken of without accusing somebody or other (whoever) of the fact that something remarkable is happening here."

In the culminating passages of his letter, Pantsulaia conveyed both his praise for Lakoba and his apparent concerns over the course of recent events: "The conclusion from all of the above is such that in principle I support without hesitation the policy that you have implemented, as I am sure that one way or another it leads – or will lead – to a final drawing together of Georgians and Abkhaz." This did not mean that Pantsulaia overlooked Lakoba's mistakes, "and there are plenty of them," although "many errors have been attributed to you while others might be guilty." "I say openly to all that you are the first among the Abkhaz who is able to govern the country and feel yourself strong," Pantsulaia continued, "may god allow that you remain in power in Abkhazia despite all of the obstacles that they throw at you; I am certain that you will successfully be the first among those Abkhaz who will genuinely lead the Abkhaz on the historically correct path." Yet at the same time, Pantsulaia warned Lakoba about being too trusting of those sycophantic people around him, "those who are not particularly able or who are able only 'to do good things' for themselves." In that regard, "no few such officials have gathered around you who will tell you 'Yes you are right, it is so!'" Pantsulaia cautioned. "You might not believe me," Pantsulaia surmised, "maybe they are all good and I am over salting (in particular regarding the so called non-party individuals);[4] for many reasons I hate them with all my soul. So yes, therefore maybe I am over salting."

Pantsulaia ended his letter by asking for Lakoba's forgiveness "if this strange continuation of our discussion will seem somewhat audacious," yet insisted that he offered "much honesty and little falsehood." "I hope that you will sort everything out and not be lazy to read to the end," Pantsulaia concluded, and that "you will accept all of my honesty as genuine respect for you; I am certain that I may speak with you openly and all that I have said will remain 'between us,' otherwise 'it is not worth the headache,' as the Georgian saying goes.[5] With honest comradely greeting."

Although this letter clearly contains an interesting and unique perspective, to my knowledge it has never been cited before; historians using the Lakoba Papers collection have been at a loss for what to make of it. In part this is because Pantsulaia remains an historically obscure figure, though judging by the *Sovetskaia Abkhaziia* public dialogue with the Abkhazian Obkom Chairman Giorgi Sturua cited above he was well enough known in Soviet Abkhazia at the time to require little introduction. The letter also represents only one episode of an ongoing dialogue: we do not know more than Pantsulaia tells us about the preceding conversation, and we do not know Lakoba's response. We know only that Lakoba deemed the letter worthy of preservation. We can also say that it represents a particular voice of a former Menshevik who had been directly involved in Abkhazia and his views (whether or not, as he claims, other former Mensheviks came to share his perspectives) about Abkhazia's recent past and about the already thorny question of the relationship between Georgians and Abkhaz and about the burning issues of the day, especially that of language and, although phrased in aa seemingly purposely opaque manner, about the Lakoba's controversial patronage entourage. These are clearly issues that would continue to reverberate throughout the Soviet period and beyond. The clear respect and esteem towards Lakoba that Pantsulaia conveys in his letter is also striking, given the more general levels of enmity during this period between the Georgian Mensheviks and the Bolsheviks, which was only exacerbated by the 1924 August Uprising. The apparent mutual respect and civil discourse between the two is even more remarkable considering that Pantsulaia had been "underground" in Abkhazia during the period between the end of the Georgian Democratic Republic in early 1921 and the 1924 uprising. We are left only to surmise if there had been interaction between them during that time. In any case, I have attempted in this brief essay to lay out the themes that Pantsulaia expressed in his missive to Lakoba, and to the degree possible to place them in the context of the place and the period.

Endnotes

[1] N.A. Lakoba Papers, The Hoover Institution, box 1, file 48, parts 1 and 2. The pagination in the original document is inconsistent, so I have not indicated specific page numbers here.

[2] *Sakme sakartvelos antisabchota partiebis paritetuli komitetis shesakheb (sabralmdeglo daskna)* (Tiflis: iustitsiis saxhalkho komisariatis gamotsema, 1925), pp. 106-108, 118.

[3] See the discussion about the language question in Abkhazia in the summer of 1925 in Timothy Blauvelt, "From Words to Action! Nationality Policy in Soviet Abkhazia, 1921-38," in Stephen Jones, ed. *The Making of Modern Georgia, 1918-2012* (Routledge, 2014), pp. 232-62.

[4] This seems to me likely an oblique reference to the *Abgostorg* chairman Ismet Kady-Zade, a businessman and relative of Lakoba's wife who was at the center of several of the political scandals of the period. See Timothy Blauvelt, *Clientelism and Nationality in an Early Soviet Fiefdom: The Trials of Nestor Lakoba* (Routledge, 2021), pp. 64-65, 126-127.

[5] In Georgian, "If the head doesn't hurt, why make it hurt".

Understanding *"unknown" tragedies*

Ucha Nanuashvili

Founder, Democracy Research Institute, Founder, Human Rights Center. Former Public Defender (Ombudsman) of Georgia (2012-2017).

3 0 years have passed since the beginning of an armed conflict in Abkhazia. As a result of the hostilities, both sides suffered irreparable losses.

Many agree today that it is futile to talk about conflict transformation or reconciliation without a critical review of the past. The future of our society and state depends a lot on how much we refuse to embellish history and admit our mistakes and crimes.

The war in Abkhazia was preceded by the gravest events, which have not been properly realised, investigated or assessed in the context of the conflict so far: The Tbilisi civil war, violent dispersal and killings of peaceful demonstrators, executions in Samegrelo [aka Mingrelia in western Georgia – Ed.], the war in South Ossetia. The Russian influence on the Georgian government that came to power as a result of the military coup in January 1992 significantly damaged the interests of the State. Military forces of the Illegitimate State Council started an operation in Abkhazia on 14 August.

Nevertheless, none of these heinous crimes have been investigated and no one has been held accountable.

It is impossible to resolve a conflict and start the process of reconciliation when the truth has not been properly assessed or established. One of the first steps towards reconciliation should be to start the process of joint-search for the truth by the parties to the conflict. To date, no government has had the will or power to evaluate properly or investigate these processes, which makes it impossible to achieve reconciliation.

The fact is that for years the political élite avoided (and is avoiding) even the mere talking about such uncomfortable topics – the concept of critically dealing with the past has not become popular (let alone a need) for the general public of Georgia.

Today we, Georgians, Abkhazians and Ossetians know much more about the developments in distant countries than about each other, even about the tragedies of our recent past. It has been almost three decades since the atrocities of war, and we need to realise the significance of those days. It is true that nothing can bring back the Georgian, Ossetian or Abkhazian lives lost during the war; however, we have to realise our mistakes and crimes and, where possible, remedy them.

The tragedies of Dzari and Eredvi are one of the most painful pages of the Georgian-Ossetian conflict for Ossetians, and the Lata tragedy is the hardest episode of the Georgian-Abkhazian conflict for Abkhazians.

The tragedy that took place on 14 December 1992, near the village of Lata in the Gulripshi District of Abkhazia, was one of the most difficult days for Abkhazians. A shell fired from the territories controlled by the military units of the State Council of Georgia shot down a helicopter flying from Tkvarcheli, killing 87 people on board, including 35 children and 8 pregnant women.

Other similar stories can also be recalled from the recent past.

In March 1991, in response to the burning of 4 Georgians in a car by ethnic Ossetians, members of the then Georgian armed forces buried 12 ethnic Ossetians alive. On 18 March, people traveling from Dmenisi, Khelchua and Zemo Kere to Tskhinvali by Ural vehicle were dropped off near the village of Eredvi. There were 25 people in the vehicle. Women and children were released, while 12 men went missing that day. Their remains were found only in 1993, with the help of the Gori Prosecutor's Office.

The murder of 4 Georgians on Mount Tsveriakho shortly before this event as well as the Eredvi tragedy remain uninvestigated and black spots in the history of the Georgian-Ossetian conflict.

On 20 May 1992, a convoy of vehicles driving from Tskhinvali to North Ossetia was attacked and fired on by unidentified individuals in the village of Dzari in the Java District, leaving 32 people dead, including children; 16 others were injured.

Similar tragedies can be recalled by both sides, although people mostly think about their own tragedy and pain. The war created mistrust and alienation, as a result of which, we do not know much about the pain of the "other side". We have forgotten how to share grief and mourn together. Many similar stories have been erased from our memory.

The tragedies of Sokhumi and Tskhinvali, the numerous victims and displacement of thousands of people over the decades are issues that we all remember, or should remember. Neither have these tragedies been investigated. We people always mourn only our own tragedies, feel only our own pain, but we cannot share the tragedy of others, of the other side.

The tragedies of Lata, Dzari, Eredvi and others are not the tragedies of only Abkhazians or Ossetians, they are the tragedies of everyone, the tragedies of the people, the country, all Georgia.

It is tragic what happened, but no less terrible is the fact that we have put up with these tragedies that have not been investigated so far and the perpetrators have not been punished. Over the years, governments have changed, with no desire to investigate these crimes. Nor did anyone do anything to inform all Georgian citizens of these tragedies.

Furthermore, we have never tried to commemorate the victims of these tragedies or to offer sympathy to their families. The authorities have not indicated any desire personally to express their condolences to the families of the victims. And this has been so for years, while the pain has not gone away.

Offering sincere sympathy over these tragedies, properly studying, investigating and evaluating these cases would be important steps towards restoring trust.

An investigation of the above-mentioned cases is at least necessary in order to prevent a recurrence of such crimes in the future. Understanding the evil of the past must unite people for changing the present situation.

Until then, it is desirable to take the following steps. The authorities should:

- state their official position on these tragedies and find some form to establish the facts and complete the investigation that began years ago;
- ensure that these facts are investigated in order to identify and punish all the perpetrators involved;
- inform the citizens of Georgia about these tragedies, as they have the right to know what happened years ago;
- declare a day of remembrance to honour all those who died on both sides of the Georgian-Ossetian and Georgian-Abkhazian conflicts.

A long time has passed since the physical violence and war, though there remain conflicts in the hearts of people. Hate and anger have been controlling people's lives for a long time. These emotions paralyse people and turn them into hostages of hatred.

When people are overwhelmed with anger and hatred, it is impossible for them reasonably to evaluate events and look ahead. Sharing human tragedies after so many years of armed conflict may be a step towards breaking the negative circle so that emotions and hatred no longer dominate people's lives. We must learn how to get out of this situation and understand and feel each other's pain and tragedy.

It is necessary to learn from the past mistakes. It is about taking responsibility for one's own role in the conflict, a conflict in which everyone suffered the heaviest loss, a conflict that still continues, and a conflict that left thousands of victims.

The memory of innocent people obliges us to take steps to find out the truth. Respecting the innocent victims will help us in rebuilding trust.

A Traveller's Notes

Uwe Klussmann

Former editor at 'Der Spiegel' -from 1990 to 2021, and from 1999 to 2009- as a correspondent in Moscow. He has been a freelance author since January 2022.

In August 1992 I was on vacation in Yalta, Crimea. I had only visited Abkhazia once before, for one day, in September 1984. At that time the region was still an autonomous republic within the Georgian Soviet Socialist Republic. In the resort town of Gagra, locals and tourists crowded the streets and beaches.

Eight years later, in August 1992, the picture was completely different. The Russian television which was on in the hotel in Yalta showed fighters armed with Kalashnikovs and civilians fleeing the war. In 1992, my knowledge of Russian wasn't good enough to understand the news. What's more, I didn't understand the conflict either. Hadn't Georgians, Abkhazians, and many members of other nationalities lived together peacefully when I visited just a few years earlier?

The armed conflict in Abkhazia initially remained a mystery to me, even after I had learned Russian and started working in the Moscow office of *Der Spiegel* at the beginning of January 1999. Some Moscow newspapers gave me the impression that it was a region of Georgia there, a part of the Georgian population, which had a problem with their central government.

In the summer of 2003, I decided to visit Abkhazia. I wanted to talk to residents of the country, but also to members of the Abkhazian political leadership. This was possible with the help of the Abkhazian diaspora in Moscow. They put me in touch with an Abkhazian, the Deputy Prime Minister, who met me in Sochi and took me across the Russian border to Abkhazia.

Almost nothing was the same as it had been in 1984. In the once overcrowded Gagra, there were only a few walkers and holidaymakers to be seen. The power went out again and again for hours, with the result that there was no hot lunch to be had in the restaurant. The people also lived without mobile means of communications and petrol-stations; rusty *zhigulis* [the standard family-car from Soviet times] ruled the streets.

Gagra showed hardly any traces of the war, unlike in Gudauta or Sukhum. There the consequences of the war could not be overlooked in entire districts. Blocks of houses with facades riddled with bullet-holes, entire blocks of flats burned out. The mental wounds inflicted by the war of 1992/93 were also noticeable. I saw in deep mourning women who, ten years after the war, still wore black and regularly laid flowers at the memorial for their husbands and sons who had died in the war. As to how unforgiving the view of Georgia was, this I learned from the response given by a female market-trader in Sukhum in answer to my questions as to whether she could imagine Abkhazia as again being an autonomous region within Georgia: "Not even our dogs would survive that!"

I learned about not only the chasms but also the nuances and subtleties of life in this war from a copy of a book by the Abkhazian writer Vitali Sharia entitled 'The tank is no more terrible than the dagger'. I bought it, slightly wrinkled by the sun at a kiosk in the centre of Sukhum. After reading this, a collection of documentary-based short stories, I understood why, after the 1993 war, Abkhazia is no longer seen as being a part of Georgia by the majority of its remaining residents.

I experienced the other side of that 'huge human tragedy', as Vitaly Sharia calls the exodus of the majority of Georgian residents of Abkhazia, in Moscow. In 2005, at a memorial service for a long-time resident of Abkhazia, I met a Georgian from the Abkhazian town of Ochamchira. As a result of the war he had lost his house there together with the homeland he felt Abkhazia to be. He recalled the peaceful coexistence of Georgians and Abkhazians, without resentment. But this world had been irrevocably destroyed by the war.

The Abkhazians accepted poverty rather than submit to the superior power of Georgia. The fact that Russia finally recognised it as an independent state in August 2008 was the result of the beginning of a new division of the world, which overarched the Abkhazian-Georgian conflict. As a result, the plans of some Western diplomats for an Abkhazian statehood within the state of Georgia finally came to nothing.

The first years after recognition by Moscow brought an upswing that was hardly imaginable in 2003. Roads and schools, hospitals and barracks had been renovated, ambulances and fire engines, police-cars and the cars of the country's political élite have been replaced with new models. However, there could only be rudimentary talk of any comprehensive upswing in the economy, in manufacturing industry and modern agriculture. And after the events in Crimea in 2014, the sanctions against Russia are also leaving their mark in Abkhazia.

Economic stagnation was felt in the years 2017 to 2018; construction-projects, even for small hotels, were frozen. Not all of the problems turned out to be the result of Moscow's cuts in funds for Abkhazia's budget, which is largely subsidised by its northern neighbour. Corruption was a frequent topic in the outspoken Abkhazian press and civil society. Unforgotten is the statement by the then President of Abkhazia Raul Khadzhimba, published by an Abkhazian weekly newspaper, to officials at the Ministry of the Interior, explaining how cars stolen in Russia were able to find Abkhazian licence-plates so quickly.

Other problems in the small country are less material than mental. The number of traffic-fatalities, according to Khadzhimba in a speech in 2017, is now a 'demographic threat'. At least the dramatic problems were not concealed. Young girls organising flash-mobs against young speedsters showed that civil society is alive in Abkhazia.

In September 2018 I visited Abkhazia for the last time. The country celebrated the 25th anniversary of the end of the war. The military parade could not hide the script of the Moscow masters. "Who else could we have learned it from?" asked an Abkhazian politician whom I know to have an independent view of the world. More interesting than the parade were the folk-festivals and concerts in the Abkhazian capital, which gave an impression of the country's inhabitants' attitude to life. The Abkhazian flag, perceived by many in Georgia only as the banner of a handful of 'separatists', was held in many hands. Pupils slung them over their shoulders, young and old adults carried them as a matter of course when strolling through the city, without any orders being issued to do so. In many conversations, I was also able to convince myself that most Abkhazians, regardless of their often critical attitude towards the government, see themselves as part of a small nation.

The opportunity for the Abkhazians to get their views and social attitudes heard in the West is even smaller today than it was before 24 February 2022. In the new, bitter East-West conflict, Abkhazia in all its historical, cultural, linguistic and political particularities is hardly being noticed in Europe. It is worth listening to the nuances of this small country, which is more than just an appendage to a northern neighbour without which it cannot exist.

What is little known in the West is that the will for Abkhazian self-determination is also expressed in conscious dissent with regard to Russian imperial thinking. The border between Abkhazia and Russia is still not contractually determined; the Abkhazians insist on the village of Aibga that the Russians consider part of their territory as belonging to them. Abkhazian civil society continues to hold discussions more freely and with fewer restrictions than Russia's. And the nostalgia for Stalin that has become fashionable in parts of Russian society is met with a cool rejection in Abkhazia. The Stalin memorabilia-trade is not forbidden in Abkhazia – it simply doesn't take place, not even at the Stalin *dachas* [country-residences] that have been turned into museums. The reaction of Abkhazian society to the suggestion of the eloquent Great-Russian writer Zakhar Prilepin that Abkhazia should join the Russian Federation fits the pattern – protest against this presumption ranged from the social networks to the Abkhazian Foreign Ministry, which issued a sharply-worded statement.

It is often through nuances that a visitor to Abkhazia comes to appreciate that a very special people is attempting to work out a way of its own there.

Prospects for International Recognition of Abkhazia

Ümit Dinçer

*President of the Federation of the Caucasian Associations (KAFFED).
Turkey.*

Yasemin Oral

*Vice President of the Federation of the Caucasian Associations
(KAFFED).*

Introduction

Although the Republic of Abkhazia declared *sovereignty* as early as 1992 (the Declaration of Independence following in 1999) and was recognised as an independent state by several UN member states including Russia, Venezuela, Nicaragua, and Nauru following the August war of 2008, it has lacked wider international recognition since then. As George Hewitt (2012) put it, the partial recognition initially brought about expectations among the peoples of Abkhazia that the path was open for Abkhazia to proceed to full membership of the international community. However, the subsequent developments have demonstrated that the partial recognition has created rather new challenges for Abkhazia.

Ambivalent Politics of State Recognition

The literature in international law is dominated by two competing theories of state-recognition – the constitutive and declaratory theories. According to the constitutive theory, "an entity becomes a state only when it is recognized as such" (Ryangaert & Sobrie, 2011: 469). In this respect, recognition becomes an essential requirement for statehood. Yet, the constitutive position has attracted severe criticisms on the grounds that statehood is a relative and subjective, rather than an absolute and objective, concept due to a number of significant questions such as how many recognizing states are needed for statehood and whether the decision should be based on facts, norms, political considerations or a combination (Ryangaert & Sobrie, 2011: 469). More specifically, the constitutive approach "lends itself to strategic manipulation by powerful states that have a vested interest in recognizing or not recognizing a political entity" (Olaizola, 2012: 64).

According to declaratory theory, on the other hand, "recognition of a new State is a political act, which is, in principle, independent of the existence of the new State as a subject of international law". (Crawford, 2006: 22) Statehood is fully determined by a set of factual conditions – a permanent population, a fixed territory, an effective government able to control its territory, and the ability to enter into relations with other states on its own account (Brierly, 1955). Recognition is, in this theory, nothing more than an official confirmation of a factual situation (Ryangaert & Sobrie, 2011: 470). That is to say, the international community does not actually grant the status of statehood but merely acknowledges what is already a fact. However, the declaratory position is not devoid of issues, either. Regarding the declaratory position, it is often pointed out that "non-recognized entities have no international legal personality and thus cannot be considered to be a state, even if they meet all the requirements outlined above" (Ryangaert & Sobrie, 2011: 470).

In addition, the aftermath of the dissolution of Yugoslavia brought about some fundamental challenges. During this process, different from the traditional legal framework, the European Community made reference to (1) the right to self-determination which was traditionally confined to the colonial contexts, (2) the democratic commitment, and (3) commitment to disarmament and nuclear non-proliferation as important principles in the recognition of new states (Ryangaert & Sobrie, 2011: 475). However, the rules were not applied in a very consistent manner (Ryangaert & Sobrie, 2011: 476). Most of the recognized republics did not fully meet the criteria – neither the traditional ones nor the new ones. For instance, neither Croatia nor Bosnia-Herzegovina had a stable government able to control their territories at that time. Furthermore, such countries as the USA and Australia did not attempt to justify their decisions of formally recognizing them in reference to these criteria. When Kosovo declared its independence from Serbia in 2008, the international reactions to it further complicated the situation. There was almost no reference to international law. States that recognized Kosovo have almost invariably justified their decision to grant recognition – if such a justification was given at all – by referring to political considerations, most notably the need for stability, peace, and security in the region, and the positive effect recognition would have on these parameters (Ryangaert & Sobrie, 2011: 480).

This paper does not intend to recount the well-known parallels between those cases but the Ahtisaari report deserves a brief reference as the arguments mentioned in the report well apply to the case of Abkhazia. On the contrary, several recognizing states stressed the 'unique' character of Kosovo in an attempt to refute the claims that a precedent was being set. A few months later, following the August war, the recognition of Abkhazia and South Ossetia added to the uneasy state of affairs. Condoleezza Rice, the US Secretary of State at the time, claimed that situations in the Balkans and Caucasus have nothing in common: "I don't want to try to judge the motives, but we've been very clear that Kosovo is *sui generis* (unique) and that is because of the special circumstances out of which the breakup of Yugoslavia came". Her Russian counterpart, Sergei Lavrov, justifying the recognition of South Ossetia and Abkhazia as independent states, did not refer to the Kosovo precedent either. However, Lavrov, like Rice, claimed that "the recognition by Russia of Abkhazia and South Ossetia as independent states does not set a precedent for other post-Soviet break-away regions. There can be no parallels here." (Müllerson, 2009:4).

On the whole, the recognition of Kosovo by several NATO and EU states and the subsequent partial recognition of Abkhazia and South Ossetia have clearly shown that the practice of state recognition is characterised by a declining role of international law and an increasing role of political convenience and interests. Despite all the strong evidence and justifications regarding the 'double standards' in this regard, there is almost no exception to the highly selective and politicized practice of state recognition worldwide. International law has clearly been demoted to a position where it is primarily used to support decisions made on the basis of purely political considerations and vested interests rather than providing a normative practice of recognition based on justice-based criteria to which prospective states would be subjected, which resulted in inconsistency, arbitrariness and uncertainty and lack of confidence in international law.

Political Placebo Effect of Partial Recognition

As Kolstø (2020a) states, all the *de facto* states that have failed to win international recognition or are recognized by only a handful of other states need a strong protector or a 'patron state' that sustains the *de facto* one financially and gives it military security. In the case of Abkhazia, this patron state has been the Russian Federation. Abkhazia is dependent on Russia militarily, politically and economically. About 90% of the inhabitants of Abkhazia hold Russian citizenship since the passport of the Russian Federation not only enables them to travel out of Abkhazia but also gives entitlement to unemployment benefits and pension payments from the Russian state budget (Kopecek et al., 2016). Almost all political actors in Abkhazia have consistently favoured maintaining strong relations with Russia, since any weakening of patron support would put the very survival of the statelet in question (Kolstø, 2020b).

Despite the understandable nature of the patron-client relationship between Russia and Abkhazia given the circumstances, the influence of Russia over Abkhazia has been reinforced by the double standards in the stance of the EU and the USA to the issue of international recognition and their subsequent lack of willingness to cooperate with Abkhazia. Their stance has naturally limited the capabilities of Abkhazia to establish relations with the international community and thus served to buttress its increasing dependency on Russia and gradual isolation from the international system. This high degree of isolation has resulted in Abkhazia in "a significant reduction of income from foreign investments, limitation of the possibility to export goods to foreign markets, a low rate of development aid and zero loans from international financial institutions" (Kopecek et al., 2016). Furthermore, as Kopecek et al. (2016) puts forward, Abkhazia represents the most likely case of successful democratisation-for-recognition strategy among the other *de facto* states. Their analysis explicitly shows that "the only *de facto* state which little by little, but constantly, democratises is ultimately Abkhazia". Yet, this has not brought about even a slightest change in the position of the West toward Abkhazia either.

On the whole, the 14-years-long partial recognition has brought about an increasing dependency on Russia and an attendant gradual isolation from the international system, taking Abkhazia even further away from international recognition than 2008. It is still considered to be a *de facto* state since it lacks international recognition although it has performed sovereign legislative, executive and judicial power over its territories. Currently, it would not be an exaggeration to say that the partial recognition of Abkhazia in 2008 has functioned like a *placebo* stimulating hopes and expectations for full membership of the international community; however, the reality seems to confirm the argument that "so as long as *de facto* states remain as *de facto* entities, they move away from international recognition" (Meydan, 2018:6).

The Iron Will

The current state of affairs does not obviously allow us to expect the international recognition of Abkhazia in the foreseeable near future. Yet, prospects for Abkhazia to transform into an internationally recognized state reside in the never-broken will of the Abkhazian people to safeguard and maintain the independence of Abkhazia. This strong will can also easily be tracked in the 'patron-client' relationship between Russia and Abkhazia.

As Kolstø (2020a) demonstrates very clearly, Abkhazia has not always been an obedient client to Russia, nor has it shied away from pursuing and maintaining its own interests despite the asymmetrical power relations between them. This was the case when the initial bilateral agreement "On Friendship, Cooperation, and Mutual Support" was sought by Russia to be replaced by a new one in 2014 and Abkhazia successfully negotiated the terms in a way that "the new treaty "On Alliance and Strategic Partnership" would supplement, not supplant, the 2008 treaty, and that it would not contradict the Constitution of Abkhazia" (Kolstø, 2020a). In a similar vein, in 2015, when establishment of a joint Russian–Abkhazian "Information and Coordination Centre to Combat Organized Crime and Other Kinds of Criminality" was on the table, it took two years to sign an agreement due to the perceived need to safeguard Abkhazian state independence against all possible encroachments within the Abkhazian side (Kolstø, 2020a). The last issue analysed by Kolstø (2020a), Abkhazia's reluctance to allow Russians to buy property in their country, despite massive pressure from the Russian authorities, has still significant currency as is evident in the recent turmoil over the issue of the transfer of a large territory in Pitsunda to Russia.

As discussed above, almost all political leaders in Abkhazia have consistently favoured maintaining strong relations with Russia, but it must not be forgotten that they have also had to convince the voting public that they are able to stand up to any kind of Russian pressure that would jeopardise Abkhazia's independence (Kolstø, 2020b). The contentious and unsecured aspects of Abkhazian-Russian relations has of course a long history. It is the very same Russian Federation which is not only the successor of tsarist Russia, the perpetuator of the Circassian genocide and exile including the Abkhazians in the 19th century, but also one of the signatory states of the embargo agreement in 1996 covering all commercial, financial, and transport connections with Abkhazia, from which it did not officially withdraw until spring 2008.

What is needed are some steps to break this vicious circle and to extend the iron will of the Abkhazian people for freedom and independence with the ultimate aim of full international recognition. Despite the dominance of the constitutive approach in practice and the ambivalence in the international politics of state-recognition, every effort still should be made to inform the world of the legitimacy of Abkhazia's case in order to forge public opinion at the international level, to demonstrate Abkhazia's commitment to the requirements of international law and to the further democratizatopm of the system in the country.

Epilogue: Diaspora as a Prospective Agent for International Recognition

The last part of this paper is devoted to the role of the Circassian diaspora in Turkey as a prospective agent for the wider recognition of Abkhazia. Yet, this first necessitates a brief overview of the Circassian diaspora. Although there are not any official figures, it is estimated that there are approximately three to seven million Circassians living in Turkey. The Circassian diaspora in Turkey is not homogenous but is rather composed of various peoples (predominantly Abkhazians, Adyghes, Ubykhs and other North Caucasian peoples) who speak different dialects and have diverse cultural identities. Furthermore, this heterogeneity extends to political thought. What characterises the diaspora is not homogeneity and monolithic structure but diversity and dynamism in terms of political thought and cultural identity. However, despite all these differences, there are strong social and historical ties which connect these groups in various ways. The term 'Circassian' (or 'Cherkess') has a wider sense of 'North Caucasian' including the Abkhazians, Adyghes and other groups in Turkey since they have all lived in close proximity to each other and believed in a common history and culture, since they are considered to be historically and spatially inseparable from one another. They have always been directly concerned about what is happening in all parts of the Caucasus; both the Abkhazian and other North Caucasian communities living in Turkey have interacted and cooperated closely at various times. It should be particularly noted that it is the maintenance of these strong ties, alongside the diversity and differences, which could make the Circassian diaspora a more influential pressure-group, a more powerful actor both in Turkey and the EU throughout the process of broader international recognition for Abkhazia.

In accordance with the complex composition of the diaspora, there are many civil organisations and foundations with which the Circassian diaspora in Turkey have contacts at various levels. Among those organisations, KAFFED (The Federation of Caucasus Organisations) is the largest associational network in Turkey with around 55 member-associations located all around Turkey. It was established in 2003 when it became possible to establish federations with the new laws and regulations introduced as a result of the democratisation process encouraged by the prospect of EU membership, but its processor, KAFDER (The Caucasian Association), was established in 1993. KAFFED commits itself to the political representation of the Circassian diaspora in Turkey as well as the development of active and effective political participation-strategies among the Circassian diaspora. KAFFED acknowledges the exile and genocide committed against the Circassian people and calls for the recognition of this historical truth and thus puts a strong emphasis on the 21st of May. Furthermore, while KAFFED is always concerned with the political processes in the homeland in general, KAFFED supports, in every possible way, Abkhazia's drive for strengthening its independence and a free, democratic and prosperous country. More specifically, KAFFED (1) considers Abkhazia as an essential part of the cultural identity and the guarantor for cultural survival/revival of the Abkhazian people, (2) acknowledges the decisive importance of the international recognition of Abkhazia for peace and stability in the Caucasus, and (3) demands the recognition of Abkhazia as an independent state by Turkey and the international community. In this regard, while being committed to undoing the historical injustices, KAFFED supports the conciliatory diplomatic methods of mutual understanding and compromise without jeopardising the prospects for the future of Abkhazia that have emerged as a result of the partial recognition of its independence. In addition, KAFFED defends the right to return of all peoples deported from their homeland and thus seeks to spread the idea of repatriation to the homeland and supports all initiatives in this respect.

This overview will now be followed by how the Circassian diaspora in Turkey can provide more political support and contribution to Abkhazia in general and to its policies aiming at wider recognition in particular. The Circassian diaspora in Turkey, which has a large population that pays strong attention to both Abkhazia and the North Caucasus, has the potential of becoming a more effective pressure-group for the interests of Abkhazia both in Turkey and in the EU. It can and must make an impact on the Turkish government and impress the European Union. On this matter, the quality of diaspora-Abkhazia relations is of great significance. There are of course certain difficulties the diaspora faces with which they have to deal on their own in Turkey and together with Abkhazia.

Firstly, this potential could be realised more easily and faster when they are united with a shared vision rather than divided down ethnic and/or micro-nationalist lines. This in fact already reflects the long-lived perception among the Circassian diaspora in Turkey. Therefore, conciliatory steps might be taken to increase a mutual understanding rather than to strengthen the negative attitudes in Abkhaz-Adyghean relations both in the homeland and in the diaspora would be of great benefit to the realisation of this potential and the fulfilment of Abkhazia's expectations from the diaspora as well as to the peace-building in the region.

Secondly, what is needed is the development of more effective, dynamic and multilateral channels of communication, which would facilitate the political involvement of the diaspora, between the members of the diaspora and Abkhazia. To be able to achieve that, it is necessary to acknowledge the naturalness of the different expectations or disagreements between diaspora members as well as between the homeland and the diaspora and the unique and complex identity of the Circassian diaspora in Turkey – just as in any other diaspora (Çelikpala, 2009: 146). It is not always realistic to expect a one-to-one correspondence between the homeland and the diaspora. The diaspora has been through its own process, created its own dynamics in Turkey while longing for the homeland and now accordingly has its own problems and prospects. Despite the increasing numbers of young people claiming their Caucasian identity in Turkey and despite all the achievements obtained so far, the diaspora is still in need of accelerating the politicisation-process, a process of transition from cultural identity to cultural-political identity. The question is how to harmonise these differences with the actions of both the diaspora and the homeland to be able to build up a common vision and perception but *not* how to nurture those differences and contradictions that might lend themselves into further tensions.

Overall, the Circassian diaspora in Turkey with a population of millions is an assurance for Abkhazia and the Northern Caucasus; Abkhazia, as the historical homeland, is always a source and aspiration for cultural survival and revival for the diaspora. We have every confidence that the independence of Abkhazia will be recognized by the international community, that Abkhazia will become a member of the United Nations one day. And, we have also every confidence that one of the major roles throughout this process shall be played by the diaspora living in Turkey.

References

Brierly, J. L. (1955). *The Law of Nations*. Oxford: Clarendon Press, Fifth Edition.

Busdachin, M. (2010). Abkhazia in International Context. In J. Colarussa (Ed.), *Independence of Abkhazia and Prospects for the Caucasus,* pp. 13-16. İstanbul: CSA Global Publishing.

Crawford, J. (2006). *The Creation of States in International Law*. Oxford: Oxford University Press, Second Edition.

Çelikpala, M. (2010). The Definition of 'Diaspora', Its Position and Processes of Evolution and Transformation. In J. Colarussa (Ed.), *Independence of Abkhazia and Prospects for the Caucasus,* pp. 143-147. İstanbul: CSA Global Publishing.

Hewitt, G. (2012). Abkhazia, from conflict to statehood. Retrieved from www.opendemocracy.net/print/67024.

Kolstø, P. (2020a). Biting the hand that feeds them? Abkhazia–Russia client–patron relations, Post-Soviet Affairs, 36:2, 140-158, DOI: 10.1080/1060586X.2020.1712987

Kolstø, P. (2020b): Authoritarian Diffusion, or the Geopolitics of Self-Interest? Evidence from Russia's Patron–Client Relations with Eurasia's DeFacto States, Europe-Asia Studies, DOI: 10.1080/09668136.2020.1806209

Kopeček V., Hoch, T. and Baar, V. (2016). De Facto States and Democracy: The Case of Abkhazia. In: Szymańska, D. and Chodkowska-Miszczuk, J. editors, Bulletin of Geography. Socio-economic Series, No. 32, Toruń: Nicolaus Copernicus University, pp. 85–104. DOI: http://dx.doi.org/10.1515/bog-2016-0017

Meydan, V. (2018). A Paradox of International (Non)recognition: The Relationship Between *De Facto* States and Patron States. International Journal of Economics Politics Humanities and Social Sciences Vol: 1 Issue: 1.

Müllerson, R. (2009). Precedents in the Mountains: On the Parallels and the Uniqueness of the Cases of Kosovo, South Ossetia, and Abkhazia. *Chinese Journal of International Law*, 8/1, 2-25.

Olaizola, M. (2012). Secession, Statehood, and Recognition: Normative Bases for International Law. *Penn State Journal of International Affairs*, 2/1.

Ryangaert, C. & Sobrie, S. (2011). Recognition of States: International Law or Realpolitik? The Practice of Recognition in the Wake of Kosovo, South Ossetia, and Abkhazia. *Leiden Journal of International Law*, 24, 467-490.

Georgian Policy Towards Abkhazia in the Period 1918-1921

Vadim Mukhanov

*Head of Caucasus Department of The Institute of World Economy and
International Relations of the Russian Academy of Sciences (IMEMO).
Russia.*

In 1917, i.e. in the first revolutionary year, when everyone was just
beginning to live according to the new rules, the principle of territorial demarcation in Transcaucasia was recognised to be based on
ethnicity (which was associated with the economic needs of the people
and topographical conditions). This is what was accepted and supported
by the main political forces in the region (in particular, the representatives of the Georgian Social Democratic and Social Federalist parties
took a similar position). Striking confirmation of this is one of the pro-
gramme-statements of the Social Democratic Party, which emphasised
that "the boundaries of territorial self-government are established on
the principle of the real settlement of one or another nationality, while
economic and living conditions are taken into account. When shifting
national borders, a referendum of those areas that are disputed in determining borders is to be applied". This principle did not cause heated
debates and discussions at numerous meetings and commissions either
during that fateful year or until the declaration of independence in the

late spring of 1918 (that is, the period of the Provisional Government and the united Transcaucasian Republic).

It is extremely indicative that, if before the declaration of independence the Georgian political élite supported the ethnic principle of division, then after May 1918 it began to advocate observing the administrative borders, since this allowed it to retain some territories. It is also significant that, if in negotiations with the Armenian side Tiflis put pressure on the old administrative-territorial division of Transcaucasia, then in the north, in relations with the Volunteer Army, on the contrary, it insisted on observing the ethnic principle. With regard to Abkhazia, the leadership of the Georgian Democratic Republic, headed by N. Zhordania, acted in the simplest way, viz. with the help of pressure through force. After the entry of Georgian troops there, the People's Council, controlled by Tiflis, recognised the presence of Abkhazia as a part of the Georgian Republic in the shape of an autonomous unit (1919). Moreover, in relation to the former Sukhum District of the Russian Empire, neither the principle of administrative delimitation nor the ethnic principle worked.

* * *

If the Georgian Republic arose on the basis of two imperial provinces, namely those of Tiflis and Kutaisi, then Abkhazia also had its own administrative-territorial unit within Russia. It met the fateful 17th year of the century in the form of the Sukhum District, which, like the aforementioned provinces located in the neighbourhood, fell within the frontiers of the Caucasian Viceregency. After the February Revolution, the Public Security Committee headed by Prince A.G. Shervashidze began to operate on the territory of the District.

In 1917, due to the understood succession of power in the capital, no acute conflict-situations arose between Tiflis and Sukhum. On the contrary, there was a sense of hope for the establishment of life in the region on a new basis. This is evidenced by the first contacts of the National Councils, which eventually came to the conclusion of the well-known agreement of February 1918 (which some Georgian experts like to refer to as evidence of the consent of the Abkhazian élite to become part of an independent Georgia!).

In the autumn of 1917, the Sukhum District joined what was then in the process of formation, namely the Union of Cossack Troops, Highlanders of the Caucasus and Free Peoples of the Steppes (the agreement on organising the union dates back to 20 October 1917). In particular it declared that "The Union was concluded with the aim of contributing to the establishment of the best state-system, external security and order in the Russian State, as well as to ensure the integrity of the members of the Union, maintain internal peace, raise general well-being and thereby consolidate the boons of freedom won by the Revolution" – (At the same time, the main goal was "to achieve the earliest establishment of a Russian Democratic Federative Republic with the recognition of the Members of the Union as its separate states").

After the fall of the Provisional Government and the collapse of regional power in Abkhazia, a general congress was held, at which on 6 November 1917, its own socio-political body, the Abkhazian People's Council (ANS [for the Russian *Abkhazskij Narodnyj Sovet*]), was elected. The latter began actively to make contact with various political forces in both the North Caucasus and Transcaucasia. It is clear that in the first place in the list of contacts were neighbours from Tiflis. Georgian politicians, we recall, dominated the regional authorities and also created the National Council of Georgia, which became their mouthpiece.

The emerging consolidation of the political forces of Transcaucasia, which did not accept the coup in Petrograd and which were anti-Bolshevik, forced Georgian politicians in early 1918 to invite their Abkhazian colleagues to distinct negotiations. In the message that came to Sukhum, it was proposed to "arrange a meeting with representatives of the Abkhazian People's Council to clarify the relationship between Georgia and Abkhazia... In view of this, the National Council of Georgia asks the Abkhazian People's Council to send its representatives to the city of Tiflis by 20 January". The letter emphasised that "the Georgians, for their part, sincerely wish to find a way to such mutual understanding and the establishment of close fraternal unity with the Abkhazians".

The ANS (headed by the chairman Prince A. Shervashidze) arrived in Tiflis, where on 9 February he took part in a meeting of the Presidium of the Executive Committee of the Georgian Council. As a result, as recorded in the protocol, the following provisions were approved on the issue "On the establishment of relations between Georgia and Abkhazia". This document, often referred to as a kind of agreement, consisted of three points:

1. To recreate a single, indivisible Abkhazia within the limits of the River Ingur to the River Mzymta, which will include Abkhazia proper and Samurzakan, or which is also the current Sukhum District.
2. The form of the future political structure of united Abkhazia must be worked out with the principle of national self-determination at the Constituent Assembly of Abkhazia, convened on democratic principles.
3. In the event that Abkhazia or Georgia wish to enter into political treaty-relations with other nationalities or states, they mutually undertake to have preliminary negotiations on this matter between themselves."

Interestingly, this small document is the basis of the Georgian argumentation about the alleged unification of Georgia and Abkhazia, and the subordination of the latter to Tiflis. However, as we can see, these three points are reminiscent of fixing intentions.

Analysing the document, it is worth paying attention to several important points. Firstly, the negotiations (which resulted in a protocol with points) were conducted by two newly-minted political organisations that were endowed with no authority at that time. There were several national councils – in addition to the Georgian, there were Armenian, Muslim, Russian ones. Their members were members of the regional authority, but the councils themselves did not represent it. Recall that at the end of 1917 the power in the region was represented by the Transcaucasian Commissariat, which in early 1918 transferred it to the Transcaucasian Seim, assembled from representatives of the major political parties of the region and deputies of the Constituent Assembly from Transcaucasia. Secondly, the Georgian Democratic Republic was proclaimed only at the end of May 1918, therefore, there can simply be no talk about any process of unification with Georgia in February. Thirdly, the February agreement confirms a certain independent status for Abkhazia and does not mention anything about a possible autonomy within the then non-existent Georgia. Fourthly, in one of the points the territory of Abkhazia is fixed in and of itself.

* * *

In March 1918, the Second District Peasant Congress was held in Sukhum, on which the Georgian Social Democrats (who saw the ANS as a threat to their plans) were betting. Sukhum mayor V. Chkhikvishvili, who was a Georgian protégé, was elected chairman by an overwhelming majority of votes. The Transcaucasian Seim was recognised as the highest body and the presence of Abkhazia in this association (and not in the North Caucasian Union) was confirmed. At the same time, it is worth noting that none of the local politicians of the Social Democratic persuasion offered to consider or support the agreement concluded with the National Council of Georgia (NSG [for the Russian *Natsional'nyj Sovet Gruzii*]) of 9 February 1918 (or to emphasise the political line on gaining independent status of Abkhazia). On the contrary, speaking at the Congress on behalf of the NSG, its representative D. Suliashvili stated that "Abkhazia will be an integral autonomous unit based on the territorial-national principle". It is clear that these statements, which demonstrated the true intentions of Georgian politicians and their vision of the future position of Abkhazia, were a threat to the plans of the ANS, but until May 1918 it seemed illusory.

A real threat and clear danger came in the first half of the year from the another side. At that time (that is, even during the existence of a single Transcaucasian space), the ANS faced other contenders for power in the shape of local Bolsheviks, their ardent opponents, and a group of local élites orientated towards Turkey.

The Bolsheviks, led by Nestor Lakoba and Ephrem Eshba, made two attempts to seize power during this short period of time – in February and April 1918. The first attempt failed immediately, whilst the second was successful. During April, the Bolsheviks took control of a significant part of Abkhazia (with the exception of the Kodor area) and proclaimed Soviet power there. Having seized Sukhum, they disbanded the Soviet and arrested its prominent representatives (interestingly both Abkhazian politicians and their pro-Georgian opponents - S. Basaria, G. Zukhbaja, I. Ramishvili, V. Shervashidze and others) were taken into custody. Priest G.D. Tumanov was sent to Tiflis to the then still common Transcaucasian government for help. The latter experienced staunch rejection of the Bolsheviks and allocated forces to eliminate the "distemper" in the Sukhum District. By government order, detachments under the command of Colonel A. Koniev and the commander of the Red Guard V. Dzhugeli entered there. In May 1918, these units took Sukhum and liquidated Soviet power, pushing back the Bolshevik forces.

This military contingent was partially withdrawn after the end of the operation, but a detachment of the Red Guards remained on the territory of the district. This is important in the light of the sharp change in the general political situation in the region associated with the collapse of the Transcaucasian Federation. It was at the end of May that Georgia, and then Azerbaijan and Armenia, declared their independence. Thus, the detachment sent by the still unified regional government to Abkhazia automatically turned into a Georgian one, which gave Tiflis a strong trump card in seizing the territory of the Sukhum District.

The second entry of troops sent from Tiflis in June of the same year to protect against the Bolsheviks turned out to be fatal for Abkhazia. The military unit under the command of General Mazniev, having knocked out the weak detachments of the Abkhazian rebels, quickly took control of the entire district. Moreover, immediately after the declaration of Georgia's independence, the Georgian units used the Abkhazian territory as a springboard for a further offensive on the Black Sea coast. Taking advantage of the beginning of the Civil War in Russia, the virtual absence of authority and the anarchy, and with German support at the same time, the Georgian units went forward in the direction of Taman, where German troops were already present.

Georgian politicians, who were in a state of euphoria after the declaration of independence of Georgia and the quick conclusion of an agreement with Germany on assistance, decided to expand the borders of the republic as far as possible, and the Black Sea coast became the most attractive direction for expansion in the light of the presence of German troops in the Ukraine, the outbreak of the Civil War in Russia, as well as anarchy in the South Caucasus. The newly formed Georgian government decided to expand the traditional border of the Kutaisi Province (and, accordingly, the Sukhum District) along the River Bzyp.

Mazniev, having dispersed the detachments of the Abkhazian rebels, quickly cleared the territory of the Sukhum District and reached the border of the Black Sea province. Taking advantage of the fact that the armed forces of the Kuban-Black Sea Soviet Republic were linked through battles with the Volunteer Army pressing upon them, the Georgian units invaded the Sochi District of the Black Sea Province, and on 3 July 1918, they occupied Adler, and on the 5th – Sochi. By 26 July General Mazniev (virtually unopposed) captured the territory of the Black Sea coast as far as Tuapse. On 27 July Tuapse, which became a Georgian border-town, also found itself under his control. As the modern researcher V. Tsvetkov rightly emphasises, «[D]istracted on fighting the 'Denikin gangs', the Red Guard detachments were not ready to repel the offensive of the Georgian regular division, reinforced by detachments of the People›s Guard.» It should be noted that the plans for the advance of the Georgian troops were coordinated with the German command (which was informed of this offensive), especially since already in June 1918 German occupation-units had landed on Taman.

As General A.I. Denikin wrote, "[I]n the first period of the Turkish-German occupation, the desires of Georgia were directed towards the Black Sea Province. The reason was the weakness of the Black Sea." Another leader of the White movement, General A.S. Lukomsky in September 1918 gave the following explanation of the Georgian plans (and actions), very fairly by the way: "... for Georgia, the Sochi District was of great importance in the sense of the zone separating the Sukhum District, inhabited by the freedom-loving Abkhazian people, from the Volunteer Army. The Georgian government feared that, if the Sochi District became part of the Black Sea Province, then this could have an influence on the secession of Abkhazia from Georgia."

In order to resolve controversial issues, the command of the Volunteer Army offered the Georgian government to negotiate, but the two-day meeting in Ekaterinodar did not bring any positive result, rather, on the contrary, it aggravated Denikin's already difficult relations with the Transcaucasian Republic.

Unfortunately, the political leadership of Georgia did not show any will or desire to compromise, which led to the deepening of the conflict between Denikin and Tiflis. It should be noted that, if the newly emerged Georgian politicians who had seized power were disposed to such an adventure, then some experienced representatives of the national élite opposed such steps and provocative operations with sad consequences for Tiflis. For example, Zurab Avalov, one of the most famous Georgian international lawyers and diplomats of that era, emphasised that "the accession of the Sochi District to Georgia created a new plane of friction, and there were already enough of them ... complications that were not caused by necessity should have been avoided in the position of Georgia", and therefore firmly stated that "not only in Tuapse, but also in Sochi, the Georgians had no business." Unfortunately, such sound thoughts were not understood and accepted by the leadership of the republic.

It is clear that Denikin did not want to follow the lead of the Georgian politicians, but he had neither the time nor the means immediately to resolve the controversial issue by force (due to the difficult situation on other fronts, he tried to avoid a war with Georgia). The main result was that the Russian border on the Black Sea coast after the so-called Sochi Conflict was established, effectively, along the indicated line of demarcation of 1919, i.e. along the River Psou. This was also established in the Moscow Treaty with Georgia of 1920 – this border, having been administrative, passed into the Soviet border, and it was preserved after the collapse of the USSR. At present, the Gagra District is the Republic of Abkhazia's border-region with Russia.

* * *

The territory of the Sukhum District in the same June 1918 was declared a general-governorship [*gubernia*] within the Georgian Republic, headed by Mazniev, who had distinguished himself there. This was a direct contradiction with the statements of the ANS, which, after the collapse of the Transcaucasian Republic, became a local government that had the support and trust of the population. According to the decision of the ANS of 2 June 1918, in view of the collapse of the Transcaucasian Republic, the council assumed "all power within Abkhazia". At the same time, it was noted that "from the moment of the collapse of the Transcaucasian Federal Republic and the declaration of Georgia's independence, Abkhazia has lost the legal basis for ties with Georgia, and the detachment of the Transcaucasian Red Guard, being currently a military unit of the Georgian Republic, has found itself outside the borders of its state, but all fullness of power has effectively come to lie in its hands".

According to the documents issued at that time, it is clear that the ANS tried to settle its relations with Tiflis through negotiations. However, the Georgian politicians who had just come to power, on the contrary, preferred to talk with the Abkhazians from a position of strength, which was already there in the person of the Mazniev detachment.[1]

Members of the ANS, sent to Tiflis at the beginning of the summer, signed the well-known agreement of 11 June 1918, which Georgian historians declare as key in the process of Abkhazia's joining the Georgian Republic. It should be noted that at that time the politicians of Georgia were in some euphoria after the bright declaration of the independence of the GDR, the conclusion of a peace treaty with Turkey and the receipt of support from Germany, and therefore they acted so decisively in the Abkhazian issue, considering it both less significant in comparison with the above and also simpler. At the same time, they needed an agreement (that is, an official document) with Abkhazia in order legally to establish their actual presence there (in addition to having further confirmation of their jurisdiction over this territory during the process of the international recognition of Georgia). In particular, Tiflis especially needed such a document in its relations with Turkey, which supported the Mountain Republic, which also claimed an alliance with Abkhazia. Abkhazian researchers believe that this document was written under strong pressure from the then Georgian politicians (with which is hard to disagree).

Here is the full text of the agreement between the government of Georgia and the Abkhazian People's Council from the date specified:

"The Abkhazian People's Council decided to empower its representatives R.I. Kakubava, G.D. Tumanov. V.G. Gurdzhua and G.D. Adzhamov to conclude the following agreement:

"The Government of the Georgian Democratic Republic, represented by its representatives (Minister of Justice Alekseev-Meskhiev and of

Agriculture Khomeriki) and the Abkhazian People's Council, represented by representatives Razhden Ivanovich Kakubava, Georgij Davidovich Tumanov, Vasilij Georgievich Gurdzhua and Georgij Davidovich Adzhamov, in the furtherance and supplementation of the agreement between the Georgian National Council and the Abkhazian People's Council held on 9 February 1918, concluded the following agreement:

"1. The concluded agreement will be reviewed by the National Assembly of Abkhazia, which will finally determine the political structure and fate of Abkhazia, as well as the relationship between Georgia and Abkhazia.

"2. Attached to the Government of the Georgian Democratic Republic is an authorised representative of the Abkhazian People's Council, with whom the Georgian Government communicates regarding the affairs of Abkhazia.

"3. The internal administration in Abkhazia is in the hands of the Abkhazian People's Council.

"4. In matters of foreign policy, Georgia, being the official representative of both treaty-parties, effectively acts in conjunction with Abkhazia.

"5. Credits and funds necessary for the administration of Abkhazia are released from the funds of the Georgian Democratic Republic for disposal by the Abkhazian People's Council.

"6. For the speedy establishment of revolutionary order and the organisation of a firm government, the Georgian Democratic Republic sends a detachment of the Red Guard to help the Abkhazian People's Council and to remain at its disposal until the end of the need for it.

"7. The Abkhazian People's Council will organise military units, and the equipment, uniforms and means necessary for these units will be released by the Georgian Democratic Republic to be at the disposal of the Council.

"8. Social reforms will be effected by the Abkhazian People's Council on the basis of common laws promulgated by the Transcaucasian Seim, but in relation to local conditions.

"This document is taken into account and is attached to the agreements concluded between the Georgian National Council and the Republic of Georgia, on the one hand, and the Abkhazian People's Council, on the other hand. City of Tiflis, 11th day of June 1918."

It is impossible not to pay attention to one clear trend in the actions of the Georgian politicians. Inspired by the support of Germany and the newly declared independence, they began to put pressure on the Abkhazians, since the territory of Abkhazia and further along the Black Sea Province gave them direct access to German troops, and one cannot discount the simple desire to "round out the borders". They tried to realise this understandable desire in the course of the Paris Conference and the actions of their own delegation there (in the form of territorial claims for a significant part of the Black Sea coast as far as Tuapse).

Moreover, for the Georgian politicians who declared independence, Abkhazia turned into the most important outpost against any threat from the north, whether White or Red. Even if the campaign in the Black Sea Province was recognised by many as an adventure, control over Abkhazia was assessed as a vital necessity for Georgia. Thus, from the very beginning of independence, the GDR government exerted serious pressure on Abkhazia, its élite and population, which only intensified after the actual occupation by Georgian troops and the announcement of the creation of the Sukhum General-Governorship.

In particular, strong pressure was exerted on the small Abkhazian delegation that arrived in Tiflis in early June to discuss the current situation. The Abkhazian delegates were immediately frightened by the cessation of assistance from Tiflis, which was provided to them when they were in the Transcaucasian Republic, and also by the fact that Abkhazia might be occupied by Turkish troops. Delegate Kakubava, in his telegram from Tiflis, demanded authority to sign a treaty with an already independent Georgia, without waiting for "a congress of plenipotentiary representatives of Abkhazia". He emphasised that "according to the statement of the Government of Georgia, the urgent issue of our relations is caused by this extremely serious political moment which can often change within several hours". For this reason, the Georgian side insisted on the urgent signing of an agreement. As Kakubava reported to Sukhum, "[W]ithout such an agreement, the Government of the Georgian Republic does not find it possible to speak with foreign powers on behalf of Abkhazia. If the Government of Georgia is deprived of this opportunity, it has no doubt that Turkey will occupy Abkhazia in the coming days. Neither this nor any other treaty, of course, can we sign without authority from you; so let us know as soon as possible whether the Council gives us the necessary authority." Furthermore, Sukhum was requested to select one of the delegates as temporary representative of Abkhazia to the Georgian government. Kakubava asked for an answer promptly - "no later than tomorrow".

Well-known is the draft-treaty between the government of the GDR and the Abkhazian People's Council (dated 8 June)[2], which was, in all probability, submitted for discussion – it is interesting that some Georgian historians take it as the final one, despite the existence of a later version dated the 11th. The well-known text of the final agreement between the parties, signed on 11 June, allows us to speak of the great haste this document with which this document was agreed and signed – it was essentially unchanged.

The haste and psychological indoctrination of the Abkhazian delegates had their effect. In a telegraph-conversation with Sukhum the next day (starting at 10 pm!), these insisted on the need to conclude an agreement with Tiflis as soon as possible: "The delegation once again confirms the categorical need for the immediate conclusion of the proposed agreement. The information we have received here gives us the right to say that the political situation of the moment is clearer to us than to you, and we find the moment catastrophic." "Take all measures so that the People's Council agrees to conclude an agreement, especially since this temporary agreement does not bind Abkhazia in any way. Such a temporary agreement gives the Georgian Government the right to speak on behalf of Abkhazia. We are all deeply convinced that the Georgian Government will act and speak only in favour of Abkhazia. If you are afraid of responsibility before the People's Council for the proposed treaty, then we can take responsibility before the People's Council for the proposed treaty," was what the Abkhazian delegates said by telegraph from Tiflis.

To discuss the draft-treaty and the current situation, on 10 June 1918 a meeting of the ANS was held, which, having accepted the arguments of the delegates, instructed them to conclude the draft agreed with them in order to stabilise the situation. Although there was no unity among the members of the Council, since an alternative opinion was also recorded in the minutes of its meeting: "In view of the fact that the draft-treaty proposed by the Georgian Republic between Abkhazia and Georgia has the character of an ultimatum, hindering the possibility of deliberate, free discussion, and in view of the fact that an important act such as the proposed treaty between Abkhazia and Georgia is being effected by force, with a limited number of members of the Abkhazian People's Council and without the knowledge of the population of Abkhazia, which thinks of its political freedom without any guardianship on anyone's part, I propose that the Abkhazian People's Council respond to Georgia's ultimatum with the request that an opportunity be given to the population to arrange an Abkhazian National Congress, authorised finally to determine the political structure of Abkhazia, assuring the Georgian Democratic Republic that Abkhazia, as an independent national organism, will certainly enter into good-neighbourly, treaty-alliances and agreements with Georgia."

However, due to the haste and pressure of the Georgian side, it was not possible to hold a congress or at least a public discussion of the treaty in Abkhazia, and on 11 June it was signed in the version close to the original, sent from Tiflis.

Nevertheless, the agreement can be designated as preliminary, since it practically did not contain specifics in matters of the division of the powers of the parties, their obligations to each other (it declared a kind of union between Georgia and Abkhazia; however, all the elaboration was left to the Constituent Assembly of Abkhazia, which should soon have been convened). For obvious reasons, there were no specific mechanisms for interaction, since the ministries and departments of the GDR were just being formed, and the main legislative documents were at the initial stage of development.

According to the June agreement, under the Georgian government the post of a Minister for Abkhazia was established, who was supposed to coordinate the activities of local authorities with the republican ones; all external relations passed into the hands of Tiflis[3], while all issues of internal administration remained in the hands of local bodies (the ANS being recognised as the highest of them). Thus, the subordinate position of Abkhazia was consolidated. At the same time, one of its members, Isidore Ramishvili, who represented the Social Democratic faction of the Council, became the official Georgian representative under the ANS. However, this idyll did not last long, since General Mazniev, having taken into his own hands control of Abkhazia, already in August 1918 actually dissolved the Council, which had no real levers of influence.

* * *

A conflict between the People's Council and the Georgian high command, headed by General Mazniev, arose immediately, because a situation of dual power developed, whilst real power, for obvious reasons, ended up in the hands of the Georgian military leader.

Mazniev's first orders were already a direct violation of the agreement between the ANS and the government of the GDR. The latter, referring to the order of the Minister of War of Georgia, announced the creation on the territory of Abkhazia of the Sukhum General-Governorship under his command. Following this, he publicly informed the population that the laws of the GDR were in force throughout Abkhazian territory and demanded unconditional obedience to them.

The next conflict-situation arose during the presence in Abkhazia of the Turkish landing force in Abkhazia and its liquidation. Members of the ANS were able to agree with part of the *mukhajirs* who had landed from this detachment on the surrender of weapons and their departure back to Turkey. However, Mazniev, considering the surrendered military property (weapons, cartridges and horses) as his military booty, immediately ordered the Georgian units to take control. In addition, he announced the introduction of the death-penalty, in accordance with the law adopted by the National Council of Georgia. In this regard, on 4 July 1918, a protest was sent to Tiflis, signed by the chairman of the ANS, Prince V. Shervashidze, in connection with violations of the terms of the Agreement of 11 June by the Georgian army. Addressing the head of the government of the GDR, Prince Shervashidze asked "to point out to the general that the only source of power and emergency-powers on the territory of Abkhazia is the Abkhazian People's Council ... The above actions of the Governor-General in Abkhazia essentially create mistrust in the masses of the population of Abkhazia towards the Government of the Georgian Republic. According to paragraph 8 of the Agreement, the laws issued by the Transcaucasian Seim in Abkhazia are implemented by the Abkhazian People's Council with regard to local conditions. As for the law on the death-penalty, issued by the National Council of Georgia, it cannot be extended to the territory of Abkhazia until the Abkhazian People's Council has spoken about it".

It should be noted that Turkey became another power that took part in the struggle for Abkhazia, since a significant number of

Abkhazian *Mukhajirs* and their descendants lived there. The news of the occupation of Sukhum by Georgian troops and the announcement of Mazniev's general-governorship there prompted part of the Abkhazian élite to take action. On the night of 27 June 1918, an armed landing-force from Turkey landed near the River Kodor (part consisted of Abkhazian *Mukhajirs*, part of Turkish *askers*) and was supported by Princes Alexander Shervashidze and Tatash Marshania.

Istanbul was not averse to gaining control over the Abkhazian territory, and primarily over the port of Sukhum. However, nothing came of this venture, since the *mukhajirs*, after meeting with members of the ANS, handed over their weapons and ammunition[4] and abandoned military operations in their homeland (some of them went back, whilst the others remained in Abkhazia). The Turkish contingent, on the contrary, was ready for clashes, but by mid-August, after several days of fighting, Mazniev dispersed it.

The participation of the Abkhazian princes in this adventure and the meeting of the members of the ANS with representatives of the landing-force served as a pretext for accusations of treason and betrayal of national interests, which, in turn, allowed the Georgian administration to break up the composition of the Abkhazian Council, which was unacceptable to them, and even to place under investigation some of its members who were not ready to cooperate with Tiflis. The work of the ANS was completely terminated by October 1918.

* * *

Recall that the first Abkhazian Soviet appeared in November 1917, and was dissolved by the Bolsheviks during their seizure of power in April 1918. It was able to recover only after the capture of Sukhum by a detachment of the Transcaucasian Red Guard in May of the same year.

On 20 May, in the newly liberated Sukhum, at the initiative of the command of the guard, a meeting of the ANS was held. An important circumstance was the absence of Prince A. Shervashidze, who went to

Batum to defend the interests of the Abkhazians who wanted to be in the Union with the Mountain Republic (its delegates were invited by the Turks to participate in the peace-conference). Georgian politicians, who in those days had just begun negotiations with the Germans regarding support for the recognition of Georgia's independence, could not approve such activity on the part of the head of the Abkhazian Council.

The composition of the ANS was modified by diluting it with new pro-Georgian socialists, and a new chairman was elected – Varlam Shervashidze, who was set on a close alliance with Georgia and locating Abkhazia in the Transcaucasian political orbit. The modern historian B. Mailjan believes that "the diplomatic intrigues that unfolded around the fate of Abkhazia in May-August 1918 arose because of the German-Turkish rivalry in the Caucasus. All the efforts of the Turkophile part of the Abkhazian leaders for the recognition of Abkhazia as part of the Mountainous Republic remained without consequences, since Germany took over the patronage of the Georgian independent state proclaimed on 26 May 1918". An interesting sketch of the behaviour of the Abkhazian delegates is given by the Georgian researcher L. Bakradze, who relied on documents of the German Foreign Ministry: "... German sources note with regret that the Abkhazian delegates were under Turkish influence to such an extent that they did not even approach the German delegation."

Difficulties in relations with Tiflis after the declaration of independence and the arrival of Georgian troops quickly led both to a conflict within the Council between supporters of joining Georgia as well as of their own independence, and to its actually being pushed out of real control. The shameless intervention of the Georgian authorities in the socio-economic and political life of Abkhazia led to protests from the ANS, which referred to the articles of the June Agreement.

An extremely harsh resolution was adopted on 4 August 1918 in response to the Georgian government's order to introduce a monopoly on the sale and export of tobacco to Germany (under the Georgian-German agreement). In particular, it was rightly noted that "according to the design of the agreements of 9 February and 11 June 1918, the Abkhazian People's Council was granted the inalienable right independently to manage the natural wealth and sources of income of Abkhazia, which follows from paragraphs 1, 3 and 4 of the Agreement of 11 June 1918". Attention was also drawn to the fact that "economic relations between the Republic of Georgia and Abkhazia, i.e. everything related to issues of industry, railways, telegraph-lines, the system of customs' fees and taxation of export- and production-items has not yet been determined by any agreements".

The ANS demanded that Tiflis immediately cancel this order, which led to a split within the Council itself. The pro-Georgian group headed by V. Shervashidze was afraid of an open break with Georgia and its possible consequences, and therefore, in response to the adoption of this resolution, they (namely, Varlam Shervashidze, Dzhoto Shervashidze, Vladimir Emukhvari, Arzakan Emukhvari, Lavrenti Khonelidze and others) left the Council on the same day. However, their return to the Council proved to be imminent. Immediately after the liquidation of the Turkish landing-party in mid-August, the Georgian command dispersed the ANS by force, making a number of arrests. Its members were accused of complicity with the enemies of the republic, particularly of being pro-Turkish.

The backbone of the new composition was the group of Varlam Shervashidze, who advocated autonomy for Abkhazia as part of the Georgian Republic. He stated that "the political position of Abkhazia and relations with Georgia in the future will be determined by a people's representative assembly".

The composition of the ANS was seriously diluted by the Georgian authorities with representatives of the non-Abkhazian population of the district in order finally to exclude their ardent opponents (for example, S. Basaria and D. Marshania disappeared from it). Thus, the original national character of this body was destroyed, since the remaining national councils of the district delegated two of their representatives to the ANS. Thus, it became both multinational and more predictable in his actions and, most importantly, came under strong Georgian influence. In other words, the Georgian authorities managed quickly to change the ANS: from being a socio-political body that defended Abkhazian interests, it turned into a standard body of local self-government.

Such dismissive behaviour on the part of the Georgian authorities towards the ANS against the backdrop of a reverent and respectful attitude towards their own national body, the NSG, which, we recall, became the actual basis for the formation of the main authorities in Georgia itself (transforming into the parliament and government of an independent republic!), is extremely indicative. The Abkhazians were not given a similar chance – quite the contrary, Tiflis did everything to prevent a real chance from even appearing ...

* * *

Even G.N. Andzhaparidze, who was the representative of the NSG in Abkhazia, insisted on this very option. HE considered both the holding of elections to the separate Constituent Assembly of Abkhazia and, even more, its further convocation and operation to be unnecessary and counterproductive for Georgian policy in the district. Andzhaparidze advocated the election of a new Soviet, which should be turned into an ordinary *zemstvo*-body. In one of N. Zhordania's messages, he insisted on the creation in Sukhum of only a local organ of self-government, requesting "the fulfilment of our desire as soon as possible, namely to have a representative body from the population of the whole of Abkhazia, adopting our point of view as its stance".

Thus, he, like many other Georgian politicians, advocated the creation of a standard local self-governing body in Sukhum, and not the convening of a separate Abkhazian parliament, which would be a serious threat to the plans of the Georgian political élite to turn Abkhazia into one of the provinces of the republic. This point of view found full support and understanding in Tiflis. The Georgian leadership, having gained real control over the territory of the district by the summer of 1918, no longer wanted to take into account the signed agreements and promises previously given to their Abkhazian counterpart.

As Mikhail Tarnava, one of the prominent members of the ANS, noted: "In the towns military command-offices have been created: in the centre there is the district military administration going by the name of defence-headquarters and headed by Colonel Tukhareli; in the counties military units operate at their discretion, replacing the local administration – in a word, the entire military administrative control of the country is in the hands of the military agents of the Georgian government."[5]

The second membership of the ANS also did not last long – until October of that year, when it was dissolved for the second time by the Georgian armed forces, some of its active deputies being arrested and sent to Tiflis (imprisoned in Metekhi Fortress).

The Georgian government decided finally to dissolve the Council on 10 October 1918. This happened after a stormy meeting on 9 October when the opposition group raised the question of confidence in the presidium of the ANS, headed by Varlam Shervashidze. As a result of the election, a vote of no confidence was expressed in him. As Mikhail Tarnava, one of the ANS deputies, recalled: "At this meeting of the Council it proved possible to vote for a chairman, namely Var[lam] Aleks[androvich] Shervashidze. And then the opposition demanded that he leave, i.e. to give up his chairmanship to a representative of the opposition, as whom, it seems, Semjon Mikh[ailovich] Ashkhatsava was selected. But the elected chairman Shervashidze did not yield to this, and he arranged a break in the meeting, during which he secretly called the regiment to send a military unit to eliminate the 'disturbances' in the Soviet. Having established contact with the military authorities, the same chairman resumed the meeting of the Council, during which soldiers gradually began to enter the meeting-room singly and in twos. So gradually, in a short time, ranks of soldiers formed along the walls and inside the premises of the Council. The opposition felt something was wrong and untoward - the betrayal and treachery of the Chairman of the Council were understood. But before anything could be done, the Chairman of the Council raised the question of treason against the State and the danger stemming from some deputies, pointing to the leaders of the opposition ... However, at this meeting of the Council no more drastic measures were taken, and the meeting of the Council was closed, and the military units that had arrived left peacefully at the direction of the Council.

"But on the same night, or the next day, soldiers or policemen were sent to the apartments of the most active opposition-deputies, and these deputies were arrested. They turned out to be Sem[jon] Mikh[ailovich] Ashkhatsava, Iv[an] Nik[olaevich] Margania, Dm[itrij] Iv[anovich] Margania and Georg[ij] Dav[idovich] Adzhamov. They were immediately sent to Tiflis and imprisoned in the Metekhi Fortress. After that, the Council was effectively dissolved and was no longer convened with this membership ...

"This shows that it was dangerous after the arrest of the leaders of the opposition to convene the Soviet with the participation of the rest of the opposition, so that they would not reveal from the deputies' rostrum the lawlessness committed by the Mensheviks by seizing the deputies physically. It would also have been inappropriate officially to announce the dissolution of the Council with its present composition, i.e. its disbandment. This was done cunningly and behind the scenes, without any official act. But in fact the Soviet was dissolved by the most surreptitious act of arresting some deputies and not convening others. ... Thus did the second Abkhazian People's Council end its existence and its struggle / in terms of the opposition/ with the occupying Georgian Menshevik authorities in Abkhazia without any results."

One of the instigators of the vote of no confidence in the chairman of the Council was Semjon Ashkhatsava, who made the following statement, which served as the beginning of events (as recorded in the Sukhum newspaper *Novoe Slovo*): "... [T]he working population of Abkhazia has definitely determined to take power into their own hands, for which they sent their representatives. The existing order cannot continue. Talk about Turkophilia is nonsense and deceit: if it continues like this, then indeed the people will take any orientation, not only Turkish, even devilish, if only to get rid of the invaders, and therefore it is necessary to re-elect the Presidium. People who have neither the trust nor the respect of the people cannot rule the country."

It was this Semjon Ashkhatsava, formerly one of the leaders of the anti-Georgian struggle in the Soviet, who conveyed in his memoirs interesting details of its actual liquidation: "The Mensheviks, having suffered a complete collapse on their favourite parliamentary front, decided to resort to military force, especially since they had it available. On the next day, the 10th, the Menshevik government decreed the dissolution of the Abkhazian People's Council with its then-membership and the appointment of new elections for the third time. On that day, in the morning, S. Ashkhatsava and I. Margania were arrested, kept at the headquarters of the regiment until the evening in order to be sent to Tiflis at night by steamer [via Batumi? – Trans.] (so as not to be taken across Abkhazian territory, where they could be beaten off by local residents – author) and detained for this purpose from the morning. Also, Abkhazia was placed under martial law, and an extraordinary commissar V. Chkhiktishvili was appointed, and guards were placed on the roads to the city so that there would be no raids from the population. At about 1 o'clock on the same day a meeting gathered on the boulevard, at which G. Tumanov spoke with a sharp accusatory speech against the Menshevik outrages. The rally was dispersed and Tumanov arrested. In the following days, D. Alania, G. Adzhamov, V. Chachba, M. Schlatter and others (up to 16 people) were arrested for anti-Menshevik agitation and speeches. Thus, for Tiflis, the situation in the ANS in October 1918 turned very unpleasant, and therefore the most severe decision was taken: the ANS lost control and was immediately liquidated by the local Georgian administration.

Now Tiflis staked everything on a serious transformation of the Soviet via new elections on a proportional basis (across the entire territory of the district). Obviously, in the case of applying this election-formula, persons of non-Abkhazian origin ended up in the Council, and Georgian representation there increased (both directly and indirectly, thanks to protégés of the Georgian administration). Consequently, the Abkhazians would lose their majority in the ANS. Thus, Tiflis wanted finally to close the issue of Abkhazian independence by creating a representative body under its control, which would focus on issues of local self-government and would not peddle the idea of self-determination for Abkhazia.

In March 1919, new elections were held to the People's Council (which were kept under total control by the Georgian administration), with the result that most of the seats were taken by representatives of the political parties of Georgia (primarily, of course, the Mensheviks). The new cycle was opened by the oldest member of the Council, a well-known Menshevik in Abkhazia, Isidore Ramishvili, who, in addition, was the official representative of Georgia in the ANS. At the very first meeting of the new composition of the ANS, the 'Act on the Autonomy of Abkhazia' was adopted, which allowed the Georgian government legally to consolidate its presence in Abkhazia. Soon, alongside the Soviet there arose the Commissariat of Abkhazia, which was conceived as an executive authority, standing next to the legislative, i.e. the ANS. However, the commissariat turned out to be largely a decorative body that did not have real levers of influence on the situation.

Thus, in the period from October 1918 to March 1919, the entire administration of the former Sukhum District was conducted with the direct support of the Georgian military units.

* * *

So, the third council was renamed the People's Council of Abkhazia (NSA), and formed under the total control of Tiflis in March 1919, which allowed it to exist until the end of the democratic republic, i.e. almost two years, until March 1921. It was this Council, under pressure from the Georgian administration, that on 20 March 1919 adopted the 'Act on the Autonomy of Abkhazia', where Tiflis finally managed to carry through the provision it needed, to wit: "Abkhazia is part of the Democratic Republic of Georgia, as an autonomous unit of it." The second paragraph of this act served as a kind of straw to soften the blow, insofar as it announced the start of work on a constitution for Abkhazia, the main provisions of which would later be included in the Georgian constitution − (+ to coordinate the powers and relations between Tiflis and Sukhum, the creation of a mixed commission was announced to be made up from the Constituent Assembly of Georgia and the People's Council of Abkhazia in equal measures). The modern Abkhazian historian Stanislav Lakoba rightly emphasises that "in essence, it remained on paper, and three different drafts of the Constitution of Abkhazia were not approved due to disagreements between the ANS, on the one hand, and the Georgian government and Constituent Assembly, on the other". In fact, this document legitimised the Georgian military-political presence in Abkhazia, establishing the supremacy of the legislation of the GDR and its power there.

Abkhazians, dissatisfied with the actions of the Georgian government and the military command in Abkhazia, left the Social Democratic faction of the People's Council, and there arose there a separate group of Social Democrats - Internationalists, consisting exclusively of Abkhazian representatives. It was during this period that they proposed three draft constitutions for Abkhazia, the adoption of which was much discussed from the rostrum of the Council. However, everything ended with their discussion in Sukhum, because the further process turned out to be blocked in Tiflis, since the peddling of this issue logically resulting in the form of an agreement and approval of one of the options would actually have undermined the reality of Georgian power in Abkhazia.

It should be noted that the autonomous status of Abkhazia within Georgia could not be legally formalised for a long time by its then leadership, and this happened only on the eve of the Sovietisation of 1921. Only in the last days of the existence of the Georgian Democratic Republic, did its Constituent Assembly, the elections of which, by the way, were boycotted by the majority of the Abkhazian population, adopt a Constitution of Georgia, which spoke of the autonomous governance of Abkhazia.

The Georgian government needed a document stating that Abkhazia was part of the republic (it is clear that it was an autonomy), and when it received it in 1919, the activity of its representatives abruptly dwindled. At that time, the drafting of the Constitution of Georgia was in full swing, in which Abkhazia was allotted a very small place.

The politicians from Tiflis were not interested in working out the specific powers and functionality of the People›s Council itself, so the matter did not go further than this document. The desire of the Abkhazian leaders to receive legislative functions for the Council remained an unfulfilled dream. The Georgian administration was able to keep the Abkhazian Council within the framework of an ordinary representative and advisory body. The formal declaration of autonomous status without a specific legal elaboration of the relationship between Sukhum and Tiflis created uncertainty and contributed to the escalation of the conflict.

After March 1919, only the dispute over the status of Abkhazia within Georgia remained relevant. By and large, the Georgian authorities, who felt themselves masters of the situation, managed to localise this dispute within the framework of the Council. Ethnic Abkhazians, united in an opposition-group, demanded the status of "broad political autonomy", referring to the equality of subjecthood for Georgia and Abkhazia and to the Agreements signed in 1918. Tiflis, in turn, supported the local Social Democrats, as well as the Social-Revolutionaries and Social-Federalists, who lobbied for the idea of "administrative autonomy" for Abkhazia.

Therefore, no Abkhazian constitution was ever considered or supported by Tiflis. Members of the People's Council were deprived of the right independently to adopt a constitution. Otherwise, a format of equality would have arisen between the Abkhazian and Georgian sides, something which the latter feared and did not want.

The adoption of the constitution of the GDR and the "Temporary regulation on the management of the autonomy of Abkhazia" in February 1921 was clearly belated, given that the Republic was already rolling towards collapse ...

* * *

The misunderstanding between Tiflis and Sukhum that arose in 1918 quickly turned into an escalating conflict.

So, the ANS was dissolved by Mazniev on 9 October 1918, some of its members being arrested and sent to Tiflis. By order of the general, a number of punitive expeditions were carried out on the territory of the district, some of them even ended with the burning of the houses of local residents. In October of the same year, the Minister for Abkhazian Affairs R. Chkhotua was removed from office and, together with the district commissioner I. Marshania, was accused of conspiracy against Georgia (after which there followed the arrest of the aforementioned).

The actions of the Georgian authorities and the military contingent caused massive discontent among the local population. This trend is recorded in the intelligence of the Volunteer Army. In particular, in the report of the head of the Intelligence Department of the Headquarters of the Commander-in-Chief of the Volunteer Army, Colonel S.N. Rjasnjanskij, of 22 October 1918 it was noted that "all Abkhazians are extremely hostile towards the Georgians and the Georgian Government.

The following circumstances served as the reason for the dissatisfaction: some part of the population of Abkhazia, back in ancient times, moved to Turkey, but at present they decided to return to their compatriots in Abkhazia, especially since the population of the latter agreed to accept them. For this purpose, a delegation of 200 people was sent to the Georgian Government in order to obtain permission from it to re-settle in Abkhazia. The Georgian Government refused the request of the Abkhazian deputies, which was the first reason for the dissatisfaction of the Abkhazian population towards the Government of the Georgians. The second reason, which finally sowed irreconcilable enmity between the Abkhazians and Georgians, was that the latter, in view of the large grain harvest in Abkhazia, requisitioned almost all food-supplies for the population for Georgia. In addition to bread, the Georgian Government also requisitioned from the Abkhazians cattle, horses, saddles, and in general everything needed by Georgia. The latter circumstance finally brought the Abkhazians to the end of their tether, and in some places of Abkhazia they raised an armed uprising against their oppressors".

According to the head of Denikin's intelligence-service, such demonstrations, "having an unorganised character, were quickly suppressed by the Georgian troops, and the Government of Georgia officially styled them a Bolshevik movement among the Abkhazians. Weapons amounting to 4,000 rifles and 40,000 cartridges for them were brought to the Abkhazians from Turkey by the delegates. At present, some detachments of the rebellious Abkhazians are hiding in the mountains, and the Georgian Government is in no position to do anything with them".

Dissatisfaction with the Georgian government and the presence of its troops grew and resulted in the appeal of the Abkhazians to Denikin, who then commanded the Volunteer Army. As S. Danilov stresses: "Finally, the Abkhazians could not stand it and sent their representatives to the command of the Volunteer Army with a request to help them free themselves from the new conquerors. Many Abkhazians, officers and horsemen, secretly left Abkhazia and joined the ranks of the Volunteer Army of Gen. Denikin, which was successfully operating in the North Caucasus and in the south of Russia."

Having received such an appeal ("Appeal of representatives of the Abkhazian people to General Denikin" dated 1 February 1919), Denikin immediately wrote a special appeal to the two most influential British generals, J. Forestier-Walker and J. Milne, wherein, in particular, he noted, that "the hatred of the Abkhazians towards the Georgians is so great that no cohabitation of these two peoples is possible, but all the same, through bloody struggle the Abkhazians will achieve their freedom ...". In connection with such an understandable trend, he asked the Allied command "for the immediate withdrawal of Georgian troops from Abkhazia in order to save the Abkhazian people from violence ...".

The outrages of the Georgian units both in the Abkhazian and Armenian villages of the district caused open discontent. For example, on 22 June 1918, Georgian soldiers robbed the cash-desk of the Lykhny Credit Association. An investigative commission was created, which confirmed the fact of the robbery and bringing the fireproof cash-desk "into a state of complete disrepair" – the cost of the damage was estimated at 2 thousand roubles.

This commission was specifically engaged in identifying victims of the robbery and compiling a general statement of losses to the population of Abkhazia caused by Georgian troops in the summer of 1918. In particular, the population of the Gudauta province alone, according to the register drawn up on 17 August, suffered losses totalling 85,718 roubles. In addition to money, a large number of horses (as well as saddles, bridles, whips), gold rings and bracelets, watches, daggers, carpets, and household-utensils were stolen. All the necessary food-supplies and alcohol were taken from the local residents (many complained about the theft of several buckets of wine or vodka, and about the disappearance of flour and sugar). Moreover, the Georgian soldiers were not averse to stealing small and low-value items – in other words, everything that just lay about - clothes, bedding, even handkerchiefs. Serious damage was also caused to the inhabitants of the Kodor district as a result of robberies and arson committed by soldiers.

Periodically, indignant residents sent letters to Tiflis demanding the removal of the presumptuous "defenders" from Abkhazia. For example, a similar goal was pursued in a memorandum of the chairman of the Sukhum Armenian Council Kh. Avdalbekjan (March 1919) to the Chairman of the Government in Tiflis, where, in particular, it was said that "the recent speeches of the Georgian regular military units have created in the Armenian population a feeling of deep resentment from the unlawful manifestations of cruelty on the part of these units. Murders, robberies, illegal removal of horses from peasants and rape of women accompanied the path of the military units, mainly the cavalry division". The document lists a number of villages that had suffered at the hands of Georgian units: "In the village of Atara, a flying detachment carried off 11 horses and the population was robbed of the amount of 62,500 roubles, according to the calculation of the district commissariat. The losses of the peasants of the village Lechkop were, by their account, 32 thousand roubles. The losses of the peasants of the villages of Gumista and Eshera were, by their account, 196 thousand roubles. The losses of the peasants of the village Kavakluk were, by their account, more than 200 thousand roubles. ...".

Discontent ripened and resulted in an appeal by a delegation of 14 deputies of the People's Council addressed to the head of government, Noë Zhordania, (dated 29 September 1919), where there was a demand to deal with "the arbitrariness and violence of the authorities". This message, also brought to the Georgian capital, listed the excesses and facts of the arbitrariness of the representatives of the Georgian administration, the military command and individual detachments.

In particular, General Mazniev and his chief of staff, Colonel Tukhareli, organised an expeditionary detachment to carry out punitive operations. He, according to the statement of the deputies of the People's Council, broke into "peaceful Abkhazian villages [in the Kodor District – commentary in footnote], taking everything of even the slightest value, and committing violence against women. The other part of this detachment, under the direct supervision of Mr. Tukhareli, was engaged in bombing the houses of those persons who had been denounced. Similar violence was carried out in the Gudauta Region. The head of the Georgian detachment, Lieutenant Kupunia, a former bailiff of the city of Poti, beat up a gathering of the entire villege in Atsy, forcing everyone to lie down under machine-gun fire, and walked on their backs, striking with the flat surface of a sabre; then he ordered the gathering to group together in a mass and rode at full gallop into the crowd, inflicting beatings with the whip. Members of the former Abkhazian People's Council, Abukhba and Dzukua, who turned to him ub protest against such atrocity and violence, were arrested and locked up in a barn.

Widespread discontent among the local population was also caused by the actions of the Georgian detachment in the Gumista District. There, "in the Dranda region, the head of a separate detachment, officer Chargishvili, systematically is provoking the population on ethnic grounds, resorting to blatant measures for this purpose. So, for example, for 11 days Abkhazians travelling from the Kodor and Samurzakan Districts were not allowed to pass over the Kodor bridge; Mr. Chargishvili referred to the order of Colonel Tukhareli. Neither of them cancelled their order even after instruction from the Commissar of Internal Affairs of Abkhazia, Mr. Lordkipanidze".

Extraordinary Commissar Chkhikvishvili, who was appointed Head of the Georgian administration of Abkhazia by Tiflis after the dissolving of the People's Council, repeatedly "distinguished himself" in Abkhazia. "Like General Mazniev, he organised a detachment from the dregs of Samurzakan, which, being sent to the village of Dzhgerda (Kodor District) in order to catch the killers of Mamatsov (instructor for elections to the People's Council of Abkhazia), limited himself to robbing literally the entire civilian population of Dzhgerda. On the way back, this detachment robbed the Armenian village located between Dzhgerda and the village of Atara. The losses caused by this detachment were expressed in millions," the Abkhazian deputies said in a statement.

The authors of the appeal write bitterly that: "The peoples of Abkhazia have not yet seen anything but punitive expeditions, arson, flogging and violence against women ... Thus, in a short time, in all respects, representatives of the Georgian government have not only failed to establish friendly relations between the peoples of Abkhazia and the Georgian government, but, on the contrary, have alienated those who sincerely supported the Republic of Georgia in its democratic aspirations."

* * *

The negative consequences of the shameless intervention of Tiflis in the life of Abkhazia (dictatorship, if you like) were felt by the population and its various circles rather quickly. For example, the decision of the Georgian government to ban the export of tobacco from Abkhazian territory led to a sharp drop in prices for it and actually brought down the previously flourishing industry. As early as July 1918, tobacco-prices fell by almost 40%. This was in direct violation of the June Agreement, which left all matters of internal administration in the hands of the ANS.[6]

The attempt to introduce the Georgian language as an official language did not find understanding either: Tiflis demanded the translation into Georgian of all office-work in state-institutions, as well as at the post office and telegraph. In particular, the government of the GDR, based on clear nationalist ideology, demanded that within 3 months the activities of all government-agencies and, of course, postal and telegraph services, be completely translated into Georgian. This directly affected the issue of personnel, since people of non-Georgian origin, specifically those with no knowledge of the Georgian language, had to leave the service within the same three months. The ANS was categorically against such an unacceptable innovation, considering it important to preserve linguistic freedom in Abkhazia; therefore, on 3 August 1918: "In view of the multi-tribal population of Abkhazia and the impossibility of nation-alising government institutions, the Abkhazian People's Council decided temporarily to keep the Russian language as the common language of government institutions on the territory of Abkhazia", and, in addition to this, to announce "for general information that in the territory of Abkhazia the dismissal of employees on a national basis cannot be al-lowed". Therefore, already on 2 August, the ANS had suggested that "the heads of the institutions of Abkhazia freely accept telegrams and written correspondence in all languages only with the Roman or Russian script".

A sharp protest was also caused by the announcement of a state-mo-nopoly on the export of tobacco, which had previously been one of the main sources of income for Abkhazia (this led to a conflict between Tiflis and Sukhum, which, referring to the Agreement, demanded that this in-dustry be left in its jurisdiction). The introduction of additional taxes and payments (many were of an emergency-nature), as well as various prohibitive decrees by the Georgian administration, had an extremely negative impact on the socio-economic life in Abkhazia, and on the al-ready rather low level of trust in Tiflis. In particular, the "one-time emer-gency land-tax" introduced in the autumn of 1919 caused unrest and grumbling among the Abkhazian population.

The sanitary tax had similar consequences. For example, the newspaper *Nashe Slovo* describes the current situation in Gudauta in November 1919 as follows: "The city is now, more than ever, experienc-ing a food-crisis: there is no meat, which is explained by speculation on the part of butchers, taking advantage of the lack of a butcher's shop in the city, doing their dark deeds like slaughtering stolen cattle and selling them to some restaurateurs, etc. The sanitary tax caused a lot of talk among merchants, who called it 'an invention of the mayor'. The san-itary tax is not going particularly well because of distrust in the City Duma on the part of the irresponsible part of the merchants ... With the announcement of the sanitary tax, prices for all consumer-goods have increased significantly... In connection with this increase in food-prices, the poor and service people are doomed to starvation: the only way out is to supply their products at a reasonable price.»

Danilov notes that: "Since the country has come to be ruled by the Georgian authorities, the economic situation in Abkhazia has begun noticeably to worsen. There was no influx of the public (from Russia) to the resorts; the main branch of the country's economy, tobacco growing, was experiencing an acute sales-crisis due to the closure of borders. The main consumer for Abkhazian tobacco was the Russian tobacco-industry. Now, when this main buyer was no more, tobacco-prices have fallen sharply: local small factories (for example, in Tiflis) could absorb no more than 5% of the finished tobacco-crop. All this hit the well-being of the population of Abkhazia hard. The closure of markets with Russia caused yet other, extremely negative consequences: the supply of flour and foodstuffs ceased. Prior to this, the bulk of food-products had come to Abkhazia from the Ukraine (flour, butter, livestock, etc.), down to bran and hay, not to mention industrial goods."

It should be noted that by the autumn of 1919 the socio-economic situation in Abkhazia had become serious. As recorded in the order of the ANS delegation sent to Tiflis for negotiations (dated 28 November 1919): "The financial and economic crisis of Abkhazia has reached catastrophic proportions; private initiative has become predatory – industry, especially tobacco, as well as any organic work under In the current order of things, is excluded – as a consequence of which the population and local democracy are in the most difficult position. As a result of this, local democratic institutions – the People's Council of Abkhazia and its executive body - the Commissariat, as well as local organs of government and economy - *zemstvos* and city-administrations are on the verge of extinction and, in view of threatening indications, no creative work or development of the productive forces of the region is conceivable unless urgent action is taken.»

The ANS demanded that Tiflis leave the foreign trade in tobacco (at least 50 thousand *poods* of tobacco-leaf!), nuts (hazelnuts) and wine (since tobacco-growing, wine-making and collecting nuts were traditional Abkhazian industries) under their jurisdiction, to provide a monopoly on logging activities (i.e. harvesting timber and exporting it abroad for sale), as well as harvesting corn, beans, hay and pork. In addition, in order to intensify trade and economic activity in Abkhazia, the Council asked the Georgian government for a loan of 10 million roubles.

Tiflis paid attention to Abkhazia and provided it with financial support only on a residual basis, obviously not meeting the wishes and requests of the ANS. In extreme cases, when it was completely indecent or insulting for the Georgian government to refuse, a half-hearted decision was made. Sukhum's demands were never fully supported, despite their moderation.

In particular, the financial and economic delegation sent to Tiflis at the end of 1919 was able to obtain official permission only for the export of 20 thousand *poods* of small nuts abroad. Independent export of tobacco abroad was prohibited (the ban was announced personally by the Minister of Supply of Georgia, G.P. Eradze, in connection with the announcement of the state's monopoly on tobacco-leaf).

However, after the meetings of the delegation with members of the government, it was possible to change the position of the Georgian side. As recorded in the report of the delegation: "On the first issue of granting the right to export 50,000 *poods* of tobacco-leaf abroad, the delegation was not fully satisfied, either in terms of quantity or in terms of export. It is allowed to prepare only 25,000 *poods* of tobacco and export it in conjunction with the central government for sale abroad. Moreover, sharing in the net income from the sale are both the Commissariat and the central Government, which assumes responsibility for insurance and the costs of moving the delivered tobacco from the place of loading to the destination, where the sale is to be completed. Their sharing in this income is determined by the percentage-balance, namely: the Commissariat receives 40%, and the remaining 60% goes to the central Government."

Success can be considered to be the conclusion by the said delegation of two agreements in the Ministry of Supply of Georgia: "On the purchase and preparation of a monopoly for tobacco, corn and *lobio* [beans – Trans] within Abkhazia. Under these agreements, in addition to all expenses for the purchase and procurement of tobacco and corn, the Commissariat of Abkhazia receives in the form of net income for the production of operations 5% of the purchase-price from tobacco, 10% from corn, and 20 roubles for the procurement of *lobio* per *pood*.

* * *

However, during the years of Georgian dictatorship, the situation in the socio-economic field did not change for the better. An assembly of the Abkhazian intelligentsia, which met at the end of February 1920 in Sukhum, stated "that among the Abkhazian masses, as well as among the peasants of other nationalities inhabiting Abkhazia, there is complete poverty and an extreme need for factory-made items; that locally produced products are devalued due to abnormal marketing; that public education, medical and agronomic assistance to the population are at a low level or completely absent; that the observed negative attitude towards the existing political order is mainly due to the unsecured material situation of the population".

By the autumn of 1920 the situation in Abkhazia was still serious. The Council of Civil Servants repeatedly appealed to the People's Council of Abkhazia with a demand to improve their financial situation, which had put them on the brink of survival and poverty. In one of the Council's statements, dated 7 September, it is emphasised that "the extreme cost and lack of basic necessities, coupled with completely insufficient maintenance, barely enough to last 10 days, create extremely difficult living conditions for employees, leading to gradual physical exhaustion".

It should be noted that dissatisfaction with the local administration and anti-Georgian sentiments in Abkhazian society only grew in the period 1919-1921. The characteristic of the situation in Abkhazia in the autumn of 1920, which is given by intelligence of the 9th Kuban Red Army, based on data from agents, is indicative: "All power in Abkhazia is concentrated in the hands of the Commissar of Internal Affairs of Abkhazia Ubiria, who appoints the entire administration (commissars of towns, districts and etc.). He himself is a mere tool, an agent of the Georgian government... Ubiria enjoys absolutely no authority among the masses. At the? Com[mittee] of Ext[ternal] Affairs of Abkhazia, a Special Detachment (Georgian counterintelligence) is working, headed by Eshba; agents of this organisation are scattered in all corners of Abkhazia. It is enough to arouse the slightest suspicion in the eyes of a special constable to end up spending 2-3 months in prison when entirely guilt-free. The Sukhum prison is constantly overcrowded (up to 400 people are imprisoned), mostly by legally innocent Abkhazians. Bribery among the administration has reached its climax – people are often arrested in order to squeeze out a bribe. Therefore, the entire population is full of dissatisfaction with the administration ... The Abkhazian people are certainly not in a position to oppose Georgia, but they are waiting for the right moment, an external onslaught, to reveal their inner bitterness ...

"A small part of the Abkhazians cleave to Turkish orientation – princes (nobility) and Mohammedan Abkhazians, whilst the rest of the Abkhazians, who reside in the Samurzakano, Gudauta and Gagra regions, are on the side of Soviet Russia."

A similar negative attitude towards the Georgian authorities was also recorded by Mustafa Butbaj (who made an extended trip to the Caucasus in 1920 and visited Georgia and Abkhazia); he left behind interesting travel-notebooks, collectively known as "Memories of the Caucasus". For example, in the entry dated 21 August, there are the following lines: "An old man came to visit me today. He talked a lot about Georgians for a very long time. About how they took tobacco from the peasants without paying anything, and things like that, about how the Abkhazians are very embittered with regard to the Georgians; he spoke of it with great bitterness and pain."

* * *

After the adoption by the People's Council of the document so desired by the Georgian leadership (the "Act on the Autonomy of Abkhazia" March 1919), more than a year passed, and the situation regarding the official formalisation of relations between Sukhum and Tiflis, as well as the creation of a legislative framework for Abkhazia itself, essentially did not change. The Georgian leadership in every possible way delayed the process of adopting the constitution of Abkhazia, and the legislative delimitation of powers between Tiflis and Sukhum. In total for the period 1919-1920 three delegations of the NSA visited Tiflis, bringing with them three different drafts of an Abkhazian constitution, but none of them was considered on its merits, and, moreover, was not adopted. The deputies of the Constituent Assembly of Georgia considered simple fixation in law of the autonomous status of Abkhazia within the GDR sufficient.

In the note of the Abkhazian delegation, submitted to N. Zhordania in November 1920, it was emphasised that "the People's Council of Abkhazia, based on aforementioned Agreements, Acts and government-assurances, repeatedly sent delegations to the Constituent Assembly to finalise relations between Georgia and Abkhazia – indeed an Extraordinary Commissioner of the Republic of Georgia took part in the preparatory work in the People's Council. However, these delegations did not achieve the desired result. ... Relations between Georgia and Abkhazia have not yet been formalised and therefore are not legally binding on either side".

The delegation publicly accused the Georgian side of regular violations of the signed Agreements: "All the Government's assurances about the inviolability of autonomy were in practice far from reality. In essence, since 1918, the Government of Georgia has been increasingly expanding the scope of its intervention in all spheres of life in Abkhazia, quite often violating even those of its rights about which there was no dispute in the commissions that developed the Draft Constitution of Autonomous Abkhazia. This contradiction, expressed, on the one hand, in the repeated assurances of the organs of the Republic about the inviolability of autonomy, and on the other hand, in the interference in the internal affairs of Abkhazia, created in Abkhazia distrust not only in the national authorities, but also in the local legislative body – the People's Council of Abkhazia which believed, by a large majority, its immediate tasks lay in organising power in Abkhazia and in achieving the people's peace of mind, which had been disturbed by the aforementioned contradictions.

The delegation headed by I.N. Margania arrived in the Georgian capital in the autumn of 1920 (as recorded in a note) "with a certain expressed desire to receive clearly and precisely documented answers on the merits of the Act of 20 March 1919, and also insists on the need for the immediate formation of a mixed commission made up in equal numbers from the People's Council and the Constituent Assembly to consider the Draft Constitution of Abkhazia, which draft should be hastily approved by the Constituent Assembly. The goal of the delegation was not achieved this time either. The Constituent Assembly of Georgia was not going to consider a separate Abkhazian constitution, let alone approve it. It was during this period that the work on the republican constitution was being completed, where Abkhazia (also called the "Sukhum Region" = *oblast'* – Trans.) was allotted a very modest place. Along with other outlying areas, it received the right to "autonomous government in local affairs" (according to the 107th article). The Georgian political élite simply did not want to treat the Abkhazians as equals and bother with their demands for broad autonomy.[7]

* * *

Officially unscheduled relations between Tiflis and Sukhum were in a essentially broken state. The gulf between the aspirations of the Abkhazian and Georgian élites had only widened since 1918. In real life, anti-Georgian sentiments in Abkhazian society had grown stronger and stronger. Tiflis could not do anything to smooth out these sharp contradictions. And soon after the departure of the last Abkhazian delegation, Tiflis welcomed the year 1921 followed by new guests wearing Red Army uniforms.

It is important to emphasise that the mass-dissatisfaction with the Georgian policy, both by Abkhazian society and its élite, naturally led to an increase in the feelings of protest in society and sympathy for the Bolsheviks (Soviet Russia). As the Soviet military attaché in Georgia Pavel Sytin reported (in a report dated 25 January 1921): "Since the return of the delegation of the Abkhazian People's Council from Tiflis, the Council has not yet met, despite the fact that the majority of members insist on convening the Council, but the Georgian government is afraid that the Abkhazian People's Council at the very first meeting will renounce Georgia due to Georgia's violation of the Act of 20 March 1919, which states that Abkhazia is part of Georgia as an autonomous unit. All this causes revulsion in the masses of Abkhazia and creates a fertile ground for us. Robberies are going on in Abkhazia and anarchy is intensifying. The population is waiting for a call to revolt."

Such sentiments greatly facilitated the military operation of the Red Army on the territory of Abkhazia in 1921, when the Georgian troops found themselves without any support from the population and were forced to retreat rapidly beyond the River Ingur. Moreover, such a clear victory was largely the result of the direct actions of the Abkhazian rebel-detachments. Modern scholar of the Caucasus A.B. Krylov rightly notes that "the establishment of Soviet power in Abkhazia in March 1921 was perceived by the population primarily as deliverance from national oppression and Georgian occupation". Let us emphasise that the Abkhazians most actively participated in the operation of the Red Army against the Republic of Georgia and made a significant contribution to the defeat of its armed forces and the final victory, which led to the Sovietisation of Georgia.

Sources and Literature

Sources

Abxazskij Narodnyj Sovet. 1917-1920 gg. Dokumenty i materialy [The Abkhazian People›s Council. 1917-1920 Documents and Materials], Compiled with foreword by R. Khodzhaa. Sukhum, 2007.

Abxazija – dokumenty i materialy (1917-1921 gg.) [Abkhazia – Documents and Materials (1917-1921)], Compiled by R.H. Gozhba. Sukhum, 2009.

Avalov Z.: *Nezavisimost' Gruzii v meždunarodnoj politike. 1918-1921 gg.* [The Independence of Georgia in International Politics. 1918-1921]. Reprint of the 1924 edition. New-York, 1982.

Amia M.: *Put' gruzinskoj žirondy. Fakty, dokumenty, materialy iz istorii pereroždenija men'ševikov i izgnanija ix iz Gruzii* [Amia M.: The Way of the Georgian Gironde. Facts, Documents, Materials from the History of the Rebirth of the Mensheviks and their Expulsion from Georgia]. Tiflis, 1926.

Bammat G.: *Kavkaz i russkaja revoljutsija: Političeskij aspekt* [The Caucasus and the Russian Revolution: Political Aspect]. Translated from English. Makhachkala, 2000.

Baturin G.: *Krasnaja Tamanskaja armija* [Red Taman Army]. Krasnodar, 1940.

Bor'ba za Oktjabr' v Abxazii. Sbornik dokumentov i materialov 1917-1921 gg. [The Struggle for October in Abkhazia. Collection of Documents and Materials 1917-1921]. Sukhum, 1967.

Bor'ba za pobedu Sovetskoj vlasti v Gruzii. Dokumenty i materialy (1917-1921) [The Struggle for the Victory of Soviet Power in Georgia. Documents and Materials (1917-1921)]. Tbilisi, 1958.

Bor'ba za Sovetskuju vlast' na Kubani v 1917-1920 gg. Sbornik dokumentov i materialov [The Struggle for Soviet Power in the Kuban in 1917-1920. Collection of Documents and Materials]. Krasnodar, 1957.

Bor'ba za Sovetskuju vlast' v Abxazii v 1917-1921 gg. [The Struggle for Soviet Power in Abkhazia. 1917-1921]. Sukhum, 1957.

Butbaj M.: *Vospominanija o Kavkaze. Zapiski turetskogo razvedčika* [Memories of the Caucasus. Notes of a Turkish Intelligence Officer]. Makhachkala, 1993.

Vorobjov N. *O neosnovatel'nosti pritjazanij gruzin na Suxumskij okrug (Abxaziju) (Rostov n/D, 1919) // Materialy po istorii Abxazii. Vyp. 1* [On the Groundlessness of the Claims of Georgians to the Sukhum District

(Abkhazia) (Rostov on Don, 1919), in *Materials on the history of Abkhazia. Issue. 1*]. Sukhum, 1990.

«Vse abxaztsy krajne vraždebno nastroeny protiv gruzin»: Raport načal'nika denikinskoj razvedki". Publ. A. Ganina // *Rodina. 2008. No. 11* [«All Abkhazians are extremely hostile towards the Georgians»: Report of the Head of Denikin›s Intelligence. Publication of A. Ganina. *Motherland. 2008, No. 11*].

Glonti T.: *Men'ševistskaja i Sovetskaja Gruzija* [Menshevik and Soviet Georgia]. Moscow, 1923.

Gruzija: Dannye o vooružennyx silax i kratkij obzor političeskogo, èkonomičeskogo i meždunarodnogo položenija Gruzii (po sostojaniju k 1 janvarja 1921 g.) [Georgia: Military Data and a Brief Survey of Georgia›s Political, Economic and International Situation (as of 1 January 1921)]. Moscow, 1921.

«Demokratičeskoe pravitel'stvo» Gruzii i anglijskoe komandovanie [«Democratic government» of Georgia and the British Command]. Tiflis, 1928.

Denikin A.I.: *Očerki russkoj smuty. V 5 t.* [Essays on Russian Troubles. In 5 Volumes]. Paris, 1921; Berlin, 1924, 1926.

Dzhugeli V.: *Tjaželyj krest* [Heavy Cross]. Tiflis, 1920.

Dni gospodstva men'ševikov v Gruzii (dokumenty i materialy) [Days of Menshevik Domination in Georgia (Documents and Materials)]. Tiflis, 1931.

Dokumenty i materialy po vnešnej politike Zakavkaz'ja v Gruzii [Documents and Materials on the Foreign Policy of Transcaucasia in Georgia]. Tiflis. 1919.

Zhordanija N.N.: *Moja žizn'* [My life]. Stanford, 1968.

K istorii revoljutsionnogo dviženija v Abxazii. Sbornik Glavpolitprosveta Abxazii [On the History of the Revolutionary Movement in Abkhazia. Collection of the Works of the Chief Education Committee of Abkhazia]. Sukhum, 1922.

Kavkazskij kalendar' na 1917 g. [Caucasian Calendar for 1917]. Tiflis, 1916.

Kvinitadze G.I.: *Vospominanija. 1917-1921*. Paris, 1985.

Mazniashvili G.: *Memoirs*. Tbilisi, 1927. (In Georgian)

Materials from the History of Relations between Georgia and the North Caucasus (1917-1921)] (ed. M. Bakhtadze, G. Mamulia). Tb., 2005. (In Georgian)

Materialy po istorii Abxazii sovetskogo perioda. SSR Abxazija v pervom desjatiletii (1921-1931 gg.). T. 1 [Materials on the History of Abkhazia in the Soviet period. Abkhazian SSR in the First Decade (1921-1931). Vol. 1]. Sukhum, 2012.

Makharadze F. *Diktatura men'ševistskoj partii v Gruzii* [Dictatorship of the Menshevik Party in Georgia]. Moscow, 1921.

Makharadze F. *Sovety i bor'ba za Sovetskuju vlast' v Gruzii 1917-1921* [Soviets and the Struggle for Soviet Power in Georgia 1917-1921]. Tiflis, 1928.

Meshcherjakov N. *V men'ševistskom raju. Iz vpečatlenij poezdki v Gruziju* [In the Menshevik Paradise. From the Impressions of a Trip to Georgia]. Moscow, 1921.

Meshcherjakov N. *V men'ševistskom raju. Iz vpečatlenij poezdki v Gruziju* [Frivolous Traveller]. Moscow, 1921.

Mirnyj dogovor meždu Rossiej I Gruziej [Peace Treaty between Russia and Georgia]. Moscow, 1920.

Okkupatsija i faktičeskaja anneksija Gruzii. Dokumenty i materialy [Occupation and *de facto* Annexation of Georgia. Documents and Materials] (Compiled by A. Menteshashvili, and edited by A. Surguladze). Tbilisi, 1990.

«On logičen v svoix orientatsijax»: abxazskie bol'ševiki N.A. Lakoba i E.A. Èšba o svoej poezdke v Turtsiju v kontse 1920 – načale 1921 g. // (Publ. V.V. Novikova: Kavkazskij sbornik. T. 8(40) ["He is logical in his orientations": Abkhazian Bolsheviks N.A. Lakoba and E.A. Eshba about their Trip to Turkey in Late 1920 - Early 1921, in Publ. by V.V. Novikov: *Caucasian collection. Vol. 8(40)*]. Moscow, 2014.

Orakhelashvili M.D.: *Sergo Ordžonikidze: Biog. očerk* [Sergo Ordzhonikidze: Biographical Essay]. Moscow, 1936.

Ordzhonikidze G.K.: *Biografija* [Biography]. Moscow, 1962.

Ordzhonikidze G.K.: *Stat'i i reči. T. 1* [Articles and speeches. Vol. 1.]. Moscow, 1956.

Revoljutsionnye komitety Gruzii v bor'be za ustanovlenie i upročnenie Sovetskoj vlasti (fevral' 1921 g. – mart 1922 g.) [Revolutionary Committees of Abkhazia in the Struggle for the Establishment and Strengthening of Soviet Power (February 1921 - February 1922). Collection of Documents and Materials]. Sukhum, 1961.

Revoljutsionnye komitety Gruzii v bor'be za ustanovlenie i upročnenie Sovetskoj vlasti (fevral' 1921 g. – mart 1922 g.). Sbornik dokumentov i materialov [Revolutionary Committees of Georgia in the Struggle for the Establishment and Strengthening of Soviet Power (February 1921 - March

1922). Collection of Documents and Materials]. Sukhum, 1963.

RSFSR i Gruzinskaja demokratičeskaja respublika. Ix vzaimootnošenija [RSFSR and the Georgian Democratic Republic. Their Mutual Relationship]. Moscow, 1922.

Sokolov K.N.: *Pravlenie generala Denikina (iz vospominanij)* [The Rule of General Denikin (from Memoirs)]. Moscow, 2007.

Sojuz ob'edinennyx gortsev Severnogo Kavkaza i Dagestana (1917-1918 gg.), Gorskaja respublika (1918-1920 gg.). Dokumenty i materialy [The Union of United Highlanders of the North Caucasus and Daghestan (1917-1918), the Mountain Republic (1918-1920). Documents and Materials]. Makhachkala, 1994.

Stalin I.V.: *Kontrrevoljutsionery Zakavkaz'ja pod maskoj sotsializma // Sočinenija. T. 4* [Counter-revolutionaries of Transcaucasia under the Guise of Socialism, in *Works. Vol. 4*]. Moscow, 1951.

Stalin I.V.: *Položenie na Kavkaze. Beseda s sotrudnikami gazety «Pravda» // Sočinenija. T. 4* [The Situation in the Caucasus. Conversation with Employees of the Newspaper «Pravda», in *Works. Vol. 4*]. Moscow, 1951.

Trudjashchiesja Abxazii – V.I. Leninu (1918, 1921-1924 gg.). Sbornik dokumentov / Sost. G.A. Dzidzarija [Workers of Abkhazia – V.I. Lenin (1918, 1921-1924). Collection of Documents. Compiled by G.A. Dzidzarija]. Sukhum, 1970.

Učastniki osvoboditel'nogo dviženija v Abxazii 1917-1921 gg. Vospominanija kiarazovtsev, krasnogvardejtsev i krasnyx partizan [Participants in the Liberation-movement in Abkhazia 1917-1921. Memoirs of *Kiarazovites*, Red Guards and Red Partisans]. Sukhum, 2007.

CK RKP(b) – VKP(b) i natsional'nyj vopros. Kniga 1. 1918-1933 gg. / Sost. L.S. Gatagova, L.P. Koševeva, L.A. Rogovaja [Central Committee of the RCP(b) - VKP(b) and the National Question. Book 1. 1918-1933 / Compiled by L.S. Gatagova, L.P. Kosheleva, L.A. Rogovaja]. Moscow, 2005.

Elde.: *Zakavkaz'e i Edinaja Rossija* [Transcaucasia and United Russia]. Rostov on Don, 1919.

Literature

Abxazy/ Otv. red. Ju.D. Ančabadze, Ju.G. Argun [Ju. D. Anchabadze, Ju. G. Argun (eds.): The Abkhazians]. Moscow, 2007.

Adamia V.I.: *Iz istorii anglijskoj interventsii v Gruzii (1918-1921 gg.)* [From the History of British Intervention in Georgia (1918-1921)]. Sukhum, 1961.

Anchabadze Z.V., Dzidzarija G.A.: *Družba izvečnaja, nerušimaja. Očerki iz istorii gruzino-abxazskix otnošenij* [Friendship is Eternal, Indestructible. Essays from the History of Georgian-Abkhazian Relations]. Sukhum, 1973.

Baberovski J.: *Vrag est' vezde. Stalinizm na Kavkaze* [The Enemy is Everywhere. Stalinism in the Caucasus]. Moscow, 2010.

Badaljan Kh.A.: *Turetsko-germanskaja èkspansija v Zakavkaz'e (1914-1918 gg.)* [Turkish-German Expansion in Transcaucasia (1914-1918)]. Erevan, 1980.

Bakradze L.: *Abxazija 1918 g. v dokumentax germanskogo MIDa: Aspekty gruzino-abxazskogo konflikta 5. (Materialy gruzino-abxazskoj konferentsii «Preemstvennost' kul'tur v kontekste gosudarstvennogo stroitel'stva». Adler, 26-28 avgusta 2000 g.)* [Abkhazia in 1918 in the Documents of the German Foreign Ministry: Aspects of the Georgian-Abkhazian Conflict 5. (Materials of the Georgian-Abkhazian Conference "Continuity of Cultures in the Context of State-building". Adler, August 26-28, 2000)]. University of California, Irvine, 2001.

Bakradze L.: *German-Georgian relations during the First World War (Activity of the Georgian National Committee 1914-1918)*. Tbilisi, 2009. (In Georgian)

Bgazhba M. *Nestor Lakoba*. Tb., 1965. (In Russian)

Bezugolny A.Yu. *Demokratičeskaja respublika Gruzija i ee vooružennye sily. 1918 – 1921 gg.,* // *Voprosy istorii No. 10* [Democratic Republic of Georgia and its Armed Forces. 1918 – 1921, in *Questions of History No. 10*]. 2009.

Borisov E.: *Zakavkazskaja mikroimperija* // *VPK. № 38(55). 6-12 oktjabrja 2004* [Transcaucasian Micro-empire, in VPK. No. 38(55). October 6-12, 2004].

Bortsy za Sovetskuju vlast' v Abxazii [Fighters for Soviet power in Abkhazia]. Sukhum, 1973.

Bortsy za Oktjabr' v Abxazii. Očerki [Fighters for October in Abkhazia. Essays]. Sukhum, 1981.

Volkhonsky M.A., Mukhanov V.M.: *Kavkazskoe namestničestvo,* // *Bol'šaja Rossijskaja Èntsiklopedija T. 12.* [Caucasian Governorship, in *The Great Russian Encyclopaedia, Vol. 12*]. Moscow, 2008.

Galojan G.A.: *Oktjabr'skaja revoljutsija i vozrožodenie narodov Zakavkaz'ja* [The October Revolution and the Revival of the Peoples of Transcaucasia]. Erevan, 1977.

Galojan G.A. *Rabočee dviženie i natsional'nyj vopros v Zakavkaz'e. 1900-1922 gg.* [The Labour-movement and the National Question in Transcaucasia. 1900-1922]. Erevan, 1969.

Gambashidze G.L.: *Gruzinskij vopros v planax imperialistov Antanty* [The Georgian Question is in the Plans of the *Entente* Imperialists]. Tbilisi, 1970.

Ganin A.: *Ot voenpreda tovariša Sytina. Sovetskaja voennaja razvedka v Gruzii o Belom Kryme, // Rodina. 2014. № 5* [From Military Representative Comrade Sytin. Soviet Military Intelligence in Georgia about White Crimea, in *Motherland 2014. No. 5.*]

Ganin A.V.: *Sovetskaja voennaja razvedka v Gruzii v 1920-1921 godax. Missija Pavla Sytina // Gosudarstvennoe upravlenie. Èlektronnyj vestnik. Vypusk № 43. Aprel' 2014 g.* [Soviet military intelligence in Georgia in 1920-1921. The Mission of Pavel Sytin, in *Public Administration. Electronic Bulletin. Issue No. 43. April 2014*]

Germanskie okkupanty v Gruzii v 1918 g [German Invaders in Georgia in 1918]. Tbilisi, 1942.

R.G. Suny, T. Martina (eds., & translated from English by V.I. Matuzova): *Gosudarstvo natsij: Imperija i natsional'noe stroitel'stvo v èpoxu Lenina i Stalina* [The State of Nations: Empire and Nation-Building in the Era of Lenin and Stalin]. Moscow, 2011.

Grishanin P.I.: *Vnešnepolitičeskaja strategija komandovanija Dobrovol'českoj armii 1918 god., // Novyj istoričeskij vestnik 11* [Foreign Policy Strategy of the Command of the Volunteer Army in 1918., in *New Historical Bulletin. No. 11*], 2004

Gubelidze B.: *Krax men'ševizma v Gruzii* [The Collapse of Menshevism in Georgia]. Tbilisi, 1979.

Gubernii Rossijskoj imperii. Istorija i rukovoditeli. 1708-1917 [Provinces of the Russian Empire. History and Leaders. 1708-1917]. Moscow, 2003.

Daudov A.Kh., Meskhidze D.I.: *Natsional'naja gosudarstvennost' gorskix narodov Severnogo Kavkaza (1917-1924)* [National Statehood of the Mountain- peoples of the North Caucasus (1917-1924)]. St.-Petersburg, 2009.

Dzhangveladze G.: *Bankrotstvo antiproletarskix partij v Gruzii* [Bankruptcy of Anti-proletarian Parties in Georgia]. Tbilisi, 1981.

Dzidzarija G.A.: *V.I. Lenin i Abxazija. Sukhumi* [V.I. Lenin and Abkhazia]. Sukhum, 1977.

Dzidzarija G.A.: *Ephrem Eshba.* Moscow, 1967. (In Russian)

Dzidzarija G.A.: *Iz istorii sovmestnoj bor'by gruzinskogo i abxazskogo narodov za vlast' Sovetov (1917-1921 gg.)* [From the History of the Joint Struggle of the Georgian and Abkhazian Peoples for the Power of the Soviets (1917-1921)]. Tbilisi, 1983.

Dzidzarija G.A.: *Nikolai Akirtava.* Sukhum, 1985. (In Russian)

Dzidzarija G.A.: *Očerki istorii Abxazii. 1910-1921* [Essays on the History of Abkhazia. 1910-1921]. Tbilisi, 1963.

Dzidzarija G.A.: *Očerki istorii bor'by za Sovetskuju vlast' v Abxazii 1917-1918 gg.* [Essays on the History of the Struggle for Soviet power in Abkhazia 1917-1918.]. Sukhum, 1958.

Dzidzarija G.A.: *Rol' Sovetov i «Kiaraza» v istorii revoljutsionnoj bor'by v Abxazii. 1917-1921 gg.* [The Role of the Soviets and «Kiaraz» in the History of the Revolutionary Struggle in Abkhazia. 1917-1921]. Sukhum, 1971.

Dzidzoev V.D.: *Ot Sojuza ob'edinennyx gortsev Severnogo Kavkaza i Dagestana do Gorskoj ASSR (1917-1924 gg.)* [From the Union of the United Highlanders of the North Caucasus and Daghestan up to the Mountain ASSR (1917-1924)]. Vladikavkaz, 2003.

Drabkina E.: *Gruzinskaja kontrrevoljutsija* [Georgian Counter-revolution]. Leningrad, 1928.

Enukidze D.E.: *Razgrom i izgnanie interventov iz Zakavkaz'ja* [The Defeat and Expulsion of the Interventionists from Transcaucasia]. Tbilisi, 1960.

Zhvanija G.K.: *Velikij Oktjabr' i pobeda Sovetskoj vlasti v Gruzii* [Great October and the Victory of Soviet Power in Georgia]. Tbilisi, 1987.

Zhorzholiani G., Lekishvili S., Toidze L., Khoshtaria-Brosse E.: *Istoričeskie i politiko-pravovye aspekty konflikta v Abxazii* [Historical and Politico-legal Aspects of the Conflict in Abkhazia]. Tbilisi, 1995.

Istorija Abxazskoj ASSR (1917-1937) [History of the Abkhazian ASSR (1917-1937)]. Sukhum, 1983.

Istorija Gruzii. V 3-x t. [History of Georgia. In 3 volumes. Vol. 2, 3.] Tbilisi, 1968, 1973.

Kadishev A.B.: *Interventsija i graždanskaja vojna v Zakavkaz'e* [Intervention and Civil War in Transcaucasia]. Moscow, 1960.

Karpenko S.V.: *Očerki istorii belogo dviženija na juge Rossii (1917 – 1920 gg.)* [Essays on the History of the White Movement in the South of Russia (1917 - 1920)]. Moscow, 2003.

Karpenko S.V.: *«Rossija na Kavkaze ostanetsja navsegda»: Dobrovol'českaja armija i nezavisimaja Gruzija (1918-1919 gg.) // Novyj istoričeskij vestnik № 2(18) 2008.* «Russia in the Caucasus Will Remain Forever»: The Volunteer Army and independent Georgia (1918-1919), in *New Historical Bulletin, No. 2(18)*]. 2008.

Kirmel' N.S.: *Belogvardejskie spetsslužby v Graždanskoj vojne. 1918–1922 gg.* [White Guard Intelligence Services in the Civil War. 1918–1922]. Moscow, 2008.

Kodzhaman O.: *Južnyj Kavkaz v politike Turtsii i Rossii v postsovetskij period* [The South Caucasus in the Policy of Turkey and Russia in the Post-Soviet Period] (Translated from English by I. Stamova). Moscow, 2004.

Krylov A.B.: *Religija i traditsii abxazov* [Religion and Traditions of the Abkhazians]. Moscow, 2001.

Krylov A.B.:. *Gruzino-abxazskij konflikt: istorija i sovremennost' // Kavkazskij sbornik. T. 2 (34)* [The Georgian-Abkhazian conflict: History and Modernity, in *Caucasian Collection. T. 2 (34)*]. Moscow, 2005.

Kuznetsova S.I.: *Ustanovlenie sovetsko-turetskix otnošenij* [Establishment of Soviet-Turkish Relations]. Moscow, 1961.

Lakoba S.: *Očerki političeskoj istorii Abxazii* [Essays on the Political History of Abkhazia]. Sukhum, 1990.

Lakoba S.: *Abxazija posle dvux imperij. XIX – XXI vv. Očerki* [Abkhazia after Two Empires. 19th – 21st Centuries. Essays]. Moscow, 2004.

Lakoba S.Z.: *Krylis' dni v Suxum-Kale...* [Days were Flying in Sukhum-Kale ...]. Sukhum, 2011.

Lezhava G.P.: *Iz istorii rabočego klassa Abxazii 1921-1941 gg.* [From the History of the Working Class of Abkhazia 1921-1941]. Tbilisi, 1978.

Lezhava G.P.: *Texnologii ètničeskoj mobilizatsii. Iz istorii stanovlenija gruzinskoj gosudarstvennosti (1987 – 1993 gg.)* [Technologies of Ethnic Mobilisation. From the History of the Formation of Georgian Statehood (1987 - 1993)]. Moscow, 2000.

Mailjan B.V.: *K voprosu o političeskom statuse Abxazii (mart 1917 – fevral' 1921 gg.) // Vestnik RAU (Serija – Gumanitarnye i obshchestvennye nauki, №º 2)* [On the Issue of the Political Status of Abkhazia (March 1917 - February 1921), *Reporter RAU (Series - Humanitarian and Social Sciences, No. 2)*]. 2009.

Mailjan B.V.: *K voprosu o territorial'nom konflikte na černomorskom poberež'e Kavkaza (ijul' 1918 – maj 1920 g.) // Istoričeskoe prostranstvo. Problemy istorii stran SNG* [To the Question of the Territorial Conflict on the Black Sea Coast of the Caucasus (July 1918 - May 1920), in *Historical Space. Problems of the History of the CIS Countries*]. Moscow, 2013.

Makharadze N.: *Pobeda Velikogo Oktjabrja v Gruzii* [Victory of Great October in Georgia]. Tbilisi, 1967.

Matsaberidze M.: *Razrabotka Konstitutsii Zakavkazskogo Sejma i Natsional'nyj Sovet Gruzii // Kavkaz i globalizatsija* [Development of the Constitution of the Transcaucasian *Seim* and the National Council of Georgia, in *The Caucasus and Globalisation, Vol.2*]. 2008.

Menteshashvili A.M.: *Iz istorii vzaimootnošenij gruzinskogo, abzazskogo i osetinskogo narodov (1918-1921 gg.)* [From the History of Relations between the Georgian, Abkhazian and Ossetian Peoples (1918-1921)]. Tbilisi, 1990.

Menteshashvili A.: *Raspad Rossijskoj imperii i Zakavkaz'e // Rossija v XX veke. Problemy natsional'nyx otnošenij* [The Collapse of the Russian Empire and Transcaucasia, in *Russia in the XXth Century. Problems of National Relations*]. Moscow, 1999.

Muzaev T.M.: *Sojuz gortsev. Russkaja revoljutsija i narody Severnogo Kavkaza, 1917 – mart 1918 g.* [The Highlanders' Union. Russian Revolution and the Peoples of the North Caucasus, 1917 - March 1918]. Moscow, 2007.

Mukhanov V.M.: *K istorii sovetizatsii Zakavkaz'ja (1920-1921 gg.) // Kavkazskij sbornik. T. 8(40) / Pod red. V.V. Degoeva* [On the History of the Sovietisation of Transcaucasia (1920-1921), in *Caucasian collection. T. 8(40)* (Ed. V.V. Degoev)]. Moscow, 2014.

Mukhanov V.M.: *«Sotsializm vinogradarej», ili Istorija Pervoj Gruzinskoj respubliki, 1917-1921* [«Socialism of winegrowers», or History of the First Georgian Republic, 1917-1921]. Moscow, 2019.

Očerki istorii Abxazskoj ASSR (1917-1964 gg.). Č. 2 [Essays on the History of the Abkhazian ASSR (1917-1964). Pt 2]. Sukhum, 1964.

Puchenkov A.S.: *Natsional'naja politika generala Denikina* [National Policy of General Denikin]. St.-Petersburg, 2012.

Sagarija B.E.: *K voprosu o granitsax Abxazii s Gruziej 1917-1921 gg. (sbornik dokumentov i materialov s kommentarijami)* [On the Issue of the Borders of Abkhazia with Georgia in 1917-1921. (Collection of Documents and Materials with Comments)]. Sukhum, 1998.

Sarkisjan A.E.: *Velikij Oktjabr' i neproletarskie partii Zakavkaz'ja* [Great October and Non-proletarian Parties of Transcaucasia]. Erevan, 1990.

Sef S.E.: *Bor'ba za oktjabr' v Zakavkaz'e* [Struggle for October in Transcaucasia]. Tiflis. 1932.

Sef S.E.: *Revoljutsija 1917 g. v Zakavkaz'e. Dokumenty, materialy* [Revolution of 1917 in Transcaucasia. Documents, Materials]. Tiflis, 1927.

Stavrovsky A.: *Zakavkaz'e posle Oktjabrja. Vzaimootnošenija s Turtsiej v pervoj polovine 1918 g.* [Transcaucasia after October. Relations with Turkey in the First Half of 1918]. Moscow-Leningrad, 1925.

Surguladze A.N.: *Zakavkaz'e v bor'be za pobedu* sotsialističeskoj *revoljutsii* [Transcaucasia in the Struggle for the Victory of the Socialist Revolution]. Tbilisi, 1971.

Surguladze A.N.: *Gruzinskaja demokratičeskaja intelligentsija v trëx revoljutsijax (1900-1921)* [Georgian Democratic Intelligentsia in Three Revolutions (1900-1921)]. Tbilisi, 1986.

Traskunov M.B.: *Geroičeskij boevoj put' 11-j armii na frontax graždanskoj vojny (1918-1921 gg.)* [The Heroic Combat-path of the 11th Army on the Fronts of the Civil War (1918-1921)]. Tbilisi, 1958.

Traskunov M.B.: *Kavkazskaja Krasnoznamennaja* [Caucasian Red Banner]. Tbilisi, 1961.

Tjutjukin S.V.: *Men'ševiki // Političeskie partii Rossii: istorija i sovremennost'* [Mensheviks// Political Parties of Russia: History and Modernity]. Moscow, 2000.

Khachapuridze G.V.: *Bor'ba gruzinskogo naroda za ustanovlenie Sovetskoj vlasti* [The Struggle of the Georgian People for the Establishment of Soviet Power]. Moscow, 1956.

Tsvetkov V. *Kapkan tiflisskogo kovarstva. Osobennosti političeskogo kursa Belogo dviženija v otnošenii Gruzii v 1918-1920 godax // Rodina No. 11* [The Trap of

Tiflis Treachery. Features of the Political Course of the White Movement towards Georgia in 1918-1920, in *Motherland No. 11*]. 2008.

Tsutsiev A.A.: *Atlas ètnopolitičeskoj istorii Kavkaza (1774-2004)* [Atlas of the Ethno-political History of the Caucasus (1774-2004)]. Moscow, 2006.

Charkviani K.: *Ob antinarodnoj èkonomičeskoj politike gruzinskix men'ševikov* [On the Anti-people Economic Policy of the Georgian Mensheviks]. Tbilisi, 1962.

Chokheli A.I.: *Politika Frantsii v otnošenii Gruzi. 1917-1921 gg.* [French Policy towards Georgia. 1917-1921] Tbilisi, 1980.

Shafir Ja.: *Graždanskaja vojna v Rossii i imperialističeskaja Gruzija* [The Civil War in Russia and Imperialist Georgia]. Tiflis, 1921.

Shafir Ja.: *Očerki Gruzinskoj Žirondy* [Essays on the Georgian Gironde]. Moscow-Leningread, 1925.

Allen W.E.D., Muratov P.P.: *Caucasian Battlefields. A History of the Wars on the Turco-Caucasian Border 1828-1921*. Cambridge, 1953.

Jones S.F.: *Socialism in Georgian Colours: The European Road to Social Democracy, 1883 – 1917*. Cambridge, 2005.

Kazemzadeh F. *The Struggle for Transcaucasus (1917-1921)*. New York, 1951.

Marshall A. *The Caucasus under Soviet Rule*. London – New York, 2010.

Suny R.G.: *The Making of the Georgian Nation*. Indianopolis, 1994.

Stephen F. Jones (ed): *The Making of Modern Georgia, 1918-2012: The First Georgian Republic and its Successors*. London, 2014.

R.G. Suny (ed.): *Transcaucasia: Nationalism and Social Change: Essays in the History of Armenia, Azerbaijan and Georgia*. Ann Arbor, 1996.

Endnotes

[1] As the modern historian B. Mailjan rightly notes, "[A]t the time of the declaration of independence of Georgia, Abkhazia was ruled by the command
of armed detachments subordinate to the NSG. Thanks to this circumstance, the Georgian government not only established its hegemony in the
region of Abkhazia, but also gained a significant advantage in the ongoing
discussion about the possible status of the District [*okrug*]."

[2] "The Government of the Georgian Democratic Republic, represented by its representatives, Ministers of Justice Sh.V. Alekseev-Meskhiev
and Agriculture N.G. Khomeriki, and the Abkhazian People›s Council,
represented by representatives Razhden Ivanovich Kakuba(va), Georgij
Davidovich Tumanov, Vasilij Georgievich Gurdzhua and Georgij Davidovich
Adzhamov, in furtherance and supplementation of the agreement between
the People›s Council, held on 9 February 1918, concluded the following
agreement:

"1. A Minister for Abkhazian Affairs is invited to the Government of the
Georgian Democratic Republic upon submission of the Abkhazian People's
Council.

"2. The internal administration and self-government in Abkhazia is in the
hands of the Abkhazian People's Council.

"3. Credits and moniess necessary for the administration of Abkhazia are
issued from the funds of the Georgian Democratic Republic and are at the
disposal of the the Abkhaz People's Council for the needs of Abkhazia.

"4. For the speedy establishment of revolutionary order and the organisation of a firm government, the government of the Georgian Democratic
Republic is sending a detachment of the Red Guard to help the Abkhazian
People's Council and to be at its disposal. The equipment and funds necessary for the detachment are issued by the government of Georgia.

"5. An international detachment is being organised in Abkhazia, which is
at the disposal of the Abkhazian People's Council.

"6. Social reforms will be carried out by the Abkhazian People's Council on
the basis of common laws, but taking into account local conditions.

"7. A Congress of the population of Abkhazia will be convened on democratic principles as soon as possible for the final resolution of issues relating to organisation in Abkhazia, and

"8. The agreement will be reviewed by the National Assembly of Abkhazia.

    Noë Georgievich Khomeriki

    Shalva Vladimirovich Alekseev-Meskhiev

    Georgij Davidovich Adzhamov

    Vasilij Georgievich Gurdzhua

    Father Georgij Davidovich Tumanov

    Razhden Ivanovich Kakuba(va)."

[3]   It should be noted that from the very beginning of its march towards independence, Tiflis in every possible way prevented contacts between Abkhazians and the outside-world, especially outside the former imperial space – for example, with Turkey, Germany, Great Britain, France and other countries. Georgians, starting from 1918, tried to block such contacts for Abkhazians, to prevent their presence at international conferences and meetings. The goal here was simple and clear: to tie the Abkhazian élite to Tiflis and bind all their external ties to itself. A vivid example is the meeting of the Abkhazian delegates with Zhordania in Istanbul, where they were asked to go home immediately. On the way to the Turkish capital, various obstacles and difficulties had been created on Georgian territory, and problems arose also on the way back ...

[4]   Representatives of the ANS were issued with 180 rifles and more than 1 million rounds of ammunition.

[5]   It is indicative that even Georgian authors, who considered Abkhazia as an ordinary territory of Georgia, recognised the fact of gross interference by the Georgian command, characterising it as frankly a *diktat*: "Even the most flagrant interference of the military authorities in civilian life, the restriction of the autonomous rights of Abkhazia can be qualified in any appropriate way (for example as: arbitrariness of the military, violation by them of the Agreement, failure to fulfil statutory duties, a manifestation of indiscipline, even sometimes even as a crime, etc.), but only not by the term 'occupation' of their own territory."

[6]   In response to this, on 4 August 1918, the Council adopted a resolution with a protest «Against the prohibition by the Georgian government of the removal of tobacco or other products of industry from the borders of Abkhazia" and emphasised Tiflis' lack of the right to "interfere in the economic life of Abkhazia". The said proceedings just prompted the Abkhazian Council to split, and soon it was dissolved for the first time by Georgian administration (see above).

[7]   As B. Mailjan rightly emphasises, "Abkhazian politicians could not provide for their country more favourable conditions in relations with Georgia than those dictated by Tiflis. Actions of individual members of the ANS involuntarily contributed to the desire of the Georgian side to bring Abkhazia to the state of administrative subordination to Georgia. The Government of Georgia, using various levers of pressure, including diplomatic ones but, at the decisive moment, without promising not to use armed forces, was able to take control of the territory of Abkhazia."

Georgian-Abkhaz War in the Context of the Georgian-Abkhazian Conflict

Vitaly Sharia

Honoured Journalist of Abkhazia. Editor-in-chief of the independent newspaper Echo of Abkhazia and author of the Ekho Kavkaza. Abkhazia.

A t dawn on 14 August 1992, the Georgian-Abkhazian war began with the entry into Abkhazia of a group of troops of the State Council of Georgia. It lasted 413 days, or thirteen and a half months. It was only in its very first days that the majority in Abkhazian society avoided pronouncing this word "war", hoping that everything would be settled through negotiations in the coming days. But very soon it became obvious that this was a war, and many Abkhazians were enraged for a very long time when they heard that somewhere, in particular on the Georgian side, they called what was happening a "conflict". The same thing happens to this day; however, for some in Abkhazia confuse the concepts. After all, there really is a "Georgian-Abkhazian conflict", which has not yet been resolved, and the war of the early 1990s was the hot phase of this conflict.

It should also be remembered that the prerequisites for the Georgian-Abkhazian war of 1992-1993 took shape many decades after the territory of Abkhazia was largely deserted in the last third of the 19th century, after the catastrophe of the *makhadzhirstvo* [or Great Exile].

The end of the 20th century and the beginning of the 21st in terms of the triangular relationship «Abkhazia - Georgia - Russia» very much resembled the parallel relations at the beginning of the 20th century, except that everything, according to the law of the spiral, developed much further and sharper. This recurrence can be confirmed, for example, by a brochure of an unidentified author, published in 1908, "Abkhazia is not Georgia" as well as by notes of a Russian lawyer, Deputy of the State Duma of the Republic of Ingushetia Alexander Demjanov, entitled "In Abkhazia and the Georgian Socialist Republic", which covers events from March 1918 to March 1921. These notes, previously unpublished, were published as a separate book in 2021 by the famous Abkhazian historian Stanislav Lakoba. Upon acquaintance with them, one is struck by the coincidence of many arguments voiced by the parties to the conflict now and a century ago.

Some are trying to trace the roots of the current Georgian-Abkhazian conflict to much more distant times. For example, I remember, a speaker at one of the Abkhazian rallies at the turn of the 80s-90s of the last century reproached the first king of the Abkhazian Kingdom (from about 787 to 975), Leon II, who lived thirteen centuries ago, for starting the process of annexing the lands inhabited by the peoples of the Kartvelian language family. continued by his successors. And we, they say, modern Abkhazians, are now disentangling the consequences of these territorial acquisitions, because the distant descendants of the annexed Kartvelians never tire of repeating now that Abkhazia is Georgia...

In fact, of course, the centuries-old history of relations between Abkhazians and Georgians, as well as most of all neighbouring peoples in the world, includes periods of hostility, territorial disputes and wars, as well as cooperation, military alliances, and good-neighbourly relations. And over the millennium that has passed since the existence of the Abkhazian Kingdom, such periods in relations between our two peoples have replaced one another more than once. The roots of the current period of conflict go back to the last decades of the 19th century, when immigrants from Georgia, mainly its western region(s), began intensively to populate Abkhazia, depopulated after the *makhadzhirstvo*. But it cannot be said that this immediately led to the Georgian-Abkhazian confrontation. It matured in proportion to the rise in the numerical superiority over the remaining Abkhazians in Abkhazia of the Georgian [or Kartvelian] population arriving from the east and to the increase in Tbilisi's attempts to assimilate the Abkhazians. It is noteworthy that in our days some among the Abkhazians began, including in the press, to "issue criticisms" of the Abkhazian leaders of the twenties and thirties of the last century for their "policy of compromise", as a result of which, they say, Abkhazia was united in December 1921 with Georgia as a "treaty republic" and then in 1931 entered fully the Georgian SSR as an autonomous republic. But sane people had to explain to these (to put it mildly) eccentrics that the leaders criticised by them lived in a different era from the one in which we live, and did not know – could not know – either about such future developments as: Beria's repressions of the late thirties in order to destroy the Abkhazian political and cultural élite; the transfer in 1946 of Abkhazians from Abkhaz-language schools to schools where Georgian was the language of instruction; or the fierce Georgian-Abkhazian war of the early nineties. That is, they simply looked at the prospects for relations between the two ethnic groups in many ways with different eyes from those of their critics today...

But what can I say, if for us, representatives of the current generation, much over time begins to be perceived quite differently than before. There is nothing to say about such turning points as wars, and the collapse of previously united states. But if we compare how the future was imagined by the participants in the conflict immediately after the end of its hot stage (viz. the Georgian-Abkhaz war), thirty years ago, then, perhaps, there is one thing that unites all of them, no matter how and in what else their interests and views differed. For no one in Sukhum or Tbilisi on the eve of 1994 imagined that everything would be left "hanging between heaven and earth" for so long, in a state of "neither peace nor war", that in 2022 Abkhazia would exist as a partially recognised state for 14 years, and Georgia is still striving to restore its territorial integrity within the borders of the Georgian SSR...

It is naturally easier for me to judge what mindsets were in the very first post-war period in Abkhazian society - because I saw all this "from the inside".

But it is not difficult to guess that in Georgia after 30 September 1993, despite the most severe military defeat, they still hoped for a military revenge and restoration of the aforementioned territorial integrity. But there was clearly no unity regarding the means and methods of achieving this goal, as the next episode clearly shows. On 13 January 1995, Tengiz Kitovani, with the support of Tengiz Sigua, gathered about 700 armed supporters and set off on a new campaign against Abkhazia. He was stopped by the Georgian police and arrested, then convicted of organising illegal armed groups and sentenced to eight years in prison in October 1996, and in May 1999 he was pardoned by Georgian President Eduard Shevardnadze "on medical grounds." This is the same Kitovani who, during his first campaign in Abkhazia, two and a half years before the second, with the rank of Minister of Defence of Georgia, brought there three thousand Georgian guardsmen, members of the paramilitary unit "Mkhedrioni" ("Cavalry"), etc. But if the first campaign turned out in the end to be a gamble, then the second initially looked absurd and insane... However, when Mikheil Saakashvili came to power in Georgia as a result of the "Rose Revolution" of 2003, he, inspired by the expulsion of Aslan Abashidze from Adzharia, proclaimed publicly that very soon he would extend the power of Tbilisi to Abkhazia and South Ossetia. Although any sober-minded observer perfectly understood and understands that there was "a huge disparity", because there was no ethnic conflict in Adzharia but simply an intensified struggle for power. In 2008, Saakashvili decided to start with what he probably thought was the weakest link - South Ossetia. But he failed, because the Russian army came to the rescue of the Ossetians. Since that time, the Georgian leadership and civil society have adopted exclusively peace-loving rhetoric, repeating as a mantra the words that Georgia should return "our Abkhazian and South Ossetian brothers" with kindly words. But when on social networks Georgian users start "discussing" with Abkhazians, most of them immediately switch to the language of hatred, insults and threats. At the same time, even if one believes in the absolute sincerity of those bearing "good will" among Georgian society, one must, being realists, understand that with any hypothetical "return", there will be immeasurably more of the latter.

As for the ideas about the future on the Abkhazian side, at first they did not doubt that the outcome of the war logically entailed the recognition of Abkhazia's independence by Georgia, and then by other states, plus its acceptance into the UN. True, for quite a long time this was combined with fears that over the River Ingur, having come to their senses after the crushing military defeat, maybe not today, but tomorrow they would attempt revenge. Many residents of Abkhazia admitted that they woke up in the morning for at least six months with anxious fears: has the Georgian army moved in a new campaign against North-western Georgia (this is how Abkhazia was called in their texts in the late 80s by Zviad Gamsakhurdia and his associates)? But since this did not happen, they started increasingly asserting themselves in an optimistic scenario. Namely: after some time, Tbilisi will recognise the independence of Abkhazia, and, following after it, all other states. Well, such was the way, let's say, after the wars of France with Vietnam and Algeria, which had belonged to it... Well, in fact, here after all, it is, as they say, "either - or." It is surely impossible to find oneself stuck forever between heaven and earth.

True, some in Abkhazia recalled at that time the saying of Kozma Prutkov "There is nothing more permanent than temporary." By 'permanent' they did not understand, of course, nothing is endless. It was understood that the negotiation-process could drag on for an unexpectedly long time. The biggest skeptics, answering one of the interview-questions of the newspaper "Echo of Abkhazia" in the mid-90s, to wit: "When will the independence of Abkhazia be recognised?", assumed that this would happen in five years. Others went lower – two, three years...

Can all these people be called naive? No way. They simply relied on the previous experience of mankind. But it was at the end of the 20th century that the world reached such a degree of interconnectedness and interdependence and its division into spheres of influence of the leading powers took place in such a way that the concept of geopolitical ambivalence appeared and the number of so-called partially recognised states began to grow. One of them – the Turkish Republic of Northern Cyprus – will soon be half a century old. Approximately the same applies also to the Saharan Arab Democratic Republic in north-west Africa. But these are cases that stand apart. All the remaining partially recognised entities are the product of the bloody collapse of two multi-ethnic countries of the former Eastern bloc – Yugoslavia (1991-2008) and the USSR; on the territory of the latter, it continues even now, in the form of the Russo-Ukrainian war. Kosovo, Abkhazia, South Ossetia, DPR, LPR... Here we should add Transnistria and Nagorno-Karabakh, which are not recognised by anyone but have three decades of *de facto* independent existence.

Recall that during these decades, after lengthy wars against the mother-countries, Eritrea and South Sudan achieved independence... Why were they recognised without any long delay by the world-community, just like East Timor, which bloodlessly achieved independence? Yes, because neither of these states, which joined the UN family, nor their former mother-countries were involved in the orbit of confrontation between the leading world-powers. But, let's say, in the early 90s, even though Yeltsin's Russia seemed to be in partnership and almost friendly relations with the Western coalition, it never occurred to anyone in the West to support the so-called separatists who decided to secede from the former Moldavian, Georgian and Azerbaijani SSRs. And the fact of the matter isn't only that Chisinau, Tbilisi and Baku were not going to let go of the controlled territories in peace, as Moscow did with the former Soviet republics (which was such an unexpected turn-out for many). Another factor – and indeed the main point – was that the Russian Federation, as the legal successor of the USSR, was still implic-itly perceived in those years as a rival of the collective West, whilst the former Soviet republics were viewed as a natural counter-balance to it. Accordingly, the separatist republics within the former union-republics became a natural counter-weight to them and thus Russia's allies. Here, as they say, is the whole story in a nutshell. Well, except that in the case of Nagorno-Karabakh it was still somewhat different; there the role of patron was performed by Armenia and the influential Armenian diaspo-ra of many countries. That is why the NKR did not join the Society "For Democracy and the Rights of Peoples", which was established in 2006 by Tiraspol, Sukhum and Tskhinval but which quietly died after 2008 and is almost forgotten today. More precisely, Stepanakert formally joined it and then left it...

In addition to the aforementioned "naive" ideas in Abkhazian society in the mid-90s, I'll say what I personally imagined then: after the set-tlement of Georgian-Abkhazian relations (based, of course, on the rec-ognition of the independence of Abkhazia), the Tbilisi-Sukhum passen-ger-train will again run and we shall ride it just as in Soviet times. The only difference is that along the way, border-guards and customs-officers will enter the wagons for checks. By the way, at one time it was very con-venient to travel on the trains along this route in both directions: you would go to bed in the evening and get up in the morning ... after all, don't a variety of modes of transport go between many countries that fought each other, including, it seems, those recently completely con-quered, as, for example, in the former Yugoslavia?

But, as you know, not only did the restoration of this passenger-route not happen, but even the railway-bridge over the Ingur, blown up on the night of 14 August 1992, has not yet been restored. (It has never been officially stated who carried out this explosion; there are only speculations in the media that it was Zviadist rebels under the command of Loti Kobalia).

By the way, now in the Abkhazian segment of social networks, sometimes there are really naive statements from those who are perplexed: the participants in the Second World War reconciled a long time ago, so why are there no changes for the better in Georgian-Abkhazian relations? They begin to explain the obvious to these eccentrics: in the first case, there is no subject of dispute, but how can reconciliation occur if none of the parties to the conflict agrees and in the foreseeable future will not agree to the version of the state-status of Abkhazia on which the other side insists?

In this case, a paradoxical picture is observed. In the very first post-war years, when the spiritual wounds of those who buried relatives and friends in the war were still fresh, at the same time quite intensive contacts were observed between the Georgian and Abkhazian sides. Suffice it to recall the meetings of the so-called Schleining Process that took place in Western Europe, in which representatives of both civil society and state-structures of Georgia and Abkhazia took part. Everything was interrupted in 2006, after the entry of the Georgian army into the upper part of the Kodor Gorge and the translocation there by Mikheil Saakashvili of the structures of the so-called government of Abkhazia-in-exile/the Autonomous Republic of Abkhazia, who, however, were clearly in no hurry to do this and preferred to stay in comfortable conditions in Tbilisi. Well, shortly after that, the August war of 2008 broke out, which led to the recognition of the independence of South Ossetia and Abkhazia by the Russian Federation and a number of other countries.

This partial recognition prompted many in Abkhazian society solemnly to proclaim that the conflict with Georgia is over and assert that we and Tbilisi have nothing to talk about now. But this was, of course, far from being the case; one stage of the Georgian-Abkhazian confrontation simply ended and another began.

For the last nine years after the Georgian Dream party came to power in Georgia, the positions of the parties in this ethno-state-conflict look like this. Sukhum did not accept anything other than the recognition of independence, and this was, one might say, initially, during and after the war. Georgian-Abkhazian negotiations with the aim of creating some kind of "common state" were conducted in the second half of the 90s under the obvious pressure of Moscow, with the mediation of [the late] Boris Berezovsky and other Russian politicians of the time, and Sukhum was extremely satisfied when it was Tbilisi that refused to sign an already seemingly agreed version of the agreement. And the reason for that refusal was once again the following - "all or nothing!". In today's Georgia, however, noble-hearted rhetoric ("We must return not the territories, but our Abkhazian and Ossetian brothers and sisters, and this return can only be a peaceful one") coexist perfectly with the fact that any, so to speak, compromise-proposal from the Georgian side is immediately branded as national betrayal.

So it was, for example, with the idea of the political scientist Mamuka Areshidze, who was persecuted in Tbilisi for the idea of recognising the independence of Abkhazia while simultaneously returning *en masse* Georgian refugees and their descendants to it. Moreover, in Abkhazian society they clearly saw this as a trap. Another thing is that no one seriously discussed such a proposal in Abkhazia, since it was rejected in Georgia while still in bud: how can one, they say, even talk about some kind of recognition of the independence of the "breakaway regions"?! And in vain did Areshidze draw for the Georgian public an analogy with the puppet-state of Manjou-Go that had sunk into oblivion in the thirties of the last century, thereby (of course) confirming the very suspicions of the Abkhazian public.

A couple more examples. Shortly after the end of the Georgian-Abkhazian war, a certain map was shown on Abkhazian television, according to which it was proposed to divide Abkhazia along ethnic lines into western and eastern parts. Here is what the first president of Abkhazia, Vladislav Ardzinba, writes about it in his posthumously published book of memoirs "My Life" (2018, p. 293):

> *"Imagine my surprise and bewilderment when I saw the map attached to the report of the UN Secretary-General dated 6 August 1993, on which the Republic of Abkhazia was shown divided along the Gumista River. The eastern part of it, according to the principle of 'new ethnic distribution', was called Abkhazeti. The Georgian name of Abkhazia left no doubt that the map was prepared by Georgian representatives advocating the dismemberment of Abkhazia along ethnic lines."*

Quotations are also cited there, confirming that this option was then supported by a number of Georgian figures.

It is curious that similar "compromise"-options with the partition of Abkhazia along the Gumista were in the air on the Georgian side even on the eve of the war. Well, though not hovering in the air, then this is exactly what I heard in the summer of 1991 from one of the leaders of the Georgian national movement in Abkhazia, when we were standing together in the editorial office in Sukhum near the map of Abkhazia hanging on the wall and I asked where, according to his opinion, if it came to it, it would be fair to draw such a border. His answer, of course, roused a fury in my heart: that is, Sukhum, the capital of Abkhazia, which then accounted for about a quarter of the population of the republic, he kept for his own people, and in their number he himself was going to stay here, while thereby proposing to me that I leave my native city and settle somewhere then on the right bank of the Gumista. But I didn't see any point in entering into a discussion with him and didn't argue ... By the way, that's what I ended up having to do a year later, when the Georgian-Abkhazian war began, and to live in the city of Gudauta, working there as deputy-editor of the *Republic of Abkhazia* newspaper, for the thirteen and a half months of the war.

And now, many years later, in one of the publications on the radio *Echo of the Caucasus*, I mentioned this memorable "Q&A", and recklessly gave the name of my interlocutor of long ago, although I could have safely dispensed with such specification without prejudice to the meaning. I just didn't imagine that it could do him any harm... So what happened? He burst into an interview in some Tbilisi Russian-language online-publication, where he categorically denied that any such conversation had taken placed! Well, well, it happens that one person remembers something from a conversation with another, whilst that other one completely forgets this moment. Therefore, I will not reproach my old interlocutor for insincerity. But this unexpectedly furious reaction of his made me think about something else – that, apparently, in modern Georgian society, such "compromises" are already deemed to be exclusively seditious – but what about, they clamour, our Bichvinta (that is, Pitsunda), our Akhali-Afoni (that is New Athos) [these locations lying on the 'Abkhazian' side of the putative divide – Translator]? Let me once again draw attention to this paradox: the further the hot phase of the Georgian-Abkhazian conflict has moved into the past, the more all compromise has been excluded in the public consciousness, and more and more often the statements of politicians and political scientists have rung out for internal consumption, so as not to anger the radicals.

Here's a more recent example. I was told that one middle-aged Tbilisi resident wanted to come forward three years ago with such an initiative: Georgia's recognition of the independence of Abkhazia in exchange for the transfer by Sukhum of the Gal region within its pre-war borders to the control of the Tbilisi authorities. But when he first decided to acquaint his high-ranking acquaintances with his idea, they were horrified, saying: "Are you out of your mind?"

The preservation of the status quo, in general, suits Abkhazians well enough. The Georgians have, apparently, decided to follow the ancient Chinese wisdom - to sit on the banks of the river and wait for its current to carry the corpse of your enemy away. We shall, they say, wait... In rhetoric, they have realised, it seems that everything is there; no deviations from the Georgian national project should be voiced.

Indeed, just as any war ends sooner or later, such an "ambivalent state" also ends. Not in this century, but in the next. And experts both in Sukhum and Tbilisi have long agreed that this will most likely happen after some global upheaval, when one of the world powers acting as patrons to the parties to the Georgian-Abkhazian conflict will prevail in the course of their rivalry. Might this possibly be the third world war resulting from the development of Russo-Ukrainian hostilities, as some political scientists are croaking? This has already been discussed in both Abkhazian and Georgian societies, although not a single person of good will can possibly wish for this.

In 2003, in a number of Tbilisi publications there appeared a publication based on the materials of a discussion club in the journal *Dro Mshvidobis* (Time of Peace) which outlined five possible options for resolving the Georgian-Abkhazian conflict. Almost twenty years later, it can be said that none of them has been realised. The fifth option turned out to be closest to reality – "Conservation of the conflict with its attendant problems continues," but at the same time, none of the participants in the discussion could have imagined that in this case Abkhazia would become a partially recognised state (the most important thing, of course, being recognition by Russia).

I will express the following thought: if today someone proposes twenty variants of the aforementioned settlement, then, most likely, some twenty-first will be realised at some future point. That's how life works.

And another question, which, of course, inevitably faces experts and futurologists: will the period of enmity and confrontation between the Abkhazian and Georgian peoples change into one of good neighbourliness, and if so, when? It is well known that everything in the world has developed and is developing very differently here. For example, the British, French, Germans, Russians and other Europeans for centuries fought, then became reconciled and "were friends against someone else". But in relations between the Turks and the closely related Azerbaijanis, on the one hand, and the Armenians, on the other, nothing is visible at the end of the tunnel... In the relations between the Abkhazians and Georgians in the past, we repeat, things were different, but there is something which, like a splinter, is acting as an irritation for the future, and this is the impossibility of finding a compromise on the issue of Abkhazia's state-status.

The peculiarity of this ethnic conflict is that it cannot be qualified as a territorial dispute, such as lies at the heart of most such conflicts on the planet. Let's take the Armenian-Azerbaijani conflict over Nagorno-Karabakh, the Georgian-Ossetian conflict over the territory of South Ossetia, the Russian-Ukrainian conflict over the Donbas plus some other territories... In Abkhazia, as already noted, there is no territorial dispute: Georgia simply denies the right of the Abkhazian people to self-determination.

Russia and the Caucasus: Paradoxes 1991–2022

Vladislav Bugera

*Philosopher, political publicist, and independent left-wing activist.
Russia.*

Today Chechens and Abkhaz are fighting in the Donbass alongside Russian soldiers and troops of the Lugansk and Donetsk People's Republics. Thirty years ago Chechens and Russians were fighting in Abkhazia alongside Abkhaz combatants. Indeed, not only Chechens – representatives of many peoples of the Northern Caucasus took part in defending Abkhazia from the Georgian occupiers. However, they themselves were called occupiers by Georgian nationalists. Just as the Russian soldiers, including the Chechens fighting in the Russian army, are now called occupiers by Ukrainian nationalists.

And it was only two years after the war in Abkhazia that Russian soldiers in Chechnya became the same sort of occupiers as were Georgian soldiers in Abkhazia and South Ossetia and as are Ukrainian soldiers in the "Lugansk and Donetsk People's Republics" today. And the same Chechen fighters who not long before were defending Abkhazia with Russian support became partisans fighting against the Russian occupiers -- occupiers just as cruel to the civilian population of Chechnya as the Ukrainian occupiers are now to the civilian population of the

Donbass. The Russian mass media today often recall 'Odessa's Khatyn' – Trade Unions House in Odessa.[1] But nor should we forget the 'Chechen Khatyn' – the village of Samashki.[2]

Unlike the government in Kiev, the Kremlin has shown itself capable of coming to agreements its adversaries. In 1996 Moscow concluded a peace agreement with insurgent Chechnya, and just over three years later, during the second Chechen war, it turned out that most of Moscow's former enemies were now its allies and their leaders loyal vassals of the Kremlin. In the first Chechen war too, there were some Chechens – inhabitants of the Nadterechny County of the Republic of Ichkeria[3] – who supported Russia, but they were in the minority. In the course of the second Chechen war everything changed. Permanently?

From 1991 to the present Chechens have often fought Chechens. In the Donbass today, for example, some Chechens fight under Russian command while others fight for the government in Kiev. A quarter of a century ago some of them were comrades-in-arms.

Russia and the Caucasus... How different are the attitudes of the various peoples of the Caucasus toward Russia, and how often have those attitudes changed over the last two hundred years!

The Russian state and its policy in the Caucasus have also undergone enormous changes over these two hundred years. But one thing in this policy has remained constant: neither the tsarist empire nor the Soviet Union nor the Russian Federation has ever allowed the various ethnic groups of the Northern Caucasus to unite in anything like a federation encompassing the whole or at least large parts of the Northern Caucasus. St. Petersburg and Moscow have offered the peoples of the Northern Caucasus first tsarist provinces (*gubernii*), then a conglomerate of small autonomous units within Georgia and the Russian Republic (RSFSR) of the USSR and then within the Russian Federation, and finally gradual recognition of sovereign statehood (as in the cases of Abkhazia and South Ossetia after the disintegration of the Soviet Union) – but never a federation. And yet within the framework of a federation the peoples of the Northern Caucasus could try to find a common language not just in accordance with the paternal guidance of the wise northern arbitrator but in direct interaction.

In the absence of a federation this has always somehow not turned out very well. The ethnic groups of the Northern Caucasus continue to quarrel among themselves, not to mention the internal quarrels within each group. Are they really so irreconcilable? And do we not find here another paradox? Does Russia not unite the peoples of the Northern Caucasus while at the same time dividing them?

To unite while dividing. To reconcile while dividing. In Transcaucasia it would seem that Moscow has been trying for the last thirty-five years to reconcile Armenia and Azerbaijan as they wrestle over Artsakh.[4] Yet ever since the disintegration of the Soviet Union Russia has been arming both these states, preparing them – as it turns out – for new wars. Efforts to reconcile the Azerbaijanis and Armenians have got nowhere. Does this mean that Russian diplomacy has failed? Or perhaps it has not failed and the Kremlin has simply not been trying very hard?

Or perhaps, if only the Transcaucasian federation (ZSFSR) created in the 1920s had not so soon been destroyed by Stalin and his Politburo, Armenia and Azerbaijan would have grown accustomed to tackle problems arising in their mutual relations peacefully within its framework? Perhaps Georgia too, within the framework of that federation, would gradually have rid itself of that bellicose chauvinism which had already manifested itself in all its repulsiveness under the Menshevik government [of 1918-21], flourished under Stalin and Beria, persisted under Khrushchev and Brezhnev, and during the disintegration of the Soviet Union prompted Georgia to unleash colonial-racial wars of the kind that Ukraine has been waging in the Donbass for the last eight years? Questions worth pondering.

No United States of the Northern Caucasus has ever yet arisen in any form. But does it follow from this that such a slogan is unrealistic in principle? And if such a federation were to take shape, then would it not succeed in bringing the peoples of the Northern Caucasus closer together—including the ethnic Russians, who have long been an indigenous people of the region? And is a federation of peoples of the Northern Caucasus possible inside Russia? And if so, then under what conditions and with what consequences? How many important questions for social scientists to investigate!

Investigations that should aim to resolve a practical question: how to reduce the number of tragic paradoxes in the life of the peoples of the Caucasus?

Endnotes

[1]   Khatyn was a village near Minsk where almost all inhabitants were massacred on March 22, 1943 by German troops. On May 2, 2014, some scores of Russian-speaking activists who had taken refuge in Odessa's Trade Unions House were burned alive after Ukrainian nationalists set the building on fire, or died or were killed while trying to escape.

[2]   Samashki is a village in western Chechnya where Russian troops massacred up to 300 civilians on April 7 and 8, 1995.

[3]   In north-western Chechnya, along the border with Ingushetia.

[4]   Formerly known as Nagorno-Karabakh.

Abkhazia 1992-2022: Reminiscences from England

Zaira Khiba

Linguist & Translator. United Kingdom.

On 13 August 1992 my family and I drove back to our home in Yorkshire from Kilmarnock, Sukhum's twin-town at that time, where we had joined a visiting delegation from Abkhazia. The next day, the fateful 14 August, we drove down to London to visit members of the (Turkish-)Abkhazian community there. In the late afternoon in the house of one of our friends, while I was engaged in conversation in Abkhaz with our host, my husband George sat watching the news with the volume turned down. Suddenly, he asked us to be quiet and switch up the volume, because he recognised the pictures being broadcast of streets in Sukhum where men with guns were clearly engaged in fighting – the war had not only started but was already on the world's TV-screens.

That night began the series of frequent phone calls to Moscow to ascertain news of the latest developments from Madina, daughter of Abkhazia's war-leader and future first president, Vladislav G. Ardzinba.

But Madina was not our only source of information. The Abkhazian delegation's interpreter in Kilmarnock had been Liana Kvarchelia, who had not flown straight back to Abkhazia but had chosen to spend some time with her sister in Moscow. The outbreak of war meant that she had to stay there much longer than planned. However, being in the Russian capital, she was an ideal voice for Abkhazia to the (particularly English-speaking) world after the establishment of Abkhazia's Moscow-based press-centre. Faxes came thick and fast not only from this agency but also from the one later set up in Gudauta. All information thus received was passed (for the duration of the war and beyond) to a contact in the British Foreign Office's Research Department and other interested parties.

Naturally, I was most concerned for members of my large family, most of whom lived in Ochamchira or Sukhum. At some (much later) stage we discovered that my family-home had been commandeered by a Kartvelian group led by a Svan. When they arrived, they asked my elderly mother, who was there with my older sister, who else was living in the house. She lied, saying: "There's only me and my daughter." They did not believe her and began a search. Now, one of my brothers was hiding in an outhouse behind a stack of fruit. Luck was on his side, for when the occupiers entered the outhouse and found that there was a Lada (Zhiguli) parked inside there, their joy was unconfined at the realisation that such a 'trophy' of war had fallen into their possession, and they searched no further. My brother then sneaked away and managed to make his way by following country-pathways to a safe area. As for my mother, she was eventually included in a population 'swap', ending up in the mining-town of T'q^w'archal, where she remained under siege until the end of the war.

Over the 13 months of fighting as I was living on my nerves in a permanent state of worry, family-news trickled out, but it was only when we returned in the mid-90s that we discovered the details of the full horror of those dreadful months. Entering the family-home, we did not recognise any of the fittings, because all our furniture and belongings had been packed up and carried off to Georgia. Returning at the end of the war and finding the family-house still standing but bare, my brothers had had no option but to take furniture from the houses abandoned by local Kartvelian residents when they fled in panic across the Ingur frontier with Georgia before the Abkhazian fighters and their allies arrived, possibly intent on taking revenge for any assistance afforded to the invading troops.

Back in 1992, towards the end of July before leaving Abkhazia, which was palpably in a state of high tension, to return to the UK, George [Hewitt] had left some academic books already wrapped and addressed to be posted by my younger sister to Yorkshire as time allowed. Looking for them in the mid-90s he couldn't find them and asked our immediate (Mingrelian) neighbour, who had stayed in Ochamchira during the war and who, having an Abkhazian husband, had seen no reason to flee, what had happened to them. "Well," she said, "during the cold of winter fuel was needed for heating, and so, in addition to chopping down trees, anything combustible was burnt, including, I noticed, several books from your house…"

But (most) books can be replaced, lost lives cannot. Though, mercifully, none of my brothers was killed, three male cousins died. Two were shot in battle, but the third met a grizzlier end.

On the morning of Sunday 15 July 1989 when large numbers of Kartvelians (including prisoners from Zugdidi who had been deliberately set free and armed by nationalists in order to go and fight the Abkhazians) were heading along the highway from Gal in the direction of Sukhum, the head of the Gal District, Vakht'ang Q'olbaia, had rung his counterpart in Ochamchira, Abkhazia's later 2nd president, Sergej Bagapsh, to warn him of the impending danger represented by the approaching convoy. Bagapsh and my cousin Tolik hurriedly managed to manoeuvre a tanker onto the bridge over the River Aaldzga (in Georgian Ghalidzga) just outside Ochamchira town and blew it up, thereby preventing the horde from crossing and perhaps starting their projected killing-spree in Ochamchira, where we were awoken by the sound of the explosion and some gunfire. Tolik's part in this action was not forgotten.

It seems that shortly after the start of the war, he was captured further along that same highway in the village of Tsagera. The story is that he was tortured and murdered by means of a Winnie Mandela "necklace"...

Аԥсны зхы акәызҵакәаз хашҭра рықәымзааит. Нагҙара аҟəзааит Аԥсны ахьыԥшымра!

Republic of Abkhazia (Apsny)

www.abkhazworld.com

Abkhazia is situated on the Eastern coast of the Black sea, bordering Russia in the North and North Caucasus along the Caucasus Mountains Range and Georgia in the East. Abkhazia is divided into seven administrative districts: **Gagra, Gudauta, Sukhum, Ochamchira, Gulripsh, Tquarchal and Gal**. Due to its mountainous nature, Abkhazia has many rivers and lakes, and rich fertile soil. The climate is very mild, averaging around 15 degrees Celsius. Higher elevations experience a more varied climate, with significant snow and even glaciers in some parts. The capital city is Sukhum (Aqw'a in Abkhaz) which lies on the Black Sea coast.

History Early Development

6th Century B.C.: The Greeks established trading posts in Abkhazia, a Caucasian land, then part of the region known as Colchis at the Eastern end of the Black Sea. Their cities, especially Dioscurias (modern day Sukhum) grew to be a prosperous trade center.

In 55 AD Saint Andrew and Simon the Zealot came to Abkhazia to preach Christianity where they were both buried. First Century B.C.: The Romans fortified Sukhum. The peoples' longevity was reported.

523 A.D.: Abkhazia became part of the Byzantine Empire. Christianity was adopted.

780 - 978: The Kingdom of Abkhazia flourished and the Abkhazia Dynasty extended its sway over much of what is now Western Georgia.

978 - 13th Century: Abkhazia, as a result of dynastic inheritance, is united with Georgian-speaking regions in the mediaeval kingdom whose rulers carried the title ‹Sovereign of the Abkhazians and Georgians›.

1300-1500: A portion of Abkhazia was under Mingrelian Rule.

1500 - 1680: The Abkhazian Chachba Dynasty drove the Mingrelians out and established the southern boundary that exists to this day.

1578: Abkhazia was invaded by the Ottoman Empire

18th Century: Abkhazia, in alliance with Georgia, made repeated efforts to drive out the Turks.

Russian Empire

1801 - 1804: Various Georgian areas (Kartli and Kakhetia-1801, Mingrelia-1803, Imeretia and Guria-1804) came directly under Russian Rule (voluntarily seeking protection from Ottoman Turks and Iran).

1810: Tzar Alexander the First, issued a Charter to the ruling Prince of Abkhazia acknowledging Abkhazia as an autonomous principality under the protection of Russia.

1864: After prolonged fighting across the entire region of the Caucasus, Abkhazia was the last Caucasian principality to be forcibly annexed to the Russian Empire. Russian oppression was so severe that over the next few decades more than half of the Abkhazian population fled to Turkey and the Middle East.

1917 - 1918: Abkhazia joined the Mountainous Republic of the Northern Caucasus. The Mensheviks took over the government of

Georgia and annexed Abkhazia by a mixture of political manoeuvring and the application of 'fire and sword' by General Mazniashvili's troops.

Soviet Abkhazia

March 1921: The Bolsheviks overthrew the Mensheviks in Georgia. The Abkhazian Soviet Socialist Republic was established independently of Georgia and headed by Nestor Lakoba.

1922: Abkhazia was a signatory to the formation of the USSR acting as a sovereign Abkhazian Republic.

1925: Abkhazia adopted its first Constitution under which it was united by a Special Treaty of Alliance with Georgia.

1931: Stalin (Georgian) and Beria (Mingrelian) reduced Abkhazia to the status of an autonomous Republic within Georgia.

1937 - 1953: Forced mass immigration into Abkhazia was carried out from Western Georgia (Mingrelia) by Stalin and Beria. In Abkhazia, as well as other regions of the USSR, mass oppression was carried out, thousands of intellectuals were persecuted. Before the enforced georgianisation of the 20th century, Abkhazia had a highly diverse demography with many Turks, Armenians, Jews, and Greeks, among others. Abkhazia celebrated its diversity, and the strict homogenization under Georgian rule greatly contrasted with the traditionally tolerant Abkhazian culture. During the period of enforced georgianisation (1937-1953), the Abkhaz were deprived of the right to teach their children in their native language; all Abkhaz schools and institutions were closed from the school-year 1945-46. The Abkhaz were only compelled to study in Georgian schools. The Abkhaz script (originally based on Cyrillic and then on Latin) was altered, against the will of the Abkhaz people, to one based on Georgian characters in 1938. Despite the reintroduction of schooling in Abkhaz and a reformed, Cyrillic-based script following the deaths of Stalin and Beria in 1953, in 1978 Abkhazian intellectuals signed a letter of protest to the Supreme Soviet of the USSR complaining about the status of Abkhazia and blamed the Georgian leaders for pursuing a "Beriaite" policy aimed at the "Georgianisation" of the Republic. Major demonstrations at Lykhny (a sacred place in Abkhazian tradition) followed. The Abkhazian campaign, to be incorporated in the Russian Federation, was rejected by Russia and Georgia. Instead, concessions were made to the Abkhaz, including the opening of the Abkhazian State University and TV broadcasting for 15 minutes twice a week in the Abkhaz language. During that year (1978), Moscow allocated millions of roubles to help Abkhazia. The Abkhazian government never received the money. The sum was dispersed to constrain the Abkhazian people's protest at existing conditions.

Post Soviet Period

1988 - 1989: Leaders of the National Movement in Georgia demanded the abolition of the "Autonomies within Georgia together with secession from the USSR.

1988 - 1990: The Georgian Soviet Socialist Republic unilaterally adopted a number of measures which essentially effected the secession of Georgia from the USSR, abrogating in the process all legal acts that united Georgia and Abkhazia under Soviet jurisdiction.

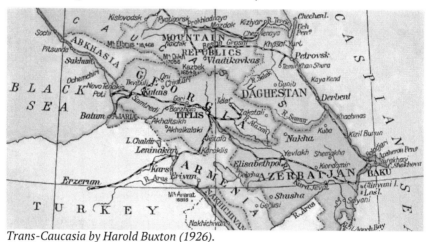

Trans-Caucasia by Harold Buxton (1926).

1990: On the eve of the signing of the new Soviet Union Treaty, Abkhazia, like all of the other autonomous republics, declared its sovereignty. On the next day, Georgia declared the abrogation of the Abkhazian Declaration of Sovereignty. Georgia abrogated the autonomy of Ossetia, leading to armed conflict between South Ossetia and Georgia.

1992: Abkhazia declares the sovereignty of its own territory and proposes a federative treaty to Georgia to fill the "legal vacuum" that resulted from Georgia's unilateral abrogation of all Soviet legal documents. On August 14th, exactly 20 days after being accepted by the United Nations, Georgian troops entered the territory of Abkhazia without any notification to the Abkhazian government and launched a land and air attack on the southeast part of Abkhazia and its capital city. Bloody fighting continued for 13 months.

1993: On September 30th, Abkhazian forces - backed by the Confederation of the Peoples of the North Caucasus Organization, finally ousted the Georgian troops from the territory of Abkhazia.

1994: In April, a joint Declaration of the Political Settlement was signed by the parties to the conflict - the UN, Russia and OSCE, in the presence of the UN Secretary General. The Declaration outlined principles for the peaceful settlement of the conflict on the basis of equality between the parties. In May, negotiations under the auspices of the UN sanctioned the deployment of the CIS peace-keeping troops to separate the parties to the conflict.

Recent history of Abkhazia

After Georgia annulled all Soviet legislation, Abkhazia, as a temporary measure, re-enacted its 1925 constitution, and a new constitution was acclaimed by popular referendum on November 26 1994, restating Abkhazia's national sovereignty, which was not recognised by Georgia or any other state, as were the elections in November 1996; the Constitution was amended in 1999, at which point Abkhazia finally declared its formal independence Later, a regime of economic sanctions was imposed on Abkhazia by Russia, Georgia and the CIS states. This had a severe impact on the economic growth and development of Abkhazia. Until 26th August 2008, when Russia (followed by Nicaragua, Venezuela, Nauru, Vanuatu, Tuvalu and Syria) recognised both Abkhazia and South Ossetia as independent states, Abkhazia continued to act as a de facto sovereign state, constantly making its case for international recognition, having finally declared its full independence from Georgia in 1999.

Politics and Issues in Abkhazia's Relations with Georgia

After the end of the conflict in 1993, Georgia made several military attempts to take Abkhazia back (e.g. in 1998 and 2001). The introduction of troops (masquerading as police) of the Georgian Army in the upper part of the Kodor Gorge of Abkhazia effectively put an end to the already fragile peace process. Until the troops fled from the Gorge after bombing and prior to a land-attack on 12th August 2008, Georgia continued to claim that part of Abkhazia to be part of Georgia by relocating there the so-called "Government in exile" (The Georgian-recognised Government of the Autonomous Republic of Abkhazia never had any actual jurisdiction over, or relevance in, Abkhazia). Georgia and the international community (apart from Russia, Nicaragua, Venezuela, Nauru, and Syria) refuse to recognise the Sukhum-based government, despite the fact that it exercises sovereign rule over its territory and people, whilst Georgia has been unable to do so since the end of the war on 30th September 1993.

Abkhazia demands reparations from Georgia for destruction during the 1992-93 war as well as for the economic damage suffered due to the sanctions placed on Abkhazia by the CIS states. Within Georgia, there are high numbers of internally displaced people (IDPs, or refugees) from the war, mainly Mingrelians who fled in fear of what the post-war chaos would mean for those who supported the Georgian invasion. Georgian President Saakashvili (like his predecessor, Eduard Shevardnadze) often uses the IDPs as a bargaining chip for humanitarian assistance from the

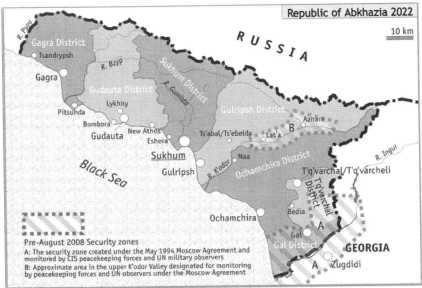

Republic of Abkhazia (2022)

world-community. Abkhazia argues that during the 1992-93 war, many local Georgians living in Abkhazia fought on the Georgian side against the Abkhaz. According to the 1951 UN Convention on Refugees, those who use arms in an armed struggle and then flee do not fall under the international definition of refugees. Experienced Abkhazian expert Liana Kvarchelia writes that Abkhazian society can allow the return only of those Georgians who did not fight on the Georgian side and only after they recognise Abkhazia as an independent state. She also says that the same right for return should be given also to descendants of Abkhazian refugees from the Russian-Caucasian War of the XIX century and the Russo-Turkish War of 1877-78, who live mostly in Turkey. Abkhazia demands for recognition as a sovereign state both by Georgia and by the international community have been substantially strengthened by Russia's recognition of 26th August 2008.

Population

According to the data of the census, conducted in February 2011, the population of the republic stood at 240,705.

The urban population of the Republic represents 50.3% or 121,255 persons, whilst the rural population represents 49.7% or 119,450 persons.

The ratio of men to women was 46.4% and 53.6% respectively. The population-figures for the most numerous nationalities break down as follows: Abkhazians – 122,069; Russians – 22,077; Armenians – 41,864; Georgians – 43,166; Megrelians/Mingrelians – 3,201; Greeks – 1,380.

Abkhazians in the Republic make up 50.71%, Armenians 17.39%, Georgians 17.93%, Russians 9.17%.

There is also a large Abkhazian Diaspora of over half a million, based in Turkey but with populations in Syria and Jordan.

Languages

Abkhazians speak Abkhaz, though Russian is also common and shares co-official status, - whilst Mingrelian and Georgian are widely spoken in the Gal district, where most of the returned 'Georgian' refugees live. Written Abkhaz, based on the Cyrillic alphabet, first appeared in 1862.

Religion

The majority of Abkhazians within Abkhazia are Orthodox Christians, comprising approximately 75% of the population. Another 10% of Abkhazians are Sunni Muslims, and there are small numbers of Jews, Lutherans, Catholics and followers of new religions. Abkhazian historian Stanislav Lakoba, when asked about the religion of Abkhazia, answered that the *Abkhaz are eighty percent Christian, twenty percent [Sunni] Muslim, and one hundred percent pagan!*

Culture

The majority of Abkhazians live in rural areas, mostly in large family homes where they grow and process their own food. Horses have an important place in Abkhazian culture. Equine sports and equestrian activities are popular with Abkhazians and often play a central role in festivals. Song, music, and dance are also important to Abkhazian culture. There are joyous songs for weddings, ritual songs, cult songs, lullabies, healing songs, and work songs. There are special songs for the gathering of the lineage, for the ill, and songs celebrating the exploits of heroes. All of the arts are represented in Abkhazia. There are drama and dance companies, art museums, music schools, and theatres for the performing arts. Poetry and literature are also held in high regard. It has recently been acknowledged that there is a disproportionately high occurrence of nonagenarians and centenarians in certain areas in the Caucasus, including Abkhazia. These long-lifers are known for continuing their active lifestyles, continuing to work the fields, dance, sing, and walk for miles long past their ninth decade.

Economy

Abkhazia is mostly rural and boasts a variety of abundant agricultural natural resources, primarily citrus fruit, tobacco, tea, and timber. It also has some energy resources with coal mines and hydro-electric plants. Abkhazia's economy is heavily reliant on Russia, using the rouble as its currency, and relying mostly on Russia as export market, a trading partner and investor. Turkey is another big economic partner for Abkhazia. Economic and travel sanctions were imposed on Abkhazia in 1996 by the CIS countries after its declaration of sovereignty and the removal of Georgian troops from the country. The economic blockade following years of military conflict devastated the Abkhazian economy. No foreign direct investment was able to breach the blockades, and international trade is highly restricted. Lifting of the embargo by Russia opened new horizons for the country's economic growth. Tourism to Abkhazia is on the rise, with the number of tourists reaching almost 2 million visitors in 2007 and the expectation that this number will continue to grow in coming years. Fishing and construction industries are increasing their volume annually.

Nature & Environment

Despite the years of isolation, Abkhazia managed to preserve its unique and virgin natural parks and resources. Abkhazia is rich in freshwater and may become one of its biggest exporters. The fast-growing tourism industry is challenging Abkhazia's environment. Years of isolation, however, deprived Abkhazia of its access to international know-how on environmental protection standards.

Further Reading

Publications

Hewitt, B. G. (1999). *The Abkhazians: A Handbook.* London & New York. Palgrave Macmillan.

Hewitt, B. G. (2013). *Discordant Neighbours: A Reassessment of the Georgian-Abkhazian and Georgian-South Ossetian Conflicts.* Leiden, Netherlands. Brill.

Shesterinina, A (2021). *Mobilizing in Uncertainty: Collective Identities and War in Abkhazia.* New York, Cornell University Press.

Junge M. & Bonwetsch B. (2015) *Bolschewistische Ordnung in Georgien: Der Große Terror in einer kleinen kaukasischen Republik.* Berlin, Germany. De Gruyter Oldenbourg.

Francis, C. (2011). *Conflict Resolution and Status: The Case of Georgia and Abkhazia.* Brussels. Brussels University Press.

Harlz, Benedikt (2018). *The Law and Politics of Engaging De Facto States: Injecting New Ideas for an Enhanced EU Role.* Washington D.C. Brookings Institution Press.

Shnirelman, V. A. (2001). *The value of the past: myths, identity and politics in Transcaucasia.* Osaka, National Museum of Ethnology.

Tekushev, I., Markedonov S. M., Shevchenko K. V. (2013). *Abkhazia : between the past and the future.* Prague. Medium Orient.

Articles

Hewitt, B. G. (1993). *Abkhazia: a problem of identity and ownership History and Documents.* London. Central Asian Survey.

Hewitt, B. G. (2014). *History in the Context of the Georgian-Abkhazian Conflict.* Leiden, Brill, Iran and the Caucasus.

Sonmez, M (2010). *'Absence of Will': A commentary.* Retrieved from http://abkhazworld.com/aw/

Shenfield S. D. (2008). *Origins and Evolutions of the Georgian-Abkhaz Conflict.* Retrieved from http://abkhazworld.com/aw/

Shenfield S. D. (2010). *The Stalin-Beria Terror in Abkhazia, 1936-1953.* Retrieved from http://abkhazworld.com/aw/

Auch, E. M. (2005). *The Abkhazia Conflict in Historical Perspective.* Baden, OSCE Yearbook 2004.

Coppieters, B. (1999). *The roots of the conflict.* London, Conciliation Resources.

Coppieters, B. (2004). *A Moral Analysis of the Georgian-Abkhaz Conflict.* 'Contextualizing Secession: Normative Studies in Comparative Perspective' Richard Sakwa (Ed.) Oxford. Oxford University Press.

Kaiser, P. C. (2019). *What Are They Doing? After All, We're Not Germans": Expulsion, Belonging, and Postwar Experience in the Caucasus.* 'Empire and belonging in the Eurasian borderlands.' Ed. Krista A. Goff and Lewis H. Siegelbaum. New York. Cornell University Press.

Smith G. (1998). *The Georgian-Abkhazian confrontation.* 'Nation-building in the Post-Soviet Borderlands'. Cambridge University Press.

Garb P. (2009). *The view from Abkhazia of South Ossetia ablaze.* London. Central Asian Survey.

Lakoba S. (1995). *Abkhazia is Abkhazia.* London. Central Asian Survey.

Ennals D., Farrar M., Pinto A. S., Maell L., Praag W. M. Hille C. (1993). *Report of a UNPO mission to Abkhazia, Georgia, and the Northern Caucasus.* London. Central Asian Survey.

www.abkhazworld.com

www.reflectionsonabkhazia.net

www.abkhazia.co.uk